MW00572437

WILMETTE PUBLIC LIBRARY
1242 WILMETTE AVENUE
WILMETTE, IL 60091
847-256-5025

The Conscious Brain

PHILOSOPHY OF MIND SERIES

Series Editor
David J. Chalmers, Australian
National University/New York
University

Self Expressions
Mind, Morals, and the
Meaning of Life
Owen Flanagan

The Conscious Mind
David J. Chalmers

Minds and Bodies
Philosophers and Their Ideas
Colin McGinn

Deconstructing the Mind
Stephen P. Stich

What's Within?
Nativism Reconsidered
Fiona Cowie

The Human Animal
Personal Identity without
Psychology
Eric T. Olson

Consciousness and Cognition
Michael Thau

Dreaming Souls
Sleep, Dreams and the
Evolution of the Conscious
Mind
Owen Flanagan

A Place for Consciousness
Probing the Deep Structure
of the Natural World
Gregg Rosenberg

Three Faces of Desire
Timothy Schroeder

Identifying the Mind
Selected Papers of U. T. Place
Edited by George Graham and
Elizabeth R. Valentine

Purple Haze
The Puzzle of Consciousness
Joseph Levine

Gut Reactions
A Perceptual Theory of Emotion
Jesse J. Prinz

Ignorance and Imagination
The Epistemic Origin of the Problem
of Consciousness
Daniel Stoljar

Thinking without Words
José Luis Bermúdez

What Are We?
A Study in Personal Ontology
Eric T. Olson

The Conscious Brain

HOW ATTENTION ENGENDERS EXPERIENCE

Jesse J. Prinz

WILMETTE PUBLIC LIBRARY

OXFORD
UNIVERSITY PRESS

OXFORD
UNIVERSITY PRESS

Oxford University Press is a department of the University of Oxford.
It furthers the University's objective of excellence in research,
scholarship, and education by publishing worldwide.

Oxford   New York
Auckland   Cape Town   Dar es Salaam   Hong Kong   Karachi
Kuala Lumpur   Madrid   Melbourne   Mexico City   Nairobi
New Delhi   Shanghai   Taipei   Toronto

With offices in
Argentina   Austria   Brazil   Chile   Czech Republic   France   Greece
Guatemala   Hungary   Italy   Japan   Poland   Portugal   Singapore
South Korea   Switzerland   Thailand   Turkey   Ukraine   Vietnam

Oxford is a registered trade mark of Oxford University Press
in the UK and certain other countries.

Published in the United States of America by Oxford University Press
198 Madison Avenue, New York, NY 10016

© Oxford University Press 2012

All rights reserved. No part of this publication may be reproduced,
stored in a retrieval system, or transmitted, in any form or by any means, without
the prior permission in writing of Oxford University Press, or as expressly
permitted by law, by license, or under terms agreed with the appropriate
reproduction rights organization. Inquiries concerning reproduction outside the
scope of the above should be sent to the Rights Department, Oxford University Press,
at the address above.

You must not circulate this work in any other form and you must impose this
same condition on any acquirer.

Library of Congress Cataloging-in-Publication Data
Prinz, Jesse J.
The conscious brain: how attention engenders experience /Jesse J. Prinz.
    p.   cm.—(Philosophy of mind)
ISBN 978-0-19-531459-5 (hardcover: alk. paper) 1. Consciousness. 2. Experience.
3. Attention. I. Title.
B105.C477P75   2012
153—dc23   2011030961

9 8 7 6 5 4 3 2 1

Printed in the United States of America
on acid-free paper

153
PR

8-5 11/12/12

To Eary

CONTENTS

PREFACE

Much of this book was written while sitting in my house in Chapel Hill, North Carolina. There, gray squirrels regularly scurry across my balcony, hoping to receive a nut. I've reinforced this behavior by feeding them regularly, and now, squirrels peer inside all day when I am there, clinging to the screen door and following me as I move about in the house. They seem to be attending to my every move, and when I toss a few nuts out, they bound off looking for them, retaining the knowledge that there are nuts to be found in working memory. If consciousness could be inferred from behavior, it would be obvious that these little creatures experience the world around them. But, famously, no such inference is possible. Consciousness cannot be read off of behavior. To know whether another creature is conscious, we must first figure out what mechanisms produce consciousness in us. In the chapters that follow, I will not address the question about squirrels, but I'll try to offer an answer to the question on which it hangs: what is the source of consciousness in human beings?

I began thinking about this question in the 1990s, when consciousness studies came of age. Two important things happened then. First, a number of neuroscientists, spearheaded by Francis Crick and Christof Koch, began actively searching for correlates of consciousness in the brain. Second, David Chalmers crystallized and enhanced the major philosophical arguments against the possibility of reducing consciousness to something functional or physical. Thus, two poles emerged: those who sought a scientifically informed reduction of consciousness and those who thought such an enterprise was impossible. I am so constitutionally attracted toward the first of these poles that I see the second on a par with skeptical challenges. It's true that consciousness might not be part of the physical world, but that is a possibility that we can usually ignore. Since the 1990s, the psychological and biological processes associated with consciousness have been exposed in sumptuous detail. The reductive program is clearly a fertile one, and questions about nonphysical remainders can be postponed until the details are in—a strategy I follow here. The details do not render the dualist challenge inert but help to show that there are many important questions about consciousness that can be answered, and they even help explain why dualism has so much appeal.

Chalmers called his defense of dualism *The Conscious Mind*. *The Conscious Brain* is intended not as an antidote but rather as a celebration of the explosion in consciousness studies that Chalmers helped to bring about. Where he sought to synthesize two decades of dualist argumentation, I try here to synthesize two decades of empirical exploration. The impetus for this work has always been the apparent perplexity of explaining consciousness, a perplexity that Chalmers has done so much to articulate. So this synthesis can be regarded as an afterword or addendum. It is also an addendum to Dan Dennett's *Consciousness Explained*, a seminal philosophical foray into the science of consciousness, and it is an extension of the pioneering ideas in Ray Jackendoff's *Consciousness and the Computational Mind*. Without these authors, this book would not exist. I've also gotten feedback from Chalmers, Dennett, Koch, and Jackendoff over the years. Koch and Chalmers have developed some of the most powerful arguments against a central thesis of this book: the claim that consciousness essentially involves attention.

There are many others to whom I am indebted. Murat Aydede got me thinking about consciousness when I was in graduate school. David Rosenthal has spent countless hours discussing the topic with me, offering valuable challenges at every turn. Bill Lycan has long been a favorite interlocutor—a perfect colleague when this book was taking form. Ned Block has provided more feedback than anyone else, and his work has been a source of constant inspiration; it represents an ideal union of philosophy and science.

This is just the tip of the iceberg. I am grateful to my superb collaborator, Felipe de Brigard, and to numerous talented philosophers who have provided comments. These include Andy Clark, Jake Davis, Anya Farennikova, Chris Hill, Andreas Keller, Joshua Knobe, Miriam Kyselo, LeeLoo Liu, Chris Mole, Bence Nanay, Declan Smithies, Carolyn Suchy-Dicey, Michael Tye, Robert Van Gulick, Wayne Wu, Ben Young, and Dan Zahavi, among others. I was also lucky to get written feedback from Ned Block, Takayuki Suzuki, and Hakwan Lau. I owe special thanks to Tim Bayne for pages upon pages of detailed comments. His insights, corrections, and challenges were my roadmap in bringing the manuscript to its final form. In addition, I received extremely helpful editorial feedback from Katie Tullmann and Amanda Bryant as well as exceptionally careful copy editing from Wendy Keebler at Oxford University Press. Lucy Randall, Ryan Sarver, Venkat Raghavan, and the rest of the Oxford team were an absolute pleasure to work with, and Peter Ohlin, my editor, could not have been more patient and supportive.

Although most of the material in this book is new, four chapters reproduce or extend earlier work, and I am grateful to the publishers for allowing me to incorporate this material, which is reproduced with their permission. The following articles form the foundations of chapters 2, 3, 5, and 7, respectively:

Prinz, J.J. (2007). The intermediate-level theory of consciousness. In S. Schneider & M. Velmans, eds., *Blackwell Companion to Consciousness*. Oxford: Blackwell.

Prinz, J.J. (2011). Is attention necessary or sufficient for consciousness? In C. Mole, D. Smithies, & W. Wu, eds., *Attention: Philosophical and Psychological Essays*. Oxford: Oxford University Press.

Prinz, J.J. (2011). The sensory basis of cognitive phenomenology. In T. Bayne & M. Montague, eds., *Cognitive Phenomenology*. Oxford: Oxford University Press.

Prinz, J.J. (2011). Waiting for the self. In J. Liu, ed., *Consciousness and the Self: New Essays*. Cambridge, U.K.: Cambridge University Press.

All four of these volumes are full of papers worth reading, and I am grateful to their editors for including me and for feedback that has helped improve the present work.

I saved my three greatest debts for last. I am, as always, grateful to my family for enduring my manic work habits and especially to my partner, Rachel Bernstein, who, by some strange miracle, puts up with me and reminds me of the things that matter most. I am grateful to the hundreds of authors on whose work I draw—this book is about what they've achieved. And I am grateful to the squirrels of North Carolina, especially Eary, a beautiful and dignified recluse, whom I miss dearly.

The Conscious Brain

1

Do We Really Need Another Theory
of Consciousness?

Over the last quarter-century, consciousness went from being an unmentionable topic in science to being one of the trendiest. PubMed, a comprehensive science and medicine database, lists 2,516 articles with "consciousness" in the title between 1985 and 2010. That's about two articles every single week. If that's not impressive, consider the fact that there were only 1,369 articles with "consciousness" in the title between 1900 and 1984. Likewise, the psychology database PsycINFO records 4,582 articles with "consciousness" in the title between 1985 and 2010, with only 1,858 published before that, going back to 1900. That's about an eight-fold increase in publishing rate on this topic. Unsurprisingly, the last quarter-century has also seen a profusion of new theories of consciousness and countless experimental results. Rarely do so many fields within the academy turn their attention to a single topic with such enthusiasm.

This book is a kind of progress report. I will argue that these twenty-five years of inquiry have borne much fruit. Stepping back from this great mass of research, one can find various strands of evidence that point toward a satisfying and surprisingly complete theory of how consciousness arises in the human brain. The theory I will present is based on recent empirical work and guided by a set of desiderata that are widely accepted. In that sense, I am merely offering a synthesis of ideas that are already both present and popular in the literature. But this is an area where controversy reigns, so my litany of established truths will include claims that some researchers regard as demonstratively false. Much of my burden will consist in rebutting alleged refutations. I will also have the less happy task of dissenting from other esteemed theories of consciousness, theories that reflect considerable toil and achievement. One might think that there is no need for a new theory, even one that synthesizes extant ideas. There is a handsome selection of well-wrought theories on the market, which have been developed by distinguished philosophers, psychologists, and neuroscientists. While it would be nice if we could simply pick one of these, I think the most publicized theories face objections that cannot be met. At the same time, each has much to teach us; each is guided by some aspect of consciousness that any adequate theory must accommodate. My goal in this chapter is to survey the limitations and lessons of leading theories.

1. Consciousness Characterized

Before surveying theories, something must be said about what researchers in this area are aiming to explain. The term "consciousness" is notoriously difficult to define and, some would say, multiply ambiguous. I think, however, that there is a more or less univocal concept here, even if it resists definition. The theories I will survey tend to have the same declared aim. They want to explain *phenomenal* consciousness. That term, introduced by Block (1995), refers to the mental states that feel like something. Philosophers have multiple technical terms to talk about such states. Conscious states are said to have phenomenal qualities, qualitative character, or subjective properties. They are also said to divide up into basic building blocks, called qualia, or raw feels. Sometimes more colloquial terms are used: Block equates phenomenal consciousness with "experience," and Nagel (1974) says that a state is conscious if its possessor can know "what it's like." I will use all of these terms, although I concede that they wouldn't be very helpful in explaining what "consciousness" means to someone who has just encountered the concept.

One strategy that can be helpful in explaining what we're talking about is to think about conditions in which consciousness is absent. Consider fusion effects in vision. One example is flicker fusion. The images we see on television actually flicker on and off, but when the flickers are fast enough, we don't experience them. Also, if two colors flicker alternately, such as red and green, we seem to experience a fusion of the two, in this case yellow. Such chromatic fusion also occurs if each eye is presented with a different color at the same time (Grimsley, 1943). Or consider implicit rule learning. When presented with sets of random dot patterns that diverge from slightly different prototypes, people eventually become very adept at classifying new patterns as belonging to one of the training sets, but they have no idea how they do it. Such category learning seems to depend on motor routines deep beneath the cortical surface (Ashby and Casale, 2003). Likewise, people have no direct access to some rules used in parsing sentences or riding bicycles. An even more obvious example of unconscious processing is subliminal perception. When stimuli are presented very briefly and followed by a "mask," they go undetected, but they still have a psychological impact. For example, masked happy faces can cause people to pay more for a beverage (Winkielman et al., 2005), masked fear faces can trigger neural and dermal signatures of fear (Williams et al., 2004), and masked pictures of money can influence how much force people exert when squeezing a handle in a gambling task (Pessiglione et al., 2007). One can also mask a stimulus by presenting it in one eye while presenting a brighter, flashier, higher-contrast stimulus in the other, a method called interocular suppression. One can mask pictures of nudes in this way, and people will not know that they've seen them (Jiang et al., 2006).

In all of these cases, people insist that they cannot experience something—a flicker, a rule, a masked picture—no matter how hard they try. When masking methods are used effectively, people have no idea that there has been any stimulus other than the mask, and they are at chance in distinguishing trials with such a stimulus and without. It's not a matter of forgetting; in interocular suppression, one stimulus can be masked by another for long durations, and people will report ignorance of the masked stimulus while it is present. There is simply no experience to be had. Imagine how disappointed you would be if I offered to show you a picture of your favorite celebrity naked and then suppressed it with an interocular mask. This would be no better than presenting the picture behind your head, at a mile distance, or in a pitch-dark room. No definition of consciousness is required to see that there is a radical difference between seeing a nude with and without a mask. Theories of consciousness can be understood as attempts to specify the psychological or neural processes that kick in when the mask is lifted. Most theorists hope that the processes in unmasked vision can also be implicated in supraliminal perception in other sense modalities and even in conscious thinking. An intuitive distinction between conscious and unconscious can be found across a range of psychological processes, and most theories of consciousness are intended to cover the full range.

That said, some researchers also distinguish several different kinds of consciousness, and such distinctions might call out for different explanations. I think this proliferation of species is unnecessary. Alleged kinds of consciousness are either not forms of consciousness at all or just different facets of the same thing.

Consider, first, a distinction that Block (1995) draws between phenomenal consciousness and access consciousness. As we have seen, phenomenal consciousness can be equated with experience. Access consciousness is what we have when information is poised for reporting and deliberation. Block thinks these two can come apart. For example, we might have phenomenality without access when we hear the background buzz of an air conditioner but fail to notice it. Access without phenomenality is alleged to arise in pathological cases in which a person can act on sensory information in the absence of experience. For example, some people with blindsight have brain injuries that prevent visual experience, but they nevertheless avoid obstacles when walking, and, we can imagine, they might come to report reliably the placement of those obstacles (de Gelder, 2010).

I reject this distinction. I don't believe there is any form of access that deserves to be called consciousness without phenomenality. After all, access is cheap.

When an ordinary desktop computer calls up information from a hard drive or responds to inputs from a user, it is accessing information, but there is little temptation to say that the computer is conscious. Information access seems conscious in the human case when and only when it is accompanied by phenomenal experience. When we retrieve memories or deliberate, we experience mental imagery and inner speech. Presumably, people with blindsight who can readily report on the locations of obstacles also experience inner speech before issuing such reports. In saying that they are conscious, we implicitly presume that they are having experiences. If it turned out that obstacle avoidance in blindsight was totally devoid of experience, in the way that we might imagine insects having no experience when they fly from place to place, the temptation to say that such people are conscious of obstacles would disappear. The other half of Block's distinction can also be challenged. Phenomenal consciousness may always involve access or at least accessibility. But, with Block, I don't think this link is conceptually obvious. That task of establishing the link will have to await empirical evidence.

Turning to another distinction, consider Dretske's (1995) contrast between thing-consciousness and fact-consciousness. There is a difference, he suggests, between being conscious of a Beethoven sonata and being conscious that there is a Beethoven sonata being played; the latter requires the deployment of concepts, and the former does not. This might lead one to think that there are different mechanisms at work when we become conscious of facts as opposed to things. But such an inference is unwarranted (as Dretske might concur). When we consciously recognize a sonata as Beethoven, we phenomenally experience the thought "Oh, that's Beethoven." And given that the thought can be experienced phenomenologically, there is no pretheoretical reason to conclude that this is a different species of consciousness from nonconceptual cases, rather than concluding that the mechanisms underlying the phenomenal experience of music can also operate on cognitive states. To draw a distinction in consciousness rather than the contents of consciousness would require further demonstration.

A related distinction involves first-order consciousness and higher-order consciousness (Armstrong, 1968). To be conscious of the sushi on your plate may seem different from the consciousness that you are seeing sushi. The latter might be said to involve some kind of inner monitoring. But again, the fact that we can be conscious of inner and outer states does not entail that there are two species of consciousness, and in fact, most theories of consciousness treat these by appeal to the same kind of mechanisms (see, e.g., Rosenthal, 1997). I'd say the same thing about introspective consciousness. The faculty of introspection may work using the same resources by which we experience things in the world (compare Dretske, 1995). Elsewhere I argue that the term "introspection" labels not a single phenomenon but many, and each can be accommodated using the same resources that explain first-order consciousness (Prinz, 2004a). For example, introspection can involve first-order awareness of a verbal self-narrative. The narrative may also qualify as second-order insofar as it represents ongoing mental events, but as a type of experience, it is a first-order sensory state (inner speech is an auditory experience), and it presumably becomes conscious the way any other first-order state becomes conscious.

The final distinction I want to consider is drawn between state consciousness and creature consciousness (Rosenthal, 1997). State consciousness refers to those mental states, such as supraliminal visual perceptions, that are consciously experienced. Creature consciousness refers not to individual mental states but rather to the global condition of an organism. We are conscious when wide awake but can be knocked unconscious. Sleep is sometimes regarded as a form of unconsciousness, as is coma. One might think that creature consciousness is orthogonal to state consciousness, but the former can be readily defined in terms of the latter. A creature is conscious if it is experiencing conscious states. When we lose consciousness, phenomenality is lost. The question of whether we are unconscious when we sleep can be addressed by asking whether sleep always feels like something. Vivid dreaming certainly does, but the presence of conscious states in so-called slow-wave sleep is a matter of controversy. If we found a creature that had no conscious states—insects might be examples—I don't think it would make sense to refer to them as conscious in any sense. When a fly falls after being swatted and then recovers, we sometimes say it was stunned, but there is little temptation to say it was knocked unconscious.

In summary, I think the term "consciousness" in contemporary usage refers to phenomenal consciousness. If we can account for phenomenal consciousness, we'll have what we need to account for consciousness in general. In making this claim, I've relied on conceptual intuitions. In most of what follows, intuitions will play a less central role. Building theories on intuitions is risky, because intuitions are not always shared, and even when intuitions in this domain are shared, they reveal more about how we think about consciousness than consciousness itself. In saying that there is just one concept of consciousness, I leave open the possibility that there may be empirical reasons for saying that this one concept refers to several phenomena. The flip side of this is that there may be an empirical argument for unity. One can resist alleged conceptual distinctions without simply appealing to intuition by showing that there is a single mechanism underlying paradigm cases of phenomenal consciousness and then showing that same mechanism is at work wherever we are tempted to use the word "conscious" and its cognates. This book can be read as an empirical case for a unified theory (see especially the arguments in part II).

2. Philosophical Theories of Consciousness

In the dark ages, when scientists weren't allowed to talk about consciousness, philosophers had no such gag rule, and important work was done in this area. There has also been a flowering of philosophical theories during these last decades of scientific exploration, and several approaches have come to dominate the field. Our tour of theories will begin with these. I hereby beg for the patience of nonphilosophers.

2.1. DUALISM

The first stop on our tour is dualism, which was once considered outmoded but is now very much in vogue. According to a recent survey, 27 percent of philosophers deny that physicalism is true (http://philpapers.org/surveys/results.pl), and we can presume that most of these subscribe to some form of dualism. That doesn't mean that they accept the old Cartesian variety. Descartes conceived of mind and body as fundamentally different kinds of substances, and he thought that these substances could exist independently; thus, for Descartes, minds can exist without bodies, and each of us has an immortal soul. Ironically Descartes's dualism was not motivated by the same concerns that drive contemporary dualists. He doesn't dwell on the idea that it is difficult to explain the qualitative character of experience in physical terms. Indeed, Descartes (1633) explains perceptions as images in the brain, which are then conveyed by animal spirits (chemical transmitters) to the soul via the pineal gland. Although it's unclear from the text, he may think that the character of these perceptions has a physical explanation, which the soul can come to know. Descartes's dualism is motivated by his desire to explain rationality and the will; he did not see how a thinking thing, the author of thoughts and deliberative actions, could be contained in the brain. With the advent of modern computer science, which translated reasoning into logic and logic into electronic chips, there has been less anxiety about explaining reasoning mechanistically.

Contemporary dualists are generally *property* dualists; they say that some of our brain states have nonphysical properties, and they posit such properties to explain consciousness. Kripke (1980), Jackson (1982), and Chalmers (1996) have been especially influential in promoting this view. I will take up Jackson's argument in chapter 10, and my response there can be adapted in response to the others, but to see what's at stake, let's take a brief look at Kripke's argument.

Kripke begins by noting that mental-state terms (e.g., "pleasure") and brain-state terms (e.g., "striatal innervation") are usually *rigid designators*, meaning that whatever they refer to in the actual world they also refer to in all possible worlds. Identity statements between rigid designators are necessary, because if they are true here, they are always true. But every alleged identity between mental states and brain states (e.g., pleasure = striatal innervation), seems as if it could be false, because we can imagine one side of the identity existing without the other. Normally, when necessary identities appear contingent, it is because one term of the identity is associated with a contingent reference-fixing description. Thus, when we imagine that water might have been something other than H_2O, we are really imagining a perfectly possible state of affairs in which something that looks like water—a clear, tasteless liquid—isn't H_2O. Kripke argues that this strategy for explaining apparent contingency won't work with psychophysical identities. There is no way to imagine something that seems like pleasure but isn't, because we recognize pleasure by its essence rather than some contingent reference fixer; we recognize pleasures by their pleasurableness. Thus, if pleasure were really striatal innervation, then whenever we imagined pleasure, we'd be imagining a situation in which striatal innervation was taking place. If so, we are left with no explanation for why it seems as if the two can come apart. Absent such an explanation for why the two states would merely seem dissociable, Kripke concludes that they are dissociable, and if so, they are not identical.

This argument is based on the assumption that all imaginable states of affairs are possible, but this can be challenged. When we imagine that pleasure could exist without brain states, we are imagining a feeling of pleasure while also imagining (e.g., visualizing) an inert brain. If materialism is right, what we are imagining here is impossible, because the pleasure we experience is a brain state, which means that we couldn't have an inert brain. But imagination is cheap. It is easy to imagine feelings without realizing that they are brain states, because feelings, whether imagined or real, do not reveal their neural identity. From Kripke's perspective, that's a fatal concession. If pleasures are brain states, then, according to Kripke, we should be able to realize that from experience. But this premise is precisely where his and other dualist arguments go wrong. To block these arguments, physicalists need to show only that our epistemic relationship to feelings tells us what they are like without thereby allowing us to articulate what they are. There are numerous epistemic relations that seem to allow for such an epistemic gap: acquaintance versus description, knowing how versus knowing that, demonstrative versus nondemonstrative referring. The literature is full of suggestions about how to use such distinctions to combat dualism. My own attempt is in chapter 10.

We can also see from the start that dualism is implausible. The simple reason is that there is no empirical evidence for the view and overwhelming empirical evidence against it. Dualism entails that mental states and brain states can come apart. But there is no evidence for such dissociations in the actual world, not a single known example. Dualists might say that they come apart in other possible worlds, but what empirical test could possibly establish this if it can't happen in the actual world? No scientific instrument can show that they are separable. Thus, the view is woefully immune to empirical confirmation. Worse still, positing mental states that are not physical would require an expansion of physics. It requires laws that link brain states to a nonphysical realm, a realm with no mass or extension, no gravity or spin, no decomposition into atoms, no known form of energy, and so on. The awesome explanatory power of the physical sciences should give us strong reason to think that nothing lies outside their scope. If we had empirical evidence for such mental states, we might consider revising physics, but without any hope of finding such evidence, such a revision is radically unmotivated, even reckless. The dualist is forced to abandon the basic principles of scientific method and posit entities based on human imagination.

In response, dualists might counter that conscious mental states *establish* the incompleteness of physical science, because science fails to explain how brain states can be conscious. But this move confuses the ontological role of science for the epistemic one. Science establishes identities by counting entities; if two alleged posits, such as the morning star and the evening star, never come apart under any testing conditions or manipulation, then we should assume that there is only one entity there. Identities need not explain anything other than this co-occurrence. Furthermore, dualists live in a glass house when it comes to explanation. They say that brains produce consciousness by correspondence laws (Chalmers, 1996). Nothing about the brain explains why such laws exist. And when it comes to explaining why conscious states have the character that they do, dualists are again forced to posit brute facts. Phenomenal qualities are basic posits, so their character is not explained by anything. To make matters worse, dualists are left with further unsavory implications. For every measurable event, there is a physical cause, so conscious states seem to be causally inert, and if they are causally inert, it is unclear how we can gain epistemic access to them. Dualism digs out a swamp of explanatory lacuna, while offering to explain just one thing: why there is an epistemic gap between knowing what our experiences are like and knowing about correlated brain states (Levine, 1983). If we could find an alternative explanation of this gap without incurring the exorbitant costs of a dualist ontology, we'd be better off. This leaves us with the following desideratum on a theory of consciousness:

> **Phenomenal Knowledge**. An adequate theory should provide an account of how we epistemically access phenomenal states that blocks standard arguments for dualism.

In other words, given the unlikelihood that dualism is true, we need a tool for explaining why the material nature of consciousness resists discovery through introspection.

For the remainder of this chapter, I will assume that dualism is false and survey physicalist theories. Before embarking on that track, one small hurdle needs to be recognized. Physicalism is not easy to define (Jackson, 1998; Montero, 1999). One standard approach is to say that the mental *supervenes* on the physical in some way. On one definition of supervenience, this amounts to the claim that, necessarily, any two worlds that are indiscernible in their mental properties are also indiscernible in their physical properties. This definition captures the idea that mental differences always entail physical differences, but it doesn't take us all the way to physicalism. The problem is that supervenience is a correlational construct, and, at most, it tells us that mental and physical properties necessarily co-occur. As Kim (1998) points out, this is compatible with certain dualist forms of emergentism. Supervenience is satisfied by a theory that says that some physical properties necessarily produce specific nonphysical effects. Kim tries to get around this worry by defining physicalism as the view that all things can be composed into physical parts with no nonphysical remainders, but this leaves us with a worry about circularity: what counts as a physical part? The problem becomes more pressing when you notice that some dualists advocate extending physics to include primitive mental entities, and on such an expansion, irreducibly mental items could qualify as physical parts.

I offer the following working definition:

Physicalism is the conjecture that the fundamental laws and elementary parts that we find in things that lack mentality are the only fundamental laws and elementary parts in the universe.

The motivating idea behind the definition is that mentality does not require an expansion of fundamental science. One can capture the gist of physicalism by echoing a quip that Fodor (1985) made about intentionality: if mentality is anything at all, it is something else. Applied to consciousness, this means that physicalists must be able to say what consciousness is without appealing to any qualitative mental states. Some physicalists define consciousness in psychological terms, but the assumption is always that these terms can be cashed out nonpsychologically, by appeal to, say, causal relations or using vocabulary from some branch of neuroscience. The entities and processes postulated by neuroscience can then be decomposed into stuff found outside living organisms, such as chemical compounds, atoms, and laws of physics.

2.2. REPRESENTATIONALISM

One of the chief challenges for any theory of consciousness is to explain the phenomenal character of conscious states. Why do our conscious states feel the way they do? What is the nature of these felt qualities or qualia? Phenomenal character is sometimes seen as a foothold for dualism because it is tempting to posit irreducible mental items corresponding to each quale. Lewis (1929), who introduced the term, defines "qualia" as irreducibly subjective states that are ineffable and infallibly given in experience. They are not objective features of the world or representations of objective reality; we must infer the existence of objective properties by observing complex patterns in our qualia. The term "qualia" is now used to refer more broadly to the felt qualities that make up our experiences without any definitional commitment to what these qualities are. The question for physicalists is whether we can account for such qualities without positing irreducibly subjective states.

The most popular answer to this question is that qualia can be accommodated within a physicalist framework by identifying them with representational
properties (e.g., Harman, 1990; Lycan, 1996; Dretske, 1995; Tye, 1995). The
qualitative character of an experience is constituted, on this view, by what the
experience represents. A blue quale is not a mental item that has the property
of being blue but rather a representation of blueness, which is then characterized as an objective property in the world. The character of a quale can be
completely specified by saying what that quale represents. This view is called
representationalism, or sometimes intentionalism. Most representationalists
are also naturalists about representation. They assume that the representation
relation can be analyzed in physical terms. For example, Dretske says that a
mental state represents that about which it has the function of carrying information. Functions are determined by learning history or evolution, and carrying information can be characterized in terms of nomological connections
with the instantiation of properties in the world. On this view, a blue quale
represents blue in virtue of the fact that mental states of that type evolved to be
activated when blue is instantiated in the environment of their possessors. As I
like to put it, mental states represent what they are set up to be set off by. If
Dretske and other representationalists are right, qualitative character is utterly
unmysterious.

Several arguments can be advanced in favor of representationalism. One
source of appeal is that qualitative states seem to have accuracy conditions.
When you experience blueness during a perceptual episode, you thereby experience the world as being a certain way. One can say that some of our experiences
accurately capture the world, while others don't. The sea is not really blue; it
just reflects the blue sky. This suggests that qualia represent things. Of course,
representationalists are committed to the stronger thesis that qualitative differences are representational differences. But this, too, fits with accuracy intuitions. Byrne (2001) puts the point in terms of how things seem: if qualia change,
the world seems to be different. If you are experiencing blue while looking at a
circle on a computer screen in a psychology lab, and your experience changes to
yellow, you will say that the circle seems to have changed colors. You attribute
the difference in experience to the world. Likewise for any other phenomenal
changes. Even when you know that the change comes from within, as when a
night of heavy drinking makes you see double, the change is experienced as a
difference in how the world seems to be.

This argument supports the view that qualitative differences are taken to
have representational import, but it's too weak to support the stronger representational thesis that qualitative differences are nothing but representational differences. One might imagine that qualia present by means of certain purely
experiential qualities and, thus, that every experience has two aspects: it represents some aspect of reality, and it does so by means of a special model of presentation. Byrne's appeal to how things seem does not rule out this possibility.

One might say, "Gee, that circle seems to have changed, because I am experiencing it in a different way." In fact, Byrne embraces this possibility. He is open to the idea that there is "mental paint," analogous to the idea that paintings depict the subjects using pigment on a canvas, and in seeing a painting, we are, in some sense, aware of both content and the painting itself (see Block, 1996). Byrne points out that one can accept mental paint while remaining true to the letter of representationalism. For example, one can adopt a "Fregean representationalism," according to which qualia represent via "modes of presentation," a concept borrowed from Frege's philosophy of language (Thompson, 2006; Chalmers, 2004). On one version of this, qualia are individuated by their representational content, but they represent response-dependent properties, such as the property of causing blue experiences, and it is by means of these experiences that we represent the property of causing such experiences. Here, blue experiences present the property of being blue, which is nothing but the property of causing such experiences.

Such an approach would undermine the ambitions of those representationalists who hope to provide a reductive account of mental qualities in terms of representational content. If qualia represent the property of causing qualia (as Thompson suggests), then, on pain of circularity, we need some independent account of how qualia are individuated that is not representational in nature. By analogy, if the state of amusement represents the property of being amusing, then we need a nonrepresentational account of what it is for something to amuse. We might define the property of being amusing as disposing one toward laughter, and then we can escape the circle by saying that amusement represents that disposition. Likewise, if experiences of blue represent the power to cause such experiences, then there must be a way to pick out blue experiences in nonrepresentational terms. This form of representationalism cannot be a complete theory of qualitative character until we specify a way to individuate experiences in nonrepresentational terms. I will return to this option below, but for now, let me turn to arguments for a more thoroughgoing kind of representationalism, which says that qualia are individuated by the *mind-independent* properties that they represent.

One argument for thoroughgoing representationalism is that it offers a needed prophylactic against dualism (Lycan, 1996). If you have a green afterimage, there is nothing in your brain that is green and also nothing green in the physical world. This has led some dualists to posit green sense data. Representationalists can avoid this ontological extravagance by saying that the green afterimage is an "intentional inexistence." There is nothing green in the world or in the mind; we simply represent greenness. The Fregean representationalist cannot make this move so easily. For Fregeans such as Thompson, green is the property of causing certain kinds of experiences. What kind? The green kind, of course, and this brings us back to the question of where the green is if it's neither in the brain nor in the world.

This argument is alluring, but it suffers from an important limitation. There is a parallel move for blocking sense data, which does not require representationalism. The move, found in Place (1956) and Smart (1959), uses a "topic-neutral" approach to qualia individuation. It says that an experience of greenness is an experience of the kind one has when seeing green things, such as leaves, limes, and leprechauns—no need to say that the experience represents any entities. To choose between this topic-neutral approach and its representationalist cousin, we need to consider whether there are good reasons for resisting thoroughgoing representationalism. I think there are, as we will see after considering one more argument.

The most common argument for representationalism appeals to the so-called transparency or diaphanousness of experience (Harman, 1990; Tye, 1995; Dretske, 1995). When we try to examine our mental states, we never seem to find anything identifiably mental. Instead, we are immediately taken to the world. Perceptual experience seems to present us with the world in an unmediated way. Common sense might lead us to believe that we have direct access to external things. It is only rare and exotic experiences, such as afterimages and illusions, that lead us to realize, contrary to appearance, that there may be psychological intermediaries between mind and world. Representationalism offers a tidy explanation. If qualitative character is representational content, then any effort to look within will take us back out, and we will discover only those mind-independent properties that our experiences denote.

The transparency intuition is hard to shake, but it can be explained without assuming that qualitative character is exhausted by intentional content. An old and appealing alternative story says that experience seems transparent because we have acquired the habit, or innate predisposition, of using it to identify external objects (Reid, 1764; Kind, 2003). When we inspect our experiences, we immediately know which features of the world they correspond to, and this knowledge, though not intrinsic to the character of experience, makes it seem as though experiences are putting us in direct contact with the world. One might think of the habits in question as resulting in a kind of projective error. We mistake qualities of experience for external things, because we use them so successfully and automatically as a guide. By analogy, think of how the feeling of vibrations in your body is projected onto the surface of the road when driving.

This alternative view explains the sense of transparency by appeal to an automatic projection that gives us the illusion of qualia being external. This explanation may even be better than the explanation offered by thoroughgoing representationalists. Recall that they explain transparency by proposing that the content of qualia is exhausted by representational content. This fact, on its own, may not account for the experience of transparency. Notice, for example, that many philosophers of language believe that the content of words is exhausted by what they represent. It doesn't follow that we experience words transparently, somehow seeing the world directly through them. A further premise would be needed to explain transparency. We would need to say that when it comes to qualia, unlike words, we experience the message but not the medium. Nothing about the thesis that qualia represent guarantees such a premise, and indeed it is puzzling to understand how this could be true, since it is so radically different from the linguistic case where the medium always mediates. Thoroughgoing representationalists must say that qualia give us the world and nothing more, and they do this by simply representing the world, while other representations of the world lack this remarkable property. It is far less mysterious to assume that qualia give us the world, because we are disposed by habit, or innate reflex, to respond to their qualities as if they are out there in the world.

If this alternative view is correct, and transparency is a kind of projection, there should be special circumstances under which that projection breaks down, making it easier to appreciate that sensory qualities are not really external. Consider, for example, the experience of people who have vision restored after many years of blindness. For them, vision is disorienting and difficult to interpret (Cheselden, 1728; Sacks, 1995; Fine et al., 2002; Held et al., 2011). When Cheselden removed cataracts from a teenager born blind, the boy thought that all visual objects were touching his eyes. Similar disorientation occurs when first adjusting to cochlear implants. Or consider ordinary visual imagery. If I instruct you to imagine a pink elephant, you might do so without forming any impression that the elephant appears to be out there in the world. It is, paradoxically, occupying a space that is nowhere. The image is representational, of course, but it is also recognized as an item in the mind. It is difficult to see the phenomenal qualities caused by external objects as mental because they are under external control, but if you squint while looking at an external object, there is little temptation to interpret the object as changing; the blurring and distortion are experienced as features of the seeing, not the seen. This is not a decisive reply to the argument from transparency, but it suggests that there may be a nonrepresentationalist explanation, and that weakens the argument, especially if it can be shown that representationalism is implausible on other grounds.

I think there are good reasons to reject thoroughgoing representationalism, although some of the most widely discussed objections are unconvincing. There have been many attempts to devise counterexamples, but representationalists are skilled at explaining these (e.g., Peacocke, 1983; Tye, 1992). There are also elaborate spectrum-inversion cases, designed to show that qualia and content can come apart, and to these, there are elaborate representationalist replies (e.g., Block, 1998; Tye, 2000). Rather than reviewing this vast literature, I will here just indicate four general worries that I consider especially damaging.

The first worry is that there are no convincing candidates for the mind-independent properties that our qualitative states could represent. Mind-independent properties should have identity conditions that can be specified without reference to an observer. The trouble is, our sensory states don't seem to be reliably related to any such properties. Consider color. One famous problem is metamers: because of the way our visual system is built, pairs of very different wavelengths can cause the same color experience. Inventive stories have been proposed about how two metamerically matched wavelengths can be regarded as belonging to the same complex property, but in principle, the properties in question have no integrity without reference to the visual systems of perceivers. That may spell trouble for representationalists, because it concedes that the qualities we experience depend on our physical constitution, and that threatens the ambition to explain inner experience by outer features of the world (see Kuehni and Hardin's 2010 reply to Churchland, 2007). Less discussed is the fact that color experiences change with mood, energy, and context. Depression apparently makes the world grayer (Bubl et al., 2010), as does sleep deprivation (Sheth, Nguyen, and Whittaker, 2010). The color we experience when looking at a surface also depends profoundly on surrounding surfaces together with prior statistical information culled from the environment (Purves and Lotto, 2003). Such findings prove that color experiences are fully determined not by the wavelengths that cause them on a given occasion but by highly variable disjunctions of wavelengths, which overlap with the disjunctions of wavelengths that cause extremely different color experiences. One might take this as evidence for there being an objective property that colors aim to track, but which property? Is it the wavelengths we respond to when happy and well rested? Unlikely, since smiling and sleeping well were not necessarily the norm during evolution. Another problem is that the similarity space of experienced colors has no objective correlates. For example, we perceive color boundaries categorically, so that pairs of colors on either side of a boundary look more different than pairs on the same side that are at the same distance by objective measures. Representationalists might reply that this is simply a case of misrepresentation; we represent boundaries that are not really there. This is clearly right in some sense, but it is difficult to say which of our color experiences are misrepresenting: do categorical boundaries *stretch* the gaps between two nameable colors, or do they *shrink* the differences between colors that have the same name?

Such problems are not limited to color. Shape, which is traditionally considered a primary quality, is also experienced in a way that defies objective explanation. For one thing, shape is very much like color, in that shapes are made up of lines and shades, and these have qualities that go beyond what is represented; there is no reason the way we experience darkness has to represent darkness as opposed to lightness. In addition, we see shapes from a particular point of view, which means that the shapes we experience are not the shapes things have. Representationalists often respond by saying that the content of our shape experiences corresponds to something like the two-dimensional projections caused by shapes on a flat surface, comparable to the pictures we would produce if we were to put a piece of glass in front of our eyes and trace the outlines of what we saw. One problem for this suggestion is stereopsis. The lines we experience have depth, so their phenomenal spatial properties are not limited to the lengths that would be depicted on a corresponding two-dimensional projection. What is the phenomenal length of a line that seems to recede in space? Another problem is that lines on a glass tracing of space have measurable sizes; we can count the centimeters. But what is the metric of visual lines? The lines given to us in experience have sizes relative to one another but no objective length. This point can be made vivid by considering figure 1. The hat depicted there is, in reality, as tall as it is wide, but we perceive the height and width as different. Now ask which one of these two perceived lengths is the erroneous one. There seems to be no answer. We cannot even specify a mental length as a fixed fraction of the visual field, since the field expands and contracts with changes in attention. Nor would it help to say that the qualitative character of a mental line is a relative length, since we can experience the qualitative character of a mental line in isolation without comparing it with any other. Mental lines represent relative lengths, but they do so by having mental lengths that differ in comparison with each other, and mental lengths seem to have no determinate external content. This suggests that there is no simple mapping from the way space is experienced phenomenally to spatial properties of external objects or even projections of external objects on two-dimensional surfaces.

FIGURE 1 The height of this hat looks longer than the width of its base, but they are the same length.

These points can be summarized by comparing visual states with pictures. Visual states are like pictures in that their parts are spatially arranged (Kosslyn, 1994). Their parts also correspond to colors and shades, much like dashes of paint on a canvas. But visual states also differ from pictures. Some of these differences are obvious: there is no viewer; they have depth; their lines are bound together into coherent contours, whereas pictorial lines are not intrinsically bound; contiguous parts of distinct objects in a picture are not connected parts of the same object. Moreover, mental pigments have no color (they don't reflect light), and therefore, they cannot represent colors the way paintings do (paintings represent colors by resemblance). Moreover, as noted, the lines in mental images differ from pictorial lines in that they lack objective extension. One can measure a line in a painting, but mental lines are unmeasurable; they can be described only in relative terms, as longer or shorter. Pictorial content might be exhaustively analyzed representationally; one can specify what features pictures represent their objects as having, and one can specify the way they present those objects by listing the pigments they use and the extensions of the lines they contain. We cannot do this with mental images. We can specify what objects they represent in the world, but there is no obvious procedure for specifying how they represent those objects by appeal to pigments and measurable shapes.

The second worry is that distinct senses sometimes seem to represent the same properties in qualitatively different ways. The same texture can be seen and touched, and these differ phenomenally; consider the look and feel of razor stubble. The same location (e.g., to my upper right) can be seen, heard, felt, or smelled, and spatial representation across the senses exploits different brain mechanisms (Kaas, 1997; Macaluso and Driver, 2001; see Lopes, 2000). We can also see and hear the same quantity; three tones and three cookies both feel like three but in different ways. Some representationalists admit that such differences require a nonrepresentational treatment (Lycan, 1996), but others attempt to argue that the senses have no precise overlap in their representational content. One strategy is to say that each represents a different physical magnitude: light, sound waves, chemical structures, and so on. But this is unpromising. It is ad hoc to say that our senses represent these physical magnitudes rather than ordinary macro-features such as shape, size, and location, given that it is these latter that explain what we use our senses for and why they evolved. Moreover, there may be cases in which the same physical magnitude feels different across the senses (sourness may smell and taste different) and across submodalities (pressure may feel different to pain receptors and to touch receptors; light may feel different to visual pathways that register color and value). Carruthers (2000) suggests that senses differ in their temporal profiles: in vision, we can see the whole shape of an object while feeling its texture, whereas touch may not give us access to the whole shape at once. But this won't work for some cases. Scott (2007) rightfully complains that the proposal cannot explain visual and auditory experiences of space, and it also stumbles when explaining differences between the basic units of experience: a local bit of visual smoothness differs phenomenally from a local bit of tactile smoothness, regardless of how surrounding bits may happen to get disclosed over time. It seems more plausible to say that the proprietary phenomenology of the senses is intrinsic rather than representational. Once we say this, however, we may need to introduce resources that are sufficient for explaining all qualities in nonrepresentational terms.

The third worry is that representation is a relation between mind and world, and the conditions under which that relation can be altered or undermined differ from the conditions under which qualia change. The point relates to color-inversion cases and other thought experiments, but such cases are best seen as illustrations of a more principled point. Consider brains in a vat, which could be wired up to the world in very different ways from our brains. For example, one could wire a brain so that color cells fired when and only when orchestral instruments played. On any theory of reference, there is some such arrangement that would have semantic impact, but there is absolutely no theory-independent reason to suppose that it would have an impact on the character of experience. Or you could imagine two humans living in worlds with different light waves, such that each could encounter only one of two metamerically matched colors and not the other. An independently motivated semantic theory might say that their resulting experiences represent different wavelengths, but there is no reason to deny that they are qualitatively alike. Some representationalists deal with such cases by saying that representation depends on what's in the head rather than external relations (e.g., Horgan, 2000), but it's hard to see how this could work. To get reference to supervene on brain states, one could say that qualitative character itself determines reference, but that undermines representationalism by reversing the explanatory order. Or one could say that the content of a qualitative state is a function from worlds to external properties, which would deal with the metamer case but not the vatted brain. Vatted brains serve to show that it is the inner states themselves that matter for experience, not anything relational. One can bite the bullet and say that vatted brains have different qualia, but this flies in the face of the scientific evidence correlating experiences with neural responses: for every measurable change in experience, there is some measurable change in the nervous system.

The fourth and final worry begins with an obvious point that most representationalists readily acknowledge. Representation can occur outside of consciousness. In fact, the very same types of sensory representations that we experience consciously can generally occur unconsciously. When this happens, these representations don't seem to feel like anything at all (see chapter 3 for more discussion). They seem to lack phenomenal character. This has led most representationalists to recognize that a theory of consciousness needs two parts: an account of the content of conscious states and an account of how those states become conscious. Representationalism is best construed as an answer to the first question, and some further bit of machinery is needed for the second (Lycan's approach is discussed below in section 2.3 and Tye's in section 3.1 of this chapter). But these two components are also interrelated. The mechanisms that make us conscious also endow representations with their phenomenal character. If so, we can ask, how do they do it? Most theories assume that mental states become conscious by virtue of a change that takes place within the organism: a difference in how our mental representations are processed. That raises the possibility that representations also gain the qualitative character by virtue of something within the organism. Something about the conscious mode of processing endows representations with their character. Since these representations represent the same things both consciously and unconsciously, this change in their character is best explained by appeal to something other than their representational qualities. Some representationalists say that the quality of a representation depends on its content *plus* whatever makes it conscious (Tye, 1995), but there is something puzzling about this. It seems odd to say that character depends on some inner change and some outer relation. Once we admit that an inner change endows a representation with phenomenal character, why not say that that inner change is constitutive of its character? The purely inner story would be simpler and more cohesive.

Let me summarize with a sketch of a positive view. I think it is indubitable that our conscious states normally represent things, and they have probably even evolved to represent objective features of the world. But they seem to do so by means of appearances, and these appearances cannot be exhaustively characterized in representational terms. A visual image of a line represents an objective length by means of an apparent length. And an image of a colored surface represents light waves by means of apparent colors. People can report on both objective properties and appearances (e.g., Gogel, 1990). Objective properties can be expressed linguistically by naming some mind-independent property that one takes a visual state to represent (e.g., that stick is probably about a meter long). Appearance can be expressed in relative terms (e.g., the stick lying on the ground looks shorter than the one planted in the ground, even though it is longer objectively). Appearances cannot be cashed out by appeal to objective properties; for example, they cannot be characterized in terms of the features that a two-dimensional projection would have. Instead, appearances must be specified by reference to response-dependent properties. Qualitative orange is a mental response that orange things cause in viewers like us, not a property of the external world.

Putting this all together, we can say that our conscious states have two layers of content. They represent objective properties by representing (or "registering") appearances, where appearances are characterized as response-dependent properties. Different sensory states can represent the same objective properties via different response-dependent properties, as in the cross-modal cases or in cases of sensory constancies. Qualitative character corresponds to response-dependent properties insofar as qualitative differences and similarities align with differences and similarities in our responses.

The story so far points to a Fregean account of qualitative content. We can think of appearances as modes of presentation, and we can say that qualia are individuated by reference to these modes. But I think that Fregean accounts don't go quite far enough. If we simply equate qualitative character with appearances, we will imply that two stimuli with the same appearance will always be qualitatively alike. There is a simple reason to reject this view. Plausibly, the same appearance can be instantiated both consciously and unconsciously. If we unconsciously perceive a shape or color, then it will presumably have the same appearance that it would have if consciously presented. But the unconscious appearance will not have qualitative character; it won't feel like anything. Therefore, appearances alone do not account for qualitative character. If we think of appearances as modes of presentation, then Fregean representationalism is out.

To address this worry, we need to make a small but important amendment to the Fregean account. To have qualitative character, a mental state must not only present the world as having some appearance, but it also must do so consciously. Qualitative character is a property that representations acquire when they become conscious. Thus, the qualitative character of a mental state is not its mode alone but the conscious instantiation of a mode. Qualia are neither objective properties that we represent nor appearances but are rather appearances as consciously experienced.

The main points that I have been arguing for can be stated as a two-part desideratum:

> **Subjective Character**. On an adequate theory, qualitative character should be located in states that represent appearances, and those states have their character only when they are conscious.

This formulation leaves open the question of whether some form of representationalism is true, although it also makes it hard to see how any standard formulation of representationalism could work. If the relevant mental states always have their representational content but sometimes lack qualitative character, then qualitative character cannot be simply equated with representational content. What representationalism gets right is that we can distinguish qualitative states by what they represent, but here, too, there is an important proviso: qualitative mental states must have a kind of content that is deeply perspectival.

2.3. HIGHER-ORDER REPRESENTATION

I said that representationalism is not a theory of consciousness but a theory of the qualitative character of conscious states. Theories of qualia focus on the differences among consciousness states, and theories of consciousness focus on the differences between conscious and unconscious states. Merely representing something is not enough to make a mental state conscious. Something more is needed. There is no consensus about what that extra ingredient might be, and all of the theories discussed in the remainder of this chapter provide very different answers. Within philosophy, however, one class of theories is particularly popular: higher-order-representation (HOR) theories.

According to HOR theories, a mental state becomes conscious when and only when it is represented by another mental state. Theories diverge with respect to which kind of higher-order states confer consciousness and what relationship lower-order states need to have in relation to these higher-order states, beyond merely being represented by them. I will consider the two dominant versions here.

The first version is the higher-order perception theory of consciousness (HOP), which follows up on Locke's (1690: 2.I.xix) suggestion "Consciousness is the perception of what passes in a Man's own mind." In its modern guise, the theory was most influentially advanced by Armstrong (1968) and has been most forcefully defended by Lycan (1987; 1996). The basic idea is that mental states become conscious when some perception-like inner monitor represents them. Lycan (1996: 14) describes the inner monitor as an internal attention mechanism. Like perception, it can be used to scan and focus in on what passes through the mind. More particularly, the inner monitor scans perceptual states, and it outputs representations of the states that it scans at an equally fine grain. By so doing, the monitor makes its possessor aware of those states.

The second kind of HOR theory trades in higher-order perceptions for higher-order thoughts (HOTs). The principle architect of the HOT theory is David Rosenthal (1986; 1997; 2005). He argues that consciousness arises when a mental state causes, in some noninferential way, a higher-order thought representing that state. On this view, there is no inner monitor, and the higher-order states are thoughts, which is to say, they are conceptual. Like Lycan, Rosenthal does not think that we are aware of these higher-order representations unless there is some third-order representation representing them. Unlike Lycan, Rosenthal does not imply that consciousness is restricted to perception; HOTs can target other thoughts.

Lycan and Rosenthal both offer reasons for preferring their own views, but there is also a more general argument designed to show that some kind of HOR is needed for consciousness. The argument is suggested by Rosenthal's (1986: 335) remark that "Conscious states are simply mental states that we are conscious of being in." This sounds like a point of definition. If conscious states are defined as states of which we are conscious, then HORs may be seen as essential, for how else can we become conscious of something except by representing it? A more explicit version of the argument is advanced by Lycan (2001: 3). It can be rendered as follows:

P1. A conscious state is a mental state whose subject is aware of being in it.

P2. The "of" in P1 is the "of" of intentionality.

P3. A state has a thing as its intentional object only if it represents that thing.

C1. Therefore, awareness of a mental state is a representation of that state.

C2. Therefore, a conscious state is a state that is itself represented by another of the subject's mental states.

In what follows, I will begin by raising some objections to this general argument, and then I offer more specific objections to HOT and HOP theories.

There is reason to doubt Lycan's argument from the outset. We are trying to figure out what distinguishes conscious and unconscious states. It is hard to imagine why that could be determined a priori, as Lycan would have us believe. He describes the first premise as a point of definition. But "definition" is just a fancy word for a common sense conception of something, and common sense can be profoundly mistaken (some people conceptualize the world as flat, gorillas as ferocious, dolphins as docile, various ethnic groups as having traits that they lack, and so on). To find a substantive theory of what makes some states conscious, we need to begin with some paradigm cases and then investigate what makes them distinctive. The definitional move in P1 is neither necessary nor sufficient for that endeavor.

P1 can also be challenged on conceptual grounds. Conscious states feel like something, but it doesn't follow that we are aware of them. It could work out that feeling like something is an intrinsic property. Granted, we are often aware of our feelings, but this does not seem like a conceptual truth. For example, it seems conceptually possible that I might be feeling depressed and not realize it, or I might experience an increased state of intoxication without being aware of it.

P2 is also questionable. When we talk about "awareness of" mental states, we might be using a grammatical construction that doesn't reveal anything about the real way we gain access to our mental states. Just as the German language forces users to postulate a subject when they say "es gibt" ("there is"), English seems to have a syntactic transformation that goes from "state S is conscious" to "someone is conscious of S," which we can rephrase as "someone is aware of S." This may not be admissible in every language. In Russian, talk of awareness is predominantly used for cognitive states (akin to "I realize that P"), and instead of talking about "consciousness of S," Russians talk about "S being felt." Russians can talk about having a feeling of pain (the preposition is translated using a declension on the word for pain), but here the "of" is classificatory, not intentional, as in a "brand of detergent."

Even P3 is problematic. Let's suppose that the "of" in "aware of" is intentional. It still might not be representational in the sense of requiring a mental representation. Representations are used by the mind to keep track of things in the external world, but for things inside the mind, representations may be unnecessary. Intuitively, a subject can become conscious of a mental state simply by having the state. The conscious state might be experienced by virtue of its intrinsic properties rather than any representation of it. It would still make sense, in this picture, to say we become "aware of" our conscious states, because they are items that we experience, but we don't become aware of them by representing them; they are, as it were, self-illuminating.

With three dubious premises, I think we can safely put Lycan's argument to rest. HOR theories should be assessed on their empirical merits rather than their conformity to English. I will begin that assessment with Lycan's HOP theory. One reason for resisting this theory is that the analogy to perception is very problematic. For one thing, outward perception admits of a conscious/unconscious distinction, but if the HOP theory is right, inner perception is always conscious. In addition, inner perception has no transducers, no breakdowns characteristic of perception (such as agnosias), no hierarchical organization, and no systematic illusions. Dretske (1995) also complains that if there were an inner sense, it should have its own phenomenal qualities, but the qualities we experience consciously are just those of our first-order states. Lycan admits that the idea of inner perception is just an analogy, so these complaints are not fatal, but they do suggest that we need a better, perhaps less metaphorical, account of what inner monitoring consists of. One helpful suggestion already mentioned is that inner monitors are used to *attend* to inner states. Attention is a much better analogy. As Lycan (2004) points out, consciousness can come in degrees just as attention does, the phenomenology of consciousness makes it feel like attending to our perceptual states, and we can willfully control which ones we attend to. The problem here is that the analogy is so apt that it points to an alternative theory of consciousness. If inner monitoring seems like attending, then perhaps it *is* attending. If that's so, then it's hard to see why this is a higher-order theory at all. Standard accounts of attention (see chapter 3) do not assume that we attend by representing our sensory states. Attention works by simply changing the way first-order states are processed. This would explain why consciousness has the same grain of resolution as perception and introduces no new phenomenal qualities. This point can be restated as an objection. The HOP theory says that inner monitors represent first-order states in a mental code that is just like those first-order states, but it seems woefully inefficient to re-represent representations that are already there. Thus, in its most plausible form, the HOP theory collapses into a first-order theory of consciousness.

HOT theories, in contrast, are stably and decidedly second-order. But they face more serious objections as a result. Some of these objections were already implicit in discussing the HOP theory. The HOT theory has difficulty explaining why consciousness can come in degrees, why it can arise by act of will (we can't choose our beliefs), and why introspecting feels like attention (Lycan, 2004). Another common complaint is that thoughts are more coarse-grained than conscious experiences (Lycan, 2004): the range of things we can consciously discriminate outstrips those we can recognize from one occasion to another (Raffman, 1995). Concepts are generally regarded as endowing us with recognitional abilities (Millikan, 2000; Prinz, 2002), so this suggests that we don't have concepts for the full range of things that we can consciously experience, and hence we can't have thoughts corresponding to every conscious experience. Rosenthal (2005: 188) replies by proposing that we make fine sensory discriminations using *comparative* concepts. We lack concepts that could be used to recognize an exact shade of green from one occasion to the next, but when we see it next to another green, we can apply concepts such as "brighter than" or "yellower than" to distinguish it in experience. This strategy is unpromising, however, because we can experience specific colors in isolation, and it would be odd to say that comparisons arise when we do so. Some cases of sensory discrimination also defy comparison. Imagine tasting rosemary and sage for the first time; you might fail to form a concept to recognize them on the next occasion, and you might lack comparative concepts to articulate how they differ, but you would have no difficulty telling them apart. Likewise, if you are inexperienced with wine, two bottles may be easy to discriminate even if you lack concepts to characterize the differences.

Rosenthal would counter by arguing that the wine case actually favors the conceptual commitments of the HOT theory. When we learn to taste wine, concepts such as "tannin" seem to transform our experience. Rosenthal (1997) infers that these taste components are not experienced prior to acquisition of the concepts. But this phenomenon can be explained by assuming that concepts have first-order effects, a fact that is well supported by neuroimaging studies of people who become expert classifiers (Tarr and Gauthier, 2000). Perhaps the concept of tannin allows us to attend to the tannins in a sip of wine, and attention alters the sensory input by magnifying the intensity of that component. Interestingly, in the case of wine experts, such conceptual labels do not seem to play a crucial role in their superior tasting skills. Rather, expertise seems to come with perceptual skills, such as improved imagination, not the acquisition of verbally expressible categories (Parr, White, and Heatherball, 2004). This suggests that concepts may not be the source of phenomenal change when we learn to taste wine.

Furthermore, Rosenthal needs it to be the case that concepts are necessary for conscious experience, and that seems unlikely. Experience is often the basis of concept acquisition rather than the other way around. Someone can teach us how to recognize tannins by pointing out a phenomenal quality that has not yet been conceptualized ("Focus on how the wine makes your mouth pucker"); that experience can ultimately be stored in memory as a concept for recognition, but it is initially encountered nonconceptually. This can be understood as another argument against the HOT theory: experience is often prior to sensory concept acquisition and even a precondition for it.

A further worry is that the HOT theory is committed to the possibility of conscious thoughts. Just as we can have a HOT represent a perception, we can have a HOT representing our most sophisticated cognitive states. Rosenthal considers this an argument in favor of the HOT theory, saying that perception consciousness seems to fall between unconscious perception and introspective awareness of our own thoughts—a three-way comparison that could be elegantly explained by assuming that HOTs iterate at the third order. This is unpersuasive to those of us who doubt that higher cognition has a distinctive phenomenology (see chapter 5). What do nonperceptual concepts feel like? To me, it's a striking fact that I usually become aware of my own thoughts by means of inner speech, which means that I am decidedly not ascending to third-order awareness but rather kicking my ideas downstairs to the first order, where they can be experienced like sounds.

There are also problems stemming from an empirical commitment of the HOT view that has not been brought out explicitly. To have a higher-order thought, we need to deploy mental-state concepts. To think that you are seeing a sunset, you need a concept of seeing. This implies that people who have difficulty with mental-state concepts, such as individuals with autism, should suffer from corresponding deficits in consciousness. There is no evidence for that. People with autism seem to perform normally when it comes to actions that require perceptual consciousness, such as tying shoelaces or spontaneously responding to an object presented before their eyes.

More generally, there has been little effort to provide empirical support in favor of the theory, and few scientists have openly embraced it (see Weiskrantz, 1997; Rolls, 2004; and Lau, 2008, for exceptions). Weiskrantz (1997) does not offer a direct empirical demonstration of the HOT approach; his main source of evidence seems to be that individuals with blindsight cannot "comment" on the stimuli presented in their blind fields, which suggests that consciousness is linked to the operation of a commentary system, which Weiskrantz likens to a capacity for higher-order thoughts. But this is a large inferential leap, given that the brain damage that causes blindsight is in the sensory system, not in a commentary system, so the disorder may be caused by a sensory deficit, which eliminates the ability to comment, rather than the other way around. Rolls (2004) does not offer empirical support for higher-order theories but instead advances the theoretical claim that consciousness is linked to reportability and instrumental reasoning, and this in turn leads him to surmise that language centers are involved in consciousness. But there is no empirical support for this claim; language centers do not correlate with consciousness, and linguistic impairments have not been demonstrated to eliminate consciousness. Indeed, the empirical work by Rolls that bears most directly on consciousness indicates that the difference between conscious and unconscious states can be associated with neural integration within sensory systems; in a study of backward masking in monkey brains, he found that consciousness is associated with an increase in spiking frequency and duration among visual neurons (Rolls and Tovée, 1994). Rolls does not provide neurobiological evidence for thinking that these first-order changes are insufficient for consciousness.

Lau and Rosenthal (2011) have recently argued that a higher-order theory of consciousness can be defended empirically, although Lau prefers talk of higher-order processes rather than higher-order thoughts. This distinction is crucial, because, empirically, it amounts to the claim that the prefrontal cortex is implicated in consciousness. I will endorse a qualified version of this thesis in chapter 4, so much of the evidence that Lau and Rosenthal cite can equally be regarded as evidence for the theory that I will be defending, even though it is not a higher-order-thought theory. To see why their evidence does not favor the HOT approach, let me consider what I take to be the most direct line of evidence in their review. Lau and Rosenthal cite a study in which transcranial magnetic stimulation is applied to the dorsolateral prefrontal cortex (DLPFC), and that results in a reduction of self-reported "clearness" of visual stimuli but not a reduction in perceptual discrimination (Rounis et al., 2010). To use this as evidence for a HOT theory, the finding must be interpreted as follows: one must assume that the DLPFC is the locus of higher-order thoughts and that disruption to this area has an impact on experience because such thoughts are necessary for experience. But this interpretation can be challenged. First, the DLPFC has functions other than metacognition. In fact, it is primarily a working-memory hub. "Working memory" refers to our capacity to store information briefly. Such storage does not require metacognition; working memory stores by maintaining information, not representing it (chapter 10). The DLPFC has occasionally been implicated in studies of metacognition, but metacognition is more frequently associated with other brain structures: the temporoparietal junction, precuneus, superior temporal sulcus, and medial prefrontal cortex (Dodell-Feder et al., 2011). None of these brain structures has been implicated in consciousness, and there is little reason to suppose that they would alter experience under transcranial magnetic stimulation. As for the effect on visibility when magnetic stimulation is applied to the DLPFC, it is possible that working memory serves to reactivate, enrich, and retain sensory representations of stimuli, when they are accurately detected. Impairing the DLPFC reduces these effects and thereby lowers vividness when objects are presented. This does not imply that the DLPFC is necessary or a correlate of consciousness, only that it can enhance first-order states. Indeed, there is no evidence that frontal damage has a major effect on visibility, even if it can have a subtle impact.

In summary, there is strong evidence against the HOT theory and little empirical support. But there is also a powerful philosophical argument in favor of the theory that needs to be addressed. Rosenthal (1997) argues that higher-order thoughts are required to explain why conscious mental states are always reportable. All of the items in conscious experience, unlike those that are processed unconsciously, seem to be available for reporting. This is readily explained by the supposition that every conscious state has a corresponding HOT. Rosenthal suggests that reports of conscious states always report HOTs. If conscious states are reportable, and they report HOTs, then conscious states are always accompanied by HOTs, and that can be explained by assuming that HOTs make them conscious. In response, one can take issue with the claim that conscious states are always reportable. When we see a rich visual scene, we can report on some of its details, but many are too fleeting and too ineffable to comment on. Many details are experienced but go unnoticed, as in some cases of change blindness, a phenomenon in which clearly visible features of pictures are altered without viewers realizing it. If consciousness required HOTs, we might expect all of the details of experience to be poised for immediate reporting, but there is little evidence for that. The intuition that conscious states are reportable is not completely unfounded, however. When you look at a complex scene, there is no conscious component that you couldn't potentially comment on if current task demands required it. This suggests that conscious states are not all immediately reportable but are poised to be reportable. Think of Sperling's (1960) experiments with briefly displayed arrays of letters. Viewers seemed to experience all of the letters but could report only a few, suggesting that only a few got encoded in a format conducive for reporting. But Sperling showed that all of the letters were poised to be reportable, by telling people which row to report after the array was removed. People performed successfully, suggesting that all of our conscious experiences can become reportable with the right cue but are not reportable simply by virtue of being conscious.

This last point reveals an important kernel of truth in the higher-order approach. The alleged link between consciousness and awareness that is so central to HOR theories can be captured by a weaker variant: ordinarily, when we are conscious of something, we are in a position to become aware of that fact. It might even be ventured, more strongly, that we can become noninferentially aware of our first-order states only when they are conscious. Note that these are not conceptual claims. I am not endorsing a definitional link between a state's being conscious and our being aware of it. Nor am I suggesting that consciousness requires awareness; the opposite may be true. But if the opposite is true, that itself implies an important connection. It seems that consciousness puts us in position to become aware and may be necessary for doing so.

Despite the kernel of truth in higher-order theories, my main goal here has been to argue that consciousness does not require meta-representation. I think this conclusion is so likely to be true that it should be adopted as a desideratum:

First-Order Consciousness. An adequate theory should explain how mental states can become conscious without requiring that they are represented by some other mental states.

In setting out this condition, we mustn't lose sight of the factors that motivate higher-order theories, such as the fact that reportable states are conscious. The theory I ultimately endorse owes much to this tradition. But I think that first-order theories are preferable. First-order theories have also been favored by scientists.

3. Scientific Theories

3.1. GLOBAL WORKSPACE

As we saw at the beginning of this chapter, scientific interest in consciousness has grown steadily over the last quarter-century. Physicists, biologists, psychologists, and all manner of neuroscientists have gotten in on the game. There are almost as many theories as authors, although many are variations of the same basic ideas. Here we'll look at the scientific theories that seem to have attained the greatest visibility. Our tour begins with the global workspace theory, originally advanced by Bernard Baars (1988; 2002), a pioneer of contemporary consciousness studies and cofounder of a leading organization and journal in the area.

According to the global workspace theory, consciousness arises when mental states, including perceptions, images, thoughts, and memories, are made available to a global workspace. The global workspace is a short-term memory that makes the contents of those states available to numerous psychological systems, including systems involved in cognition, memory, motivation, and behavioral control. The workspace is part of working memory, which is where we store information temporarily for active use, such as when entering a phone number. But not everything in working memory is conscious. Consciousness is restricted to those items that win in a competition for attention.

Baars often introduces the global workspace theory by comparison to a theater. Working memory is a stage, attention is a spotlight, conscious states are performers, and they play for a large unconscious audience of psychological systems. These metaphors have been cashed out in psychological, computational, and neurobiological models over the years, making Baars's theory one of the most detailed in the literature (Baars and Franklin, 2009; Newman and Baars, 1993). Similar ideas have also been developed in philosophical terms. Tye (1995) defends the PANIC theory of consciousness, whose name stands for poised, abstract, nonconceptual, intentional content. This account contains a theory of which states become conscious and a theory of how they become conscious. The states that become conscious are perceptual (hence nonconceptual) representations (hence intentional content) whose contents do not include particular concrete entities (hence abstract). They become conscious by being poised, which Tye (1995: 138) defines as standing "ready and in position to make a direct impact on the belief/desire system." Similarly, Kirk (2004: 151) defines conscious mental states as those that are "directly active on the system's processes of interpretation, assessment, and decision-making (its 'central processes')," where being "directly active" is defined in terms of immediately allowing for the spontaneous behavior. Both of these philosophical theories echo the core idea behind the global workspace account. Baars's approach complements Tye's and Kirk's nicely by identifying empirically verified mechanisms, such as working memory, that underwrite cognitive accessibility. These psychological mechanisms have also been associated with neural correlates that are implicated in conscious experience.

Baars has long speculated on subcortical involvement in consciousness. In particular, he implicates the brain-stem reticular formation and the nucleus reticularis of the thalamus. These two structures project to a wide range of cortical areas, play a role in regulating cortical processes, and result in loss of consciousness when damaged (Newman and Baars, 1993). Baars recognizes that these structures do not encode sensory information with enough detail to be the centers of consciousness, but he thinks that they work together with the neocortex to allow global access. On this model, consciousness arises when the thalamus and reticular formation make information in certain parts of the neocortex, such as sensory pathways, available to other neocortical areas, such as executive control. The circuitry is sometimes described as a "thalamocortical loop."

The global workspace theory has gained some popularity in cognitive neuroscience. One of its most ardent champions is Stanislas Dehaene (Dehaene and Changeux, 2005; Dehaene et al., 2006). Dehaene agrees with Baars that thalamocortical loops are involved in consciousness, although he suggests that the subcortical structures may serve to put us in conditions of vigilance or awakeness that allow conscious states, rather than serving as global broadcasting mechanisms (Gaillard et al., 2009; Kinomura et al., 1996; Paus et al., 1997). This move away from subcortical structures is well motivated because they lack the rich anatomical connections needed to control activity in sensory cortices (Koch, 2004) and are more likely involved in sustaining the level of general arousal needed for actual mechanisms of consciousness to operate. Dehaene sensibly associates the global workspace with areas of frontal cortex, which have been implicated in studies of working memory. One might say that, for Dehaene, consciousness arises when and only when perceptual states get encoded in frontal cortex.

The case for the global workspace view begins with the observation that conscious states seem to have a widespread impact. When you see an object consciously, you can reason about it, talk about it, and perform intentional actions in response to it. Baars (2002) observes that these capacities are exactly the ones that have been associated with working memory. He also surveys evidence that unconscious processing is superficial; for example, we can process individual words but not phrases in masked priming studies. This suggests that consciousness is needed for more advanced cognition, which integrates information from multiple sources.

Dehaene has supplemented Baars's case by appealing to neuroimaging experiments. In a review, Dehaene et al. (2006) show that conscious access to perceptual stimuli is associated with activation in lateral prefrontal cortex, a known locus of working memory. When people are presented with masked words, there is increased activation in the visual system but not in frontal areas. When masks are removed, frontal areas come online. In the same paper, Dehaene argues that we should distinguish two ways in which a stimulus can be unconscious. Masked stimuli are subliminal: they are both unconscious and incapable of becoming conscious. Sometimes we also fail to experience unmasked stimuli, as when we divert attention. In these cases, the unconscious stimuli are preconscious; they can be conscious if we attend. From a neuroimaging perspective, these preconscious states show greater activation in the visual system than subliminal states, but neither show increases in frontal cortex. Thus, Dehaene's account has a three-part distinction among states that make it into the global workspace, those that are accessible, and those that are inaccessible. He identifies consciousness with states in the first category.

The global workspace theory is very attractive, but prevailing versions are hampered by subtle difficulties. Let's begin with the evidence. Dehaene tells us that activation in frontal cortex is correlated with consciousness. This is true, but the correlation is imperfect. Frontal cortex comes into play when people are asked to report on what they are perceiving, that is, when they are asked to make active use of a conscious state. But we often have conscious experiences that are ephemeral, unclear, peripheral, or irrelevant. In these cases, there isn't much use for frontal cortex. One way to induce such cases in the laboratory is to present people with clearly visible stimuli but instruct them to ignore those stimuli. Under these conditions, people are not motivated to process the ignored stimuli cognitively, although they do see them. Thus, we should predict consciousness without frontal cortex, contrary to what the global workspace theory entails. Ironically, some of the strongest empirical evidence for this comes from Dehaene and his collaborators. Kouider et al. (2007) conducted an fMRI experiment in which two words were present in succession. Subjects were told that they would be asked a question about the second word but should ignore the first. They also manipulated visibility of the first word, masking it in some conditions. The results showed that visibility of the first word is correlated with increased activity in visual areas but not with frontal activity. Realizing that this seems to contradict the global workspace account, the authors suggest that we should call these clearly visible stimuli "preconscious," and they even suggest that they are "visible but unseen." This is highly implausible. The ignored words are readily experienced; they are presented for half a second in the middle of a screen that is being vigilantly watched. Instead, we should conclude that they are consciously seen but not yet in the global workspace. I will provide further evidence for this possibility in chapter 3.

What about Baars's observation that consciousness is functionally similar to working memory? Here, too, caution is needed. The fact that conscious states can guide decisions does not show that they are actually in working memory. It shows only that they are *available* to working memory. This echoes my earlier remarks about reportability. Many of our conscious states never have a significant impact on our decisions or other psychological operations. Many brief and peripheral experiences are decidedly local, in this respect, not global. Moreover, working-memory storage has a totally different time course. Conscious experiences tend to be very short-lived, but we can sustain items in working memory for several minutes or more. Baars responds to this by saying that conscious items are made up of just that portion of working memory that is in the spotlight of attention. But this is an anachronistic use of attention. Attention does not operate on working memory; it operates on the world, and it does so by altering perceptual states, not stored states. There is no empirical evidence for the claim that working memory contains within it a further memory system, which is more fleeting and modulated by attention.

The best evidence for the global workspace theory may be Baars's observation that consciousness is a precondition for integrative processing; complex stimuli, such as phrases, are not processed in an integrative way when presented unconsciously. But this shows, at best, that consciousness is necessary for such processing, not that it is sufficient. Briefly flashed phrases that are visible but unrecognized are not deeply processed. Furthermore, processing of phrases is notoriously unconscious; we have little access to grammatical rules or the rules by which we assign meanings to sentences. More emphatically, complex decision making seems to take place outside of consciousness. There is a massive literature suggesting that we don't know how we make decisions, even when we know what those decisions are (Wilson, 2002). But decision making is a paradigm case of a global process. It makes use of multiple sources of information and influences a wide range of psychological systems. This suggests that globality is not a good predictor of consciousness.

I think that global workspace theory mislocates consciousness by looking for it in frontal cortex or other systems that make information broadly available. Consciousness is decidedly absent in our "central systems." This can even be regarded as a desideratum:

> **Noncentrality**. An adequate theory should restrict consciousness to processes that lie outside of those systems that underwrite our highest cognitive capacities.

Happily, I think Baars might agree. The fundamental insight behind the global workspace theory is that consciousness is a precondition for globality, and this is compatible with saying that conscious states are not actually global, that is, not states of central systems involved in deliberation, decision making, reporting, and so on. The precondition view fits with Baars's favorite examples of conscious states, which are perceptual inputs, and even with one of his favorite metaphors: conscious states are broadcast. The fact that they are broadcast does not entail that they are received.

3.2. THE LEFT-BRAIN INTERPRETER

The next theory I want to consider is no longer prominent in consciousness studies, but it deserves special mention because it was one of the first theories to emerge from neuroscience to gain prominence, and its impact can still be felt. The theory has been developed by Michael Gazzaniga (1988; 1992). Gazzaniga began his career assisting Roger Sperry, who won a Nobel Prize for advances in commissurotomy surgery. In a commissurotomy, the two hemispheres of the brain are split by sectioning the connective corpus callosum, which can remedy dangerous epileptic seizures. Remarkably, commissurotomy patients appear to function normally after surgery, but curious hemispheric dissociations can be observed under experimental conditions. Sperry and Gazzaniga studied split-brain patients using a tachistoscopic display, which could rapidly present words or images to one visual field without allowing time for the eyes to shift. Without a corpus callosum, stimuli presented to one visual field are processed in just one hemisphere, the one on the contralateral side. Using this method, Gazzaniga and Sperry found that split-brain patients usually fail to report items present on the left, which are processed in the right hemisphere. They insist that they haven't seen anything in these cases, although they may produce behavior relevant to the stimuli that are presented. The left hemisphere sometimes invents explanations of these behaviors, unaware of their actual cause. Gazzaniga interpreted such results as showing that mechanisms of interpretation and report are largely restricted to the left hemisphere, and this led him to consider the possibility that the left hemisphere is the seat of consciousness or at least has a form of consciousness that is fundamentally different from what one would find in the right.

There are many colorful examples (Gazzaniga and LeDoux, 1978). If the right hemisphere sees a nude photograph, the patient will blush or giggle without knowing why. Under such circumstances, one patient said, "That's a funny machine!" as a rationalization of his laughter. When the right hemisphere sees a command to laugh, split-brain patients comply without knowing the real reason; one patient chortled and said, "Oh, you guys really are something!" In one study, a split-brain patient was presented with two pictures simultaneously: a chicken claw in the left hemisphere and a snow scene in the right. Then an array of depicted objects was presented in full view of both hemispheres, and the patient was asked to select an object that went with the earlier picture. The patient chose a shovel with the left hand, triggered by the snow scene, but explained the choice by saying that you need a shovel to clean out a chicken shed.

Taken at face value, such findings can be regarded as evidence for two conclusions: these patients are unaware of what their right hemispheres are seeing, and the left hemisphere interprets what the right hemisphere does. Gazzaniga originally interpreted these results as indicating two streams of consciousness (Gazzaniga and LeDoux, 1978) but eventually rejected the double-consciousness view (Gazzaniga, 1992), suggesting that the consciousness is located in the left hemisphere. On this view, the right hemisphere blindly and automatically responds to instructions, while the left consciously observes, interprets, and reports. In some more recent writings, Gazzaniga (2002) has conceded that the right hemisphere might be conscious to some degree, but the left hemisphere has a qualitatively different kind of consciousness, which far exceeds what's found in the right.

One interesting feature of Gazzaniga's account is that he doesn't tell us how consciousness arises—for example, the precise neural mechanism or mental computations—but rather tells us what consciousness is for. He emphasizes the importance of taking an evolutionary stance toward the mind, and this implies that consciousness evolved to make sense of what we do (1992). Put differently, consciousness serves a narrative function. Its fundamental role is to weave a story that renders us intelligible to ourselves. This idea echoes others in the literature, including Dennett's (1991) proposal that consciousness can be compared to a "draft" that achieved "cerebral celebrity," although Dennett would reject the hypothesis that conscious drafts are located solely in the left hemisphere or any other single location in the brain. Gazzaniga's interpreter theory also fits with Ramachandran's (1995) work on anosognosia. Some patients who suffer injuries in right parietal cortex become paralyzed on the left side but lack insight into their condition. When asked why the paralyzed arm isn't moving, they confabulate, saying that it is moving or that they don't feel like moving it or even that it belongs to someone else. Ramachandran explains this in terms of the sense-making tendencies of consciousness. With Gazzaniga, he claims that the left hemisphere seeks to make rational sense of what it observes, but Ramachandran also argues that the right hemisphere contributes to conscious sense making by detecting anomalies, which can require new explanations. When the right hemisphere is injured, it can't tell the left that something is badly wrong, so the left goes on thinking the body is intact.

Gazzaniga's critics are probably right to resist the idea that consciousness is restricted to the left hemisphere (but see Morin, 2005, for a sympathetic discussion). As Gazzaniga has shown, the right hemisphere can respond to complex instructions, draw pictures, and generate simple verbal reports—all behaviors that normally depend on consciousness. Patients with severe left-brain injuries can also remain highly functional and responsive to the world around them. In cases of extreme epilepsy, children sometimes undergo left hemispherectomies, which have very good outcomes; within days of surgery, these children are active and alert, and they cooperatively participate in demanding tests. They do also recover language function over time, but their cognitive and sensory abilities are evidently intact before that (Boatman et al., 1999). Gazzaniga relies too much on verbal reports when concluding that the right brain is unconscious, less conscious, or endowed with a qualitatively different form of consciousness. The evidence simply isn't there.

But what about Gazzaniga's central thesis about the function of consciousness? Is consciousness primarily in the business of interpreting what we do? Again, there is reason for doubt. It is certainly true that human beings feel compelled to explain their actions, but, as Gazzaniga would no doubt agree, we arrive at such explanations unconsciously. What we get in consciousness is the result of unconscious processes of interpretation. The claim that consciousness evolved to let us know what these interpretations are is highly dubitable. On that view, consciousness primarily serves the highest aspect of human cognition: reason giving. It is more likely that consciousness evolved for much simpler functions. I offer several reasons for this conclusion. First, there are huge individual differences in the desire for reasoning and rational explanation (Nair and Ramnarayan, 2000), but these are not known to correlate with differences in consciousness. Second, interpretations occur only after prior perceptual and behavior episodes, and those are presumably conscious. Third, the deficits that arise when consciousness is absent include capacities that are more basic than interpretation. When consciousness is disrupted, we don't simply fail to interpret our actions; we fail to act. Consciousness seems to be a precondition for voluntary behavior. Behavioral interpretation occurs only after voluntary behavior has taken place, so it seems likely that consciousness has a function that precedes any contribution it may make to interpretation.

My suspicion is that Gazzaniga links consciousness to interpretation because he is not thinking about consciousness as mere phenomenal experience. He does say that consciousness essentially involves the feelings that our mental states bring about in us, but he seems to think of consciousness as also involving something at the level of judgment: our propositional knowledge that we have the mental states that we do. In this way, Gazzaniga may have something like Block's notion of access consciousness in mind. But I have already argued that "consciousness" always refers more fundamentally to phenomenal experience and that any cognitive access we have to our mental states deserves to be called a form of consciousness only if those cognitive states have phenomenal qualities. If we want to explain the function of phenomenal consciousness, we should look for an explanation that subsumes its most rudimentary, precognitive forms. Gazzaniga is no doubt right to say that human beings are compulsive interpreters, but he may be wrong to think that this trait has any special connection to consciousness.

Despite these reservations, I think we should welcome Gazzaniga's effort to offer an account of consciousness that places emphasis on its function. There are researchers, as we will see, who deny that consciousness serves any special purpose. But while making a wish list, we might hope to arrive at a theory that assigns consciousness an important role. After all, loss of consciousness seems to have a dramatic effect on behavior. But I think our search for the function of consciousness must resist the overintellectualizing of Gazzaniga's account. Consciousness is likely to serve functions that are more primitive. As a desideratum, I propose:

> **Basic Function**. On an adequate theory, the function of consciousness should be identified with something that is more basic than high-level interpretation.

We will now turn to a theory that assigns a more primitive role to consciousness.

3.3. TEMPORAL BINDING

Within contemporary neuroscience, the most renowned approach to consciousness is the temporal binding theory. The theory was brought into the limelight by Francis Crick and Christof Koch (1990), who also deserve special credit for helping to make consciousness a central topic in cognitive neuroscience. Crick and Koch begin with the observation that no single cell in the brain corresponds to a consciously perceived object. When we see a flamingo, for example, we see multiple parts and features, which are processed by hundreds or perhaps thousands of cells in the visual system. To make matters more complicated, features such as shapes, colors, and direction of motion are processed in separate anatomical regions, yet we experience all of these features inhering in one lanky pink bird flying gently across the horizon. Crick and Koch further surmise that feature binding is an aspect of conscious experience. More strongly, they imply that features come into consciousness when and only when they are bound. That is the first major tenet of their theory.

The second major tenet concerns the mechanism of binding. Here Crick and Koch follow von der Malsburg and Schneider (1986), who had earlier conjectured on theoretical grounds that neurons bind together by firing in synchrony. By firing together, visual neurons can be processed as corresponding to parts of the same object. Subsequent empirical work (to be described below) by Gray et al. (1989) had found supporting evidence for this along with an intriguing further detail. Not only did synchrony seem to play a role in binding, but the cells that synchronized together during perception oscillated at a predictable rate. In particular, the cells oscillated between forty and sixty times per second (hertz), which falls within what's called the "gamma" frequency. Crick and Koch attached themselves to this idea, suggesting that the neural correlate of consciousness is synchronized activity within the gamma range, often abbreviated as 40 Hz.

Some further details of the model are also worth mentioning. Like Lycan and Baars, Crick and Koch speculate that attention may be important for consciousness. They propose that visual inputs to the nervous system generate a saliency map, specifying the regions of space that should be prioritized for further processing. They associate such maps with attention. The visual cells that fall within salient regions are then bound together by means of neural synchrony. To determine which cells to synchronize, the visual system makes use of stored object templates. Crick and Koch admit that the details of this process are sketchy, but they offer these speculations to guide research. They later abandoned various features of this model, including the 40 Hz hypothesis itself (Crick and Koch, 1995). Nevertheless, the model has been hugely influential, and the authors responsible for some of the initial empirical results continue to defend and extend that research (e.g., Gray, 1999; Singer, 1999; Womelsdorf et al., 2007; see also Llinás, 2002).

Those initial empirical results were striking. Gray et al. (1989) measured cellular responses in the visual cortex of several cats as they looked at moving, oriented lines. They discovered that cells responding to the same line tended to oscillate in sync and that these oscillations were in the gamma range. This was true even for cells at a considerable distance with nonoverlapping receptive fields. When comparing two sites with different receptive fields, Gray et al. included the following three conditions. In some cases, they used two different lines, one in each receptive field, moving in different directions; in other cases, the two lines moved in the same direction; and in still others, there was a single long line spanning the two receptive fields. They found no synchrony for lines moving independently, some synchrony for two lines moving together, and the highest levels of synchrony for a single line, indicating that object binding was the best predictor of neural coherence.

This cat study did not directly explore the link between gamma oscillations and consciousness, and critics complained that the cats' level of consciousness is unclear, because they were partially anesthetized. But subsequent work has linked gamma to consciousness. For example, Fries et al. (1997) found that gamma was associated with the consciously perceived stimulus in a binocular-rivalry paradigm (in binocular rivalry, each eye is presented with a different stimulus, but only one stimulus is experienced). Likewise, Summerfield, Jack, and Burgess (2002) found gamma for unmasked but not masked words. Thus, there is evidence that gamma does binding and that gamma correlates with consciousness, just as Crick and Koch would predict.

Despite this impressive research, I think the temporal binding theory is problematic. The most important problem concerns the alleged correlation between binding and consciousness. In using binding to find the neural correlate of consciousness, Crick and Koch (1990) imply that perceptual states are bound when and only when they are conscious, but that is not plausible. There is ample evidence that binding can occur outside of consciousness. Consider masked priming. Stimuli used in priming studies often have multiple parts. Words are an obvious example. To extract meaning from words, the letters must be bound together. This can happen unconsciously. For example, the Summerfield, Jack, and Burgess (2002) study that found 40-Hz oscillations for conscious presentations of words also found that unconscious presentations influenced behavior. Words that produced "no conscious experience whatsoever" were still recognized above chance on a forced-choice test. Likewise, masked emotional expressions, which must be processed holistically in order to be interpreted, produced significant galvanic skin responses (Williams et al., 2004).

Conversely, conscious states can be unbound. If a pair of colored shapes is presented very quickly, viewers often fail to recognize which shape had which color, and they may make erroneous judgments (what Treisman, 1998, calls "illusory conjunctions"). This suggests that briefly presented stimuli are unbound, and viewers must guess which colors and shapes go together. Binding failures can also arise with certain brain injuries. Associative agnosia is a condition in which people can faithfully copy line drawings but cannot determine what they represent. These individuals often report that it is painstaking to make these copies, because they cannot tell how all of the lines in the original drawing hang together (Farah, 1990). This suggests a binding deficit. But associative agnosics are visually conscious. In fact, their consciousness may be perfectly normal, as evidenced by their drawings. Information about binding may lie outside of conscious phenomenology. Consider the handle on your teacup and the saucer under it. One is bound to the teacup, and the other is not. This difference has functional implications; for example, you don't expect the saucer to rise with your cup when you lift the handle, and if you were to draw these objects, you would draw one and then the other. But phenomenologically, it's not clear that the difference has any impact at all. If you were agnosic, drawing a cup and saucer would be difficult, because you could not use unconscious binding information to decide in what sequence to draw these two objects, but they might appear the same phenomenologically. This is a controversial claim, but it doesn't matter for our purposes. Even if binding contributes something to consciousness, agnosia shows that it isn't necessary.

There is also evidence that neural synchrony is not the mechanism of binding (see LaRock, 2007). It turns out that synchrony is found across all of the neurons that constitute a conscious percept, not just those that are bound. For example, studies that use textures and plaid patterns have shown that neurons corresponding to an object in the foreground and one in the background fire at the same rate (Lamme and Spekreijse, 1998; Thiele and Stoner, 2003). Temporal binding is not even feasible in a noisy human brain. Visual scenes are very complex, and each tiny bit of any surface has both a color and a form that must be bound, in addition to shading, motion, and other features. For each of these bits, there would need to be a distinctive firing rate, unique to that bit and distinguishable from the random fluctuations in spiking patterns that are rampant in noisy neural systems. It seems unlikely that this strategy could be deployed without frequent cases of accidental synchronization (Shadlen and Movshon, 1999).

Temporal binding theory may also be unworkable in principle. Suppose I see a red soda can of Coca-Cola. Here there are two things that must be unified: I see the can as red, and I see the logo on the can as white. But notice that both colors are bound to the can. Suppose the red color is bound to the can by oscillating at the same frequency as the can representation, and suppose the white logo is also bound to the can by oscillating at the same frequency. That entails that the red and the white are also firing at the same frequency as each other. But if so, then the temporal binding theory entails that these two colors are bound to each other and to the can. That clearly isn't the case, because I don't see the can as simultaneously red and white throughout.

There is another approach to binding that I find more plausible. Two components of an experience, such as shape and color, can be linked by means of mental maps. There are two kinds of maps that might be used: spatial maps and object maps. A spatial map is a population of neurons that are spatially arrayed like the visual field (or neurons that function as if they are spatially arrayed). By causally interacting with the same map location, neurons corresponding to color and shape can be bound, even if they are not processed in the same part of the brain. Such a view has been proposed by Treisman (1998), and it is consistent with the finding that there are multiple retinotopic spatial maps in the brain. In addition to spatial maps, there may be object maps. An object map can be defined as a structural description of an object—perhaps a high-level perceptual representation—that is causally linked to surface colors, shapes, and textures, in order to keep track of which bits form unified, bound wholes. Damage to these object maps may be the primary cause of the unbound experiences in associative agnosia. Ironically, Crick and Koch implicitly recognize the need for object maps when they say that templates are used to determine which neurons should fire together. Once such templates are in place, temporal binding would seem to be superfluous.

The maps that allow binding may operate outside of consciousness. They are, arguably, not items in experience but rather unconscious bookkeepers that tell us which parts of experience go together. When we experience a red circle, we need not experience a third thing, which is the unity of red and circularity. We experience red and circularity in the same place, and we are able to make use of their collocation in unconscious decision making. If maps are impaired, as in associative agnosia, the experience remains largely the same; agnosics would paint an accurate picture of a red circle, but they would not be able to report that the shape and color are united or use this fact in recognition and recall. Of course, experiences are, in some sense, integrated. We experience the circle in the same place that we experience the color, but this only shows that experiences of different object features are spatially arrayed, and the items we are conscious of have multiple features at once. We can be co-conscious of redness and circularity in the same place at the same time. Notice that we are simultaneously conscious of the background on which the red circle sits, so this form of integration has nothing special to do with binding in the Crick and Koch sense. The case of agnosia shows that experience can be integrated without being bound. Binding is neither essential to consciousness nor present as an aspect of conscious experience.

What about the impressive evidence for the 40 Hz view? Doesn't the cat study show that neurons synchronize only when responding to the same object? One problem with this study is that it doesn't control for allocation of attention. When two lines are moving in different directions, it takes effort to watch both of them attentively. Consequently, the cats in the study may have attended to just one line in this experimental condition. If gamma oscillations reflect attention, rather than binding, these results can be readily explained. But this interpretation would save gamma only if it could be established that attention is crucial for consciousness, and gamma is the correlate of attention. In either case, this move would abandon the link between consciousness and binding, which is under consideration here.

Crick and Koch were barking up the wrong tree, but they may have been in the right neck of the woods. Their main misstep is in thinking that a theory of consciousness must explain binding, but there is a related phenomenon that an adequate theory should explain. Conscious states seem to be unified. Unity is puzzling, because, as Crick and Koch emphasize, different components of our conscious states are processed in different parts of the brain, and there are even differences in the speed at which the senses respond to their inputs (Zeki and Bartels, 1998). There is a deep puzzle about how these highly distributed bits get integrated into a single stream of consciousness. The binding problem is something different, something that does not pertain to consciousness as such. But it draws attention to the problem of integration and thus leads us to an important desideratum:

Conscious Unity. An adequate theory should explain how states that are distributed in space and time get unified into coherent conscious experiences.

3.4. THE FEELING OF WHAT HAPPENS

The next approach I want to consider was put forward by Antonio Damasio (1999), and it belongs to a family of views that have an important feature in common. On these theories, consciousness is said to arise when perceptual information is related to information about the self (Edelman, 1992; Kriegel, 2005; van Gulick, 2006). I use Damasio to illustrate, because his views are worked out in some neurobiological detail.

Like Baars, Damasio begins with a theatrical metaphor. Consciousness is like an inner movie screen, he says, in which sensory information is presented.

For Baars, conscious performances are played for an unconscious audience. Damasio demurs, saying that the audience is the self, and the self is present in experience. This raises a question. How is it that the self can be both the viewer of the inner movie and an item in experience? Damasio's answer is that we experience the self in much the way that we experience the movie; the self is just another sensory state. In particular, the self is experienced as a pattern of activity in the body. Damasio's hypothesis is that consciousness arises when these bodily experiences of the self are joined with our perceptual experiences of external objects. External objects are represented by maps that register features in our outwardly directed sense modalities, and the bodily self is represented by maps that register the co-occurrence of activities in different somatic systems, such as our visceral organs and our skeletal muscles. These two maps continuously alter each other as body and world interact. Damasio postulated second-order maps that register these ongoing interactions. Consciousness is equated with activity in these second-order maps.

Damasio locates first-order maps of objects in sensory and motor cortex, as well as hippocampus, for objects drawn from memory. First-order maps of the body can be found, he says, in the hypothalamus, the basal forebrain, the brain-stem nuclei, the insula, and both the primary and the secondary somatosensory cortex. The all-important second-order maps, which related these two, are postulated to be in the cingulate cortex, the thalamus, and, more tentatively, the superior colliculus. There is no single seat of consciousness for Damasio, but these latter structures are all places where consciousness can arise, on his view, because all of them bring together sensory and somatic information.

Damasio's primary source of evidence comes from observations of people with brain injuries and abnormalities that seem to disrupt normal conscious experience. Damasio is impressed by conditions in which people seem to be awake but are nevertheless absent or vacant in some way. One example is epileptic automatism, in which people carry out behaviors such as walking around but lack awareness of what they are doing. Another is akinetic mutism, in which people are mute, inactive, and utterly lacking in motivation but nevertheless perceive the world around them. In both cases, attention is minimally preserved: people undergoing absence seizures avoid obstacles as they walk, and people with akinetic mutism periodically track objects with their eyes and heads. In some other cases, such as persistent vegetative states, the sleep cycle is preserved, but there is no evidence for minimally attentive perception. Finally, there are cases in which even wakefulness is lost, including coma, fainting, deep sleep, and the states induced by some forms of anesthesia. Damasio is struck by the fact that these disorders tend to be associated with dysfunction in the cingulate cortex and the thalamus—two areas with second-order maps. Areas that contain first-order bodily maps, such as the upper brain stem, the basal forebrain, and the hypothalamus, can also be involved. This supports Damasio's conjecture that these structures contribute to consciousness.

But should we follow Damasio in *locating* consciousness in second-order maps? The neurological evidence is open to other interpretations. Damage to the superior colliculus, Damasio's most tentative candidate for a locus of consciousness, is associated with orienting dysfunctions (such as hand-eye coordination), especially when one sense modality (e.g., touch) is used to orient another (e.g., vision) (Burnett et al., 2007). These don't seem to be cases in which consciousness is absent. Cingulate cortex lesions can cause profound disorders, such as akinetic mutism, but one can challenge the claim that people in this condition are unconscious. For example, Damasio (1994: 72) describes one of his own akinetic patients who would, with some coaxing, say her name or the names of her family members. Later, on recovery, she reported that she didn't speak because she felt as if she "really had nothing to say." One interpretation, favored by Damasio himself, is that the cingulate cortex plays a central role in emotion awareness (for more evidence, see Lane, 2000; Phan et al., 2002), and injuries here can lead to profound emotional indifference. Such individuals may be conscious, but they don't care enough about anything to act.

Injuries to the thalamus can, unequivocally, disrupt consciousness. It is difficult to know whether consciousness is lost during an absence seizure, but consciousness is almost certainly lost when people are comatose—a common result of thalamic injury. This may seem to support Damasio's theory, but we have already seen in the discussion of the global workspace view that the thalamus is likely to be a precondition for consciousness rather than a locus of consciousness. The reason for this is that it seems to play a role in general vigilance or arousal, rather than storing the contents of conscious experience (for a useful review, see Schiff, 2008). Damasio associates consciousness with the thalamus because it brings together sensory and somatic information and also results in unconsciousness when injured. But these two functions are probably subserved by different nuclei within the thalamus. The central thalamus is most likely the culprit in coma cases, whereas dorsal and anterior nuclei play a role in perception, attention, and memory. Damage to these latter nuclei can affect consciousness, by affecting what we can perceive, attend to, and recall, but they are unlikely the places where consciousness actually takes place. The nuclei don't harbor perceptual representations that are rich enough to match our experiences, and activity here is not known to correlate with vividness or other indicators of fluctuations in the degree to which we are conscious.

One can also take issue with the theoretical motivations behind Damasio's account. Let me mention two issues. First, it's unclear why consciousness should be located in second-order maps rather than first-order maps. The contents of consciousness seem to be fully available at the first order, and second-order maps in the brain probably serve to coordinate first-order maps, not to re-represent their contents. Perhaps Damasio thinks that consciousness can't arise without experiencing the fact that objects are affecting the body, and that requires awareness of the relationship between two first-order maps. But it wouldn't follow that consciousness arises in such second-order maps. Rather, these would function in the same way as the spatial and object maps that I mentioned in the discussion of how binding is achieved. That is to say, they need not be items in experience, even though they help us keep track, unconsciously, of how the items in experience are related. As with the case of associative agnosia, it seems likely that Damasio's second-order maps can be impaired, leaving consciousness largely intact. This may happen in some cases of unconscious emotion elicitation. When a social situation makes you nervous, you might experience the edginess in your body in addition to the situation, without putting the two together. If you come to realize that the two are related, your experience may remain the same, although the way you choose to cope with it may change. Thus, I see no reason to locate consciousness in the second-order maps.

The second issue cuts deeper. Underlying Damasio's entire approach to consciousness is an implicit Cartesianism. He seems wedded to the view that we become conscious when and only when we relate a sensory experience to the self. There must be an "I" there in every conscious state for Damasio, a viewer being viewed along with the inner sensory cinema. This assumption, which is shared by HOT theories, can be called into question. In chapter 7, I argue against Damasio's specific theory of self-consciousness and the thesis that the self is always present in consciousness. Here I will just plant the seed of doubt. Damasio has given no compelling reason for thinking that conscious experiences must be self-involving. It seems perfectly plausible that one could experience a stream of sensory information without having a sense of one's self as a spectator of that stream. Perhaps this is what it's like to have akinetic mutism or an absence seizure. It may also be what we experience when we are absorbed in a movie or focused on a problem or lost in a daydream. If you are convinced by these examples, you will join me in endorsing the following desideratum:

> **Selfless Experience**. An adequate theory should allow that consciousness can arise without any experience of the self.

If I am right, then Damasio's theory gets going in the wrong direction from the start, but ironically, I think his work has been very helpful in pointing to the possibility of selfless experience. The cases of mutism and absence seizures that motivate his account can be reconstrued as illustrating the possibility of conscious perception without a conscious self.

4. A Look Back and Forward

In this survey, I have focused on the theories that have been among the most visible and influential in recent years. They illustrate themes found throughout consciousness research: representation, information access, the threat of dualism, and the relationship between consciousness and the self. The neural correlates discussed here, such as gamma synchrony and the thalamus, are also the most frequently discussed. In this way, I have tried to encapsulate the state of play in contemporary consciousness research.

By necessity, many significant theories have been left out. I have not considered the multiple drafts theory (Dennett, 1991), comparator models (Gray, 2004), quantum consciousness (Hameroff, 2006), the remembered present (Edelman, 1992), neural back projections (Lamme, 2001), the ventral stream (Goodale and Milner, 1992), enactivism (O'Regan and Noë, 2001), higher-order globalism (van Gulick, 2004), same-order representational theories (Kriegel and Williford, 2006), or dispositional higher-order representations (Carruthers, 2000). Some of these will be discussed in the chapters that follow, some succumb to objections raised here, and some will be unduly neglected. I've also ignored theories that say that consciousness can be eliminated (Rey, 1988) or that we will never be able to identify the basis of consciousness in the brain (McGinn, 1991). My answer to these will be implicit in my defense of a positive theory. To the extent that my defense is compelling, such skeptical positions will lose their appeal.

One striking thing about the theories surveyed in this chapter is their diversity. The first three are stated in philosophical language and motivated by armchair observations. The global workspace theory is stated in psychological terms, although it has also been related to large-scale neural circuits and has been tested using functional imaging. Temporal binding focuses on a cellular process in populations of neurons, which have been measured in laboratory animals. Damasio's theory refers to specific neural structures and draws on patient work for support. This raises questions about what a theory of consciousness should look like and how it should be investigated. My answer to both questions is pluralism: consciousness should be explored using multiple methods, and a theory should be stated at multiple levels of analysis.

It is difficult to avoid pluralism when studying consciousness. If we want to understand how consciousness fits into the natural world, it's valuable to explore its biological basis. That brings us to the neurosciences. But the search for neural correlates depends on some prior method for identifying consciousness, and that task benefits from finding the psychological profile that distinguishes conscious states from unconscious states. Discovering such a role also helps us understand how consciousness contributes to mental life. Ideally, the story of consciousness can be told in both psychological and biological terms, with a clear understanding of how these levels relate.

One example of such an integrative theory is given by Crick and Koch (1990). What makes their approach exciting is that they begin with a psychological aspect of consciousness (binding) and then find a neural correlate (synchrony). Thus, they seek to establish that a feature of experience can be implemented in a biological mechanism, thereby revealing how matter may relate to mind. I raised issues with their account above, but some of the ideas they put forward, including neural synchrony, remain serious candidates for a final theory. Their approach and others like it leave us with an overarching desideratum:

> **Multilevel Integration**. An adequate theory should identify neural correlates of consciousness, and these should help account for some observable aspect(s) of conscious experience.

I say "multi" here, because there may be multiple levels of neural implementation. The idea that neural correlates should be related to psychological correlates may seem completely obvious, but it is not accepted by all consciousness researchers. On the one hand, some philosophers of a functionalist persuasion deny that there will be any systematic neural correlates, so they may see the search for consciousness in the brain as unnecessary (akin to the search for consciousness in particle physics). On the other hand, some neuroscientists equate consciousness with neural correlates that do not shed light in any obvious way to observable aspects of consciousness. For example, neuroscientists who have emphasized the role of "back projections" or "reentry" between populations of neurons sometimes fail to explain how such neural dynamics relate to properties of experience. Consciousness might be said to have a neural correlate that is brute, on this approach. These lines of resistance must be taken seriously, but we can still hope for multilevel integration. It would be gratifying to find a systematic correlate that coheres with properties that can be recognized at higher levels of analysis.

The desiderata that I have articulated here are largely born from criticism. Each contradicts a central tenet of at least one leading theory. Needless to say, they are not desiderata that everyone in consciousness studies would accept. At the same time, each one deals with an aspect of consciousness that every theory must address. The Phenomenal Knowledge condition exemplifies the idea that any theory of consciousness should account for how we come to know what our phenomenal states *are like*. Subjective Character expresses the fact that every theory needs an account of *qualia*. First-Order Consciousness underscores that in addition to knowing what qualia are, we need to know how they become *conscious*. Noncentrality concerns the scope of consciousness and demands that any adequate theory determine whether *cognitive states* can be conscious or whether consciousness is restricted to the periphery. Basic Function calls for an answer to the question of whether consciousness serves some fundamental *purpose* for the organisms that possess it and, if so, what it is. Conscious Unity expresses the need for an account of why conscious states seem to be *unified*. Selfless Experience takes a stand on the relationship between consciousness and the *self*. Multilevel Integration expresses the need for some position on the neural correlates of consciousness and how they relate to other *levels*.

These desiderata will recede into the background in the chapters that follow, but they will all be addressed along the way. Chapter 2 asks which of our mental states are conscious, a question that bears on the nature of qualia. I argue that consciousness arises only at an intermediate level of processing within hierarchically organized perceptual systems. Chapter 3 asks when consciousness arises and, in so doing, delivers a theory of how mental states become conscious. In a slogan, I claim that consciousness is attention; I offer an information-processing account of what attention is and survey evidence for the identity. Chapter 4 pursues the neural correlates of consciousness further by identifying brain processes that underlie attention and intermediate-level representations. Chapter 5 examines the conjecture that thinking gives rise to a distinctive kind of phenomenology, thus addressing the relation between consciousness and cognition. I argue that all consciousness is perceptual and that there is no proprietary cognitive phenomenology. Chapter 6 raises the question of what consciousness is for and, in the process, critically engages two extreme views about the relationship between consciousness and action: the enactive theory and the ventral stream theory. Chapter 7 explores the relationship between consciousness and the self, asking whether there is any such thing as an experience of the self as subject. My answer is no. Chapter 8 concerns the unity of consciousness and appeals to the importance of attention in providing an adequate account. I also argue that consciousness is less unified than we might think but that disunity is, in principle, impossible to observe. Chapter 9 examines the debate between functionalists and psychophysical identity theorists that has dominated the philosophy of mind; I argue that the two opposing views should be integrated. Chapter 10 asks why the mind-body problem seems so hard and answers with a theory of phenomenal knowledge. On this view, knowing what it's like involves the ability to hold an item in experience, a kind of mental pointing; this ability involves attention and working memory. These chapters divide into three sections: an account of perceptual consciousness, dubbed the AIR theory, is presented in the first part; the second part amounts to a defense of the claim that consciousness is limited to perception; and the third is a data-driven exploration of metaphysical questions that traditionally concerned philosophers. The concluding chapter returns to the desiderata enumerated above. These serve as a scorecard, and I argue that the AIR theory comes out ahead of the competition.

PART ONE

A Theory of Consciousness

2

Where Is Consciousness? The Intermediate Level

In 1987, Ray Jackendoff published *Consciousness and the Computational Mind*. In it, he posed an important question: where in the flow of information processing does consciousness arise? The notion of information processing derives from the computational theory of the mind. Most cognitive scientists agree that the mind is a computer, in some sense. It is a device that processes information by transforming representations in accordance with rules. Computational devices decompose into various interconnected subsystems, each of which performs some aspect of a complex task. Given such a decompositional analysis, we can ask, in which subsystems does consciousness arise? If we depict the mind as a vast flow chart and highlight the boxes whose rules and representations are conscious, which boxes should we mark? Where in this great morass is consciousness?

Jackendoff's answer is simple and elegant. He noticed that many of our mental capacities, including especially our senses and our language systems, are organized hierarchically. In each of these hierarchies, it makes sense to talk about low-, intermediate-, and high-level processing systems. We break down tasks into stages. Appealing to prevailing models of these stages, Jackendoff conjectured that the intermediate level is privileged with respect to consciousness. Consciousness seems to arise in intermediate-level processing systems and not elsewhere. If Jackendoff is right, this is a very important discovery. The hypothesis has also been sympathetically discussed by Crick and Koch (2000; see also Koch and Braun, 1996), and related views can be found in Kosslyn (2004), Tye (1995), and Bisiach (1992). In this chapter, I will review the current evidence (see also Prinz, 2000b; 2005). I will not spend a lot of time rehearsing Jackendoff's arguments. When he wrote the book, he relied heavily on the models in linguistics and computational psychology that were currently in vogue. Those models remain relevant, but they need to be supplemented by more recent research, including findings in neuroscience that were unavailable to Jackendoff when he wrote his book. I think the intermediate-level hypothesis holds up well against this evidence, although, as we will see, it remains very controversial.

Jackendoff's location question is different from the question that dominates much research in consciousness studies. Jackendoff is not asking how a physical entity like the brain could possibly underwrite qualitative experience. Indeed, he expresses skepticism about whether that question can be answered. But the location question is equally important for anyone trying to develop a theory of consciousness. An adequate theory must tell us where consciousness arises in the course of information processing. Once we know that, we can ask how such informational states become conscious. My goal in this chapter is to argue that Jackendoff is right. Consciousness arises at an intermediate level in sensory hierarchies and not at a low or a high level. Other researchers have located consciousness at these other levels or at multiple levels. I will consider the evidence for such alternatives at the end of the chapter, and I will argue that the intermediate-level hypothesis enjoys more support.

1. Locating Visual Consciousness

Jackendoff's presentation and defense of the intermediate-level hypothesis focuses on two aspects of conscious experience: language and vision. I will touch on language below, but my focus here and throughout the book will be vision. Vision is the most intensely investigated capacity in consciousness studies, and for sighted people, it is the most important sense modality. Some researchers worry that the focus on vision in consciousness studies will result in theories that lack adequate breadth. They worry that lessons from vision will not generalize. Part of the burden of this chapter will be to argue otherwise. Vision differs from other modalities in many ways but not, I suggest, with respect to where consciousness arises.

Jackendoff's views on vision were shaped by the seminal work of David Marr (1982). According to Marr, visual object recognition proceeds in three stages (see figure 2). First, the visual system generates a primal sketch of a visual scene. The primal sketch is a mental representation corresponding to local features of the stimulus. Discontinuities in light entering the retina are used to derive a patchwork of oriented edges, bars, ends, and blobs. It is useful to think of the primal sketch as a pixel array. Each pixel indicates, for example, whether there is an edge present at that point in space, but the pixels have not yet been unified with one another to generate a coherent representation of an entire object. Even stereoscopic depth information has not been encoded. At the next state of processes, the visual system generates a two-and-a-half-dimensional (2.5-D) sketch. This representation unifies the pixels into a coherent representation of an object's boundaries. It represents surface textures, separates figure from ground, and uses shading and stereoscopic information to capture information about depth. One can think of the resulting representation as an array of bounded, spatially oriented surfaces. Marr thinks that the

2.5-D sketch is not ideally suited for object recognition. Unlike the primal sketch, it does represent the bounded contours of objects, but it represents those objects from a specific vantage point. Every time we encounter an object from different vantage points, we end up with a different 2.5-D sketch. The visual system needs a way of determining that these distinct viewpoint-specific representations are images of the same object. To do that, Marr supposes that the visual system generates structural descriptions. It uses information in the 2.5-D sketch to determine what three-dimensional forms make up the object that is currently being perceived. He calls the resulting representation a 3-D model, to emphasize the fact that it captures the entire three-dimensional structure of an object, rather than merely capturing depth information from a single point of view. The 3-D models are built up from volumetric primitives, such as cubes, codes, and three-dimensional cylinders. The exact same 3-D model is derived from different 2.5-D sketches. A hippo perceived from different angles will produce the same 3-D model. In fact, 3-D models abstract away from surface textures and information about the specific (i.e., metric) size relationships among parts, so any ordinary hippo perceived under decent conditions would generate the same 3-D model. For this reason, 3-D models are ideally suited for object recognition. The visual system stores 3-D models in memory and matches these against the models generated by what we are viewing at any given moment.

With Marr's theory in hand, Jackendoff asks, where in visual processing does consciousness arise? The answer should be obvious. We don't have a visual experience corresponding to the primal sketch. We can see edges and blobs, of course, but when we look at a scene, adjacent edges blend together, and we experience them as located in depth at some distance from us. The primal sketch is not very different from the 2-D array on the retina. It is a flat, disunified jumble. Nor do we have a visual experience corresponding to the 3-D model stage. The 3-D models are invariant across viewing positions, and they abstract away from textures and other surface features. In conscious experience, objects are always presented to us from a specific point of view, and we are often vividly

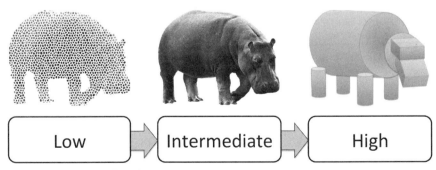

FIGURE 2 Marr's vision hierarchy.

aware of surface details. Of Marr's three levels, only the 2.5-D sketch corresponds to conscious experience. We consciously experience a world of surfaces and shapes oriented in specific ways at various distances from us. If Marr is right about the three levels of vision, then Jackendoff seems to be right about the stage at which visual consciousness arises. Visual consciousness arises at a level of processing that is neither too piecemeal nor too abstract. It arises at an intermediate level, which occurs between discrete pixels and abstract models.

One problem with Jackendoff's proposal is that Marr's theory of vision is out of date. We have learned a lot about vision in the thirty years since Marr originally developed his ideas. Much of that knowledge comes from the neurosciences, and the emerging picture departs from Marr in various respects. One difference is that there are now known to be several dozen anatomically separate areas that contribute to vision. This may seem difficult to reconcile with Marr's tripartite but mainstream vision, and researchers continue to talk about low-, intermediate-, and high-level vision. The reason for this is simple. Diverse visual areas can be grouped functionally. There are primary cortical sites that process information in a piecemeal way, others that represent more global features from a specific vantage point, and still others that abstract away from a vantage point and play a special role in object recognition. To a first approximation, the low level has been anatomically localized in primary visual cortex, or V1 (along with some subcortical structures, such as the visual nuclei of the thalamus and the superior colliculus). The intermediate level includes a family of areas with names such as V2, V3, V4, V5, and perhaps also V3A, V7, and V8; many of these are located in the so-called extrastriate areas just beyond V1. High-level vision most frequently recruits structures in inferior temporal cortex, such as the TEO, TE, and portions of the superior temporal sulcus (STS), along with the lateral occipital complex (LOC) and some structures in parietal cortex, such as the ventral and posterior interparietal areas (VIP and PIP).

The account of visual-processing levels that we get from neuroscience differs in detail from what Marr proposed. For example, we now know that the lowest levels of visual processing in the brain are not quite as simple as primal sketches. V1—the first cortical area involved in vision—can, to some degree, fill in missing contours (Seghier et al., 2000) and distinguish figure from ground (Lamme, 1995). High-level inferotemporal areas do not represent the world using 3-D models. There is little evidence for volumetric primitives of the kind that Marr proposed in object recognition. Instead, high-level vision exploits a repertoire of more idiosyncratic shapes, such as a striped triangle, a circle with a bar protruding from it, or an eight-pointed star (Tanaka, 1997), although, as on Marr's theory, high-level responses are invariant across many transformations. The neuroscientific conception of intermediate-level vision also differs from Marr's. Extrastriate cortex, which does much of the intermediate-level visual processing, divides up into a number of functionally distinct subsystems,

vhich processes a different aspect of the perceived stimulus, such as
tion, and form (Zeki, 1993). Marr's monolithic mid-level is really an
ation of different brain areas. Each of these presents a stimulus from
 vantage point, as on Marr's theory, but they divide the representa-
or.

re 2 presents some of the core structures in vision and their hierar-
ganization. V1 is the main low-level structure in the neocortex, and as
am indicates, it is something like a pixel map, registering a rich array
 and edges but not their global organization. V2 imposes more order,
g object boundaries, separating figure from ground, and in some cases
 contours that might have been difficult to discern in the raw input. V3
 less intensively studied, but it seems to be sensitive to stereoscopic
ombining information from both eyes, and may contribute to our
ability to discern shape from shading. V4 responds to colors in monkeys, and
portions of V4 seem to be color-sensitive in humans, too, although the human
color area is sometimes called V8, which may be a subregion of V4 or an area
just anterior to it. Portions of V4 also seem to be involved in texture discrimination, as indicated in the figure. V5, which is also called medial temporal cortex (MT), is sensitive to motion and plays a role in the perception of motion
trajectories. Medial superior temporal sulcus (MST) is also a motion area, but
it is more concerned with optic flow (the patterns of change as one moves
toward an object or scene) in addition to expanding or contracting motions.
Two other candidate intermediate areas, V3A and V7, will be discussed in
chapter 6. Figure 2 also includes three high-level areas: temporal area TE,
which is a principal structure involved in object recognition; area VIP, which
registers motion trajectories; and the fundus of the superior temporal sulcus
(FST), which discerns shape from motion. TE is also labeled LOC, because the
lateral occipital complex in humans may share some of the high-level recognition work associated with TE in monkeys.

Figure 3 is simplified in various ways. Some structures are left out, such as
TEO, which lies anatomically between V4 and TE but makes an uncertain contribution to object recognition. V4α, an area that may play a role in high-level
color recognition, is also excluded, because it has not been intensively
researched. Functionally specialized subregions of the included high-level
structures have not been labeled. For example, the so-called fusiform face area,
which plays a role in high-level face recognition, is probably located within TE.
Some parietal structures are also left out because their contribution to object
recognition is controversial. The figure also leaves out some connections (e.g.,
between V3 and V5), and it shows only forward pathways, although backward
connections also exist. The network is hierarchical in that a stimulus is generally fed through in the order indicated, but Marr did not appreciate the extent
to which information might also flow backward, a point I will touch on in the
final section of this chapter.

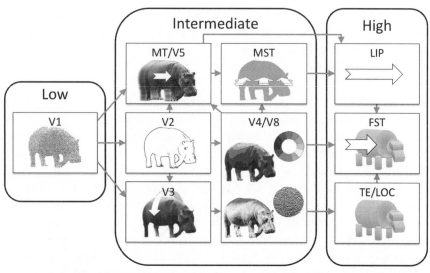

FIGURE 3 A simplified diagram of the visual system.

Despite these differences between Marr's theory and the picture that emerges from visual neuroscience, the prevailing conception of how vision works is broadly consistent with Marr on the points that matter for Jackend-off's conjecture. Low-level vision is located in brain areas with small receptive fields, so it is poorly suited for generating representations of coherent object boundaries. High-level vision is comparatively indifferent to vantage points, and it is the primary locus of object recognition. Intermediate-level visual systems generate viewpoint-specific representations that are more coherent than low-level representations and less abstract than high-level representations.

More to the point, findings from neuroscience have added support to Jack-endoff's conjecture that the intermediate level is the locus of conscious experi-ence. Most of the evidence comes from three sources: cell recordings in nonhuman primates, functional imaging studies of healthy human beings, and neuropsychological studies of people with focal brain injuries.

Recordings taken from electrodes placed in the brains of awake and anes-thetized monkeys have played a major role in visual neuroscience. More accu-rately than any other technique, single-unit electrophysiology can be used to determine what kind of information is encoded in different stages of the visual hierarchy. Such studies cast doubt on the supposition that consciousness is lo-cated in low-level or high-level areas. Cells in V1 are not promising candidates, because they do not reliably respond in ways that are consistent with features that we experience consciously. For example, while V1 is responsive to figures containing illusory contours, the cells that respond are ones that normally fire when contours of the opposite orientation are presented; V1 fires as if it were detecting illusory contours at the wrong orientation (Ramsden, Chou, and Roe,

2001). In addition, when we are presented with two color patches in rapid succession, we experience one fused color, but V1 cells respond to each color patch separately (Gur and Snodderly, 1997). Color-sensitive cells in V1 even fail to show response during color afterimages (Conway and Tsao, 2006). Cells in inferotemporal areas, the locus of high-level vision, are also bad candidates for the correlates of consciousness. They are invariant across a large range of stimulus changes. For example, inferotemporal cells are active across changes in size, position, orientation, luminance inversion, and left/right reversal (Ito et al., 1995; Baylis and Driver, 2001). This is quite striking. Each of these changes dramatically alters conscious experience, but they do not have a dramatic effect on cells in high-level visual areas. In contrast, cells in intermediate-level visual areas have response profiles that correspond more faithfully to conscious experience. Extrastriate cells respond to illusory contours (von der Heydt, Peterhans, and Baumgartner, 1984) and illusory motion (Tootell et al., 1995) and in accordance with perceived colors (Zeki, 1993). They do not respond invariantly across changes in position, size, and left/right reversal. The response profiles of extrastriate cells have not been fully investigated, but current evidence gels well with Jackendoff's intermediate-level hypothesis.

Turn now from monkey single-unit recordings to human neuroimaging. The dominant imaging method continues to be function magnetic resonance imaging (fMRI). Using this technique, cognitive neuroscientists can identify the visual areas that are most responsive to perceived stimuli. Most neuroimaging studies to date are consistent with or supportive of the conjecture that conscious visual experiences are located in extrastriate cortex. Here are several representative findings: Backus et al. (2001) found that stereoscopic depth information correlated well with activity in extrastriate area V3, rather than V1; Humphrey et al. (1999) found that color aftereffects correlated with extrastriate responses and not V1 responses; Lumer and Rees (1999) found that subjects' interpretations of bistable figures correlated with extrastriate activity; Ffytche et al. (1998) showed correlations between extrastriate activation and visual hallucinations; Braun, Balkin, and Wesensten (1997) observed extrastriate activation and V1 deactivation during REM sleep; Mendola et al. (1999) found a high degree of responsiveness to illusory contours in extrastriate areas (V3 was the main area that treated real and illusory contours alike, while also treating similar figures with and without illusory contours differently); Morita et al. (2004) found that V4 is the locus of illusory colors in the McCollough effect in which black-and-white line gradients appear chromatic; Schira et al. (2004) found that V2 registered figure-ground segmentations that are not detected by lower visual areas; Jiang, Zhou, and He (2007) used fMRI to confirm that color fusion occurs in intermediate-level areas rather than V1; Bristow et al. (2005) argue that our inability to perceive our own eye blinks is explained by the fact that the brain suppresses the visual disruptions caused by blinking, and this blink suppression doesn't occur before V3; and Konen and

Kastner (2008) confirmed that areas such as V3 and V4 are viewpoint-sensitive, while higher areas are not. Many of these studies show that conscious experiences correlate better with extrastriate activation than with activation of other visual areas.

The most compelling evidence for the intermediate-level hypothesis comes from studies of individuals who have sustained focal brain injuries. Jackendoff's conjecture makes three implicit predictions about how consciousness should be affected by brain damage, and those predictions are consistent with existing evidence. The first prediction is that damage to early-level visual areas should ordinarily eliminate visual experience. Early visual areas are the main source of input to intermediate visual areas, so damage to the former should ordinarily eliminate activity in the latter, resulting in a loss of visual experience. This is just what happens. Destruction of V1 usually results in cortical blindness. There are, however, exceptional cases of residual visual awareness after V1 damage. In some cases, individuals with V1 injuries have visual hallucinations and imagery (Seguin, 1886; Chatterjee and Southwood; 1995; Goldenberg, Müllbacher, and Nowak, 1995; Bridge et al., 2011). This is consistent with the intermediate-level hypothesis, because hallucinations are presumably generated by top-down signals into intermediate-level visual areas, which remain intact after V1 injuries. It has also been established that some individuals with V1 injuries retain a small degree of visual acuity in their blind fields as a result of a subcortical pathway that bypasses V1—the phenomenon known as blindsight. When individuals with blindsight are presented with high-contrast rapidly moving displays, they occasionally report residual visual awareness. This is explained on the intermediate-level hypothesis by presuming that such stimuli are able to activate extrastriate visual areas via the subcortical pathway. This explanation has been confirmed by neuroimaging. Under conditions in which an individual with blindsight reports residual experience, there is activation in extrastriate area V5 (Sahraie et al., 1997).

The second prediction generated by the intermediate-level hypothesis is that damage to high-level processing areas should leave experience intact. The high level is the locus of object recognition, and it is postexperiential. Subjects with high-level damage should, therefore, have vivid residual experiences but impaired visual recognition. This is exactly what neuropsychologists report. High-level visual lesions cause associative agnosia (Farah, 1990). Individuals with this condition can faithfully copy pictures presented to them in the lab, but they have no idea what they are drawing (Rubens and Benson, 1971). We should not presume that their visual experiences are exactly like ours, however. High-level areas have back projections into intermediate-level areas that may help us organize complex visual displays by selectively attending to meaningful parts. But the faithful drawings produced by associative agnosics suggest that they have no difficulty experiencing the same shapes and colors that we experience.

The third prediction provides the most direct test of the theory: if consciousness is located exclusively at the intermediate level, then extrastriate lesions and other areas that are intermediate in function should result in blindness. This prediction is complicated by the fact, mentioned above, that extrastriate cortex is not a single structure but rather a collection of functionally specialized information-processing areas. So, properly formulated, the third prediction says that damage to each of these areas should result in blindness for the information they process. This prediction has been gorgeously confirmed. Damage to extrastriate color areas causes cortical achromatopsia, a form of color blindness (Zeki, 1990); people with this condition reside in a color-free world. Damage to the extrastriate motion area causes akinetopsia, or motion blindness (Zeki, 1991); in this rare condition, the world is experienced as a series of still images. Damage to an intermediate area in parietal cortex can result in blindness to stereoscopic depth information (Ratcliff & Davies-Jones, 1972). Damage to extrastriate form areas causes apperceptive agnosia, or form blindness (Farah, 1990); apperceptive agnosics, unlike associative agnosics, cannot copy pictures accurately; they can be described as shape blind, although they can see color and motion.

The findings from neuropsychology align nicely with the predictions of the intermediate-level hypothesis. They do not support competing theories about the location of visual experience. When taken together with electrophysiological evidence and functional imaging, the intermediate-level hypothesis in vision has a very strong case. There is convergent evidence that consciousness resides at the intermediate level. Jackendoff was not aware of this evidence when he formulated the hypothesis. It is a testament to his conjectures and to Marr's pioneering model of vision that the predictions of his theory have been so nicely confirmed.

2. Beyond Vision

2.1. OTHER SENSES

In his 1987 book, Jackendoff suggests that the intermediate-level hypothesis applies equally well to all perceptual modalities. His defense of this claim is quick and speculative, because most research in perceptual psychology has been on vision. Jackendoff has little to say about audition and touch and even less to say about olfaction and gustation. There is still comparatively little research on these other senses. As we have seen, there is a large amount of neuroscientific data available now to support the claim that visual consciousness resides in intermediate-level areas, but discussions of the other senses must rest heavily on conjecture. Nevertheless, there is a growing body of research that suggests that other senses are hierarchically organized, and there is even some evidence supporting the claim that the intermediate level within these hierarchies is the locus of consciousness. This biological evidence is also well supported by introspection. Across domains, experience seems to be perspectival in nature. Consciousness presents the world from a particular point of view. When this observation is coupled with the evidence for hierarchical organization, it provides a powerful reason for concluding that the intermediate-level theory generalizes.

Let's begin with audition. The auditory pathway is organized much like the visual pathway. Vision begins when light enters the lens of the eyes and stimulates retinal nerve cells. Audition begins when sound waves stimulate the cochlea, a small structure inside the ear. Visual stimuli and auditory stimuli are both processed by the thalamus before signals are sent to the neocortex. The cortical components in both modalities are organized hierarchically, and those hierarchies can be divided into three levels of processing. We have already seen how the visual hierarchy is organized. The primate auditory hierarchy has been well described by Kaas and Hackett (2000). Cortical processing of sounds begins in a group of structures in superior temporal cortex that make up the "auditory core." The core encompasses a caudal region of primary auditory cortex (A1) and two adjacent rostral regions, labeled R and RT. Cells in caudal AI are most responsive to high-frequency tones, and those in R are most responsive to low frequencies. Both areas are tonotopically organized: similar frequencies are registered by adjacent rows of neurons, spanning from higher to lower frequencies in R and from lower to higher frequencies in caudal AI. The organization of RT is less well understood. The individual cells in these core regions respond to a narrow range of frequencies, and there are specific tones to which they are most responsive. The second level in the primate auditory pathway is called the belt, which is a collection of about eight areas surrounding the core. All of these areas are densely connected to the core, and at least some of them are organized tonotopically. Belt areas are connected, in turn, to a surrounding parabelt region, which is the presumed locus of high-level auditory processing.

Most of what we know about these areas comes from monkey research, but there is good reason to think that humans have homologous structures that function similarly in Heschl's gyrus and surrounding portions of superior temporal gyrus. Audition researchers believe that these areas process progressively more complex stimulus features. Cells in the belt region respond to pure tones, but the auditory system is also able to extract information about how tones go together to form more complex sounds, such as melodies and words, along with information about the location of a sound in space and the direction of motion in a moving sound. And, of course, the auditory system is also used to categorize sounds, including words, that vary dramatically across instances. It is natural to propose a three-stage auditory hierarchy. First, the auditory system processes elemental tones and distinguishes these from random noise; next, the system processes sequential combinations of acoustic features to arrive at representations of more complex sounds; and finally, there is a stage of categorical recognition that treats physically different stimuli as if they were alike. Hierarchical models have been suggested by Rauschecker (1998), Binder et al. (2000), Wessinger et al. (2001), and Zatorre, Bouffard, and Belin (2004) on the basis of neuroimaging studies. Some of these models differ in detail, but they all suggest that there is a progression from simple acoustic features to more complex ones, as information flows from core to belt areas. If this progression culminates in categorical representations, as, for example, Binder et al. (2000) suggest, then the auditory hierarchy is very much like Marr's tripartite hierarchy in vision.

The emerging theory of audition invites speculation about the locus of consciousness. Cells in belt regions are probably not the neural correlates of auditory experiences, because they are too finely tuned. Belt cells respond to pure tones, not polyphonic or temporally integrated sequences. In contrast, responses at the categorical level of auditory processing are too abstract; at the categorical level, acoustic stimuli that sound different are treated as alike. Once again, the intermediate level seems to be privileged. When we listen to sounds, we experience tones integrated into coherent wholes. The sounds making up a word or a melody flow together. But we do not experience sound at a categorical level. If two people utter the same word, the sound will differ phenomenologically. So, it is reasonable to locate auditory consciousness at an intermediate level.

Further confirmation of this hypothesis comes from the range of deficits that can arise as a result of damage in different parts of the auditory pathway. Lesions in primary areas can result in total deafness, while lesions in more advanced areas result in auditory agnosia. Auditory agnosia can be associative or apperceptive (Vignolo, 1982; Peretz, 1993). In associative auditory agnosia, individuals can hear sounds, but they can't identify their significance. For example, Mendez (2001) describes a patient who is perfectly good at determining whether two sounds are the same or different, but he cannot match those sounds to pictures or name them. In apperceptive agnosia, the capacity to hear sounds normally is impaired. Ayotte et al. (2000) describe two patients who do very poorly at same/different judgments when listening to music excerpts. As this example suggests, some cases of apperceptive auditory agnosia are highly selective. Some patients have a deficit in music perception (amusia), environmental perception, or perception of words (word deafness). Peretz et al. (2001) describe a patient who cannot distinguish dissonant from assonant versions of the same musical excerpts. This suggests that intermediate-level auditory areas are functionally specialized, just like intermediate-level visual areas. The functional specialization may not coincide perfectly with music, words, and environmental sounds but rather with more basic acoustic properties that happen to coincide roughly with these domains. For example, individuals with amusia also tend to have difficulty with speech prosody (Monrad-Krohn, 1947; Stewart et al., 2006).

The precise anatomical loci of these deficits are not fully clear, but the symptoms are consistent with the hierarchy that I proposed. Low-level damage should prevent any auditory information from being processed by the neo-cortex, resulting in complete deafness. Damage to the intermediate level should also result in deafness, if the intermediate level is the locus of consciousness, but, given the functional specialization of intermediate-level systems, individuals with focal lesions should become deaf to certain aspects of sound and not others. This is what we find in apperceptive auditory agnosias. Finally, damage to high-level systems should leave auditory experience intact while impairing recognition. This is what we observe in associative auditory agnosia. The fact that we find auditory disorders that parallel those found in vision suggests that the two modalities are organized in similar ways and that, in both, the intermediate level is the locus of consciousness. If auditory consciousness were located at a high level, apperceptive agnosia would be impossible, because categorical deficits would be comorbid with a loss of experience. If auditory consciousness were located at the low level, apperceptive agnosia would be impossible, because individuals whose injuries were located above the low level would experience sound normally, and they would make accurate same/different judgments when presented with pairs of sounds.

Preliminary evidence is consistent with the conjecture that auditory consciousness resides at the intermediate level. With other sense modalities, the evidence is considerably less secure. Too little research has been done. But it is noteworthy that all of the senses are organized hierarchically, and in each case, there seems to be a progression from very local features to categorical representations. In each case, an intermediate level can be postulated in between. Here's what we know.

The tactile hierarchy is located in the parietal lobe. It is well known that there is a representation of the body running along the central sulcus. It turns out that this body map is part of a hierarchically organized system (Kaas, 1993; Friedman et al., 1986). Low-level touch is associated with primary so-matosensory cortex (S1), which includes Brodmann areas 3a and 3b, 1, and 2. There may be a hierarchy within S1; area 3b, for example, feeds into area 1. S1 areas also send afferents to secondary somatosensory cortex (S2) (Pons et al., 1987), and SII sends afferents to an adjacent parietal ventral area (PV) and various parts of the insula (Kaas, 1993). S1 and S2 are organized somatotopically (Ruben et al., 2001), and both have cells that are responsive to differences in surface texture (Pruett, Sinclair, and Burton, 2000). Within these areas, different cells respond to different cutaneous features, such as pressure, flutter, and vibration (Chen, Friedman, and Roe, 2005). In addition to cutaneous response, the somatosensory system has cells that are responsive to deep somatic (inside our bodies), thermal, nociceptive, and haptic touch. Each of these features may have its own processing hierarchy. The cutaneous and haptic cells may collaborate in an object-recognition hierarchy (Bodegard et al., 2001).

In addition, some cells in SII and Brodmann areas 5 and 7b may participate in sensorimotor integration; they are responsive to movements. There are high-level cells that code categorically for manual actions such as holding or grasping.

The exact organization of the tactile hierarchies is not known, so it is difficult to confirm that we can distinguish three functional stages, corresponding to local features, complex features, and categorical representations. There is, however, evidence consistent with this supposition. I will restrict my speculations to tactile object recognition, but a comparable story can be told about other somatic senses, such as proprioception, kinesthesia, and thermoreception. In tactile object recognition, the most widely studied components of the hierarchy are S1 and S2. There is also a growing body of evidence that insula is involved (Reed, Shoham, and Halgren, 2004). Based on work with monkeys, Schneider, Friedman, and Mishkin (1993) suggest that the granular area of insula (Ig) may serve a role comparable to that of inferotemporal areas in high-level vision. It is tempting to locate low-, intermediate-, and high-level tactile recognition in S1, S2, and insula respectively. An alternative division would treat area 3b of S1 as low-level, areas 1 and 2 as intermediate, and S2 and insular cortex as high levels of processing. Time will tell which, if either, is right.

Focal brain injuries in the tactile recognition pathway lead to selective recognition deficits. The inability to recognize objects by touch is called "astereognosia." This term covers a variety of different syndromes. Some individuals are bad at recognizing microgeometrical features, such as texture and shape, and others are impaired at recognizing macrogeometrical features, such as length, suggesting that these may be functionally and anatomically distinct abilities (Roland and Mortensen, 1987; Reed, Caselli, and Farah, 1996; Bohlhalter, Fretz, and Weder, 2002). Thus, touch, like vision, is vulnerable to feature-specific deficits. In addition, patients with astereognosia differ in their performance of tactile-to-tactile matching tasks (matching pairs of objects through touch), suggesting a distinction between apperceptive and associative agnosia. Subjects who can match but can't name ordinary objects by touch can be described as associative tactile agnosics. Bohlhalter, Fretz, and Weder (2002) describe patients with an apperceptive deficit, while Platz (1996) describes an individual with an associative deficit.

The apperceptive/associative distinction in tactile agnosia supports the conjecture that intermediate-level touch systems are the locus of consciousness; high-level damage leaves experience intact, but intermediate-level damage disrupts experience. The intermediate-level hypothesis also sits well with introspective experience. When touching a surface, we do not experience isolated edges and textures but rather an integrated and interconnected array of textured surfaces. When pricked by the tiny tip of a pencil, we experience that discrete sensation as located on the larger surface of our hands. Such spatial integration suggests that conscious experience occurs beyond the primary level of tactile processing. But experience cannot reside too far past the primary level, because high-level representations presumably abstract away from features that are available in consciousness. For example, we can experientially discriminate between two differently shaped spoons, even though they belong to the same category. If high-level tactile recognition abstracts away from specific details of shape, then consciousness must reside at an earlier stage of processing. I am optimistic, therefore, that the tactile modality will conform to the predictions of Jackendoff's intermediate-level hypothesis.

Let me turn, finally, to the chemical senses of gustation and olfaction. Here current knowledge is even more limited. What matters most, at this preliminary stage, is establishing that these modalities are hierarchically organized. If hierarchies can be identified, then we may infer that the senses are organized in similar ways, and we can advance testable and concrete proposals about the intermediate level. Let me begin with taste. In monkeys, primary gustatory loci can be found in anterior dysgranular insular cortex (Yaxley, Rolls, and Sienkiewicz, 1990) and the adjoining portion of the operculum (Scott et al., 1986). This is consistent with human neuroimaging studies (e.g., Small et al., 1999; O'Doherty et al., 2002). Rolls, Yaxley, and Sienkiewicz (1990) proposed that caudolateral orbital frontal cortex is a secondary gustatory center, and Kobayakawa et al. (1999) have shown that a variety of areas become active after the primary gustatory area when humans are given taste stimuli. These areas include the frontal operculum and the anterior insula. The exact organization of these areas is unknown, but the connectional anatomy and sequential activation suggest that they are hierarchical. It is unknown whether there is an identifiable intermediate level within this hierarchy, but the anatomy invites speculation. Perhaps there is a progression from disunified maps of tastants distributed on the tongue, to more integrated taste sensations, and, finally, to repeatable taste categories. Introspection suggests that we experience taste holistically and precategorically. Sweet-and-sour soup tastes simultaneously sweet and sour, and the phenomenal intensity of these component flavors varies from chef to chef, despite being categorically alike. If this is right, then the intermediate-level hypothesis applies to gustation.

Olfaction is important for flavor, and it is possible that we have an integrated representation of taste and smell somewhere in the brain, but there is also evidence for modality-specific architecture. Smell is our oldest sense. There are creatures, such as the lungfish, that rely on smell alone. Like the other modalities, smell is hierarchical. Savic et al. (2000) found that perceiving odorants caused activation in the amygdala, piriform cortex, insular cortex, claustrum-orbitofrontal cortex, and anterior cingulate. As with all other senses, they also found activation in the thalamus. The organization of these structures in smell processing is not fully understood, but connectional anatomy in monkeys suggests that there is a pathway from the piriform cortex onto area 13 of caudal orbitofrontal cortex and then on to other orbitofrontal areas (Carmichael, Hogan, and Walter, 1994). To identify regions associated with recognition of odorants, Savic and Berglund (2004) presented subjects with odorless air, novel smells, and familiar smells. The familiar smells induced activation in frontal cortex (Brodmann areas 44, 45, and 47), along with precuneus and parahippocampus. Perhaps one or more of these areas contains modality-specific representations of smells. It is known that focal lesions can lead to smell-recognition deficits, and these deficits sometimes leave other aspects of smell perception intact. For example, Eichenbaum et al. (1983) describe an individual who, after surgery to prevent seizures, could recognize odor intensity but not odor quality.

We do not know for sure whether the smell hierarchy has three identifiable levels, but, as with the other senses, such an organization would make sense. Receptors in the olfactory bulb receive a variety of different chemical inputs in any one sniff. These need to be integrated and categorized. One would expect olfactory processing to progress from local features of the ambient chemical environments to coherent odorants and on to categorical recognition, including very abstract category judgments (e.g., food versus nonfood). Once again, introspection suggests that the intermediate level is the locus of consciousness. Consistent with this, Livermore and Laing (1998) found that people cannot consciously access the chemical components of odorants, even though they are represented at low levels of the olfactory system. This suggests that conscious representations of smell have integrated components into coherent wholes (see Young, 2011, for a theory of how primitive odorants combine). By the same token, we do experience odorants in a way that seems vantage-point-specific. For example, we can use experience to locate the source of a smell in space (Zhou and Chen, 2009). Smell experiences are coherent and perspectival. There are also associative smell agnosias in which acuity remains but recognition is impaired, suggesting that, as with vision, consciousness is precategorical (Stevenson and Wilson, 2007). Such recognition deficits with intact acuity may be common in schizophrenia (Kopala, Campbell, and Hurwitz, 1992).

At the present stage of research, evidence from neuroscience does not decisively establish the intuitive hypothesis that consciousness resides at an intermediate level in all of these sense modalities. But the existing evidence is tantalizing. The senses are all hierarchically organized, and evidence from neurological disorders suggests that each sense may be vulnerable to breakdowns like those found in vision. There can be categorical deficits without loss of experience, along with both global and selective experiential deficits. If this pattern holds up, it will support the intermediate-level hypothesis. At present, there is plenty of reason for optimism, and at the very least, looking for the locus of consciousness in sensory hierarchies other than vision promises to be a productive research program.

I have not shown that Jackendoff's account generalizes to all senses, but I hope to have fueled optimism. Existing evidence is, at least, suggestive.

2.2. EMOTIONS, DRIVES, AND PAINS

So far, I have only spoken about the senses. I have suggested that the intermediate-level hypothesis is plausible for every sensory modality. But what about other aspects of conscious experience? According to the strongest formulation of the intermediate-level hypothesis, they don't exist; all conscious experiences are sensory in nature. Call this the perception hypothesis. The perception hypothesis is a source of considerable controversy, but I think it is right. If so, every apparent case of consciousness outside the senses must turn out to be sensory in nature. We will see various examples of this along the way, but I want to begin with some obvious cases. No one would deny that we can have very intense emotions, drives, and pains. We can experience crippling despair, insatiable hunger, and agonizing injuries. In a folk-psychological taxonomy, these mental events are not always treated as perceptions. It is sometimes suggested that their phenomenal character cannot be pinned on any of the senses. I think that this folk conception is wrong.

Let's begin with emotion. Jackendoff has a puzzling account of emotional responses. He admits that they are conscious, but he makes no effort to explain them by appeal to intermediate-level perceptual states. Instead, he suggests that emotions constitute a separate class of conscious feelings that often coincide with intermediate-level perceptual experiences. When we see something disgusting, we have an intermediate-level visual representation and an "affect" marker that makes it feel disgusting. The affect marker is neither a perception nor an intermediate-level state, and Jackendoff offers no explanation of why it is experienced. This is a major departure from the perception hypothesis and the intermediate-level hypothesis with which he is associated. If emotion consciousness is not explained on the model of visual consciousness, then Jackendoff's account, by his own admission, does not generalize. I will offer a different account that conforms to the view that all consciousness, including conscious emotional experiences, arises at an intermediate level of perceptual processing.

There is considerable controversy about what emotions are. According to some researchers, emotions essentially involve judgments or other cognitive states (Solomon, 2004), and others disagree (Prinz, 2004b). The most popular noncognitive theories of emotion are somatic in nature. William James (1884) proposes that emotions are perceptions of patterned changes in the body. When we are afraid, for example, our hearts race, our eyes widen, our blood vessels contract, our breathing becomes strained, our hair stands on end, our posture stiffens. James says that the emotion of fear is nothing more than a feeling of such changes. Many authors reject this view, but we need not get embroiled in that debate. For us, the question isn't whether emotions are exhausted by bodily feelings but rather whether the experience of emotions is exhausted by such feelings. James has a simple and compelling argument for this claim. He says to imagine a state of terror without any bodily feelings. Imagine that your body is in a completely placid state. If you imagine that properly, he says, there will be no feeling left that you would describe as fear. The feeling of fear and that of every other emotion evaporate when bodily sensations are removed. Perhaps there are other unconscious aspects of emotion, but emotional feelings seem to be somatic in nature.

I have defended James's view elsewhere (Prinz, 2004b), and I will assume here that it offers an adequate theory of emotional consciousness. If it does, it is easy to see how the intermediate-level hypothesis might apply to emotions. If James is right, then emotional feelings are perceptual. They are somatic feelings—feelings of our organs and muscles. Thus, emotions pose no particular problem for the perception hypothesis. But how do they sit with the intermediate-level hypothesis?

Here's a sketch of a proposal (Prinz, 2004b). Like tactile object recognition, our somatic senses, such as interoception and kinesthesia, are hierarchically organized. Feelings of the body, I submit, reside at an intermediate level of processing. I think that emotion pathways overlap with but are not exactly identical to the pathways of ordinary body perception. Emotions are elicited by factors that typically originate outside the body, so neural structures underlying emotion elicitation are likely to reside outside our somatosensory system. And emotions also involve different effects from mere body perceptions. If you merely think your heart is racing, you may slow down, but if you think you are afraid, you may speed up and flee. This suggests that emotions have characteristic causes and effects that differ from mere body sensations. But nestled between these causes and effects, I think emotions recruit the very same systems that support nonaffective body perception. I think there is a hierarchical process that begins with domain-general detection of local bodily features and culminates with emotion-specific categorical perceptions.

Imagine again the feeling of terror, which involves changes in your musculoskeletal, circulatory, and respiratory systems. In order to go from a constellation of bodily changes to the recognition of fear, one needs to register that those changes are taking place. Muscles and organs have nerve fibers in them, and these are spatially distributed. The brain receives information from these fibers, but at the earliest stages of processing, that information is likely to be disunified in two respects. First, the fibers coming in from a single organ or muscle group may register local changes without giving a more integrated representation of how the organ is behaving. The changes may be both spatially and temporally local. To experience the heart as a whole object changing over time (e.g., the rate of heartbeats), the brain must integrate local events. Early somatic perception is also disunified in a second respect: individual organs are probably registered separately. To experience a pattern of changes in the body, one must bind together perceptions from different somatic systems. It is extremely likely, therefore, that body perception involves a second stage of processing beyond the stage at which local features are perceived. At this second stage, we bind together responses from nerve cells that have more restricted receptive fields, and we bind together responses from multiple organs, giving rise to a coherent representation of the global bodily state. This is an intermediate level of somatic processing. There must also be a high level. To distinguish a mere bodily perturbation and an emotion, we must be able categorically to recognize patterns of bodily change. Among those body patterns that we perceive to be emotional, we must also determine which affective category they express: is this state fear, fury, or elation? Moreover, the very same emotion may have different bodily correlates on different occasions. Fear can involve a flight response or a freezing response; these are somatically different but equally recognizable as fear. Thus, we must postulate high-level mechanisms that recognize and label bodily patterns.

In summary, there seems to be a three-stage hierarchy that begins with perception of local bodily changes, then integrates these into patterns, and finally assigns equivalence classes of different patterns categorical significance. Anatomically, this hierarchy probably involves the somatosensory cortices, the insula, and various parts of anterior cingulate cortex, all of which have been implicated in interoception. The emotion pathway differs from mere somatic perception at the final stage; it avails itself of emotion-specific categorical representations of the body. But these categories are probably represented in neural circuits that are involved in body perception, because emotion categories can be identified as equivalence classes of somatic states. There is evidence based on functional imaging studies of self-reported emotional states that rostral portions of anterior cingulate cortex are especially important. More caudal portions of anterior cingulate along with interoceptive regions of the insula may make up an intermediate level of emotion processing. The emotion pathways also include mechanisms that trigger bodily changes when matters of concern arise. The amygdala is the most widely studied structure that plays this role.

Now, if we ask ourselves where in this hierarchy the conscious experience of emotions arises, the answer should be obvious. We do not experience emotions as disunified changes in specific organs; the heart races in terror and euphoria, so we need to perceive a full constellation of changes to experience one or the other of these emotions. Thus, emotional experience does not reside at the low level of somatic perception. Nor do we experience emotions as categorical. The flight response feels different from the freezing response, even though both are recognized as fear. Emotional experience resides at the intermediate level. We experience emotions as coherent and specific patterns of bodily change.

This is all highly speculative but also highly plausible. There even seem to be emotion disorders that conform to the pattern of breakdowns observed in vision and other senses. Some people are very bad at identifying their emotions. When it reaches clinical extremes, this condition is labeled "alexithymia." Some alexithymic individuals also experience somatization, the tendency to misde-scribe emotional responses as mere bodily states (Shipko, 1982). These syndromes are akin to associative agnosias: the experience is intact, but people do not know how to categorize it. In addition, there are clinical conditions that seem to involve an absence of emotional experience. This can occur in schizo-phrenia, especially during catatonic episodes. The most extreme case of emo-tional flattening is akinetic mutism, which typically arises when anterior cingulate cortex is surgically sectioned to treat intractable pain (Damasio and Van Hoesen, 1983). People with akinetic mutism seem comatose—they do not respond verbally or behaviorally to the world around them—but they are actu-ally fully cognizant of the world around them. Some people who endure this condition recover, no doubt because of the brain's remarkable plasticity, and they report that during the period of mutism, they felt emotionally dead. They do not respond to the world around them, because everything leaves them dis-interested. The disorder might be likened to cortical blindness, a profound sen-sory deficit caused by brain damage. Alternatively, it might be closer to apperceptive agnosia. Perhaps low-level body monitoring is taking place, but the intermediate level is damaged, so conscious experiences of emotionally sig-nificant bodily changes are lost. Such pathologies are consistent with the three-level model of emotion processing that I have proposed. They do not prove that emotion consciousness resides at an intermediate level, but the model does pre-dict that such disorders should occur.

I have been arguing that emotions can reconcile the intermediate-level hy-pothesis and the perception hypothesis. What about the other conscious expe-riences mentioned above? Let's begin with pain. According to standard theories, pain is a compound state. It involves a sensory aspect and an emotional aspect. The sensory aspect tells us which part of our body has been injured or dis-rupted, and the affective aspect gives us a feeling of aversion. If this analysis is right, then pain can be entirely explained in terms of somatic perception. The affective component involves somatic changes that have emotional significance, such as changes in our viscera, and the sensory component will involve percep-tion of the affected part of the body. Neuroimaging studies support this conjec-ture. Pain coincides with activation in somatosensory areas, very often including the anterior cingulate and other structures that are frequently implicated in emotional response.

There may be pain-specific machinery within our somatosensory systems. There are nociceptive cells in all parts of the body capable of experiencing pain, and the sensory component of pain may involve activation in the afferents of these cells rather than in cells that register pleasant or neutral bodily sensations. As remarked above, somatosensory systems may partition into functionally separate pathways for perception of cutaneous touch, deep touch, temperature, pressure, and pain. Each of these pathways may produce different kinds of qualitative experiences. The distinctive sensory character of pain may derive from the nociceptive pathway rather than from the emotion pathway that is also engaged when we respond to noxious stimuli. Drugs, such as morphine, that inhibit the emotional response in pain leave a residual sensory experience that feels painlike but is not unpleasant.

I already suggested that the emotional pathway is hierarchical and that the intermediate level is privileged. To show that pain conforms to the intermediate-level hypothesis, I would need to establish that the nociceptive pathway is also hierarchical. Here evidence is limited, but there is reason for confidence. There are cells that respond to nociceptive stimuli in various of the neural structures implicated in somatosensory processing. This suggests that nociception proceeds in stages. Conceptually, we might understand the hierarchy as follows. First, the brain registers local activity in nociceptive cells with small receptive fields; then these responses are integrated into more complex maps that tell us the precise boundaries and character of the pain; finally, high-level representations allow us to identify the pain using broad categories such as sharp, dull, or shooting. If this hierarchy exists, consciousness resides in the middle. We experience pains as circumscribed states with specific character that outstrips our coarse categorical descriptions.

Finally, consider drives, such as hunger, thirst, and sexual urges. Here I will be very brief. Folk psychology sometimes distinguishes these states from perceptions, but it should be obvious that they are at least partially perceptual in nature. In hunger, we perceive the levels of nutrients in our blood and the state of fullness or emptiness in our digestive tracts. In thirst, we also register blood chemicals, and we perceive the level of hydration in our mouths and throats. During sexual urges, we feel emotions and arousal, along with characteristic changes in our reproductive organs. Some of the somatic changes involved in basic drives may never enter conscious awareness. It's not clear, for example, that there is a conscious experience of blood chemistry. But changes in loins, throats, and bowels are certainly experienced. Presumably, the considerations that point toward hierarchical organization in other somatosensory states apply equally well here. The intermediate-level hypothesis is, I believe, as plausible for conscious drives as it is for other forms of bodily experience.

2.3. LANGUAGE

In addition to garden-variety sensory experiences, we can have conscious experiences of language. Jackendoff (1987) devotes more time to language than to anything else. This is unsurprising, because Jackendoff is a linguist. Here I will merely summarize what he has to say.

Language processing involves a number of functionally separate subsystems. When we hear a sentence, we process phonology, syntax, and semantics (roughly, sound, phrase structure, and meaning). In the standard picture, these three components are processed in that sequence during sentence comprehension and in the reverse sequence during language production, but each system can exert some influence on the others. For example, the meaning we assign to a sentence can affect what we hear. Jackendoff begins his story by asking which of these components of linguistic processing we experience consciously. He says that the answer is obvious. We don't have conscious experiences of word meanings. Some words are associated with mental images, which we can consciously imagine, but much of the time, meanings are constructed from conceptual representations that have no qualitative character. Nor do we experience syntax, the complex tree structures that bind together words and label phrases with syntactic categories. Instead, people with intact hearing experience language via phonology, the sounds that make up a sentence.

If Jackendoff is right about this, then language conforms to the perception hypothesis. We experience just that aspect of language that is perceptual in nature. Meanings and syntax are not perceptual, and they cannot be directly experienced. Jackendoff also suggests that language conforms to his intermediate-level hypothesis. The sounds we consciously experience reside at an intermediate level of auditory processing. A raw acoustic signal is a noisy flow of sound waves with no discrete parts. We streamline this signal in experience, filtering out noise, focusing on significant features, and imposing partitions between words. But we do not experience speech sounds at the categorical level. Any given phoneme sounds different depending on the age, gender, and accent of the speaker. These differences are lost at the level of categorical phoneme perception, but they are all consciously experienced. Speech sounds are experienced at a level that lies above the buzzing confusion of unfiltered sound waves but below the level of phoneme categories. Therefore, the conscious experience of language conforms to the intermediate-level hypothesis.

In summary, it seems that all of the most obvious components of conscious experience—perceptions, emotions, and silent speech—lend themselves to an intermediate-level account. Later chapters will consider whether other contested aspects of consciousness require resources that go beyond those surveyed here. For now, I conclude that the intermediate-level hypothesis shows great promise in accounting for those aspects of consciousness that just about everyone agrees we have.

3. Some Objections

I turn now to arguments that might be marshaled against the intermediate-level hypothesis. The objections that I will consider here focus on the conjecture that the intermediate level is privileged. In later chapters, we will encounter other objections concerning the generality of this hypothesis.

Objection 1: No Hierarchies
    The intermediate-level hypothesis cannot be right because perceptual systems are not organized hierarchically.

In an influential paper called "A Critique of Pure Vision," Churchland, Ramachandran, and Sejnowski (1994) argue that Marr's hierarchical theory of vision is not merely wrong in detail but is fundamentally misguided. Their main objection is that vision is not hierarchical, as he proposed. Instead, there are dozens of different visual systems that operate in all directions: bottom up, top down, and lateral. The authors give many examples of visual phenomena that support this picture. For example, when we look at a mask photographed from the inside, it continues to look convex, even though it is concave. The nose of the mask appears to protrude, rather than recede, because our knowledge that faces are generally convex exerts top-down influence on our visual system. The intermediate-level hypothesis is prefaced on the assumption that perception is hierarchical. If this assumption is false, the hypothesis is hopeless.
    There are two decisive replies to this objection. First, I have characterized the intermediate level in terms of what information gets encoded: a world of coherent objects presented from a specific vantage point. On this characterization, the intermediate-level hypothesis could be true even if perception were not strictly hierarchical, although the presence of hierarchical organization provides evidence for vantage-point specificity; the task of perception is to transform local features into invariant representations, and that seems to require an intermediate stage in which features are bound into perspectival wholes. Second, top-down and lateral processing are entirely compatible with the claim that perception is hierarchical. Let me define an information-processing system as hierarchical if (a) it has subsystems that can be recruited sequentially, and (b) each subsystem contains representations that can be derived using transformation rules from the representations in the sequentially prior system. On this definition, nothing that Churchland, Ramachandran, and Sejnowski say about lateral and top-down effects is incompatible with the claim that perception is hierarchical. Edges are needed to derive lines, lines are needed to derive contours, and contours are needed to derive invariant object representations. It just happens that our stored object representations can also be used to generate images and bias processing at earlier levels in the hierarchy. This point about function gains further support from neuroanatomy. The synaptic distance between brain areas and eyes increases as we move from the lower to the higher levels. Information flows in all directions, but higher areas cannot respond to a stimulus without first routing through lower areas.

Objection 2: Feature Consciousness
    We can consciously experience local features even when those features are represented at a low level of perceptual processing.

Consider vision. According to the three-level account presented earlier, low-level vision extracts local edges. But local edges can be experienced. We can focus on a tiny part of a contour and have a conscious experience of it. Doesn't that show that the low level can be conscious?

This objection is based on a confusion. Of course, we can experience an edge, but when we do so, we are not necessarily experiencing low-level representations. Representations at the intermediate level have edges, and by focusing attention or moving up close to a contour, we can make a small bit of edge very vivid, while the surrounding bits of edge blur away. The fact that we can experience features that are represented at a low level does not mean that the low level is being experienced. Some of those features are re-represented. The intermediate level makes two predictions. Features that are represented only at the low level cannot be experienced, and features that are necessarily represented at the intermediate level are experienced. These predictions seem to be true.

Objection 3: V1 as Locus of Visual Consciousness

Even if consciousness resides at an intermediate level of representation, there is evidence from neuroscience that recurrent connections to low-level systems are necessary for awareness.

This objection has been forcefully advanced by Lamme (2001; 2006). It has also been sympathetically discussed by Block (2007), and I, too, defended the importance of feedback in my first publication on consciousness (Prinz, 2000b). Lamme does not think that consciousness is located in V1. He admits that the response profiles of cells there do not conform perfectly to the contents of experience. But he thinks that consciousness does not arise until higher-level areas, especially intermediate areas in extrastriate cortex, send signals back to V1. There is evidence that extrastriate areas send signals back to V1, but why think that such efferent projections are necessary for consciousness? The main piece of evidence comes from a transcranial magnetic stimulation (TMS) study by Boyer, Harrison, and Ro (2005), among others. The authors presented subjects with visual stimuli and then, 100 milliseconds after stimulus onset, used TMS to inhibit response in V1. As a result, subjects did not consciously experience the stimulus. The TMS inhibition functioned like a mask. This is striking because extrastriate representations are generated 80 milliseconds after a stimulus is presented. So inhibited V1 response prevented the stimulus from entering awareness even after activation had started in extrastriate areas. Lamme proposes that the extrastriate activity sends a signal back to V1, and if that signal does not match the incoming stimulus representation, consciousness never arises. Because V1 is inhibited at 100 milliseconds, the efferent signal fails to find its match.

This is an interesting proposal, but the evidence is too weak to support that conclusion. There are explanations of the TMS results that are more natural than the explanation proposed by Lamme. TMS is sometimes said to mimic focal brain lesions, by disabling regions of the brain. That description is really inaccurate. When TMS is applied to visual cortex, it generates phosphenes, which are experienced by subjects as bubbles of light (Kammer et al., 2005). In addition, TMS stimulation is not very focal. It is hard to localize on a small region of the brain, such as V1, and when one region is stimulated using TMS, connected regions, often quite far away, also show activation (Walsh and Cowey, 2000). Thus, it is overwhelmingly likely that stimulating V1 would rapidly generate activity in extrastriate cortex. The perceived stimulus would be immediately replaced by something similar to an intense light. The Boyer study shows something that we have known for a long time from masked priming. When one stimulus is rapidly followed by another, the first isn't experienced. This suggests that intermediate-level representations must be active for a certain amount of time before they enter consciousness (a point that I will return to below). But it does not prove that intermediate-level systems must send signals back into low-level systems in order to have a conscious experience. Indeed, there is evidence that such feedback is anatomically limited and functionally variable; this suggests that feedback plays only a modest and context-sensitive role in modulating inputs to reduce conflict or reflect visual expectation (Budd, 1998). Moreover, we have already seen that people with V1 injuries sometimes experience visual images and hallucinations. This proves that V1 is not required for consciousness. Thus, Lamme does establish the necessity of feedback. There is no strong evidence that such signals play an important role in conscious experience.

Objection 4: Perceptual Grouping

We sometimes use high-level information to impose structure on visual inputs, and doing so alters how they appear in consciousness.

Objections 2 and 3 allege that low-level visual areas contribute to consciousness. It is more common to find objections vying for the high level. Consider figure 4. It is almost impossible to make out what these gray blobs represent (the famous Gestalt Dalmatian is another example of this kind). But the indeterminacy can be resolved with some simple instructions. If you mentally rotate the image 90 degrees counterclockwise, you may be able to discern that the image depicts a tightly cropped portrait (the face of philosopher Tim Bayne). When you assign meaning to this image, it seems to change. You can tell, for example, which parts are foreground and which are background. That transformation may depend on the fact that you have been told what the picture represents, and your high-level knowledge of its meaning has an effect on the experience. This might be taken as evidence for a high-level contribution to phenomenology.

There is, however, an alternative explanation. Just as there are back projections from intermediate- to low-level visual areas, there are back projections from the high level. These may alter processing at the intermediate level. We know that the

FIGURE 4 An image that is difficult to interpret.

intermediate level can encode object contours and figure-ground separation. It is possible that the high level can impose such structure on intermediate-level representations through back projections.

We thus have two explanations of what happens when we discern the structure in pictures that look disorganized at first glance. According to one, the experience supervenes on high- and intermediate-level vision, and according to the other, the high level merely influences the conscious representation at the intermediate level. The former hypothesis might seem to enjoy support from neuroimaging studies. There is fMRI evidence that when people recognize a group of blobs as a face, there is an increase in activation in high-level visual areas but not in earlier areas (Andrews and Schluppeck, 2004). But this is inconclusive. It's not surprising that high-level face areas would be active when faces are perceived, but there is no reason to expect greater intermediate-level activity when that happens, since the picture of blobs is just as richly detailed as the same picture when perceived as a face. What we should find is not an increase in intermediate-level activity but an increase in organization. Some evidence for that can be found in scalp recordings taken when people view the Gestalt Dalmatian picture. Here researchers find evidence for greater neural coherence in occipital areas when the picture is parsed (Tallon-Baudry and Bertrand, 1999). Moreover, it's not even clear how the high level could be directly contributing to phenomenology in these cases. When we parse figure 4, we see the face from a particular orientation, at a particular size, in a particular position—features that are characteristically lost at the high level. The perspectival nature of the experience suggests that the intermediate level is the correlate.

Objection 5: Categorical Awareness

We can be consciously aware of the categories to which perceived stimuli belong, even though such categorical information is represented at the high level.

When you look at a chair, you are aware of its shape from a particular point of view, but defenders of this objection insist that you are also aware of its chairness. When you look at a coin from an angle, you experience an ellipse, but you also experience a circle. Such categorical knowledge resides at the high level, and therefore, the high level seems to be conscious in addition to the intermediate level.

This is a popular objection, but I have never quite seen the force of it. Some people insist that they have conscious experiences corresponding to categorical representations, and I just can't find them in my own experience. When I look at a chair, try as I may, I only see a specific chair oriented in a particular way. When I look at a coin, I just experience an ellipse. There is something bizarre about saying that one experiences circularity of a tilted coin in addition to the ellipse. If this were a visual experience, one might expect it to involve two overlapping shapes, an ellipse in a circle, but vision is not like that. Likewise, it's not clear what it would mean to say that one visually experiences chairness. What kind of experience would that be? A chair as seen from no vantage point? A chair from multiple vantage points overlapping? A shape possessed by all chairs? Phenomenologically, these options seem extremely implausible. Thus, the only way to defend this objection is to assume that categorical features are experienced in some nonvisual way. One might suppose that they are experienced conceptually. A response to this possibility must await chapter 5, where I critically assess the claim that there is distinctively cognitive phenomenology. For now, let it suffice to say that the visual aspects of consciousness do not seem to outstrip the intermediate level.

There is one puzzle, however, that must be addressed. Why do some people insist that they visually experience the roundness of a tilted coin or the chairness of a living-room recliner? Why do these nonretinal features seem visual to some viewers? One answer has to do with the fact that viewpoint-specific imagery can carry information about an allocentric world. Under the right conditions, an experience of an elliptical shape carries the information that there is a round object present, because that is the way round objects look from an angle. Thus, seeing an elliptical shape is seeing a round thing. The roundness is what we are visually representing. The error arises when people attribute the representational content of what we are seeing to the visual experience itself. This error has long been recognized in the philosophy of perception. When we see a stick in water, it *looks* straight in some sense, but that doesn't mean that we have a straight visual image. Rather, the curvy lines we experience happen to be what straight sticks look like when submerged, and we know this fact. Thus, "looks straight" expresses the representational content of our experience, not the qualities of the experience itself, but this way of talking makes it easy to confuse the content of experience for the quality.

Objection 6: Perceptual Constancies

   Some perceptual constancies are consciously experienced but not encoded at the intermediate level.

For example, look at a vertical line, and then bend your neck over as far as you can. You will notice that the line continues to appear perfectly vertical. Within the visual system, some high-level and, more surprisingly, low-level brain structures represent objects as they are objectively oriented regardless of body position, but intermediate-level representations change with body position (Sauvan and Peterhans, 1999; McKyton and Zohary, 2007). Likewise, if you see a wall painted white, it looks uniformly white even though there may be shadows and reflected lights that give rise to irregularly colored intermediate-level representations. Such examples might suggest that the intermediate level cannot be the correlate of experience.

I believe that we are subject to an illusion when we think that we experience certain perceptual constancies. As with the elliptical circle, looking vertical does not entail that there be a vertical object in experience. Looking vertical can be a matter of having an appearance that is perpendicular to the appearance of the ground. We also experience verticality by the fact that visual experiences co-occur with the somatic experience of gravity and body orientation (Yardly, 1990). When we tilt our heads, the column is *visually* experienced as tilted, but the overall experience presents the column as emerging vertically from the center of gravity. But these other senses do not completely make up for the visual tilt; it is well known that judgments of verticality are systematically skewed in the direction of our head position when we bend our necks (Yardly, 1990).

Color constancies can be explained, too. It's impossible to deny that we can recognize a white wall as such, even when it is cast in shadows, but this ability may not depend on phenomenological constancy. When lighting changes, people can easily report phenomenal changes (Reeves, Amano, and Foster, 2008). Color constancy most likely involves an unconscious inference about the objective color, an inference that can go wrong or vary without corresponding changes in the phenomenology. To confirm this, look at a white wall under shadowy conditions and imagine being told that the wall is actually pale gray. This change in the belief about the objective color does not seem to alter experience of the perceived color. This dissociation is confirmed by research on patients with brain injuries. Some injuries eliminate constancy but leave color experience intact (Cowey and Heywood, 1997; Rüttiger et al., 1999). In contrast, if the capacity to discriminate specific colors is lost, there may be unconscious constancy detection, but there will be no color experience (see Walsh, 1999). This suggests that constancy is postexperiential.

Color constancy is, in this respect, quite unlike color contrast effects. When color perception is altered by contextual information, the effects are experiential. For example, Purves and Lotto (2003) have developed extraordinary illusions in which gray squares appear colorful when placed on a grid of surrounding colors. They explain this by saying that the visual system uses statistical information to compute the colors of surfaces based on encounters we've had in the past. These effects can be accommodated on the intermediate-level approach, because color processing of cells in V4 is influenced by the surrounding chromatic context (Kusunoki, Moutoussis, and Zeki, 2006).

Objection 7: Perceptual Presence

When you see a mug facing you, only one side reflects light onto your retina, but you sense that is has another side. The occluded side is part of your experience, even though it probably isn't represented in intermediate-level vision.

This kind of example was popular among the phenomenologists. I'm told that Husserl used to show his students a sphere and then turn it around to reveal a point on the occluded side, causing great surprise. The idea of perceptual presence has come back into vogue under the influence of people defending the enactive theory of perception (see Noë, 2005). The intuition that vision goes this far beyond the retinal input is problematic for the intermediate-level view. Intermediate-level representations present the world from a single vantage point, which means that they leave out occluded surfaces.

The perceptual presence objection is a bit like the objection that we are conscious of categorical representations. As with the latter, I find it hard to buy the intuition here. When I look at a mug, try as I may, I don't see the occluded side. It's invisible to me, like the dark side of the moon or the organs inside my body. I can consciously imagine all of these things, but when I do so, I am generating an intermediate-level representation. Of course, most of the time, occluded parts can't be seen. Why, then, have clever people bought into the idea that occluded objects are perceptually present? In some cases, the sense of presence may simply reflect the fact that we form unconscious visual expectations and experience surprise when they are violated. This would explain Husserl's students' reaction to his trick sphere. In other cases, the sense of presence may involve the formation of imagery in other modalities. I submit that the occluded parts are not visually present, but they may be represented in other ways. When I look at a mug, I may imagine grasping it, and that could produce some kinesthetic imagery. I think this is all that is going on when, to use Gibson's (1979) term, we see what actions the objects around us afford. We don't literally see affordances, in that affordances are not represented visually. Rather, the visual system causes us to form kinesthetic images. When I see a mug, I may imagine holding it. This is consistent with the intermediate-level hypothesis. There are neuroimaging studies showing that people generate spontaneous motor and somatosensory representation when they view tools and other objects that afford manual manipulation (e.g., Grèzes et al., 2003). Thus, manipulable objects cause imagery associated with physical interactions, and that imagery may be couched at the intermediate level. Noë suggests that affordances are aspects of our visual experiences (he even says that vision supervenes on the body). But this radical claim is unnecessary (see chapter 6).

Affordances seem to arise in distinct neural pathways, and there is no reason to think that visual experience is dependent on them.

Objection 8: IT as Locus of Visual Consciousness
 Neuroscientific research on binocular rivalry proves that visual consciousness is located in the high level.

This objection is based on work by Logothetis and his colleagues (Leopold and Logothetis, 1999; Sheinberg and Logothetis, 2007). He presented monkeys with two pictures simultaneously, one in each eye. When rivaling stimuli are presented binocularly, monkeys (and humans) experience just one image at a time, but they shift randomly back and forth. Monkeys can be trained to report what image they are seeing, and by measuring cellular activity at different stages of the visual system, Logothetis sought to discover the correlates of conscious experience. To do this, he found populations of cells at different stages of processing that are responsive to each of the stimuli that he presented. Then, when presenting both stimuli at once, he could measure which of these cells were active and whether their activations correlated with what the monkey reported seeing. Logothetis discovered that only 40 percent of the active cells in intermediate-level areas corresponded to what the monkeys reported seeing, whereas 90 percent of the cells in high-level areas corresponded to what the monkeys reported. Logothetis concluded that visual consciousness is located at the high level.

These findings have been harder to establish in human beings, where there is some fMRI evidence that the intermediate level is the locus of consciousness in binocular rivalry (Tse et al., 2005). But one can even bracket that evidence and expose a fallacy in Logothetis's reasoning. The claim that the intermediate level is the locus of consciousness does not entail that every cell active at this level contributes to consciousness—a theme I will take up in the next chapter. Thus, let's suppose that some intermediate-level cells are conscious and others are not. Perhaps the cells that Logothetis found to be correlated with the percept in intermediate-level areas are the conscious cells. For this proposal to work, it would have to be the case that there is something special about those cells. In particular, it would have to be the case that their pattern of activation differs from those of the other cells that don't correspond to what the monkeys report. Logothetis does not report any distinctive pattern of firing among the cells that correspond to the percept in intermediate-level areas, but those cells *must* be firing in a distinctive way. Otherwise, it wouldn't be the case that 90 percent of the high-level cells fire in conjunction with the reported percept. If all cells at the intermediate level behaved the same way, then they would all be able to send afferent signals to the high level, and 60 percent of the cells there would fire in ways that did not correspond to the reported percept. The fact that Logothetis finds some intermediate-level cells that correspond to what the monkeys report is sufficient for establishing that consciousness could reside at the intermediate level. The total proportion of cells doesn't matter. Here's an analogy. Suppose we want to know when a certain style of dancing originated, and we find that in 1961, a small group of people were doing the dance in question, and the next year, everyone was dancing that way. It would be absurd to infer that the dance originated in 1962.

Objection 9: Subliminal Perception

Intermediate-level perceptual representations may be necessary for consciousness, but they cannot be sufficient, because in cases of subliminal perception, there are unconscious intermediate-level representations.

This is the only objection to the intermediate-level hypothesis that I find compelling. Cases of unconscious perception response establish demonstratively that intermediate-level activation is not sufficient for consciousness. Something more is needed. One can make the point by saying that Jackendoff has identified the contents of consciousness, but he has not identified the process by which these contents become conscious. He has told us *what* we are conscious of but not *how* we become conscious. How do intermediate-level representations pass the threshold of experience? That is the topic for the next chapter.

In this chapter, I surveyed evidence in favor of the view that all consciousness resides at the intermediate level of hierarchically organized perceptual systems. The intermediate-level hypothesis enjoys considerable support in the case of vision. When Jackendoff first advanced the hypothesis, most of the existing evidence was behavioral. We now have a large body of corroborative evidence from neuroscience. Neuroscience is also revealing the organization of other sense modalities, and it is clear that all senses are hierarchical. Time will tell whether consciousness is associated with intermediate-level representations in each case, but there is reason to be optimistic. Sensory hierarchies seem to proceed from more local to more categorical representations, and consciousness arises between these extremes. The intermediate-level hypothesis should be considered a serious contender.

I also addressed important objections to Jackendoff's account and offered strategies for addressing each. None of these objections is decisive. This does not mean that the intermediate-level hypothesis offers a complete theory of consciousness. The last objection that I considered raises an insuperable challenge. I pointed out that mere activation of intermediate-level representations is not sufficient for conscious experience, even if it turns out to be necessary. This objection is consistent with the thesis that all consciousness resides at the intermediate level, but it suggests that a full account of conscious experience requires something more. Jackendoff's account is the cornerstone of an adequate theory of consciousness, but it is not sufficient on its own.

3

When Are We Conscious? Attention and Availability

In chapter 2, I argued that consciousness arises at a particular stage of sensory processing. More specifically, I endorsed Jackendoff's (1987) prescient conjecture that consciousness occurs at an intermediate level of representation that lies between a low level of processing, which represents local features of a stimulus in a disunified way, and a high level, which abstracts away from vantage-point and surface details in the service of object recognition. The low level might be compared to a pixel map, and the high level might be compared to the structural descriptions used by some computer-aided design programs, whereas the intermediate level is more like a 3-D movie: it represents whole objects with rich surface details, located in depth, and presented from a particular point of view. If the intermediate-level hypothesis is right, it is a major boon for the search to find the neural correlates of consciousness (NCCs). When we identify the neural mechanisms underlying intermediate-level perceptual processing, we have, in effect, located consciousness in the brain. One might think this is enough. If our goal is to find the NCCs, then we need look no further. Intermediate-level processing areas are well known in the brain, and we have overwhelming reason to think that consciousness resides there.

Unfortunately, it is premature to pop open the celebratory champagne. For while there is good reason to think that activation of intermediate-level representations and their neural realizers is necessary for conscious experience, there is equally good reason for thinking that such activations are not sufficient. The reason is simple. We sometimes perceive things in the absence of conscious experience. When we do so, we are presumably engaging the entire perceptual hierarchy, from low level to high; otherwise, we would not recognize objects that we unconsciously perceive. That means there is activation of intermediate-level representations in cases of unconscious perception, and therefore, mere activation at this level is not sufficient for conscious experience (see also Kanwisher, 2001).

The intermediate-level hypothesis gives us an account of *where* consciousness arises in the flow of information. But it doesn't tell us *when* these representations become conscious. We need a theory of the conditions under which intermediate-level perceptual states come to be consciously experienced. Without such a theory, we'll have an incomplete story about the psychological conditions that are necessary and sufficient for consciousness. Once we figure out which representations are candidates for consciousness, we still need to figure out what makes them conscious. Answering that question is the goal of this chapter. And to dispel any unpleasant suspense, I will reveal the answer now: consciousness arises when and only when we attend.

1. Evidence for the Necessity and Sufficiency of Attention

1.1. UNCONSCIOUS PERCEPTION

In 1957, James Vicary instigated a consumer panic when he reported that he had dramatically increased soft-drink and popcorn sales at a New Jersey movie theater by inserting subliminal messages. Evidence later suggested that these results were fabricated, and Vicary himself admitted that he did not collect enough data to consider the results reliable. Since then, however, there have been numerous studies establishing that stimuli can be subliminally perceived.

In studies of subliminal perception, the subliminal stimulus is presented either very briefly, in a degraded form (e.g., with low intensity), or in competition with another stimulus or task demand. Afterward, researchers must measure two things: consciousness and perception. Consciousness is measured either objectively or subjectively (Szczepanowski and Pessoa, 2007). On objective measures, subjects are asked to make a forced-choice guess about what they have seen; errors suggest that the stimulus was not consciously perceived. On subjective measures, subjects are asked to report on whether they saw anything and, sometimes, on what they saw; if the subject reports not having seen anything, that is taken as evidence that stimulus was unconscious. Sometimes subjective and objective measures are combined. For example, Kunimoto, Miller, and Pashler (2001) say that a stimulus is unconscious if confidence judgments about having seen it fail to predict accuracy in recall.

There are many ways to test for stimulus perception, but they generally involve some form of priming, the preactivation of representation that influences performance on a subsequent task. Most priming studies present a meaningful stimulus very quickly, followed by a mask (a screen of meaningless visual noise), which prevents an iconic memory from forming. In some cases, the stimulus is so brief that subjects are unaware that anything has been presented at all, but there is still evidence, under such conditions, for semantic processing (van den Bussche et al., 2009). For example, Naccache and Dehaene (2001) presented masked numbers and then asked subjects whether a consciously presented target number was higher or lower than five. If the masked number was in the same direction from five (higher or lower) as the test number, reaction times improved. In the study, the masked stimuli were presented for 43 milliseconds, which is below subjective thresholds, meaning that subjects report seeing nothing. Naccache et al. (2005) have also demonstrated priming below objective thresholds: they found that emotionally significant words generated activity in emotion centers in the brain even when presented at 29 milliseconds, at which point subjects' ability to guess whether a stimulus was presented is at chance. Such unconscious priming can even influence consumer choices, adding credible support to Vicary's dubious movie-theater study. Winkielman, Berridge, and Wilbarger (2005) showed pictures of faces to subjects that were angry, happy, or neutral for a mere 16 milliseconds, followed by a mask. Afterward subjects were given a soft drink and asked to rate it, pour as much as they desired into a glass, and say how much they were willing to pay for it. All of these measures were influenced by the valence of the prime.

Unconscious perception can be found in all sensory modalities. For example, Hillyard et al. (1971) had subjects listen to auditory noise and try to determine whether a brief tone had been played in the background. Even when subjects failed to detect the tone, electrical activity measured on their scalps indicated that the tone had been unconsciously perceived. Berti et al. (1999) found that a patient with somatosensory extinction could make accurate same/different judgments when holding an object in each hand even though he had no tactile experience of the one on the left. Wen et al. (2007) found that neutral faces were rated as more or less likable if paired with pleasant and unpleasant odorant presented below the level of conscious detection.

In short, researchers have found evidence for unconscious perception using a wide range of experimental methods across all modalities that have been examined. In each case, it is clear that stimuli are being semantically processed and hence represented up to the highest levels of perceptual processing, even in the absence of conscious experience. And this leaves us with a question. What makes the difference between perceiving consciously and perceiving unconsciously?

1.2. ATTENTION IS NECESSARY AND SUFFICIENT FOR CONSCIOUSNESS

One way to answer the question above is to consider pathological cases. One can look for brain injuries that lead to subliminal perception under ordinary viewing conditions. If such cases can be found, one could identify the locus of the injury to generate a hypothesis about the mechanisms that matter for consciousness. In taking this approach, one might immediately think of blindsight, which is one of the most celebrated neurological disorders (Weiskrantz, 1986). People with blindsight have injuries in their primary visual cortices, which prevent them from consciously seeing things presented in the visual field corresponding to the injury, yet they can correctly guess the location of objects presented in these blind fields. Blindsight is certainly intriguing, but it's not exactly what we are looking for, because people with the disorder cannot recognize objects in their blind fields, even on implicit measures. This suggests that they are not perceiving those objects in the sense under consideration here (representing those objects as such), and they are not using the full extent of their visual-processing hierarchies in response to those objects. Instead, the residual capacity probably involves subcortical structures and, perhaps, a select subset of spatially sensitive cortical visual areas. We need a condition in which objects are in fact recognized in the absence of consciousness.

The best example of this is unilateral neglect. Neglect is a disorder typically caused by injuries to the right inferior parietal cortex (for reviews, see Driver and Mattingly, 1998; Driver and Vuilleumier, 2001). People with this condition seem to have no conscious experience in the left visual fields or, sometimes, of the left sides of objects. When asked to copy a line drawing, they leave out details from the left side; when asked to find the vowels in a letter array, they ignore letters on the left; when asked to bisect a line, they draw the division too far to the right; and when asked to judge two figures that differ only on the left, they insist that the figures are identical. Phenomenologically, these patients seem to be blind on the left. But there is good evidence that many people with neglect retain a capacity for unconscious perception. For example, Marshall and Halligan (1988) presented a neglect patient with two vertically aligned pictures of houses that were exactly the same except that one of them had flames shooting out on the left. The patient insisted that the houses were the same, but when asked which one she would rather live in, she chose the one without flames on nine out of eleven trials. Some neglect patients do not show this pattern of performance on the house task (Bisiach and Rusconi, 1990), but the result has been replicated. Doricchi and Galati (2000) tested a neglect patient who showed a preference for the intact house on seventeen of nineteen trials, despite seeing the houses as the same. They found similar results on a wide range of items, with the patient preferring the intact object in a pair of pictures that she perceived as identical.

Other experiments have obtained further evidence for unconscious perception in neglect. Peru et al. (1996) presented neglect patients with pictures of animals that were either normal on the left side or abnormal: having either no left side, the left side of a different species, or the left side of a vehicle (figure 5). Their patients insisted that all of these pictures were identical, but when asked to guess which picture was most realistic, some patients reliably selected the correct one. When asked to explain this preference despite having said that the pictures were identical, patients would sometimes confabulate. For example, one patient explained his preference for the correct horse picture by saying that one had the eyes of a thoroughbred. This result clearly shows sensitivity to the abnormalities on the left side of the pictures without consciousness, but it does not show that the information on the left is being fully processed. A more telling result comes from Berti and Rizzolatti (1992), who showed that information in the neglected field can cause semantic priming. They presented neglect patients with pictures containing pairs of objects, which were either fruits or animals; the patients were able to categorize a visible fruit or animal on the right side if there was an invisible item from the same category presented on the left. This suggests that items on both sides are processed through the entire visual hierarchy.

Direct support for this conclusion comes from brain-imaging studies. Rees et al. (2000) found that objects that were unseen when presented to a neglect patient nevertheless caused visual activation. Important for our purposes, the activations included intermediate-level visual areas, confirming that mere activity here is not sufficient for conscious experience. Similar results were obtained by Vuilleumier et al. (2001), who found normal processing from V1 on up into the temporal cortex in the blind field of a patient with neglect.

Patients with neglect offer just what we are looking for: unconscious visual object recognition and unconscious activity in cortical visual areas. We can move toward a theory of consciousness by asking what is preventing conscious experience in neglect. The answer is that neglect is an attention deficit. The in-ferior parietal brain areas that usually cause the disorder are known to play a role in allocating attention. Neglect is also sometimes associated with injuries to the frontal eye fields, which are frontal cortex structures associated with both saccadic eye movements and attention (Husain and Kennard, 1996; Thompson, Biscoe, and Sato, 2005). Patients with neglect cannot consciously perceive things on the left, because they can't attend to them. The reason we rarely see neglect for the right visual field is that attention mechanisms in the right hemisphere, but not the left, seem to be capable of allocating attention to either side, so damage to the left hemisphere, as opposed to the right, leaves attention comparatively intact (Posner and Raichle, 1994).

Research on unilateral neglect gives us a candidate mechanism for consciousness: attention. When attention mechanisms are damaged, consciousness is lost, even though perception remains. But there is always some risk in inferring normal mechanisms from pathological cases. There is always a chance that the injuries in neglect compromise something other than attention. To confirm the hypothesis that attention is responsible, it is important to test people with intact brains. It has been shown that one can induce neglect symptoms in healthy

FIGURE 5 Some people with visual neglect see these as identical but the first as more real (reproduced from Peru et al., 1986, with permission).

people by delivering transcranial magnetic stimulation to attention areas in the parietal cortex (Meister et al., 2006; Kanai, Muggleton, and Walsh, 2008).

The hypothesis that attention is necessary for consciousness has been corroborated by behavioral research. Three phenomena are especially relevant. First, consider motion-induced blindness. When several fixed spots are positioned over a moving grid of crosshairs, the spots appear to flicker in and out of existence. One explanation of this is that the moving grid captures attention, making it unavailable for the dots, and that results in their disappearance (Bonneh, Cooperman, and Sagi, 2001). Second, there is a phenomenon called the attentional blink. This occurs when a subject is asked to detect two target stimuli in a series of rapidly displayed stimuli (typically presented at a rate of ten per second). Under such conditions, the first stimulus captures attention, and the second stimulus is not consciously perceived if it appears soon afterward (typically within 200 to 500 milliseconds of the first stimulus). Electrical recordings from the scalp suggest that the second stimulus is perceived unconsciously, but it does not reach consciousness because attention is consumed by the first (Luck, Woodman, and Vogel, 2000). Research on the attentional blink has led to the discovery of a related phenomenon called the emotional blink. Arnell, Killman, and Fijavz (2007) gave people a rapidly presented series of words, including some color terms. After a color term was presented, subjects were asked to name the color. In some conditions, they included an emotionally charged word (e.g., "orgasm") shortly before the color term. When this occurred, subjects tended to miss the color term. Emotionally charged words attract attention, leading to disruptions in conscious perception.

Third, consider inattentional blindness. While conducting experiments on divided attention, Rock et al. (1992) discovered that a significant percentage of people were completely oblivious to a stimulus that would be plainly visible had attention not been consumed. This was confirmed by Mack and Rock (1998) in a book-length series of follow-up studies. Mack and Rock instructed subjects to judge which of two intersecting lines in a crosshair was longer, and while the subjects were engaged in this task, they flashed a word or a shape (see figure 6). Many of their subjects failed to detect the unexpected stimulus and had no recollection of seeing anything other than the crosshair when probed with leading questions afterward. These stimuli exhibited priming effects but seem to have had no impact on conscious experience. Similar results have been obtained by others. For example, Koivisto, Hyona, and Revonsuo (2004) flashed a circle in the center of the screen while subjects were engaged in a task that required detecting two numerals; in one condition, 92 percent failed to notice the circle.

Strikingly, inattentional blindness can even occur for stimuli that are presented for a relatively long time. Simons and Chabris (1999) asked subjects to count how many times a basketball was passed by one of two teams in previously recorded videos. Unbeknownst to the subjects, these videos also had

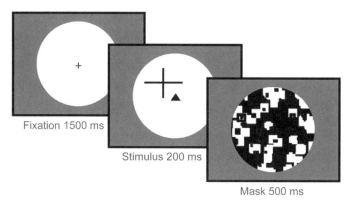

FIGURE 6 Testing procedure for inattentional blindness (based on Rock et al., 1992, with permission).

either a man with an umbrella or a woman in a gorilla suit traipse across the center of the screen for five seconds. Afterward, subjects were asked a series of increasingly leading questions about these unexpected intruders in the basketball game, and many reported no awareness: 67 percent failed to notice the umbrella man in one condition; and in two conditions, 92 percent failed to notice the gorilla. It might be objected that the intruders were consciously experienced but not recognized, since they could have been confused for the basketball players. I think this is unlikely, given that it is easy to recognize a gorilla and an umbrella, but the study is imperfect because the stimulus is very complex, and the bodies of the intruders could have been partially seen. A cleaner study was conducted by Most et al. (2005). They had subjects view an animated sequence in which black and white circles and squares slowly bounce against the side of the screen; subjects were asked to count how many times the black or white shapes bounced, and while they were doing so, a cross drifted across the center of the screen. In one condition, with a white cross and participants attending to black polygons, 100 percent failed to report the surprise stimulus when asked. Even when the cross was red, 28 percent failed to report it. The red cross differed from the other objects on the screen in color, shape, luminance, and pattern of motion, and it scrolled straight through the fixation point on the center of the screen and remained clearly visible for five seconds. In other words, the stimulus was highly incongruous, readily discernible, and impossible to mistake for anything else, yet more than a quarter of the viewers insisted that it wasn't there.

Research on unilateral neglect, motion-induced blindness, attentional blink, and inattentional blindness all provide powerful evidence for the claim that attention is necessary for consciousness. When attention is withdrawn as a result of brain injury, bottom-up capture, or top-down allocation to a demanding task, stimuli that are presented in clear view become invisible. In each case, the unconscious stimuli show priming effects, suggesting that they are represented at all levels of the visual hierarchy. Mere activation at the intermediate level is not enough. Attention is necessary.

There is also evidence that attention is *sufficient* for making intermediate-level perceptual states conscious. Consider the phenomenon of visual pop-out. If subjects are asked to find a target stimulus in a group of contrasting distracters, the target stimulus often seems to pop out. Imagine seeing a black sheep, for example, in a group of white sheep (figure 7). Pop-out is believed to occur when a target stimulus captures attention (Treisman and Gelade, 1980) and the stimulus that pops out is consciously experienced.

Similarly, conscious perception can be improved by the presence of a cue that indicates where a stimulus is going to occur. In a method developed by Posner (1980), subjects see an arrow or other cue that either accurately or inaccurately predicts where a target will appear. When the cue is accurate, conscious detection is improved. Cueing can also have an impact on which percept becomes conscious in binocular rivalry. When people are presented with two equally vivid stimuli, one in each eye, they consciously experience only one, alternating back and forth between the two. There is evidence that attention determines which we see (and the correlative absence of attention determines which is invisible). Mitchell, Stoner, and Reynolds (2004) cued one of two rival swarms of moving circles and thereby determined which swarm participants consciously perceived. Miller et al. (2000) achieved similar effects, determining using TMS or injecting liquid into one ear ("caloric vestibular stimulation"), which is known to shift attention.

Pop-out, Posner cases, and binocular switching are usually considered low-level or "early selection" phenomena. In both cases, visual forms capture or direct attention without much semantic processing. But attention can also be captured by meanings; there can be "late selection." We all know the cocktail-party effect, in which you can hear your own name being mentioned by someone

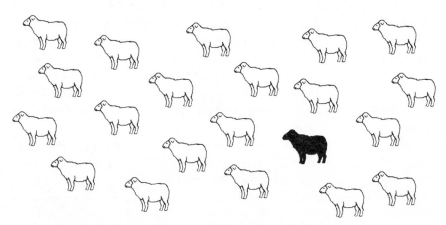

FIGURE 7   An example of pop-out. You cannot fail to experience the black sheep.

across a crowded noisy room. A moment earlier, the surrounding conversations were all an unintelligible din, but when you hear your name, it is crystal clear. That suggests that the surrounding conversations are being processed to some degree and filtered for words that might be especially relevant. When such a word is found, attention is captured. What could be more relevant to you than your own name? Mack and Rock (1998) discovered a visual analogue of the cocktail-party effect. In their crosshairs studies, they found that inattentional blindness did not occur when the unexpected stimulus was the name of the subject in the experiment. The name would capture attention and become visible as a result. Mack and Rock tested other stimuli for attention capture and made the lovely discovery that smiley faces are also relatively immune to inattentional blindness (see also Mack et al., 2002, for a replication with attention blink and other attention-demanding tasks).

Attention capture can also facilitate conscious perception in individuals with brain damage. For example, individuals with blindsight can have experiences in their blind field when presented with very high-contrast stimuli, and when this occurs, areas of the brain associated with attention become active (Sahraie et al., 1997). For some neglect patients, the locus of blindness can shift during attentional object tracking. Behrmann and Tipper (1994) showed a neglect patient a barbell picture and then rotated it 180 degrees as the patient watched it; initially, he was blind to the circle on the left, but after rotation, he was blind to the circle on the right. The blindsight case involves bottom-up attention, and the neglect case involves top-down attention. In both cases, attention helps to bring about conscious experiences in a visual region that is usually blind.

As in chapter 2, I have focused here on visual consciousness, but it must be added that attention has been implicated in consciousness across the sense modalities. For example, Koreimann, Strauß, and Vitouch (2009) found that most people failed to detect an unexpected guitar solo when counting tympani beats during Richard Strauss's *Also Sprach Zarathustra*. Such inattentional deafness suggests that attention is needed for audition (see also Macdonald and Levie, 2011). There is also compelling evidence that attention is needed for conscious touch (Schubert et al., 2006) and olfaction (Keller, 2011). It also is noteworthy that neglect can eliminate experience outside of vision, especially experience of the left side of the body, suggesting that somatosensory, kinesthetic, and proprioceptive senses are also dependent on attention. This broad pattern of findings suggests that attention and consciousness are intimately linked.

1.3. ATTENTION AND SUBLIMINAL PERCEPTION

I have been arguing that attention is necessary and sufficient for consciousness. This hypothesis was first inferred from research on unilateral neglect and then supported by appeal to studies in healthy people. But I have not yet shown that this hypothesis can explain the cases of subliminal perception with which this chapter began. Perception in neglect and inattentional blindness qualifies as subliminal in informal parlance, but the term is usually used to refer to cases in which a stimulus is masked, extremely fast, or degraded. If it cannot explain those cases, then it cannot offer the needed account of how to draw the conscious/unconscious divide.

To explain core cases of subliminal perception, we need to begin with the simple fact that attention takes time. Once a stimulus is presented, it captures attention, either because it pops out or because we are looking for it. In either case, the initial visual response to the stimulus and the attention directed to it are two distinct processes, and the latter happens after the former. We might attend to a region of space before a stimulus is presented there, but even in this case, the stimulus presentation must cause a stimulus representation to be formed before that representation can itself become an object of attention. Or, put more accurately, we attend to an external stimulus only by attentionally modulating a representation of that stimulus, not by merely attending to the location in which it is presented.

This fact has a simple consequence. The representation that is caused by a stimulus can be modulated by attention only if it endures for a temporal interval that is long enough for attention to do its work. It is known that representations of stimuli do endure in perceptual systems after a stimulus is removed. This is called iconic memory. A visual stimulus, such as a color, can get to intermediate visual areas in about 110 milliseconds (Plendl et al., 1993). Attention to color has been recorded as fast as 125 milliseconds after stimulus onset (Connor, Egeth, and Yantis, 2004). Other features might generate faster latencies for both visual response and attention, but attention always seems to lag behind (e.g., Maunsell and Gibson, 1992, find V1 responses within 20 milliseconds; and Schoenfeld et al., 2007, find attention at 90 milliseconds). When stimuli are presented faster than the time course of attention, they can still usually be consciously seen, because they produce iconic images, which can last for about 300 to 500 milliseconds if the stimuli are sufficiently intense. But fleeting stimuli do not always produce iconic images that are available for attention. Consider three cases. First, if a stimulus is followed by a mask, the representation of the mask will quickly replace the representation of the stimulus, preventing an iconic memory trace from arising. Second, if the stimulus is low in intensity or contrast, it may produce a perceptual representation that is correspondingly weak, and decay time may increase. Third, decay time is affected by stimulus-presentation time, so stimuli that are presented very briefly may leave a weak and short-lived trace. These cases correspond to the conditions that are used in subliminal-perception studies. My conjecture is that perception is unconscious in these cases because the stimulus conditions do not generate perceptual representations that are strong or long enough to be modulated by attention.

This interpretation is supported by work on visual masking by Enns and Di Lollo (2000). In traditional masked priming, the mask is placed in the same location as the stimulus; the mask, in effect, replaces the stimulus. But Enns and Di Lollo have shown that masking can be achieved by a mask that simply surrounds the stimulus without covering it. A letter followed by four dots placed in the space around where the letter was located can be masked by the four dots. Enns and Di Lollo explain the effect by proposing a new model of masking according to which attention is centrally involved. The dots attract attention before the representation of the stimulus can be attentionally modulated. This model, which they use to explain more traditional masking results, suggests that standard cases of subliminal perception may be attentional effects. In standard cases of masking, attention does not have time to set in, and in cases where the mask does not overlap with the stimulus and thus fails to wipe out the iconic memory trace, it may serve to distract attention away from that trace.

The upshot is that research on subliminal perception is consistent with the suggestion that attention is the mechanism by which consciousness is attained. Indeed, current models of masked priming explicitly hypothesize that attention makes the crucial difference. Enns and Di Lollo explicitly compare visual masking to inattentional blindness and point toward a unified account.

1.4. THE AIR THEORY OF CONSCIOUSNESS

The evidence just reviewed suggests that attention makes the difference between conscious and unconscious perception. When we attend, perceptual states become conscious, and when attention is unavailable, consciousness does not arise. Attention, in other words, is necessary and sufficient for consciousness.

To avoid misunderstanding, let me underscore that attention is an answer to the "when" question: when do mental states become conscious? It is not an answer to the "where" question: where in the flow of information does consciousness arise? The answer to the "what" question is that we are conscious of representations at an intermediate level of representation in perceptual systems. These representations become conscious when we attend. Attention is necessary and sufficient for making intermediate-level representations conscious, not sufficient for making any mental state conscious.

Putting the "where" and the "when" together, we get the following theory of consciousness:

The AIR Theory of Consciousness
    Consciousness arises when and only when intermediate-level representations are modulated by attention.

"AIR" stands for attended intermediate-level representation. Conscious states are AIRs. I will have more to say about what it means for attention to modulate an intermediate-level representation in the next section. For now, the basic idea is that when we attend, there is a change in the way intermediate-level representations are processed. That change is what makes the difference between these representations being conscious and not. Many others have suggested that attention is essential for consciousness (Baars, 1988; Crick and Koch, 1990; Evans, 1982; Lycan, 1996; Mole, 2008; Peacocke, 1998; Posner, 1994). I combine this insight with the intermediate-level view and will offer some elaborations below.

The AIR theory is a two-part theory of consciousness, because it has an account of the contents of consciousness and an account of the mechanisms by which we become conscious. There are other two-part theories. For example, defenders of higher-order theories of consciousness distinguish the target mental states that are conscious and the representations of those states that render them conscious (Rosenthal, 1997). Lycan (1996) even equates his consciousness-conferring higher-order monitors with "inner attention." But the AIR theory is not a higher-order theory; attention does not work by re-representing the attended states. To see this, I need to say more about what attention is.

2. How Does Attention Give Rise to Experience?

2.1. WHAT IS ATTENTION?

To some ears, the claim that attention gives rise to consciousness sounds utterly uninformative, because they think "attention" and "consciousness" are synonyms. Such semantic intuitions reveal a close link between attention and consciousness, but the two constructs can be defined independently. As noted in chapter 1, by "consciousness," I mean to refer to the property of having phenomenal qualities. Mental states are conscious if they feel like something or, in Nagel's (1974) phrase, if there is something it is like to have them. Attention can be defined without reference to phenomenal qualities.

I treat "attention" as a natural-kind term. It is not something that has an essence that can be discovered by conceptual analysis. Pretheoretically, we grasp the concept of attention by appeal to a range of different activities and phenomena. A couple of those have already been mentioned. There is the phenomenon of pop-out, when a stimulus seems to stand out from things around it. Pop-out is passive, but attention can also be effortful. Put differently, when pop-out occurs, we don't say that the viewer is attending; we say instead that attention was captured, but surely attending can also be a deliberate activity. For example, there is the phenomenon of search, as when you are looking for a specific object in a complex scene. Attention can also involve monitoring, as when we retain perceptual contact with an object or scene, or tracking, as when we watch an object move through space. Attention sometimes involves selection, as when we focus in on a feature of an object. But it need not. We refer to vigilance as a form of attention, but being vigilant involves remaining alert and responsive to anything that might come before our senses. Thus, attention can spread across a scene. Attention also spreads when we survey our surroundings, and even when we focus on a particular object, we may spread attention diffusely in the background.

I don't think any of these phenomena constitutes a definition of attention. Rather, they are all cases in which we say that attention is taking place. From a pretheoretical point of view, it is possible that these phenomena do not involve any overlapping mechanisms. They may be fundamentally different. But it is also possible that there is some shared mechanism running across all of these cases. There may be a common denominator that can be empirically discovered. If such a common mechanism were found, we might say that "attention" refers to that mechanism. If these phenomena share nothing in common, then we might say that "attention" should be dropped as a term from scientific psychology. We might become eliminativists.

To look for a common denominator, we might begin with one paradigm case and then see whether its underlying, empirically discovered mechanisms are also operative in other cases. When we are asked to attend to a stimulus, a number of changes take place in the brain: our visuomotor systems instruct the eyes to shift so that the stimulus can be foveated; receptive fields that include the stimulus shrink, resulting in a larger number of cells responding to the stimulus (Moran and Desimone, 1985); the cells corresponding to unattended stimuli and regions of space are inhibited; and the cells corresponding to the stimulus are modulated in a way that allows them to propagate neural activity forward in the nervous system. We might define attention as including all of these changes, since they commonly occur when we are instructed to attend, but it's possible that they are not all essential.

There is, for example, a clear dissociation between attention and gaze. Posner (1980) showed long ago that people can fixate on a point while attending elsewhere. So the fact that attention and gaze often coincide does not mean that they are the same. The intention to shift one's eyes may also be separable from attention. For example, in antisaccade tasks, people are trained to look away from a sudden stimulus; the stimulus may capture attention even if there is an intention to look elsewhere. For similar reasons, it is likely that attention does not essentially involve a change in receptive-field sizes. Receptive fields are also known to change when eyes shift, so they may not be sufficient for attention, and it is possible that fields don't shrink when we attend to very large objects (Tolias et al., 2001). Some researchers tend to equate attention with selection (e.g., Reynolds, Chelazzi, and Desimone, 1999; Van Boxel et al., 2010), but that, too, seems to be a mistake. We can attend to one object against a simple background or to a solid field of color; in such cases, it doesn't seem that there is anything to select. Correlatively, we should not assume that attention always involves competition between stimuli and inhibition of unattended objects.

Those who are skilled at meditation can put themselves in a state of being hyperattentive without attending to any specific thing. In other words, attention could be applied to everything in the visual field at once, even if, in practice, it is usually selective. Selection is not even sufficient for selection, since many selection processes take place as a precondition to attention, as in the case of pop-out or the cocktail-party effect. Here selection is the cause of attention, not necessarily the effect.

Of all of the things that occur when we attend, one seems to be an especially good candidate for the essence, or common denominator: a change in information flow. When we attend to a stimulus, it becomes available for certain kinds of further processing. When one of two stimuli is attended in binocular rivalry, for example, the representation of it can be processed by subsequent psychological systems. But what kind of processing? An unattended rivalry stimulus can also be processed further. Bahrami et al. (2010) have shown that the unseen rivalry stimuli can cause priming. This suggests that unattended stimuli can passively activate networks of semantically associated representation. But the attended stimulus does much more than that. The attended stimulus becomes available for processes that are controlled and deliberative. For example, we can *report* the stimulus that we consciously perceive, we can reason about it, we can keep it in our minds for a while, and we can willfully choose to examine it further.

Psychologists postulate the existence of a capacity that plays all of these roles associated with victory in pop-out. It's called working memory. As noted in chapter 1, working memory is a short-term storage capacity that allows for "executive control" (Baddeley, 2007; D'Esposito and Postle, 1999). Operationally, neuroscientists think of working memory in terms of stimulus-specific neural activations that remain during a "delay period" after a stimulus has been removed. Psychologists think of working memory as a place where temporarily stored information is held "online" for "controlled" information processing, that is, processing that is not automatic in the sense of being reflexive, overlearned, or driven entirely by the stimulus. For example, items encoded in working memory become available to language systems for reporting and for reasoning, planning, and comparison. Working memory can play a role in guiding effortful attention (e.g., Cowan, 1995), but it is also where attended perceptual states get temporarily stored (Knudsen, 2007). It is widely recognized that attention is a "gatekeeper" to working memory (Awh, Vogel, and Oh, 2006). Attention determines what information gets in.

Evidence for this view of attention comes from many sources. For example, consider a study by Rock and Gutman (1981) in which subjects had to attend to one of two overlapping shapes (see figure 8). Then, on a subsequent memory test, the attended shape was recalled, and the unattended shape was not, even though both were presented for the same duration of time in plain view. There is also evidence that working-memory capacity limits the allocation of attention.

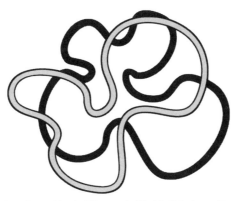

FIGURE 8 Look at the gray shape, ignoring the one behind it. Rate how attractive it is on a scale of 1 to 10 (inspired by Rock and Gutman, 1981).

When working memory is full, it is harder to attend. In fact, studies have shown that inattentional blindness increases when people have to keep many items in their minds (Klein and Acevedo, 2002; Fougnie and Marois, 2007).

Such interactions between attention and working memory suggest an intimate relationship. The simplest explanation for this relationship is an identity claim: attention can be identified with the processes that allow information to be encoded in working memory. When a stimulus is attended, it becomes available to working memory, and if it is unattended, it is unavailable.

This hypothesis might explain the fact that attention can affect the experience of a stimulus in a number of ways. Increases in attention cause greater apparent resolution, contrast, and size (Carrasco, Ling, and Read, 2004; Anton-Erxleben, Henrich, and Treue, 2007). To understand why, we might think of perception as kind of bit map, where each cell corresponds to a pixel. Attention determines how many of these pixels are available to working memory. Consequently, we might think of attention as coming in degrees, meaning that more or fewer of the pixels in a given region of the visual field are accessible at a given time. Fully attending an object would potentially make every cell responding to that object accessible to working memory. But partial attention results in a subset of cells being accessible, while the others are not. This is like viewing an object through a screen door, letting some details in but not all. The fully attended object will therefore be clearer and sharper in contrast.

The idea of working-memory access can also explain why attention can be both bottom-up and top-down. In the case of pop-out, this hypothesis amounts to the following. Pop-out occurs when the representation of one stimulus competes with the representations of surrounding stimuli and wins. When it wins, it is processed in a way that makes it available to working memory. This process is the psychological correlate of attention. It turns out that very same process—a process that makes perception available to working memory—may be implicated in all of the phenomena that we called attention above. When you visually

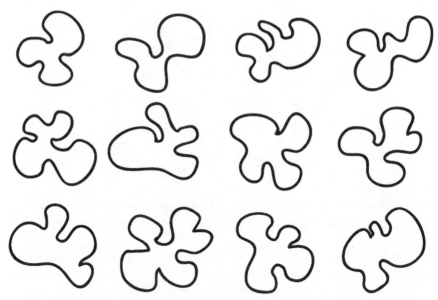

FIGURE 9 Test your memory. Which of these is the gray shape from figure 8? Which is the black shape? If you attended to the gray, it will be easier to recall.

search for an item, such as a can of Coca-Cola in a crowded room, you use a template of the sought object as a filter on the representation of the room; when a match is found, it becomes available to working memory. When you monitor something or track it, a representation of it becomes available to working memory. When you are vigilant, you are in a state that disposes any new incoming representation to become available to working memory. When you selectively focus in on some part of an object, that part becomes available.

Thus, top-down and bottom-up attention result from different control structures, but they make use of the same resource. There is some process that makes information available to working memory, and that process can be passively triggered by stimulus features (bottom-up) or actively recruited (top-down). We refer to the top-down cases as "paying attention" or "attending," implying person-level agency, but the same subpersonal process underwrites attention whether top-down or bottom-up. In the former, working memory is both the cause and the effect of attention. A representation in working memory is used to guide a search process, and a successful match makes an input representation available for working-memory encoding. Attention can be controlled by different kinds of representations. We can search for an object (the Coca-Cola can) or for a location. We can attend to color, shape, or shadow, to vision or sound. In each case, it is plausible that the same processes are taking place, even though the control structure used to guide the process differs. By analogy, there are many ways to apply paint to a canvas: by hand, brush, or spray can; in strokes, small dabs, or expansive washes. But in all of these cases, the end result is physically analogous: we have paint on a canvas. The equation of attention and working-memory access can also accommodate the observation that attention can be focal or diffuse. In focal cases, a single objection representation is accessible, and in diffuse attention, wide swaths of the visual field may be accessible. We can access small details, multiple objects, or regions of space; we can even attend focally to one object while diffusely attending to one or more items in the background. Diffuseness here involves both a spread of attention over a spatial region and a reduction in the degree of attention.

Thus, if we can equate attention with the process by which perceptual information becomes available to working memory, then we can say that all examples of attention involve that process and differ only in what attention is modulating and what allows that modulation to take place. If this is right, there exists a uniform, empirically motivated account of what attention is. This is a satisfying result, because it implies that disparate cases converge on one process. Other researchers may choose to define attention differently, but I suggest that this account provides the only common denominator across the wide range of cases that we regard as examples of attention. It explains why folk psychology has used the same term to cover all of these cases, despite obvious and dramatic differences among them. The construct of working memory is not part of folk psychology, but the folk appreciate that some of the items we perceive become available for reporting, deliberation, and so on. This idea of availability underlies all of the phenomena that we call attention. Psychological research reveals that reporting and deliberation are underwritten by a common short-term storage capacity, working memory. So the folk-psychological insight implicit in the range of phenomena that we call attention can map onto the empirical construct of availability to working memory. We need not eliminate the folk construct; we have found a functional analysis.

Against this proposal, it might be objected that attention has an influence on perceptual processing in brain areas that never become available to working memory. It is known that attention leads to increased activity throughout the visual stream, for example, including primary visual areas whose contents are neither conscious, on my view, nor capable of being stored (Posner and Gilbert, 1999). So it seems to be a mistake to say that all attentional modulation renders perceptual activity available to working memory. I think this is a misleading reading of the empirical literature. There is strong evidence that brain regions involved in the control of attention directly modulate intermediate-level areas, which then influence low-level areas through feedback (Martínez et al., 1999; Mehta and Schroeder, 2000; Bouvier and Engel, 2011). If this is right, increased brain activity in low-level areas is an aftereffect of attentional modulation in intermediate-level areas and may not qualify as attentional modulation in its own right. On this interpretation, the brain-imaging studies show a V1 increase when people attend and do not actually show attention in V1 but rather V1 enhancement from intermediate-level feedback. This interpretation fits with the account of attention on offer, according to which attention involves availability to working memory; anatomical studies suggest that V1 is too early in processing to play this role. V1 has no direct connections to Brodmann area 46, a major seat of working memory, but area 46 does connect with Brodmann area 19, which houses V3, V4, and V5. Arguably, these intermediate areas are the only ones on which attentional modulation has a direct impact.

Another worry about the hypothesis that attention is a gatekeeper to working memory concerns recent dissociations alleged to exist between working memory and consciousness. Two recent studies report that stimuli presented unconsciously can be retained in memory for several seconds. Hassin et al. (2009) presented subjects with a rapid series of disks that either formed a pattern or did not, and for each disk, they were asked to report whether it was filled; the presence of a pattern improved performance on the task, even though subjects had no conscious awareness of the pattern. In a very different paradigm, Soto, Mäntylä, and Silvanto (2011) presented subjects with a Gabor patch for less than 17 milliseconds followed by a mask; the Gabor patches slightly improved performance on subsequent orientation-detection tasks even when subjects reported no awareness of them. These studies suggest that encoding in working memory can occur without consciousness. If so, then either attention isn't the gatekeeper to working memory, or attention isn't sufficient for consciousness. Either outcome would be bad news for the AIR theory.

These results are far from conclusive, however. It is possible that they tap into a kind of short-term memory that differs from working memory (Block, 2011). Sligte et al. (2010) have shown that there are different systems for briefly storing information. Working memory is one such system, but there is another, which they call fragile visual short-term memory. Fragile visual short-term memory has a higher capacity than working memory, and it is unaffected by magnetic stimulation that disrupts activity in brain structures associated with working memory (Sligte et al., 2011). Crucially, it remains intact when attention is withdrawn (Vandenbroucke, Sligte, and Lamme, 2011). If the Hassin and Soto results depend on fragile visual short-term memory, then they put no pressure on the hypothesis that attention is the gatekeeper to working memory or the hypothesis that consciousness arises with access to working memory. Fortunately, there is reason to think that this is the case. The patterns used in the Hassin study are complex and may outstrip the resources of working memory. The Soto study used delay periods of two seconds in some conditions and five seconds in others, finding no decrement in performance. Working memory, in contrast, shows signs of decay after four seconds (Zhang and Luck, 2009). More obviously, participants in this study cannot spontaneously report on what they have seen, and this is powerful evidence that the visual inputs have not been encoded in working memory. These studies teach an important lesson, however. The term "working memory" should not be used for any short-term storage capacity. It names a specific psychological system, whose properties and neural correlates have been extensively studied. The AIR theory defines consciousness in terms of attention and attention in terms of working memory, understood as a specific system.

The foregoing analysis of attention resolves the circularity worry with which we began. According to that worry, it is circular to define consciousness in terms of attention, because "attention" and "consciousness" are synonyms. We have now seen that this is not the case. Consciousness is phenomenal in character, and attention is a process by which perceptual representations become available to working memory. The AIR theory can be unpacked accordingly:

> *The AIR Theory of Consciousness (Unpacked)*
> Consciousness arises when and only when intermediate-level representations undergo changes that allow them to become available to working memory.

This revised formation resolves the circularity, and it helps to explain why conscious states are characteristically reportable and available for deliberation and other executive processes. Those who disagree with my analysis of attention could simply drop the term "attention" and say that conscious states are *available* intermediate-level representation. But I think it is helpful and important to insist on attention being the mechanism of consciousness. Tasks that explicitly manipulate attention have been among the most effective in making consciousness come and go. The extant evidence establishes a strong link between consciousness and attention, and then it is a further and substantive empirical discovery that attention coincides with availability. This discovery, in turn, explains something puzzling about the empirical link between attention and consciousness. Although it is robust, that link may seem mysterious because the kinds of attention that have an impact on consciousness are superficially different. For example, pop-out attention is bottom-up, and visual search is top-down, but both can bring a stimulus into consciousness. This puzzle evaporates once we define attention in terms of availability, because availability is a common denominator uniting these two things that we call attention. Consequently, we need the concept of attention to apply the empirical results when taken individually, and we need the concept of availability to show how these results come together. For these reasons, the unpacked AIR theory does not replace the attention formulation but rather reveals why that formulation actually expresses a coherent and noncircular view.

In defining consciousness in terms of availability, the AIR theory allies itself with other theories of consciousness in the philosophical literature. A number of authors appeal to availability, including Carruthers (2000), Kirk (1994), and Tye (1995). The AIR theory may not coincide with any of these perfectly, however. These authors do not appeal to attention and working memory. Indeed, Carruthers thinks that availability involves the disposition to form higher-order representations, and Tye (2010) explicitly denies that attention is the mechanism of consciousness. Also, the AIR theory is based more directly on empirical evidence and can be said, for that reason, to enjoy more empirical support. But the prevalence of availability theories suggests that philosophical arguments provide converging evidence for something like AIR. I'd like to think of the AIR theory as a refinement of extant availability theories, which maps philosophically characterized notions of availability onto the mechanisms that are postulated in scientific psychology.

Although it is stated here in psychological terms, the AIR theory can also be mapped onto the brain. Figure 10 shows the basic circuit involved in visual consciousness. The circuit has three components: intermediate-level visual areas (most are included in figure 10, although a complete list may include others, such as MST); structures that control the allocation of attention (inferior parietal areas are especially important, but frontal eye fields and other areas may also contribute); and areas in the lateral frontal cortex that have been implicated in working memory. This circuit has been confirmed again and again in neuroimaging studies. When people are conscious, all three components tend to be active. This is the case, for example, in conscious change detection (Beck et al., 2001), correct trials in attentional-blink paradigms (Marois and Ivanoff, 2005), and when there is residual visual experience in blindsight (Sahraie et al., 1997). In each case, consciousness is associated with activation in the visual stream, the inferior parietal cortex, and the lateral frontal cortex.

This anatomical circuit and the unpacked formulation of AIR do leave one important question unanswered: what are the processes that allow for availability?

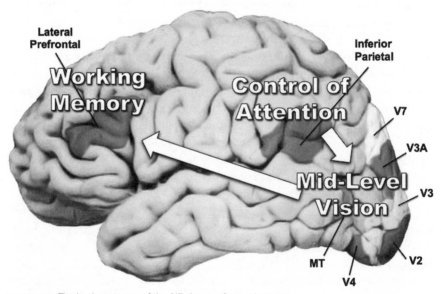

FIGURE 10 The basic anatomy of the AIR theory of consciousness.

Those processes can ultimately be specified in neural-computational terms, as we will see in chapter 4. If consciousness has identity conditions at the neural level, the current formulation will need to be unpacked even further to include those processes. I take up this issue in chapter 9.

2.2. ACCESSED OR ACCESSIBLE?

The AIR theory says consciousness arises when intermediate-level representations become available to working memory. This raises a question. Why say that consciousness involves availability as opposed to actual encoding in working memory? Metaphorically, why think that consciousness involves broadcasting from sensory systems, rather than receiving in working-memory systems? This question is pressing, because there is a popular approach to consciousness according to which receiving into working memory is necessary. This is the global workspace model, proposed by Baars (1988) and defended in neurobiological terms by Dehaene and Naccache (2001). As seen in chapter 1, these authors say that consciousness arises when information from the senses is brought into a global workspace, where it can be used to guide deliberation, reporting, and intentional behavior. The global workspace can be equated with working memory, insofar as working memory brings information in one sense modality to a functional space where it can play these disparate roles. In a similar spirit, Crick and Koch (1990) have claimed that consciousness depends on encoding in frontal cortex, where executive processes are realized. But I suggested that consciousness involves availability to working memory, rather than encoding in working memory. Conscious states are accessible to working memory but not necessarily accessed. Thus, consciousness is local (that is, located in sensory pathways), not global (that is, dependent on the involvement of "central" processes associated with higher cognition). There is considerable evidence favoring the local view over the global view. Some of that evidence was reviewed in chapter 1 when I argued against noncentrality and higher-order theories of consciousness. I will expand the case against globality here.

The most direct evidence against the necessity of working-memory encodings comes from brain injury. For decades, it has been known that frontal cortex can sustain profound injuries without causing profound sensory deficits. In the 1930s, the famed neurosurgeon Wilder Penfield removed the right frontal cortex of his sister to treat a malignant tumor; despite the destruction of working-memory structures in that hemisphere, there was no evidence of unilateral blindness after the surgery (Penfield and Evans, 1935). Nor is blindness reported in cases where working-memory structures are ablated bilaterally (Heath et al., 1949).

A second problem for the view that consciousness requires working-memory encoding is that consciousness includes things that working memory leaves out. There are many cases in which we experience something that is too complex to readily encode in working memory but not too complex to experience. Consider the displays used in visual-search experiments (Treisman and Gelade, 1980). A subject might be presented with a group of letters at various orientations, including one T and a dozen Ls. It's quite laborious to find a T in a sea of Ls. We might see such a display for well more than one second and not notice whether there is a T. We may also see such a display without having any idea afterward how many letters there were. Beyond four or five, numerosity is hard to encode in working memory without serious effort. So a typical visual-search display may have features that are not encoded in working memory. But we nevertheless experience these features. If there were thirteen big, clear letters presented to you for a few seconds, it's overwhelmingly likely that you would experience all of them. And if there was a T among them, you would experience that T even if you failed to report that you did afterward. The fact that such features go unreported suggests that they are not encoded in working memory, even though they are experienced.

A third line of evidence comes from change blindness, the widely publicized fact that people often fail to notice when something directly before their eyes undergoes a change. For example, Rensink, O'Regan, and Clark (1997) showed subjects pairs of altered photographs with a moment of visual noise in between. In each case, a central object might change color or size or disappear. People in the photos switched hats, parrots changed from red to green, buildings vanished, and yet subjects failed to notice. Simons and Levin (1997) found that people failed to notice when a stranger on the street who stopped to ask them for directions was surreptitiously switched for another person wearing somewhat different clothing. Ballard, Hayhoe, and Pelz (1994) found that people failed to notice when a stack of colored blocks changed colors during a video game in which they had to match those blocks on the other side of the screen. Change blindness is sometimes confused with inattentional blindness, but there is a crucial difference, and this is what I want to focus on here.

In inattentional blindness, subjects don't seem to have any experience corresponding to the unexpected stimulus. They are confident that they have seen nothing aside from the items they are focusing on. In change blindness, however, subjects usually experience the whole image that undergoes the change. In some cases, they stare at these images for very long periods of time, even indefinitely long. They scan the whole image strategically, hoping that they might pick up on the change. Every millimeter is examined and experienced. What subjects fail to notice is that some of the features that they experience change from one moment to the next. Thus, change blindness is essentially a deficit of memory, not of experience. People do not store what they are seeing. And the failure of storage means that they miss out on changes. They cannot match the vivid experience they have at one second with the vivid experience they have only a moment later. For example, in the Ballard study, people stare at the blocks they are trying to copy, and then those blocks change colors when they saccade away, even if just for a few milliseconds. Then, when subjects look back at the blocks, they don't notice the change. The reason is simple: they haven't stored the colors in working memory. There are too many colors to keep track of, and color usually isn't that important for object identification. Here's the rub: the colors were experienced, we can presume, but not encoded. That means that experience can occur without working-memory encoding.

A fourth reason for thinking that encoding is not necessary derives from research on subliminal perception. In these studies, there are sometimes three different outcomes, depending on the stimulus conditions. In some cases, subjects experience nothing. If you ask them whether a stimulus was presented, they are at chance in guessing. In other cases, they are confident that there was a stimulus, but they do not know what it was. And in still other cases, they know that they saw a stimulus and can readily report it (for these three outcomes, see, e.g., Kouider et al., 2007). It is obvious to anyone in these studies that the second and third cases are both supraliminal. Subjects experience something in these cases, even though they can only say what they experienced in the third case. The difference between cases two and three involves working memory. The stimulus is encoded in working memory in the third case but not in the second. This strongly suggests that encoding is not necessary for consciousness.

A final argument for accessibility rather than access is that working memory encodes the wrong things. Working memory encodes high-level perceptual representations—representations that abstract away from details of the stimuli that we consciously experience. Evidence for this comes from the sizable discrepancy that exists between discrimination and recall. Halsey and Chapanis (1951) demonstrated that people can discriminate about one million colors. When actually looking at pairs of colors, there are a million different colors that we can tell apart. But color recall is extremely limited. If we are presented with a color and then shown several similar color chips to choose from moments later, we tend to do very badly. There are only about eleven to sixteen colors that we can recognize. Since working memory is a storage system, and color storage is bad, it follows that working memory is not storing representations that are anywhere near as fine-grained as the representations that underwrite conscious experience.

In response to this last point, one might worry that the AIR theory is committed to a contradiction. I have said that consciousness arises when intermediate-level representations become available to working memory, but we have now seen that only high-level representations ever get encoded in working memory. Doesn't that suggest that the intermediate level is not, in fact, ever available to working memory? Is "attended intermediate-level representation" (AIR) an oxymoron? Here a clarification is needed. To say that a representation is available to working memory does not mean that the representation itself gets copied into working memory. Indeed, as we will see in chapter 10, it is entirely wrong to think about working memory as storing representations; rather, it works by sustaining activity in perceptual centers. An encoding in working memory is not a copy but rather a process. The neural activities in perceptual centers propagate forward in a way that allows them to be sustained after the stimulus that caused them has been removed. This process apparently loses fidelity, meaning that details registered by the initial perceptual response are lost. But that does not mean that intermediate-level representations are not available for this process. Their availability consists in the fact that they are the representations that get modulated in a way that allows this process to take place. The process itself may recruit high-level representations, and that may account for the loss in fidelity. But intermediate-level representations are the ones whose modulation allows encoding to occur. Here's how the mechanism might work. In unconscious perception, a stimulus causes activity through the whole visual hierarchy; when some attention is introduced, the affected intermediate-level representations are processed in a distinctive way; if the viewer has some reason to retain one of these, the corresponding high-level representation instructs working memory to cause a sustained intermediate-level activation when the stimulus is removed. Notice three things. First, resulting representation will lose fidelity because it results from a high-level representation. Second, the sustained representation would be conscious if and only if the viewer attends to what is being held in memory. Third, even if high-level representations are used to determine the encoding, it was the intermediate-level modulations that allowed retention in the first place. It is in this sense that attentionally modulated intermediate-level representation can be described as available to working memory. High-level representations are not modulated by attention but rather are used to mediate encoding once an attended item has been selected for retention. I will return to this story in chapter 10, so it need not detain us here. For now, it can be thought of as existence proof for the cogency of the idea that the intermediate level is available even if its representations do not get copied into working memory. The story also underscores the important fact that the encoding process is something over and above availability. Availability refers to a modulation of representations that makes encoding possible, not to the encoding process itself.

Collectively, the foregoing considerations provide evidence for the AIR theory as I presented it above. Consciousness depends on availability to working memory, not encoding. It depends on accessibility, not access. This way of putting it raises a further question, however. Why say that consciousness even involved availability at all? Block (1995) draws a distinction between what he calls access-consciousness, which arises when a perceptual state is poised for reporting and deliberation, and phenomenal-consciousness, which occurs whenever there are phenomenal experiences. He suggests that phenomenal-consciousness can occur without access-consciousness. As evidence, he cites a classic study by Sperling (1960), in which subjects are presented with three-by-three arrays of letters and have to report what they have seen. Subjects can typically report about three or four letters but no more. But which letters they report can be determined by a cue that comes *after* the stimulus is presented. If after the stimulus is removed, subjects are instructed to report the top row, they can succeed, but they cannot report the rest, and likewise for any other row. Subjects in this experiment report having an experience of the whole array, and the fact that they can report on any row they are asked about supports this. But Block says that they have access to only one row. The other rows are phenomenally conscious but not access conscious.

Block's account of the Sperling results can be interpreted in two ways: it might be read as suggesting that we lack access to each of the unreported letters considered individually or that we lack access to the array considered as a whole. The first interpretation is difficult to defend. Sperling's study firmly establishes that the unreported letters *could* have been reported. Thus, it would be wrong to imply that they are not poised for reporting. But suppose we take Block as saying merely that the array is not accessible as a whole. In his (1995) paper, he is careful to say that we do not have access to the array "jointly." This may seem plausible given that there are no circumstances in which we can report each of the letters. It may also seem plausible that we have phenomenal consciousness of the whole insofar as our experience seems to encompass the entire array. So this looks like a case of phenomenology without access. But I think this move is unstable. Once we concede that each letter of the array is accessible, I don't see what it means to say that the whole is not accessible. Subjects in the experiment report seeing a whole array, and they can report on each of its parts. What is the further thing that is supposedly inaccessible? Block says it is the array considered jointly, meaning that we don't have access to all of the parts at once. In other words, Block wants to allow, on this interpretation, that we have access to each part but not to all, and his evidence for that is that we cannot report on every item at the same time. But this evidence for an each/all distinction is undercut once we have a distinction between availability to working memory and encoding. Working memory has a very limited capacity, so we cannot report every letter, but nothing bars us from saying that all of the letters are available. Granting that each letter is available for encoding, Block ends up with a cumbersome taxonomy: the whole array is jointly phenomenal but not accessible, each letter is accessible but not accessed, and some letters are accessed. This is one distinction too many. We can capture the impression that phenomenology outstrips access by supposing that the whole array, including each of its parts, is accessible and hence phenomenal, but only some letters are accessed.

In advancing this simpler taxonomy, I still agree with Block on the most important aspect of his view. I emphatically concur that a perceptual state can be phenomenally conscious without having been accessed by centers of higher cognition. Global theories of consciousness, such as the global workspace theory, are wrong if they are intended as theories of phenomenal consciousness. But Block is wrong if he thinks that phenomenal consciousness does not essentially involve information access. It is only by virtue of being accessible that perceptual states are experienced.

Block would reject this claim and push his case for phenomenal consciousness farther back. He would say that there can be phenomenal states that are not even accessible to working memory. That, I think, is implausible. To see why, consider again the contrast between change blindness and inattentional blindness. In change blindness, the changes are not noticed, but the items that change are experienced. The items could be reported at any moment, even if the changes go unnoticed. If just after the subject looked at the pile of colored blocks, Ballard asked him to report on one, the subject would probably supply a correct answer. In inattentional blindness, the surprise stimulus is not experienced at all and is not reportable. So we have a striking contrast. In both cases, there is no working-memory encoding, but in one case, there is experience, and in the other, there is not. This difference in experience correlates with a difference in accessibility. In change blindness, the item could be reported if subjects were probed immediately after viewing. In inattentional blindness, there is no reportability. That suggests that availability to working memory is necessary for experience.

Further support for this conclusion comes from subliminal-perception studies. Consider the three cases mentioned above: no experience, experience without identification, and experience with identification. It seems utterly reasonable to say that in the first case, the stimulus is perceived but unavailable to working memory. Thus, phenomenology seems to disappear with availability. In the second case, the stimulus is available to some degree. The identity of the stimulus is not available, but when they are probed, subjects recall that they saw *something*. In some cases, they can even recall when given a forced-choice test just after the display. Here again, experience seems to come with availability.

So where Block had one distinction too many before, here he may have one distinction too few. He says there can be phenomenal consciousness without access, but "access" is ambiguous between accessibility and being accessed (see also Chalmers, 1997). In Block's view, he has not drawn this distinction, and this gives the impression that he thinks that phenomenal consciousness can arise without access of any kind—without even availability to working memory. But that would make it difficult to account for the distinction between change blindness and inattentional blindness or between the first and second cases in subliminal-perception studies. The Sperling cases that Block uses to support phenomenal consciousness without access actually provide powerful support for the conclusion that consciousness comes with availability to working memory, even though it doesn't require encoding.

Since 1995, Block has written on the distinction between accessibility and being accessed, and he offers an important challenge. In his 2007 paper, he draws a distinction between "narrow accessibility," which he defines as encoding in working memory, and "broad accessibility," which is mere availability to working memory. He argues that phenomenology overflows narrow accessibility, and I wholeheartedly agree. But what about broad accessibility? Here Block worries that the notion includes too much. After all, some stimuli that are unconscious qualify as accessible because they would be accessed were we to attend them. In light of this worry, Block (2007: 492) issues a challenge: "No doubt a functional notion that is intermediate between narrow and broad could be framed, but the challenge for the framer would be to avoid ad hoc postulation." Failure to meet this challenge would entail that phenomenology cannot be defined in terms of accessibility, which seems to be Block's view. But I think the challenge can be met, and this chapter can be read as an attempt to meet it. I have argued on the basis of empirical evidence that there is a relation of availability that arises when we attend. Availability is not a mere disposition. It is a change in formation processing that makes the difference between being a candidate for working-memory encoding and not. On this notion, items to which we have not allocated any attention are not available. Thus, there is no worry that this account will include too much. In fact, Block's account, which severs the link between consciousness and availability, runs a greater risk of being overly inclusive. In principle, his story would allow for conscious states that were entirely unavailable and hence unknowable even to those who had them. If we follow Block (2007) in restricting consciousness to those states for which there is convergent evidence for phenomenology, then I think we will be forced to conclude that consciousness coincides with an access relation.

This response to Block is not meant as a wholesale rejection. As I tried to emphasize, I think that Block is right to distinguish phenomenal states that are access-conscious from those that are not. This distinction was an enormous contribution to consciousness studies. The AIR theory does not reject this distinction; it offers an explanation. Phenomenal states can be encoded in working memory, in which case they can be reported and used in deliberative processing, but many phenomenal states are not encoded. In upholding a version of Block's distinction, I must also consider objections that have been waged against it. To my knowledge, the most powerful empirical objection comes from Kouider et al. (2010), defenders of a global workspace view. They argue that cases alleged to show phenomenology without encoding in working memory are actually cases of "partial awareness." More specifically, they argue that in the Sperling experiment and variations that they conducted, viewers encode parts of letters in addition to the few that they can report. These letter parts give the impression that experience overflows what has been accessed, but actually experience and access coincide; the letters that seem to be experienced but can't be accurately reported are unreportable simply because they are incomplete.

I think the Kouider interpretation is implausible. First, it does not seem as if we experience letter fragments—that, after all, is a distinctive experience, which can be reported. Kouider tries to address this worry by showing that people will confabulate seeing letters when distorted letters are shown, but such confabulations may arise precisely when the presented letters are not encoded in working memory. Kouider does not show that people will confabulate seeing a normal letter when presented with a letter fragment under viewing conditions that would uncontroversially result in working-memory encoding. Second, to explain why viewers access fragments rather than whole letters, Kouider proposes that the test conditions cause consciousness to access a lower level or representation that represents parts of letters without integrating them into coherent wholes. But this is implausible. For one thing, it is not clear that there is a stage at which letter parts are represented; we may move from pixel-like representations in V1 directly to whole contours. Moreover, it is unparsimonious to suppose that the locus of consciousness shifts. The task demands don't seem to invite any such shift (subjects are asked to report entire letters), and in chapter 2, I argued that there is evidence against the view that low-level perception is a correlate of consciousness. It seems much more plausible that the unreportable letters are accessible but not accessed.

Putting all of this together, we should conclude that consciousness requires availability to working memory, but it does not require encoding. This distinction may even have an analogue in order language. We sometimes reserve the word "awareness" for mental states that are encoded in working memory. When we are aware of something, we can usually report on it and deliberate about it. Some consciousness researchers assume that consciousness and awareness are equivalent. But I think that ordinary talk allows that we can experience something without being aware of it (as when we complain that someone is hearing the sounds of our words but not listening). Whether or not this distinction is fully appreciated within folk psychology, it holds up to empirical scrutiny. Block has convincingly argued that there can be consciousness without awareness. That insight is upheld on the AIR theory. But the AIR theory departs from Block by identifying phenomenal consciousness without accessibility.

The preponderance of empirical evidence favors the AIR theory as I presented it above. Consciousness arises when we attend, and attention makes information available to working memory. Consciousness does not depend on storage in working memory, and indeed, the states we are conscious of cannot be adequately stored. This contrast between availability and encoding may even be marked linguistically with the word "awareness." We can have a conscious experience without being aware of what we are experiencing. But even then, the state is a potential object of awareness. Consciousness is a kind of availability.

3. Objections

3.1. DENIAL OF THE EVIDENCE

Not everyone agrees that attention is the basis of consciousness. In fact, this has become one of the most contested claims in the empirical literature, and a barrage of studies have been designed to show that attention and consciousness come apart. Before considering those studies, however, I want to address an even more basic concern. I based my case for the AIR theory on the standard interpretation of phenomena such as inattentional blindness. In inattentional blindness, people claim that they have not seen a stimulus that was briefly presented under conditions of inattention. From this, researchers infer that attention is necessary for consciousness. But one might object that this inference is too fast. It's possible that people in these studies experience the surprise stimulus but fail to report it (Chalmers has pressed this in an unpublished commentary). Without offering any arguments against this possibility, my case for the AIR theory is tenuous.

This objection bears much in common with Block's claim that there can be phenomenal consciousness without accessibility. It amounts to the claim that people in inattentional-blindness studies are having phenomenal experiences that they cannot access. Unsurprisingly, Block (2007) has defended this possibility in print, suggesting that inattentional blindness is not blindness at all but mere inaccessibility. In response to Block's postulation of inaccessible conscious states, I argued that he fails to distinguish inaccessibility from accessibility without access, and the latter is all we need to accommodate the examples that he gives in defense of conjecture that some phenomenal states are not access-conscious. One might press Block's point, however. Isn't it *possible* that there are inaccessible phenomenal states? How can these be ruled out? And if they can't be, why accept the standard interpretation of inattentional-blindness studies?

The defender of the alternative interpretation owes us a story about why subjects in these experiments claim not to experience the stimuli if they really have experienced the stimuli. There are only two that have any plausibility, but neither one is compelling on close examination. First, the defender of the alternative interpretation might argue that participants in inattentional-blindness studies insist that they don't see the stimulus precisely because inattention interferes with verbal processing. As I argued above, attention is the gateway to working memory. It is plausible to assume that working-memory encoding is necessary for making verbal reports. That might explain why unattended stimuli are not reportable, and this explanation is compatible with the claim that such stimuli are conscious. Perhaps inattentional-blindness studies only establish inattentional unreportability and reveal nothing about consciousness. In other words, the objector will say that my theory of attention *predicts* that people in these studies will deny seeing the stimulus. If so, such denials cannot provide evidence for a link between attention and consciousness.

In response, it is important to realize that the evidence for inattentional blindness does not rely entirely on subjective reports. It's true that subjects in these studies deny that they have seen anything—that's a subjective measure of experience—but they also fail in forced-choice tests just after the stimulus has been displayed (Mack and Rock, 1998; Cartwright-Finch and Lavie, 2006). Chance performance on forced-choice tests is considered an objective measure of experience, because it doesn't require subjects to say anything about their experiences or epistemic states (e.g., their levels of confidence). Forced-choice success does not require working-memory encoding; activation of semantic networks may be enough. This suggests that subjects are not just failing to remember the stimulus; they are actually processing it in a way that differs quite dramatically from normal perception. So the claim that subjects lack experience does not depend on the assumption that first-person reports are *always* accurate. People do sometimes make false positive judgments about what they have seen, and this suggests that they *might* be making false negative judgments. But the existence of objective measures suggests that subjects are not simply misremembering what they experienced.

The second strategy for arguing against the standard interpretation of inattentional blindness makes appeal to memory. It is possible that participants in these studies experience the unattended stimulus but simply forget that it was there. If so, inattentional blindness is really just inattentional amnesia (see Wolfe, 1999). I am sympathetic to the idea that we can have experiences that we instantly forget, and I committed to this possibility when I said that consciousness doesn't require working-memory encoding. So, given that concession, it may seem that I am forced to take the inattentional-amnesia interpretation seriously. But I don't think it holds up under scrutiny.

For one thing, the amnesia interpretation is hard to square with the fact that we can be inattentionally blind for stimuli that are present for long durations (recall the five-second example from Most et al., 2005). If we were experiencing a very unusual stimulus for several seconds, why wouldn't we remember that? Furthermore, Mack and Rock (1998) conducted clever studies explicitly designed to rule out the inattentional-amnesia interpretation. In one, a shape is presented just prior to the attentionally demanding task, a short distance from where the surprise stimulus will appear. When attention is available, these two consecutive shapes induce experiences of apparent motion: the two stimuli look like one moving object. If the surprise stimulus is experienced under conditions of inattention, subjects should recall the experience of motion, since they readily recall and report the first stimulus. This is not what happened. Sixty-seven percent of subjects reported only the first stimulus and said that it was still. If the second stimulus had been experienced, the first stimulus would not be recalled as still.

It seems, then, that the most plausible strategies for explaining away the inattentional-blindness results do not succeed. There is also a deeper problem with this line of objection. The objection advances the thesis that people in inattentional-blindness studies are experiencing the unattended stimuli. Even if this possibility were impossible to rule out decisively, why take it seriously?

What positive reason is there to think that there is phenomenology in these cases, given the absence of subjective and objective evidence? The only answer that I can imagine rests on the fact that the stimuli in these experiments are perceived; they are processed by the visual system, including parts of the visual system that are operative when people are conscious. But that is not a very strong reason at all. By analogy, suppose we show that whenever someone successfully fires a gun, there is a pulling of the trigger. It doesn't follow that trigger pulling is sufficient. The gun must also be loaded. Likewise, the presence of visual activity may always accompany visual consciousness, but it does not follow that it is sufficient. There is no positive evidence for thinking that it is. On the other hand, there is powerful prima facie evidence for thinking that mere visual activity is not sufficient: sometimes people show no objective or subjective signs of consciousness in response to visually presented stimuli. There is, in other words, a great asymmetry. There is no evidence for thinking that visual activity is sufficient for consciousness, and there is evidence against this view. Therefore, we should favor the view that visual activity is insufficient. If so, alternative explanations of inattentional-blindness studies are unmotivated. There is no good reason to suppose that participants are conscious in these studies.

This conclusion is strengthened when we consider the fact that inattentional blindness is just one of several phenomena linking attention to consciousness. Recall the inattentional-blink paradigm, in which subjects are asked to detect two stimuli in a series but manage to detect only the first, which captures their attention. One could suppose that participants in inattentional-blink studies consciously experience the unattended stimulus, but again, there is no good positive reason to suppose this, and there are good reasons against: the unattended stimuli go undetected even when subjects are highly motivated to detect them. And notice that detection can normally occur immediately upon stimulus onset and can be expressed nonverbally, so it depends on neither memory nor reportability in the conventional sense. Or consider visual neglect. Here damage to attention centers seems to result in blindness for unattended items. One could propose that people with neglect really experience those items, but the evidence against that conjecture is considerable and varied. People with neglect not only fail to report items on the left, but they also fail to draw them when copying from life, and they make systematic errors in tasks that require them to draw a mark at the midpoint of horizontal lines (either making the mark too far to the right or neglecting lines located on the left-hand side). Given the fact that they fail to evidence consciousness on every overt measure, we have good reason to conclude that they are blinded by their attentional deficit and no reason to say otherwise. Those who challenge the evidence proffered in favor of the AIR theory are a bit like skeptics in epistemology; they are difficult to refute, but given the lack of positive reason to accept their position, we need not take them very seriously.

3.2. ALLEGED EVIDENCE FOR PSYCHOMETRIC DISSOCIATIONS

The considerations above suggest that we should trust the evidence from inattentional blindness and neglect. Such findings suggest that consciousness can disappear with attention. Another class of objections concedes this point but insists that it does not give a complete picture of the empirical data. Evidence of the kind that I reviewed shows that attention and consciousness sometimes go together, but, critics argue, other evidence suggests that they sometimes come apart. In a word, critics say that the two processes are dissociable (Koch and Tsuchiya, 2007; van Boxtel, Tsuchiya, and Koch, 2010). Evidence for dissociation comes in three flavors. One can show that attention and consciousness obey different psychometric properties or that there can be consciousness without attention or that there can be attention without consciousness. I will begin with the first kind of evidence, focusing for illustration on what I take to be the two best psychometric-dissociation arguments in the literature.

In one study, van den Bussche et al. (2010) tried to establish that attention and consciousness are different processes by showing that they have different effects on priming. Participants viewed a series of symbols that ended with a target numeral, and they were then asked whether the numeral was greater or lower than five. During the series, there was a prime, consisting of another numeral that was either congruent or incongruent (e.g., if the target was seven, a congruent prime would be six). The experimenters manipulated both the visibility of the prime by presenting it either very fast followed by a mask or more slowly, and they manipulated attention by presenting a cue (the symbol ++) that either accurately or inaccurately indicated the location of the prime. They found that both visibility and attention improved performance in the main task in congruent versus incongruent conditions, but they did so in different ways. Attention improved performance by facilitation, increasing speed on the main task as compared with a control condition. Visibility improved performance by interference, slowing speed on incongruent trials as compared with control. The authors consider visibility equivalent to consciousness and argue that consciousness and attention are different processes, since they cause priming in psychometrically different ways.

There is a problem with this interpretation, however. It begs the question to say that this task pits consciousness against attention. For one thing, the authors label the uncued but visible prime condition as conscious but unattended. But we cannot infer that a prime is unattended just because it is uncued. We allocate attention to uncued items all the time. So, without further argument, calling the uncued condition unattended is misleading. For another thing, on the masked trials, the primes are unconscious, and the authors still describe those primes as attended; but AIR theorists will deny that there can be attention without consciousness (see the discussion in the next section). A defender of the AIR theory will interpret the van den Bussche study as follows.

When the prime is masked but cued, it is neither attended nor conscious; the mask prevents attention from modulating the cue. Nevertheless, the cue increases the chances that the prime will be unconsciously perceived, and unconscious perception improves reaction times, because it activates semantically associated numbers in a lexical network. When the prime is unmasked and uncued, it is conscious, because attention has enough time to kick in, and the task demands that participants stare attentively at the monitor. Because attention allows access to working memory, unmasked stimuli can be used when deliberating on the main task; incongruent stimuli cause interference, because, once in working memory, they can impede deliberation.

I think that my interpretation is preferable to the one offered by van den Bussche et al. As noted, it is reasonable to assume that the unmasked stimulus is attended (because subjects are monitoring the screen) and that the masked stimulus is unattended (because attention takes time). My explanation also correctly predicts that unmasked incongruent trials will cause interference whether or not they are cued, because either way, they get into working memory. The only surprising result concerns congruent unmasked trials; these show facilitation when and only when they are cued. This is puzzling, because, on the AIR theory, all unmasked trials have access to working memory, so one might expect congruent primes to facilitate no matter what. One possibility is that participants interpret (perhaps unknowingly) invalid cues to indicate that the prime is irrelevant, so they actively try to ignore invalidly cued primes. This active-ignoring explanation would predict that invalidly cued congruent primes should, paradoxically, produce interference rather than facilitation, which is exactly what the authors found. Therefore, the AIR theory points toward an interpretation of the van den Bussche experiment that explains what might otherwise be a curious pattern of results.

In another study, van Boxtel, Tsuchiya, and Koch (2010) tried to dissociate consciousness and attention by demonstrating different effects on the afterimages. In a two-by-two design, they presented subjects with a Gabor patch that was either unconscious or conscious (i.e., either masked using interocular suppression or unmasked) and either unattended or attended (i.e., presented concurrently with a demanding letter-detection task or presented with no concurrent task where subjects were asked to report when the patch disappeared). The researchers found that the patch produced longer afterimages when it was conscious and shorter afterimages when it could be directly attended. This seems to suggest that consciousness and attention have opposite effects, contrary to what AIR would predict.

This study raises two puzzles for the AIR theory, and both can be answered. First, the authors imply that consciousness increases afterimage duration when attention is absent, which would imply that there can be consciousness without attention. But in the condition designed to show that, it would be more accurate to say that consciousness increases afterimages when *focal* attention is absent.

Subjects who are focusing on the distractor task can allocate *diffuse* attention to the Gabor patch in the periphery (see Jonides, 1983; Burnham et al., 2006). According to the AIR theory, consciousness just is attention, and the AIR theory can explain the fact that consciousness increases afterimages across all conditions by assuming that attention correlates with an increase in cellular activation, which leads, in turn, to longer afterimages. The second puzzle for AIR is that while consciousness (hence attention) always increases afterimage duration as compared with unconsciousness, *focal* attention decreases afterimage duration when compared with diffuse attention. This puzzle can be solved by appeal to the fact that the visual system contains two different kinds of cells: polarity-dependent cells, which code for hue or lightness, and polarity-independent cells, which code for boundaries. It has been shown that polarity-dependent cells generate longer afterimages than polarity-independent cells (Wede and Francis, 2007). In the focal-attention condition, van Boxtel, Tsuchiya, and Koch ask subjects to detect whether the Gabor patch is present. Object detection requires sensitivity to boundaries, not to hue or shade. As a result, polarity-independent cells presumably become more active during the detection task, and polarity-dependent cells get suppressed. Had subjects been asked to detect amorphous color patches rather than patches with clear boundaries, focus would have enhanced polarity-dependent cells, leading to long afterimages rather than short ones (a phenomenon that I have confirmed in unpublished testing). In the diffuse-attention condition (what van Boxtel, Tsuchiya, and Koch present as "no attention"), both types of cells presumably increase equally, because subjects are focusing on the distractor task and faintly monitoring the periphery for anything that might occur there. As a result, the polarity-dependent cells are enhanced and able to generate their longer afterimages. In other words, attention (which is consciousness according to AIR) always increases afterimage duration, but attending to boundaries (being more intensely conscious of them) can lead to afterimages that are shorter than afterimages caused by diffuse attention or attention to color. The alleged dissociation between attention and consciousness is actually a dissociation between diffuse attention and attention to boundaries, which can be easily accommodated by the AIR theory.

Other findings have been used to argue that attention and consciousness are psychometrically different (see Koch and Tsuchiya, 2007; van Boxtel, Tsuchiya, and Koch, 2011), but the alleged differences generally depend on defining attention in a way that differs from the definition I endorsed here. The differences often hinge on defining attention as top-down and focal, whereas I have defined attention as availability to working memory, a process that can be controlled bottom-up and applied diffusely. On my account, attention can have different psychometric effects depending on how it is allocated, but these differences show only that attention operates under multiple control structures, not that attention and consciousness are separate processes. Once we clarify what is meant by "attention," some dissociation arguments begin to look merely verbal, because they use that term in a highly restrictive way.

3.3. ALLEGED EVIDENCE AGAINST THE SUFFICIENCY OF ATTENTION

The AIR theory of consciousness says that attention is necessary and sufficient for rendering intermediate-level perceptual representations conscious. To defend the necessity claim, I argued that when attention is absent, there is no consciousness. To defend the sufficiency claim, I argued that when we attend, we are conscious. Both of these claims have recently been challenged. Some argue that consciousness can arise in the absence of attention, hence challenging necessity. Others have argued that attention can arise in the absence of consciousness, challenging sufficiency. I will consider both of these challenges, beginning with the latter.

Consider an experiment that Kentridge, Nijboer, and Heywood (2008) conducted with GY, the most-studied individual with blindsight. They presented GY with an arrow in the center of a screen, followed by either a vertical or a horizontal line in one of two locations in his blind visual field. The arrows were visible to him, but the oriented lines were not. At a tone, GY had to guess the orientation of the line that he could not see. His accuracy increased if the line was located in the direction in which the arrow was pointing. The investigators concluded that the arrow led GY to direct attention within his blind field, and it was that attention that facilitated performance. Thus, attention seems to be possible in the absence of consciousness.

It is possible that the behavior can be explained without supposing that GY attends to the unconscious stimulus. To see why, it is necessary to mention two physiological processes that typically co-occur with attention. First, attention usually co-occurs with eye movements (saccades). Overt saccades can be suppressed by asking a subject to stare at a fixation point, but even then, fast microsaccades occur. This is significant because saccades shift the position of the fovea, allowing finer resolution processing at the point of gaze. If GY microsaccades in the direction of the cue, he can get a sharper visual representation of stimulus located there. This is likely to happen because saccades remain intact even after complete movement of V1. Second, attention normally co-occurs with a shrinking of the receptive fields in the attended location in retinotopic neural areas such as V4 and V5. That means that more cells respond to the stimulus, and the resulting representation has higher resolution. Such receptive-field shifts could explain GY's enhanced stimulus detection without assuming that GY also attends to the stimulus.

These physiological responses are part of an response. Orienting and attention often co-occur, but they are dissociable processes. Informally, we can say that orienting alters what information gets in, and attention alters where it flows. In terms of processing, orienting involves a shift in the allocation of input resources, either explicitly through head and eye movements or implicitly through motor plans (e.g., the intention to saccade) or receptive-field changes. Orienting is probably a more ancient response than attention; it can be found in insects and cephalopods, creatures in which attention is difficult to demonstrate.

In human beings, orienting and attention usually go together (Tolias et al., 2001), and they behave in similar ways. Like attention, orienting can be spatially directed or object-based, as when our saccades move about within the contours of an object. But attention and orienting do not always operate in perfect synchrony. For example, we often attend to a location before saccading to it (Fischer, 1986). There can also be dramatic behavioral dissociations. Gaze is famously dissociable from attention, as Posner (1980) showed by instructing people to fixate and attend in different directions. In a study, Koivisto, Hyona, and Revonsuo (2004) found that fixation is dissociable from inattentional blindness, and Beanland and Pammer (2010) explicitly demonstrated that people sometimes orient to unseen stimuli in inattentional-blindness paradigms. Attention and orienting also involve different brain structures. Milner and Goodale (1995) distinguish visual neglect, an attention disorder, from visual extinction, which may involve a failure to change orientation; neglect is associated with inferior parietal lesions, and extinction is more superior. One can also distinguish orienting and attending by training animals on tasks that require the formation of motor intentions (hence orientation) that are orthogonal to attention (Liu, Yttri, and Snyder, 2010); intention and attention are associated with different parts of the interparietal area. Anatomical dissociations can also be found in the frontal eye fields; cells in this structure vary regarding whether they control attention, orienting, or both (Wardak, Olivier, and Duhamel, 2011). Attention and orienting may also have different effects within the nervous system. Receptive-field changes may be part of the orienting response. Receptive fields shrink when small lights are flashed on the retinas of anesthetized cats, which presumably aren't attending (Wörgötter et al., 1998). They also shrink in simpler creatures, such as fish (Umino and Ushio, 1998), which may not be able to attend.

All of this suggests that the distinction between attention and orienting is real and robust. The term "orienting" has not taken off in psychology or neuroscience, but it should. In those fields, researchers sometimes distinguish "overt" and "covert" attention, but those terms are confusing. In my terminology, so-called overt attention is overt orienting—a shift in gaze—but orienting can also be covert, as when receptive fields change or an intention to move is generated. So-called covert attention may refer ambiguously to such covert forms of orienting or to attention without overt orienting. Thus, the standard terminology cross-cuts what I have postulated as the real orienting/attending distinction.

With this machinery in place, I propose that the Kentridge results are best explained by appeal to orienting rather than attention. Orienting is intact in people with blindsight; in fact, individuals with blindsight can even track objects with their eyes (Humphrey, 1992). It is therefore plausible to suppose that GY's success trades on these ancient capacities rather than attention.

Critics might reply by stipulating that orienting is best defined as a *component* of attention—that is, by stipulating that "attention" refers to cases in which both orienting and changes in information flow occur. But this reply wouldn't save the conclusion that there can be attention without consciousness. Even if orienting is defined as a component of attention, it is not the full story. If my earlier analysis of attention is right, attention entails availability to working memory. Availability is clearly absent in blindsight, so GY cannot be instantiating *all* of the processes necessary for attention. Moreover, even if a critic were to insist that orienting is sufficient for attention, it would qualify only as a form of *spatial* attention rather than object-based attention. Recall that the cue occurs before the stimulus is presented. That could lead GY to attend to the cued region of space, but because there is no stimulus there yet, it doesn't follow that he has an attended intermediate-level object representation—an AIR. Indeed, people with blindsight have grave difficulties representing objects; they show little neural activation in intermediate-level perception centers, and their residual abilities are thought to be driven by subcortical mechanisms that bypass the usual visual pathways (Stoerig and Cowey, 1997). If GY's performance stems from a shift in perceptual fields, that shift may occur in parts of the visual system that are primarily involved in spatial processing. The shift might heighten sensitivity to primitive perceptual features in the cued location (such as orientation) by lowering detection thresholds, but we need not suppose that there is a further attentional modulation of the stimulus representation once it is presented. In summary, changes in orientation are either not a neural correlate of attention at all, not a complete correlate, or only a correlate of spatial attention. On any of these alternatives, the discovery of shrinking fields outside of consciousness would not refute the AIR theory.

In principle, the Kentridge study has two limitations when used as evidence against AIR. First, GY may suffer from a general deficit in his ability to form object representations, so his success may not reflect the presence of AIRs, and second, the attentional cue precedes the stimulus, so it is hard to confirm that an object representation has been modulated by attention rather than a region of space. Both limitations are overcome in a clever study by Jiang et al. (2006). They used a paradigm called interocular suppression to generate an unconscious stimulus. Interocular suppression works by presenting different images to each eye; if one image is dominant (e.g., brighter), it suppresses the other, making the other invisible. As their invisible stimulus, Jiang et al. used a figure that showed a naked body on one side and a scrambled version of that body on the other. Naked bodies influence attention, but in this case, the attraction was unconscious, because subjects were unaware of the stimulus. Then, in a test phase of the experiment, subjects were presented with a visible target that was either on the side where the nude had been or on the other side. The results were fascinating. For example, when presented with a female nude, heterosexual men showed an improvement in their reaction times, but gay men and both gay and heterosexual women tended to show a decrement in performance. The important finding for us here is that the nudes evidently increased attention in some conditions, despite the fact that they were invisible. And for this to happen, the nudes needed to have been recognized as such, hence processed throughout the visual hierarchy. Moreover, attention was not attracted by a cue that occurred prior to the stimulus. On the Jiang group's interpretation, the nude itself attracted attention. A similar result was obtained by Hsieh, Colas, and Kanwisher (2011), using interocular suppression together with a pop-out stimulus, but the Jiang study is even more powerful when used as evidence against the AIR theory, because the results can be explained only if we assume that the nude was processed up to the level of recognition. This suggests that there was an attended intermediate-level perceptual representation of the nude in the absence of consciousness.

Fortunately for the AIR theory, there is an alternative interpretation, which appeals to the same resources already discussed in response to the Kentridge study. Perhaps the nude is not modulated by attention but rather induces an orienting response. The experiment cannot rule out the possibility that participants had microsaccades. Nudes normally capture gaze in a way that is difficult to suppress even when we try not to look. The instruction to stare at a fixation point may not be strong enough to resist fast surreptitious glances toward the unconsciously perceived nude. Of course, nudes usually capture attention, too, but in the case of interocular suppression, that may be impossible. The competing stimulus may prevent subjects from attending to the nude. If so, there is no attended intermediate-level representation. Alternatively, the nude might trigger an intention to shift gaze, which is not fully actualized during suppression; this might result in an immediate shift in gaze after the nude is removed, facilitating detection in that location. If either of these interpretations is right, the improved performance comes from orienting, not attention.

My conjecture that the nude does not boost attention may seem ad hoc, but it is actually supported by other research on interocular suppression. Fang and He (2005) measured neuronal response during this paradigm and found enhancement in the dorsal part of the visual stream but not in the ventral part. The dorsal stream has been implicated in saccading in addition to attention, but when attention is involved, there are also detectable ventral increases (Corbetta et al., 1990). In interocular suppression, we don't seem to find such ventral enhancement. I know only one study suggesting otherwise. Watanabe et al. (2011) found a V1 increase when they asked subjects to report a target (attention trials) as compared with performing a concurrent task (inattention trials), even when the target was rendered invisible using interocular suppression. But there is a problem with their methodology. Their supporting materials reveal that the task they used for their inattention trials (detecting a letter in a rapid series) degraded target recognition, and that degradation may suggest that V1 fluctuations resulted from the quality of the stimulus encoding rather than attention. Thus, it is likely that neural activation increases associated with attention do not occur during interocular suppression. More decisively, there is also evidence that the specific cellular firing patterns associated with attention are also absent during interocular suppression (Engel et al., 1999). The details will await the next chapter, where those firing patterns are described.

There is a very powerful principled reason for thinking that interocular suppression impedes attention. Studies of binocular rivalry cited above strongly suggest that the perceived stimulus is the attended stimulus, and the unperceived stimulus is unattended. Suppression is just the limiting case of rivalry, so we have independent reason to think that suppression works by suppressing attention. Thus, the Jiang study does not establish the existence of unconscious AIRs. An intermediate-level representation of the nude is presumably generated, and it causes a shift in orientation that improves subsequent performance, but that representation is never itself the object of attentional enhancement.

There are a number of other studies attempting to establish attention in the absence of consciousness, but the response strategies presented here can be readily extended to most of those reported in the literature. For example, van den Bussche et al. (2010) implicitly argue for unconscious attention by showing that directional cues facilitate masked priming, but these cues may influence orienting rather than attention. Likewise, Kentridge, Nijboer, and Heywood (2008) try to establish attention without consciousness using a metacontrast masking paradigm, in which an arrow points toward a masked colored disk, which influences subsequent color detection, despite the fact that it isn't consciously experienced. Here again, however, the arrow may elicit orienting rather than attention; indeed, it is unlikely that attention is available, since the form of masking used in this study is believed to work by removing attention from the masked stimulus (Enns and Di Lollo, 2000).

Less obviously, the arguments made here can accommodate findings that are alleged to show that attention is necessary for priming (Naccache, Blandin, and Dehaene, 2002; Bahrami et al., 2010). For example, masked stimuli fail to prime when attentional resources have been overtaxed by a concurrent task. Such findings might indicate that we are attending to the masked stimulus and indeed that such attention is necessary. Another possibility, though, is that under attentional load, we are unlikely to orient to masked stimuli (unless the masked stimulus is ecologically significant, as with Jiang's nudes). It is plausible that orientation is necessary for subliminal perception, because orientation regulates what gets into the nervous system.

I conclude that existing research fails to establish a clear case of attention without consciousness. It might be objected that attention must be possible without consciousness, because attention is known to alter activity in V1, which, I have argued, is not a correlate of conscious vision (Posner and Gilbert, 1999). Against this, there are two lines of defense for the AIR theory. First, AIR theorists need not deny that there is unconscious attention; it is enough to show that there are no attentionally modulated intermediate-level representations. Therefore, attention modulation in V1 is completely compatible with the theory. Second, as noted above, it is not clear that the attentional effects in V1 qualify as evidence for attention directly modulating low-level vision, as opposed to feedback from other areas. There is strong evidence that attention leads to changes in V1 long after stimulus onset (Martínez et al., 1999; Bouvier and Engel, 2011), and there is also evidence that attention initiates its visual effects in intermediate-level areas (Buffalo et al., 2010). One interpretation is that attention directly modulates activity only at the mid-level, and changes that take place in V1 are aftereffects of this modulation. Recall that attention is not any increase in neural activity but a specific kind of change that allows for availability to working memory. It might ultimately be shown empirically that the changes in V1 that occur when we attend are of a different sort from those that occur in intermediate-level areas and that they are not correlates of availability. If so, it might be established that attention never occurs without consciousness. At a minimum, current evidence suggests that intermediate-level attention never occurs without consciousness, which is all that the AIR theory requires.

3.4. ALLEGED EVIDENCE AGAINST THE NECESSITY OF ATTENTION

Attention may be sufficient for consciousness, but is it necessary? I read research on inattentional blindness and inattentional blink as suggesting a resounding yes. When attention is withdrawn, consciousness also seems to go. But some researchers are unconvinced. They think that there are clear cases of consciousness in the absence of attention. This would mean that the AIR theory is mistaken.

Consider, first, an argument from Christof Koch (personal communication). Imagine that you are looking at an equally luminous, equally saturated wall of color (a "ganzfeld"). Your entire visual field is taken up by the color, and there is no variation in it and no objects to focus on. In this case, there is no need to allocate attention, because attention is a selective capacity, and there is nothing to select. So, Koch reasons, under such conditions, attention is not engaged. Yet it is obvious that we would experience the color.

The main problem with this argument is that Koch is wrong to assume that we would not use attention while looking at a ganzfeld. We might adopt a visual search strategy of scanning different parts of the field to different degrees at different times. We might let direction of gaze dictate focus of attention, in this case. Koch is also wrong to suggest that attention must be focal or selective. We can attend diffusely to a whole field, just as we can attend to an object or a region of space. Koch assumes that attention is used only when we need to select between competing stimuli, but this is not the case. Attention, we have seen, is a capacity for bringing perceptual information into working memory, and it just so happens that selection is often necessary for that. In a ganzfeld, there is no competition, but there is certainly access to working memory, and if my analysis of attention is right, this proves that attention is at work. One might put this to an empirical test by first seeing what neural mechanisms underlie attention in paradigm cases of selection and then determining whether those mechanisms are operative when we look at a ganzfeld. I will propose neural mechanisms in chapter 4, and I would predict that these are operative when we stare at a wall of color. Koch's objection is also unconvincing for another reason. The most famous fact about ganzfeld experiences is that we eventually lose visual consciousness (Metzger, 1930). Without finding anything worth attending to, we seem to go blind. This is a striking confirmation of the AIR theory.

Another piece of evidence for consciousness without attention comes from Reddy, Reddy, and Koch (2006). They devised an interesting task that combines divided attention and masking. Subjects were presented with a cluster of letters (Ts and Ls) in the center of the screen and asked to determine whether they were all the same or different. At the same time, a photograph of a celebrity was flashed in a corner of the screen, followed by a mask. Subjects could identify them, even though the central task was extremely demanding on attention. Subjects do not report having clear experiences of the faces, but they do seem to experience *something* when the faces are flashed. This looks like conscious perception without attention.

The problem with this study is that the authors do not establish that the central task consumes all available attention. In fact, they describe it as a case of perception in the "near absence" of attention. That means that some attention was available, and that might account for why the faces were consciously perceived. In fact, the experimental setup is similar in crucial ways to the Mack and Rock (1998) studies of inattentional blindness, in that both tasks show a stimulus while subjects are engaged in tasks that demand attention. We know from that work that removal of attention can completely eliminate consciousness. Why, then, does the Reddy group get different results? The answer may already be found in Mack and Rock. Recall that when Mack and Rock used a smiley face as the surprise stimulus, they found that these faces popped out and were consciously experienced. Faces are very significant stimuli, and familiar faces of people we admire are all the more so. Reddy, Reddy, and Koch do not control for facial expressions, and the image they reproduce in their paper shows Tom Cruise smiling broadly. Faces like this may capture attention and enter into conscious experience as a result. In other versions of the experiment, the investigators found that participants can also successfully detect peripherally presented animals, which may also capture attention, but not meaningless color patterns, which evidently do not. Inattentional blindness works best for meaningless stimuli because these are least likely to be attentional lures. The Reddy experimental design also differs in another crucial respect from that of Mack and Rock. The Reddy participants know in advance that there will be items presented peripherally and that they will be tested on these items. Thus, they are highly motivated to allocate diffuse attention to all corners of the computer screen. The Mack and Rock participants are given no advance warning about anything other than the main task, and this is crucial for achieving their effect; if the briefly flashed stimulus is expected, participants divide attention between the main task and the task of monitoring the rest of the screen. In other words, the Reddy experiment fails to show consciousness without attention, because its design encourages people to attend.

Van Boxtel, Tsuchiya, and Koch (2011) have replied to this objection against Reddy, Reddy, and Koch, arguing that there is no psychometric evidence for my conjecture that participants are using a diffuse attention strategy when peripheral faces are presented. In particular, they note that performance of the central task and peripheral face detection remains the same in both the dual-task condition and control conditions when each of these tasks is performed in isolation. But this reply is unconvincing. First, all participants are presented with both dual-task and control trials, which means that they may use diffuse attention in all cases. Second, the performance is near ceiling, suggesting that the measure is not adequately sensitive to performance degradation (although a nonsignificant degradation is reported). Finally, participants are subject to extensive training in a dual-task procedure before the experiment begins, which may cause them to use diffuse attention as a default strategy. These reasons reinforce my suspicion that these experiments do not adequately test for consciousness without attention.

There is one more experiment that deserves consideration. Lamme (2003) has developed a paradigm that combines Sperling's (1960) method with change blindness. Subjects are presented with a ring of eight rectangles, each of which is oriented either horizontally or vertically. Afterward, there is a blank screen, and then the circle of rectangles returns. Subjects also see an arrow pointing to one rectangle in the circle, and they have to say whether that arrow has changed its orientation. The key manipulation is when the arrow appears. In some trials, the arrow appears with the original ring of rectangles, so subjects know which rectangle to monitor; in some trials, it appears only when the ring is presented for the second time; and in some, the arrow appears on the blank screen just after the ring is removed. Unsurprisingly, subjects make few errors when the arrow is presented at the start, because they know which rectangle to monitor, and they make many errors when the arrow is presented at the end, because they do not know which rectangle to monitor, and they could not keep track of all eight. The noteworthy finding is that subjects make few errors when the arrow is presented on the blank screen. The original ring is gone at this point, but there may be a trace in iconic memory that subjects can attend to and from which they can recover information about the orientation of the rectangle that was in the location indicated by the rectangle a moment earlier. This replicates Sperling's results, and it also seems to suggest the possibility of consciousness in the absence of attention. Prior to the presentation of the rectangle on the blank screen, it seems implausible that any subjects were attending, except perhaps by chance, to the rectangle that was in the location to which the rectangle points. Yet the fact that subjects can recover information about the orientation of this rectangle and use it to judge accurately and explicitly that the rectangle changed orientation suggests that the rectangle was consciously experienced in the initial presentation of the circle. Thus, in the original display, there is consciousness of all of the rectangles but not attention to all of the rectangles, and this suggests that attention is not necessary for consciousness.

I am not convinced. Lamme's interpretation of his study echoes Block's interpretation of the Sperling studies. Following Block, he says that his study shows that there can be phenomenal consciousness without access. But this is to conflate being accessed with being accessible. Clearly, all of the rectangles are accessible. The fact that we can report on any, if cued, shows that. It is radically unlike inattentional blindness, in which people are utterly unaware of the stimulus and would presumably not be able to recover information about it if a cue were presented after the stimulus was taken away. The Lamme study also contrasts with inattentional blindness in another way: there is no attention-demanding task. Thus, attention is available to scan and monitor the display. As with the ganzfeld, one might surmise that subjects attend diffusely to the whole screen, making the total array of rectangles available to working memory. Lamme is right that subjects are not attending selectively to each specific rectangle, but he has no grounds for saying that subjects are not attending to the full assembly. And consequently, he has no grounds for saying that there is consciousness without attention. At best, he can say that the orientation of each rectangle is not encoded in working memory, but that conclusion, far from refuting the AIR theory, simply adds further support to my earlier conjecture that mere availability is sufficient for consciousness.

I have also argued that there is no compelling example of consciousness in the absence of attention. I have not surveyed every bit of counterevidence, but I hope that the replies here can be extrapolated to other studies alleging to show consciousness without attention. The evidence that attention is necessary is much stronger than any extant evidence to the contrary.

In this chapter, I have argued that attention is necessary and sufficient for making our perceptual states conscious. I also argued that attention is a process by which information becomes available to working memory and can arise without that information actually getting encoded. Finally, I addressed a number of empirical studies designed to show that attention and consciousness are dissociable. I argued that none of these provides evidence powerful enough to overturn the empirical case for the claim that attention and consciousness come and go together. There are other studies in the literature, some of which I review elsewhere, but they suffer from similar limitations (see de Brigard and Prinz, 2010; Prinz, 2010). I conclude that current evidence supports the conjecture that attention is the mechanism by which perceptual representations become conscious.

4

How Is Consciousness Realized?
Gamma Vectorwaves

In the last two decades, there have been intensive efforts to identify the neural correlates of consciousness, or NCCs (Koch, 2004; Metzinger, 2000). This enterprise has even been likened to the search for the molecular basis of life, which led to the discovery of the double-helix structure of DNA (Crick and Koch, 1990). As yet, there are many proposals, countless studies, but little consensus. This may suggest that the search for the NCCs is nowhere near completion. There is also a more optimistic perspective on the state of research. It is possible that one of the existing proposals is actually right, and what we need is not a new theory but new arguments and evidence for adjudicating among familiar options. If that is right, the NCCs may not only be within reach; they may actually be in our hands.

In this chapter, I hope to show that the AIR theory of consciousness provides helpful guidance in locating the NCCs. According to AIR, conscious states are attended intermediate-level representations, or AIRs. To find the NCCs, then, we need to find out how AIRs are implemented in the brain. The current science cannot provide a complete answer to that question, but significant progress has been made. Indeed, AIR provides a new line of support for a well-known proposal.

The search for neural correlates will also add important details to the AIR theory. In the previous two chapters, I drew heavily on neuroscientific evidence, but I stated the resulting theory in psychological terms. In other words, I gave the psychological correlates of consciousness (PCCs) but not the NCCs. One might think that a complete theory of consciousness should specify both (as I argue in chapter 9). Moreover, even if neural correlates were not essential to consciousness, it is a question of significant scientific interest to see how consciousness is implemented in the brain. As we will see, finding correlates is not a trivial task, and it raises core issues about how neurons carry information. The search for NCCs can also play a role in elaborating, confirming, and explaining aspects of a theory stated in psychological terms. We can overcome the vagueness inherent in psychological descriptions by specifying the precise way in which a given process is carried out. By pinpointing brain mechanisms, we can confirm that postulated psychological processes actually occur. Those same mechanisms may also be used to account for observable facts about consciousness. We will see examples in the final section of this chapter and in chapters to come (see chapter 8 on unity). I will argue here that the neural correlates of consciousness can account for the essential link between qualia and consciousness.

This chapter follows a simple strategy. I will assume that AIR theory is true and look for its neural correlates. I will describe these correlates at different levels of analysis, working my way down to cellular processes. The AIR theory has two parts: an account of *where* consciousness arises in information processing and an account of *when* those mental states become conscious. Each part will be considered in turn, and then I will bring both parts together.

1. Neural Correlates of the Intermediate Level

1.1. FINDING THE INTERMEDIATE LEVEL

According to AIR, conscious states arise only at the intermediate level of representation within hierarchically organized sensory systems. These representations are the ones that have qualitative character—they constitute our qualia (also known as feelings, phenomenal states, and experiences; I use such terms interchangeably). Here I want to consider how intermediate-level representations are implemented in the brain.

We can begin with neuroanatomy. As noted in chapter 2, the sensory modalities each occupy multiple interconnected anatomical components, extending from the sensory transducers to neocortex. Here I will continue to focus on vision, our best-understood sense. In vision, there are pathways from the retina into the thalamus and then into the cortex. For most visual processing, the first cortical site is the primary visual cortex (V1). V1 is called primary because it is the usual cortical starting place. The intermediate level is, by definition, not primary but secondary. Thus, one can begin to identify intermediate-level areas by identifying structures that receive afferent inputs from V1. These areas include V2, V3, V3A, V4, and V5/MT (Perkel, Bullier, and Kennedy, 1986).

It would be a mistake, however, to rely solely on this simple anatomical principle. One can also define the intermediate level informationally as the level at which discrete features are integrated into coherent representations of stimuli from a particular vantage point. Being the second place at which visual signals are processed in neocortex is neither necessary nor sufficient for being intermediate, when the intermediate level is defined informationally. For example, V1 can be bypassed for some visual tasks, as with spatial localization in blindsight.

This achievement may rely on a subcortical pathway to MT. It doesn't follow that MT is a primary, as opposed to a secondary, visual area. There may also be areas that do not get direct inputs from V1 but nevertheless function as intermediate by the informational criterion. As we will see in chapter 6, V7 is a possible candidate, because it seems to encode viewpoint-specific information about the visual scene (Konen and Kastner, 2008).

Viewpoint specificity is an improvement over connectional anatomy in pinpointing the intermediate level, but it may not be sufficient for the purposes of a theory of consciousness. To see why, we must move from systems-level anatomy (the kind of thing that can be measured by fMRI) to a smaller scale. We must consider how neurons code information. Traditionally, neural coding has been investigated by measuring action potentials—bursts of electrical activity generated when neurons send outputs from their axons (also known as spikes). Researchers establish what a given neuron codes by figuring out what causes it to fire in this way (Hubel and Wiesel, 1962). One can determine whether a given neuron is viewpoint-specific by seeing whether its firing pattern changes when a stimulus changes position. When the face of a particular person is presented at a three-quarter view, it will cause numerous cells to fire vigorously (that is to say, they produce many high-amplitude spikes at a rapid rate). Some will continue to fire as that face rotates in space, and others will stop. Those that stop are sensitive to viewpoint (e.g., Tanaka, 1997). Unfortunately, this can't be used as a sufficient criterion for intermediacy in constructing a theory of consciousness. The reason is that some viewpoint-specific cells fire in response to *entire objects*, as opposed to discrete object features. Thus, an individual cell in the fusiform face area might fire in response to seeing a specific person from a particular point of view (Perrett et al., 1991). Likewise, after learning to recognize irregular "wireframe" shapes, individual cells in inferotemporal cortex will fire when one of those shapes is presented from a specific vantage point (Logothetis, Pauls, and Poggio, 1995). Using the viewpoint-specificity criterion, we might be forced to say that an individual cell corresponds to the conscious experience of a face or of a bent piece of wire. But the idea that a single cell could be the neural correlate of the experience of an entire face is completely untenable. Faces have spatially distributed parts. When one is watching a face, some parts might become occluded as others remain exposed, as when a person puts on dark sunglasses. Phenomenologically, the lower parts of the face remain constant, even though part of the experience is different. Conscious experience must arise at a level of representation sufficiently complex to explain these componential continuities under partial transformations.

To address this worry, we need to distinguish viewpoint-specific representations of macrofeatures (such as whole faces) and microfeatures (such as edges or bits of color). It's a loose definition, since "macro" and "micro" are defined relative to our phenomenology, but the basic idea is that macrofeatures are ones that can undergo a transformation and remain partially the same in appearance.

Cells that respond to macrofeatures cannot be the correlates of consciousness, because they cannot account for these continuities. This introduces a further important criterion on being the neural implementation of an intermediate-level representation: microfeatural sensitivity. The intermediate level is not just viewpoint-specific; it is a level that represents microfeatures. By this criterion, intermediate-level representations arise in areas with topographical organiza-tion and relatively small receptive fields—that is, areas that are sensitive to small local changes.

The anatomical structures mentioned above (V2–V5 and V7) satisfy these criteria, but so does V1. To avoid the conclusion that V1 is an intermediate-level area, we need one more criterion. Intermediate structures should be sensi-tive to holistic features of the environment, such as bound object contours, rather than simply treating discrete features in a piecemeal way. V1 cells show some evidence of lateral sensitivity. For example, cells that represent color with one receptive field can be influenced by activity in cells with surrounding recep-tive fields. This can result in the phenomenon of filling in (Komatsu, Kinoshita, and Murakami, 2000). But generally speaking, it does not seem that the cells in V1 are structures. We don't see edge detectors functioning in a way that sug-gests coherent object-scale boundaries. Coherence arises only at the next stage of processing.

The combination of viewpoint sensitivity, microfeatural decomposition, and coherence singles out the brain areas that I have previously labeled intermediate-level. These criteria could also be adapted for other modalities and provide a strategy for identifying the intermediate level in the different sensory pathways. This can help in our search for neural correlates of consciousness. But merely locating the right brain structures is not enough. We also need to find the neural correlates of the representations in these structures. We need to figure out how microfeatures correspond to cellular responses.

1.2. POPULATION CODING AND VECTORWAVES

Once we start thinking about cellular responses, a serious puzzle arises, which has not been adequately appreciated in the vast scientific literature on con-sciousness. Suppose we are considering a brain area whose cells respond to microfeatures in a viewpoint-specific way. For example, there might be a cell that responds to a patch of cobalt blue in the upper right (call this a blue cell). Now we can ask, what is it about that blue cell's response that makes the or-ganism experience blue? The cell can be said to represent blue by virtue of firing when blue is present, but that is a relational property. The experience of blue doesn't seem to supervene on the external world. For one thing, there can be blue experiences without blue objects (as in dreams or hallucinations). More-over, it is very plausible that blueness is a mind-dependent property, as sug-gested in the discussion of representationalism in chapter 1. In that case, there is no external feature that could account for what it's like (Locke, 1690; see also Hardin, 1988). To explain blue experiences, the cell in question must have some distinctive property within the organism. One might distinguish blue cells by their connectivity to blue photoreceptors in the retina, but blue cells can fire when the retina is inactive. This is what happens when we dream in color, and since dreams have qualitative character, the NCC for blue experiences cannot include the retina. Long-distance connectivity won't help. To find the correlate of blue experiences, we need to identify something that goes on in the organism while the experience is taking place. One might be tempted to say that blue cells have a distinctive morphology by virtue of which they allow blue experiences, but that's a dead end, too; blue cells are structurally just like red cells and edge cells—they are pyramidal cells found throughout the central nervous system. The obvious solution, then, is to say that blue cells fire in a distinctive way.

The idea that cells impart meaning by the way they fire is a central tenet of contemporary neuroscience, but beyond this, controversy rages. It is humbling to discover that neuroscientists have not converged on a theory of how neurons encode information. Do neurons encode information in their firing rate, in the amplitude of their axon potentials, in the precise timing of their onset, in the temporal pattern over time, or in all of these? There are no settled answers to these questions. One of the central problems in this area is that much of the work on neural coding investigates how the nervous system knows *which* cells are firing, rather than on *how* cells that carry different information differ in their firing profiles. This is a bit like studying communication by devising methods for determining which person in a crowded room is speaking rather than what each person is saying. Consider the simple and popular suggestion that neurons encode information in their firing rates. On this view, a blue cell in one brain area notifies other brain areas that it is firing by spiking rapidly. But red cells broadcast by firing rapidly, too, so we must ask, what is the difference between a rapidly firing blue cell and a rapidly firing red cell? Astonishingly, this basic question about the cellular difference between red and blue has not been adequately answered or even extensively investigated by researchers interested in the neural basis of consciousness.

Given the ambiguity of rate coding, it is natural to suppose that red and blue cells differ not in firing rate but in the pattern of firing. Spikes can occur at different amplitudes and with differing temporal intervals. By analogy, think of melodies; we can think of spikes as a series of tones that rise and fall. In theory, such a temporal code could be used to differentiate the cellular responses to red and blue. In fact, there is some striking evidence to support this possibility. In an important but neglected paper, McClurin, Zarbock, and Optican (1996) used cellular recordings in monkeys to show that different colors correspond to different temporal patterns, or waveforms. These waveforms are preserved across visual areas, and, astonishingly, they are even similar across the two monkeys that they tested. This suggests that colors may be encoded by such temporal patterns in neurons. This conjecture would help to explain the fact that stimulation of the retina using temporal patterns rather than color can cause color experiences (Festinger, Allyn, and White, 1971). These temporal methods of color induction may result from the biophysics of receptor types, and the patterns caused by those receptors may then carry over into the central nervous system. Could it be that each color corresponds to a unique temporal pattern, or waveform, in the brain? This exciting possibility faces a serious hurdle. When identifying the neural responses for different colors, McClurkin, Zarbock, and Optican (1996) discovered that every color they mentioned was associated with a large family of different waveforms. Using statistical methods, they were able to show that these waveforms cluster into families of similar patterns, but even so, there were a number of distinct families for each color. This is problematic in the present context, because we are trying to find a way to distinguish colors at the neural level. If there are multiple different temporal patterns associated with a given shade of red, which of these is the neural correlate of phenomenal experiences of that shade? If we were to say that just one of them is the correlate, we would have to pick arbitrarily. If we say that each is a correlate, we are left with the odd conclusion that specific shades of red have multiple neural realizers. This would raise the embarrassing question: in virtue of what are these many neural correlates qualitatively alike? Perhaps we could find an answer by moving above neural codes to some higher level of description, but it's hard to know where to look. Therefore, we might want to abandon the temporal-coding strategy and find some other aspect of neuron firing that maps onto color qualities uniquely.

Both rate coding and temporal coding got us into trouble. Rate coding left us with no way to distinguish red neural responses from blue, and temporal coding left us with no way to say why two red responses are qualitatively alike. We need an alternative. To find one, notice that rate coding and temporal coding are properties of individual neurons. We can make progress by moving beyond individual neurons and considering "population codes." Population codes can be introduced by contrast with sparse codes. On a sparse-coding scheme, an individual neuron carries information independently of what other cells in the same brain area are doing. For example, recall those cells in higher visual areas that fire in response to whole faces. There are even cells in medial temporal structures that fire in response to celebrities; for example, an individual cell might fire in response to pictures of Bill Clinton (Kreiman, Fried, and Koch, 2002). To know that we are thinking about Bill Clinton, a downstream brain area need only register that this one cell is active. By contrast, in population codes, the information that one brain area picks up from another depends on what whole populations of cells are doing. There is evidence that cells in the motor system code for arm movements in this way. When a monkey reaches in a specific direction, many cells that are responsive to movements in that general direction fire at once. When considered individually, each of these cells has a tuning curve that covers a range of movements, including the move-ment in the observed direction; a given cell that happens to fire when the monkey reaches at a forty-five-degree angle might have fired if the monkey had reached at forty-eight degrees or forty-two degrees. But suppose you average together the tuning curves of all of the cells that fire when the monkey reaches at forty-five degrees. Then you get a response that corresponds to the direction of movement quite accurately (Georgopoulos, Schwartz, and Kettner, 1986). This suggests that direction is coded not by individual cells but by populations.

Population coding is used in some parts of the visual system. For ex-ample, Pasupathy and Connor (2002) were able to reconstruct what shape a monkey was seeing by performing population-level analyses on cells in V4, and similar results have been obtained for speed estimation in MT (Priebe and Lisberger, 2004). There is also good evidence that colors are encoded in this way; populations of neurons correlated better with perceived colors than do individual neurons (Wachtler, Sejnowski, and Albright, 2003). In addition, color-sensitive cells are spatially segregated in the nervous system, suggesting that different colors correspond to different contiguous populations (Brouwer and Heeger, 2009; Conway and Tsao, 2009; Kotake et al., 2009). It is tempting to conclude that red and blue differ because they correspond to different neu-ral populations.

Unfortunately, this won't yet solve the puzzle about color phenomenology. To analyze a population code, one usually begins with prior measurement of the tuning curves of the cells in some region (the range of inputs that cause each cell to fire). Then, to figure out what is being represented, one takes the average of all of the cells that are firing at a given time. In terms of color, this would involve finding out what wavelengths cause cells in some brain area to fire and then averaging across a current firing pattern to determine what specific color caused that pattern. This method would distinguish blue from red only by specifying which population of cells was most active for each of those colors. We might find a blue population and a red population, but we won't be told anything distinctive about these two populations aside from the relational fact that they are sensitive to different-colored stimuli in the external world. We won't be told how the red population differs from the blue population inter-nally, so we will be no better off than we were when we set out to find a differ-ence between an individual blue cell and an individual red cell.

Rate coding, temporal coding, and population coding are the three major approaches to neural coding in the literature, and none seems to solve our problem of finding neural correlates for color qualities in the brain. But we need not despair. A solution can be found if we combine these approaches. In particular, we might combine population coding with temporal coding. In the temporal-coding story, each color corresponds to a different temporal pattern in neuron firing. The difficulty with this story is that no unique waveform has been found for specific colors. But now suppose that each color corresponds to a population of waveforms. In fact, this is precisely what McClurkin, Zarbock, and Optican (1996) propose. If populations are used, readable patterns may emerge through neural noise, and colors may be equated with constellations of waveforms (figure 11). I will call a constellation of waveforms a vectorwave. In computational neuroscience, a "vector" is defined as a pattern of activity across a population of neurons. A "vectorwave" is a vector made up of waveforms. Vectorwaves may uniquely individuate color experiences. On this approach, a population of red cells and a population of blue cells will not differ simply in terms of which cells are firing. They will also differ in the temporal dynamics of those firing patterns.

The hypothesis that temporal coding can be used to distinguish colors can also be extended to other sensory qualities. McClurkin, Zarbock, and Optican (1996) demonstrate that visual patterns are associated with vectorwaves, and Victor and Purpura (1996) report similar results for other visual qualities, including contrast, spatial frequency, and texture. There is also evidence for temporal coding in the auditory modality, including pitch and timbre (Cariani, 1999), touch (Recanzone, Merzenich, and Schreiner, 1992), and gustation (Di Lorenzo, Chen, and Victor, 2009). It remains unknown whether temporal codes extend to all sensory qualities and whether the temporal patterns that correspond to stimuli occur fast enough to account for minimum discrimination latencies. Consequently, the vectorwave story remains speculative. We do know, however, that spiking patterns are, in general, nonuniform and that the brain is capable of detecting spike timing as fast as a millisecond, so brief patterns may be sufficient for discrimination, especially when populations are used. The claim that sensory qualities are population-coded is widely accepted, and if the

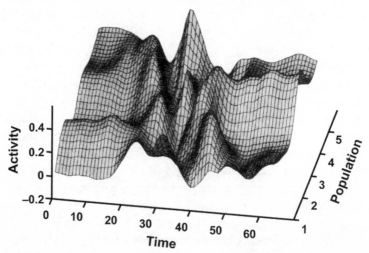

FIGURE 11 A vectorwave. McClurkin, Zarbock, and Optican's (1996) depiction of the form generated by combining the temporal pattern that several different cells exhibited in response to red (reproduced with permission).

vectorwave account doesn't pan out for every (or any) sensory quality, some other population code is likely to account for sensory differences. Hence qualia are likely to be vectors, even if not vectorwaves. The vectorwave account is just one conjecture.

Even where temporal codes have been well established, many things await future investigation. In the visual modality, it has yet to be demonstrated that temporal codes are actually used by the brain, even though they are clearly present. We do know, however, that temporal codes are sometimes used; in gustation, it has been shown that induction of temporal patterns in rat brains through microstimulation can cause behaviors associated with taste discrimination (Di Lorenzo, Hallock, and Kennedy, 2003), and it has been established that temporal codes are computationally tractable provided they don't depend on exact spike counts or interspike intervals (Shalden, 2002). It is also unknown whether the same neurons encode multiple vectorwaves. McClurkin, Zarbock, and Optican (1996) recorded color and pattern waveforms in the same neurons, but there is also considerable evidence that visual features are processed in different brain areas and can be dissociated, suggesting that some of the waveforms they observe are epiphenomenal. In addition, it is not yet known whether similarity in waveforms can reflect qualitative similarities or blends. Di Lorenzo, Chen, and Victor (2009) report that waveform blends correspond to binary flavors in taste, and there may be room for a similar story when it comes to color. On the other hand, it's controversial whether binary colors are phenomenologically simple or complex (Mizrahi, 2009).

These questions can all be answered through future research. For now, the speculative upshot is this. Rather than thinking of each cell in V4 as corresponding to a phenomenological color quale, we can think of qualia as vectorwaves. As we saw in figure 11, McClurkin, Zarbock, and Optican (1996) represent vectorwaves by plotting the temporal profile of cellular populations as three-dimensional surface forms. Such surface forms are potentially robust across variation at the level of individual neurons and can even retain their topology as neurons change their firing rate. The precise duration of the peaks and valleys may not matter. On this approach, vectorwave can be thought of in geometrical terms. This allows us to state a solution to the problem about red and blue cells very simply. Although red and blue cells are alike in many respects when considered individually, they differ geometrically when considered in populations. For colors, I've suggested, this geometry is temporal, meaning that one dimension along which it is plotted represents time, but the more basic moral is that we can think of cellular populations as collectively generating distinctive geometrical forms for each phenomenal quality.

The thesis that colors can be distinguished geometrically should not be equated with the popular hypothesis that colors are distinguished by their location in a color space. The latter idea has been advocated by a number of philosophers, including Churchland (2007), Clark (1993), and Rosenthal (2005). They believe that phenomenal states have their character by virtue of the relational structure of sensory systems. On this view, the character of an experienced color depends on its position in a similarity space rather than on some intrinsic properties of state considered in isolation from other colors. This entails a kind of experiential holism, according to which the character of any given experience depends on the character of other experiences of the same broad class. I think that experiential holism is implausible for several reasons.

First, it seems intuitively implausible that experiences have their character by virtue of the kinds of relations under consideration. An experience has its phenomenal character even when no other experiences of the same kind are occurring. For example, when we look at a ganzfeld, we might see a uniform color. That color quality is an occurrent state with temporal boundaries. The relations it has to other colors are merely dispositional, so it is not clear how they could be contributing to what it is like right now.

Second, the idea that color representations have their character by virtue of their relations to other color representations implies that two individuals with a different set of color representations will not have *any* color experiences in common, because no pair of color representations in these two systems will have the same role. There is empirical reason for doubting this. Graham and Hsia (1958) present data on a woman who is dichromatic (specifically, a deuteranope) in one eye and trichromatic in the other. They ask her to match color samples presented to each eye separately. The crucial finding is that she has no difficulty seeing samples presented in one eye as being just like samples presented in the other. She makes many errors, of course, but there are also samples that she matches correctly across. The main point is that visual experiences in a dichromatic system can be mapped onto experiences in a trichromatic system, which is at odds with the hypothesis that we grasp color experiences using representations that are individuated by relation to other color representations.

Third, there is strong evidence for thinking that color qualities are represented separately from one another in the brain. For one thing, the capacity to perceive colors doesn't always come and go as a whole. Spillmann, Laskowski, and Lange (2000) describe a patient who became color agnosic after a brain injury and then slowly recovered. Strikingly, his color perception did not return all at once. Rather, green came back first, then red, yellow, and brown, and finally blue. In addition, Kotake et al. (2009) have shown that color-responsive cells in V4 are spatially organized, such that cells responding to similar colors are clustered together. That implies that one could sustain an injury that preserved cells responsive to one color range while destroying the others. In other words, color perception seems to be relatively atomistic. Perception of one color (or perhaps one color category) does not depend on the others.

In summary, I have proposed a geometrical approach to color qualia that differs from the color-space story familiar to many philosophers. The details of the story remain sketchy and speculative, but they serve as a kind of existence proof. I've suggested that the neural correlates of distinct color experiences have to be distinguishable by features that are intrinsic to those correlates, by which I mean present when the correlates are active. Relational properties, such as being reliably caused by blue, will not suffice. Population coding combined with temporal coding provides an explanation. Color experiences can be characterized in terms of distinct vectorwaves, and the same may be true for other sensory qualities.

Pulling all of these threads together, I have argued that the intermediate level can be identified by finding brain areas that exhibit viewpoint-specific responses that are decomposable into microfeature and are also coherent. Microfeatures, in turn, are represented by vectorwaves, which are population codes defined over the temporal patterns of neurons. These criteria help to confirm that anatomical areas such as V4 correspond to the intermediate level in vision. Our functional criteria coincide roughly with anatomical criteria, placing intermediate areas at a synaptic distance from transducers that lie between primary areas and the highest reaches of our sensory systems. The exact nature of neural coding within these intermediate areas is still a topic for ongoing research, but vectorwaves are a plausible possibility.

2. Neural Correlates of Attention

2.1. THE BOLD BOOST

We have been discussing the neural correlates of conscious visual representations, but we have not yet discussed the neural mechanisms that make the representations conscious. In chapter 3, I argued that sensory representations become conscious when and only when we attend, where attention is the process by which perceptual states become available to, but not encoded in, working memory. To find the NCC, we need to find the neural correlate of attention, and to find the neural correlate of attention, we need to find out what processes allow information to flow from perceptual pathways in the brain to pathways associated with working memory.

As we have already observed, the brain can be described at many different levels of analysis, from whole systems down to cells and their components (Churchland, 1986). The neural correlates of attention have been studied at every level. Let's begin with the large-scale brain structures associated with attention and working memory. Attention is usually associated with inferior portions of posterior parietal cortex, especially the inferior parietal sulcus. Attention is also associated with the frontal eye fields in Brodmann area 8. I think it is misleading to say that attention is located in these areas; rather, they serve as control structures that can regulate the allocation of attention. Attention itself is located in the perceptual pathways. It is not a structure but rather a way of processing perceptual representations. I will discuss these processes below.

Working memory is associated with the lateral frontal cortex. It is believed that different sense modalities recruit different working-memory mechanisms, and there may be different structures associated with shapes and spatial information (Crottaz-Herbette, Anagnoson, and Menon, 2004; Funahashi, Bruce, and Goldman-Rakic, 1989). There is also considerable evidence that lateral frontal areas can be distinguished according to their specific contribution to working memory, with some areas involved in the maintenance of information and others involved in manipulation (D'Esposito et al., 1999). Both maintenance and manipulation involve projection or preservation of activity in sensory areas, which are implemented by stimulus-specific sensory responses that continue after a stimulus has been removed—often called delay-period activations.

Thus, at the level of gross anatomy, consciousness will characteristically involve a circuit that includes perceptual pathways, such as the visual pathways in occipital, temporal, and parietal cortex; attention control centers in parietal cortex; and lateral frontal structures associated with working memory. This circuitry is borne out by neuroimaging studies, as mentioned in chapter 3 (see the discussion of figure 10 above). But such systems-level observations do not tell us anything about the neural processes underwriting conscious experience. We need to delve deeper.

One thing that has been established repeatedly is that attention correlates with increased neuronal activity as measured by BOLD (blood-oxygen-level-dependent) signals in fMRI. The locus of increase is in perceptual areas corresponding to the feature dimension being attended. For example, Corbetta and Shulman (2002) recorded increases in MT, the visual area associated with motion, when subjects were asked to focus on the direction of a moving stimulus. Liu et al. (2003) found that different visual areas increased when subjects alternated attention between motion and color. Yantis et al. (2002) observed a lateral shift in extrastriate BOLD response as a function of which side of a scene subjects attended to. Such boosts in BOLD suggest that attention increases cellular activity. Given this, one might think of attention as little more than a kind of volume knob that makes cells fire more readily. This idea is deeply entrenched in neuroscience. Some researchers talk about attention as a "gain control" device, borrowing a term from electronics that refers to a device that modulates signal strength.

I think this view of attention is right but also incomplete. It would be a mistake simply to identify attention with an increase in neural activity. Brain areas fluctuate in activation all the time, and many of the increases have little to do with attention. A strong stimulus, whether attended or not, can lead to a change in activity. Indeed, any stimulus will increase firing in stimulus-sensitive brain areas, even if that stimulus is presented unconsciously. Thus, causing firing to increase is not the neural correlate of attention, much less consciousness. To find the neural correlate of attention, we need to know what is causing the attention correlated BOLD increases at a cellular level. Attention does increase signal strength, but it increases it in a distinctive way.

More information can be gleaned from cell recordings in humans or laboratory animals. One promising lead comes from a recent study by Mitchell, Sundberg, and Reynolds (2007), who trained macaque monkeys to visually track two cued shapes in a group of four shapes that moved around on a computer screen. During this task, they recorded cells in intermediate-level visual area V4. The researchers were interested in whether different kinds of cells behaved differently during this attention-demanding task. Cells were divided into two distinct groups based on the waveforms they produced. There were interneurons with basket-cell and chandelier-cell morphology, on the one hand, and pyramidal cells, on the other. The former have short-lasting action potentials and can therefore be called narrow-spiking neurons, and the latter have longer action potentials and can be called broad-spiking. Both types of cells changed from baseline firing rates during the task, but it was only the narrow-spiking neurons that consistently increased from baseline, in contrast with the broad-spiking cells, which both increased and decreased. This suggests that the net gains in activity during attention may owe more to narrow-spiking neurons than to broad-spiking ones.

It is tempting to say that the neural correlate of consciousness is activity in narrow-spiking interneurons. But this is problematic for three reasons. First, there is evidence that top-down and bottom-up attention are associated with different kinds of interneurons, which threatens to undermine our hope for a unified theory of attention and consciousness (Buia and Tiesinga, 2008). Second, narrow-spiking interneurons do not carry sensory information but rather modulate the pyramidal cells that do, and it is sensory information that gets consciously experienced. Third, interneurons operate only locally, which means that their activity is not available to the distant brain structures involved in working memory; thus, they are not good candidates for the availability relation that constitutes the attentional basis of consciousness. Thus, it is unlikely that interneuron activity is the cellular basis of consciousness. We can find a better candidate by investigating the role that interneurons play.

2.2. THE GAMMA HYPOTHESIS

Unlike pyramidal cells, interneurons are inhibitory, not excitatory. It has now been well established that such inhibition regulates how pyramidal cells fire. It makes them more orderly. Imagine a large population of pyramidal cells firing at different rates and times. Now introduce an inhibitory signal on some subset of that population. The result of that signal will be a reduction in chaos and an increase in coordination. Interneuron inhibition causes synchrony. This has been shown both in vivo and in vitro (e.g., Sohal and Huguenard, 2005). In fact, such inhibition tends to bring about synchrony within a particular frequency, the so-called gamma band. The gamma band traditionally refers to a rate of electrical signal oscillation between 30 Hz and 70 Hz, but sometimes the label also includes "high-gamma," which is in the range of 80 Hz to 150 Hz. There is no settled view about functional differences between high- and low-gamma, and the difference may not matter. I will just speak of gamma here. The suggestion I want to make is that gamma is a neural correlate of attention.

There is a large body of evidence in support of this hypothesis. In one of the most direct demonstrations of this, Fries et al. (2001) found that V4 cells fire in the gamma band when a monkey is attending to gradients presented in those cells' receptive fields (figure 12). Numerous other findings, including studies on humans, confirm this. Gonzalez Andino et al. (2005) found increased gamma during periods of expectancy. Nakatani et al. (2005) found that gamma oscillations correlated with perceived targets in attentional blink. Steinmetz et al. (2000) found that synchronized gamma activity correlated with attention across sense modalities in a vision-to-touch matching task. Tallon-Baudry et al. (1997) found gamma activity during a visual search. Ray et al. (2008) correlated gamma with selective attention in a task that involved shifting from one modality to another.

It will have not escaped notice that gamma (sometimes misleadingly abbreviated as 40 Hz) has also been associated with consciousness (Crick and Koch, 1990; von der Malsburg, 1997; Singer, 1999; Singer and Gray, 1995; Hameroff, 2007). But the association between gamma oscillations and consciousness has also been controversial. Crick and Koch (1990) originally proposed gamma as a correlate of consciousness, but they subsequently abandoned the idea, citing insufficient evidence (1995). I think their change of heart was premature. The cumulative evidence for gamma synchrony is now more impressive. For example, gamma synchrony is associated with the overall level of consciousness in an organism: it is disrupted when people undergo anesthesia (John and Prichep, 2005); it is observed during dream sleep (Llinás and Ribary, 1993); and it decreases markedly in deep sleep (Gross and Gotman, 1999). Gamma

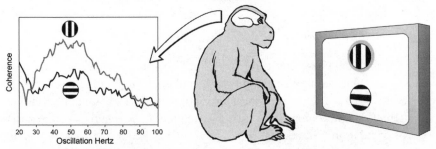

FIGURE 12 Experimental setup in Fries et al. (2001), in which a macaque attended to one of two patches, while electrodes recorded from V4. Data are just for illustration, indicating greater gamma synchrony for the attended patch.

also seems to be associated with increases in perceptual intensity: it increases with deviant auditory signals (Edwards et al., 2005) and with bright high-contrast visual displays (Biederlack et al., 2006). Finally, gamma correlates with stimulus visibility: it tracks stimulus selection in binocular rivalry (Engel et al., 1999; Fries et al., 1997); it occurs in blindsight under conditions in which a stimulus is consciously seen (Schurger, Cowey, and Tallon-Baudry, 2006); it occurs when barely visible stimuli are experienced (Wyart and Tallon-Baudry, 2008); and it co-occurs with conscious detection in masking paradigms (Summerfield, Jack, and Burgess, 2002; Gaillard et al., 2009).

This evidence is striking when coupled with the evidence that gamma is a correlate of attention. The researchers who have tested for a relationship between gamma and consciousness have generally done so independently of any presumed link between gamma and attention, and those who link gamma to attention are often neutral on questions about consciousness. So there is independent support linking gamma to both attention and consciousness. This is precisely what the AIR theory predicts: a common neural correlate. Thus, the research on gamma provides a powerful line of evidence for the AIR theory.

Some authors have suggested that consciousness also relates to other oscillation frequencies. There is evidence, for example, correlating consciousness with activity in the slower alpha band (8–14 Hz). Some have suggested that alpha synchrony is a correlate of consciousness (Palva and Palva, 2007; Sewards and Sewards, 1999), but the evidence is mixed. Alpha synchronization coincides with the suppression of distracter stimuli (Kelly et al., 2006), and when a visual target is presented in one hemifield, alpha synchronization increases in the hemisphere that is not processing it, and alpha desynchronization occurs in the active hemisphere (Sauseng et al., 2005; Thut et al., 2006). But it should not be inferred that consciousness is always associated with alpha desynchronization. Wyart and Tallon-Baudry (2008) found a dissociation between gamma synchronization and alpha desynchronization in a cueing task. When subjects saw an arrow point to one side, alpha desynchronization increased in the corresponding hemisphere, but gamma did not co-occur with that change. Instead, gamma correlated with conscious stimulus detection regardless of the arrow. The authors interpret this as a dissociation between gamma and attention, but it might be better to interpret the alpha activity as indicating *preparation for* attention: by desynchronizing alpha, the brain normally increases the likelihood that gamma will occur. In this particular study, alpha and gamma do not coincide, however, because subjects know that a stimulus can occur on either side, regardless of the cue, so they probably allocate some attention to both sides. If they happen to catch the stimulus on the uncued side, a large increase in attention will occur, and the gamma signal will come apart from the alpha.

These findings suggest that gamma is a better candidate for the correlate of consciousness than alpha. But it may be premature to conclude that alpha is unimportant. The complex and inconsistent relationship between gamma and alpha may stem from the fact that alpha waves have multiple sources and functions, some of which are linked to gamma, and others operate independently. But overall, there is evidence that gamma oscillations are characteristically *nested* in alpha oscillations. Alpha and gamma are often phase-locked, suggesting that they work together somehow (Chorlian, Porjesz, and Begleiter, 2006; Osipova et al., 2008). To say that gamma is phase-locked to alpha does not entail that they are in perfect synchrony, only that the two oscillations have a fixed relationship. As a matter of fact, gamma peaks trail behind alpha peaks, and gamma may be most likely to arise when alpha oscillations hit their low points. This pattern suggests that alpha oscillations play a role in gamma regulation. I will come back to this point in chapter 8.

Other oscillation rates may play a role in working memory. According to the AIR theory, consciousness arises when attention makes information available to working memory but does not require encoding (chapter 3). This predicts that gamma will arise during, or at least prior to, working memory but that gamma is not sufficient for encoding. This is consistent with the evidence. Gamma is associated with working memory (Howard et al., 2003; Jokisch and Jensen, 2007), but there is evidence that gamma operates locally and that slower rhythms are needed for long-distance communication (Kopell et al., 2000; von Stein and Sarnthein, 2000). Gamma has been observed to be coupled with these slower oscillations (Canolty et al., 2006; Demiralp et al., 2007), suggesting that they work together. There is especially strong evidence suggesting that gamma couples with theta oscillations (4–8 Hz) during working-memory tasks (Sauseng et al., 2007; Holz et al., 2010). Theta might be the neural signature of encoding.

Some critics worry that all of these oscillations are merely epiphenomenal, corresponding to how researchers measure the brain, rather than to actual activity in the cells that underlie conscious experience. The worry is exacerbated by the fact that neural oscillations are often measured on the scalp and thus correspond to activity in hundreds of thousands of neurons. In relating gamma to consciousness, I want to insist that gamma is a measure of an actual process in the cells that make us conscious. The oscillations measured on the scalp correspond, however imperfectly, to cellular activity. Gamma can be measured in local field potentials—electrical signals issuing from the synaptic activity on dendrites. It corresponds to both the firing rate of neurons (axon potentials) and the dendritic events that drive those axon potentials, and gamma oscillations in individual cells increase when populations of neurons fire in synchrony (Ray et al., 2008). Thus, gamma is not just a property that emerges when thousands of cells are summed. It occurs locally, and therefore it can play a role in how individual cells or small populations interact.

There are even detailed explanations of how gamma arises at the molecular level. For example, Kuznetsova and Deth (2008) have developed a model based on the observation that a certain kind of dopamine receptor (D4) can transfer methyl to a particular phospholipid called phosphatidylethanolamine, which increases fluidity around the receptor; this decreases inertia in ion channels and speeds up neural spiking. Computational models based on these biological principles show how attention-related inhibitory signals can result in 40-Hz oscillations. Whether or not these models prove correct, they illustrate the fine level of detail at which attention can ultimately be understood. We have moved from global circuits down to microenvironments, finding potential correlates of attention at every level.

The levels that we've been talking about can be regarded as levels of organization in a complex mechanism (Wimsatt, 1976; Glennan, 1996; Machamer, Darden, and Carver, 2000; Bechtel, 2001; Darden, 2001; Craver, 2007). Macro processes decompose into spatially localized components, with moving parts that decompose further and account for the macro behavior. The story about inhibition and dopamine channels explains fast synchrony in populations of neurons, which generates local field potentials. But why synchrony? What does any of this have to do with explaining attention? The answer is that synchrony facilitates communication (see, e.g., Fries, 2005). Imagine that you are on a balcony above a big crowd, and everyone is engaged in conversation with the people in their immediate surroundings. The result will be an indecipherable cacophony of speech sounds. But now suppose that some group within the crowd starts saying the same thing at the same time. Their collective voice will rise above the multitudes and be audible and discernible up above. Likewise, when neurons fire together, they are able to send signals that rise above neural noise. There is good evidence that synchrony increases output (Salinas and Sejnowski, 2001) and allows for virtual connectivity (see, e.g., Vanni, 1999). Melloni et al. (2007) found evidence for this in a masking task. They measured electrical activity on the scalp while the subject perceived a word either visibly (followed by a low-luminance mask) or invisibly (followed by a high-luminance mask). They found that in the visible condition, there was a much higher degree of synchrony across distantly connected brain areas. Thus, synchrony allows a population of neurons in one part of the brain to produce a signal that could potentially be picked up by some other part of the brain. In brief, synchrony is a correlate of availability, and availability is attention. Chemically induced changes in ion channels permit coherent signaling, which enables communication across the nervous system. I've only presented a sketch of the details, but that should be enough to see how a psychological phenomenon—attention— might be analyzed at multiple levels of organization within the nervous system.

As stated, this account remains incomplete in various ways. I have been vague about what kind of interneurons cause gamma synchrony, indicating that more than one kind may play this role (see, e.g., Tukker et al., 2007). There are also questions about where the initial interneuron inhibition comes from. There are computational models in which synchrony begins with sparse pyramidal excitation, followed by interneuron inhibition, which then leads to a pattern of reentry between these two classes of neurons, and that results in the measured oscillations (Mann et al., 2005). Grossberg (2007) has been developing a complex model that implicates thalamocortical connections in the generation of synchrony, and he also emphasizes specific laminar dynamics. Crick (1995) has also emphasized laminar organization, suggesting that consciousness might be located in a specific cortical layer, and Buffalo et al. (2011) have recently found evidence that gamma is restricted to superficial layers in the visual system. More controversially, Hameroff (2007) has proposed that quantum events contribute to synchrony, although given the plausible biological models that exist, there isn't strong pressure to invoke explanation at the level of physics. Many of the suggestions in the literature remain highly speculative, and much further investigation is needed. As an interim moral, however, we can say that we have a basic, though partial, understanding of how attention might be implemented in the brain, and there is reason to believe that gamma oscillations are a neural signature of that process.

In associating gamma with attention, I am departing from those who say that gamma is the basis of binding (e.g., Crick and Koch, 1990). In chapter 1, I rejected the synchrony approach to the binding problem, citing research showing that the cells corresponding to different parts of a perceived scene fire at the same rate, even if they don't correspond to parts of the same object. There is some evidence that attention can improve binding (Robertson, 2003; Reeves, Fuller, and Fine, 2005; Hyun, Woodman, and Luck, 2009), but its contribution may be indirect; attending to two features may reduce noise and increase the likelihood that they are both encoded and co-located in space. Attention may also be needed to bring bound features into working memory. But there is evidence that binding can occur without attention. For example, Goldsmith (1998) has shown that colors can improve shape detection in visual search, suggesting that color and shape are bound preattentively. Mordkoff and Halterman (2008) showed that unattended colored shapes can improve detection of attended objects that have the same features. Complex shapes can also be perceived without attention, suggesting that attention isn't needed to bind highly irregular contours (DeSchepper and Treisman, 1996). Such findings suggest that attention is not required for binding. This fits with the conclusion here that gamma is a correlate of the former and not the latter. This departs from the Crick and Koch (1990) model, since they associated gamma with both. My conclusion is that they were half right.

3. Correlates Combined

We have now seen a story about the neural correlates of intermediate-level representations and the neural correlates of attention. To describe the neural correlates of the AIR theory of consciousness, it remains only to put these two elements together. This task is simple but illuminating. Here I want to emphasize one thing that does *not* follow from the story I am telling, and then I'll mention five implications.

The neural correlate of an intermediate-level representation is a neural response that is viewpoint-specific and decomposable into microfeatures. The neural response to a given microfeature is not the firing of an individual neuron but rather a pattern of activity in a constellation of neurons with distinctive temporal profiles—what I called a vectorwave. Individually, none of these neurons uniquely determines a particular quality, but when combined with others in a population, a pattern emerges, which can be described as the neural correlate of particular sensory qualities.

The neural correlates of attention were specified at several levels of analysis. To relate these correlates to the correlates of intermediate-level representations, we can focus on the level of neural populations. There the story focuses on gamma synchrony. When an organism attends to an object, the cells corresponding to that object fire in synchrony with gamma oscillations. Thus, at the level of neural populations, one can say that the NCC is a population of temporally patterned neurons, which are responsive to viewpoint-specific microfeatures, firing together within the gamma range. We can call this a gamma vectorwave.

One might worry that the gamma story and the vectorwave story are incompatible. After all, both involve dynamic patters in neurons. How can a population of cells that is firing in a specific vectorwave retain its temporal dynamics when also firing in the gamma range? Shouldn't gamma synchrony undermine the more irregular patterns so crucial for vectorwaves? The solution to this problem is multiplexing. A multiplexed code is one in which a population of neurons carries different information at different time scales. Multiplexing is believed to be a widespread and important aspect of neural coding (Panzeri et al., 2010). With gamma vectorwaves, multiplexing would work as follows. Information about each microfeature in a stimulus—its various colors, for example—would be carried by different neurons by means of their distinctive spiking patterns. Then these patterned neurons would be coordinated, at a coarser time scale, into phased synchrony. The resulting activity would be a coherent undulation of distinct patterns. By analogy, imagine playing two melodies on two different radios while raising and lowering their volume in sync. Each melody would remain intact, but they would now also be heard as parts of the same overarching sound pattern. Multiplexing can bring pairs of neurons with different patterns into synchrony (as in the radio analogy), and it can also bring whole populations into synchrony (imagine the same thing with a thousand radios). It is a powerful tool for preserving information in spiking patterns, while also allowing large and disparate populations to work together. On the AIR theory, the spiking patterns give us the quality of experience, and the oscillations make those qualities conscious. This may sound like a complicated bit of dynamics, but it is actually an elegant way to encode content while also affecting information flow. It allows both qualia and consciousness to arise from temporal patterns of electrochemical activity.

The gamma vectorwave theory has a number of implications, which contribute to its plausibility. First, gamma vectorwaves help to explain how consciousness can come in degrees. I have claimed that attention can be intense and focal or ambient and diffuse. I take this to be a plausible interpretation of the phenomenology. Strictly speaking, gamma cannot be graded: cells either fire within this range, or they don't. There is no evidence linking higher rates of gamma with more vivid awareness, so as far as we know at present, consciousness comes with gamma activity regardless of the specific rate of gamma. But vividness can be explained by the number of cells in a given receptive field firing within this range. Consciousness may fade and intensify as the proportion of gamma synchrony increases. Consciousness may be focal when there is a high degree of gamma in a particular region or in the collection of regions corresponding to a specific object or feature. Consciousness is ambient when gamma spreads across a wider region. Ambient gamma may tend to be low in intensity, meaning that when spatially distributed, gamma oscillations may occur more diffusely. On this view, focus and intensity tend to come together, as do ambience and diffuseness, but they could come apart. These differences can be explained nicely on the gamma vectorwave account.

A second, related implication is that the gamma vectorwave account provides a powerful resource for testing the AIR theory. In stating that consciousness requires attention, I argued that some cases in which consciousness seems to arise outside of attention are better described as cases in which consciousness arises outside of focal attention but within diffuse attention. This move may seem ad hoc, but I don't think it is. I think it is consistent with the phenomenology. But it is also testable in principle if the gamma vectorwave view is right. If gamma is a neural signature of attention, we can see whether gamma remains diffusely distributed among background cells when attention is focused on some central foreground object. In other words, we could test whether attention can be both diffuse and intense, as I've suggested, and we can test whether the neural correlates of attention are present in those cases in which some critics of AIR would be inclined to say that we have consciousness without attention.

The next implication that I want to mention concerns the minimal physical machinery needed for consciousness. Theories differ regarding how much of the brain is required to have a conscious state. At one extreme, there are people who think that consciousness can arise in an individual neuron (Sevush, 2006). At the other, there are global workspace theories that implicate multiple sensory systems in addition to systems of higher cognition in frontal cortex. I don't think that intuitions can settle these disputes; they need to be settled empirically. The gamma vectorwave view falls between the extremes. Because conscious qualities require neural populations, consciousness cannot arise in a single cell. Because consciousness does not require working-memory encoding, frontal memory structures are probably unnecessary. Consciousness is located within sensory systems. It doesn't follow, however, that a few vibrating sensory cells could be conscious without other machinery. As we will see in the next paragraph, gamma vectorwaves may need to operate within the ambit of certain control structures. If so, the minimal physical requirements for consciousness might extend beyond sensory systems, even if the cells that become conscious are in those systems. Thus, the physical requirements for consciousness may be neither minimal nor maximal but in the middle.

The fourth implication bears on this point about minimal physical requirements, but it begins with a problem. Simply put, there is too much gamma. We can find examples of gamma synchrony in parts of the brain that do not correlate with conscious experience. For example, gamma has been recorded in the hippocampus (Colgin et al., 2009), primary visual cortex (Rols et al., 2001), and prefrontal cortex (Sederberg et al., 2007). Moreover, gamma is not just associated with attention; these studies also implicate gamma in memory encoding and retrieval. This is a fatal problem for some of those who think that gamma is the correlate of consciousness, but the AIR theory has resources to deal with it. To count as attention, gamma may need to play the right functional role within the brain. That role involves allowing information to flow (which gamma does everywhere) and operate under control of the brain mechanisms that determine which bits of sensory information can gain access to working memory. As we have seen, visual attention can be controlled by the frontal eye fields and the inferior parietal sulcus, so we might look for gamma in brain areas that have connections to these two areas. Strikingly, there is evidence that these structures have extensive connections to intermediate-level visual areas, and there are comparatively few connections to higher vision areas (Barbas and Mesulam, 1981; Blatt, Andersen, and Soner, 1990). There is also evidence that visual attention *originates* in intermediate areas and then spreads to others (Mehta and Schroeder, 2000; Buffalo et al., 2010; Bouvier and Engel, 2011). Such findings fit beautifully with the AIR theory. They also bring us to the fourth implication about gamma vectorwaves. By bringing these two components together, we can hone in on a unique neural correlate of consciousness even though the brain tends to use similar kinds of cells and processes throughout.

This last point might be expressed by saying that gamma needs vectorwaves in order to engender consciousness. That is, without playing a functional role that involves modulating vectorwaves of activation within sensory systems, gamma would not be able to do its consciousness-conferring work. The final implication I want to raise is the inverse of this. Vectorwaves need gamma. I have argued that qualitative experiences supervene on patterns of neural activity, but what, we may ask, is a pattern? Does the mere fact that neurons in some population are firing within the same general time frame add up to a pattern? Certainly not. Otherwise, every active neuron would be part of the same pattern, including not just the neurons in one person's head but all neurons everywhere. For two neurons to be part of the same pattern, their activations have to occur together, and they have to occur together nonaccidentally. Gamma synchrony achieves the required co-occurrence. It creates patterns, and without these, perception would have no character. It does not follow that synchrony is needed for perception. Individual cells carry information about perceptual features when they fire, and several cells firing within the same time window can collectively cause a cell at a subsequent stage to fire (a coincidence detector). This is sufficient for visual recognition, and that's why subliminal perception and masked priming are possible. But if I am right that qualitative character depends on the instantiation of a neural pattern, then synchrony is required for perception to feel like something.

This is a very satisfying implication because it links the two components of the AIR theory in an intimate way. I have already suggested that synchrony is needed to pass information forward to working memory, and I have suggested that synchrony functions as attention only when serving as part of a process that modulates sensory activity. Now I am suggesting that synchrony is also needed to implement neural correlates of qualitative properties. This shows that the physical implementation of consciousness is not arbitrary. The correlate of attention is needed to realize the correlate of phenomenal qualities. One needs consciousness to have qualia, and the gamma vectorwave theory explains why.

Some philosophers might resist the claim that qualia depend on consciousness. Rosenthal (2005), for example, argues that there can be unconscious phenomenal qualities, on the grounds that qualitative sensory states can occur without our being conscious of them, as when we are briefly distracted from an enduring headache. But this way of putting things raises a puzzle. When sensory states occur outside of consciousness, they don't seem to have any phenomenal qualities at all. It's not just that we don't notice them; they are entirely devoid of feeling. If we say that unconscious perceptual states are phenomenal qualities, why not say that all unconscious states are phenomenal, even states that we can never access? I think it is better to say that there can be unconscious perceptions, but perceptions don't take on qualitative character until they are conscious. The gamma vectorwave account offers an explanation of why this is so. Qualitative character comes from vectorwaves, and vectorwaves require synchrony.

If all of this is right, then the components of the AIR theory are interdependent. On the one hand, we cannot have A without IRs, because gamma can constitute attention only when playing the right role, and that role involves modulation of intermediate-level sensory activity. On the other hand, we cannot have qualitative IRs without the A, because gamma is what makes vectorwaves fire together, and vectorwaves depend on synchrony. The two ingredients that make up the AIR theory are inextricably linked when we consider their neural correlates, and a puzzle about why qualia and consciousness go hand-in-hand is solved.

PART TWO

The Limits of Consciousness

5

Which States Can Be Conscious?
Cognitive Qualia Reduced

Most research on consciousness has focused on sensory experiences, but some authors believe that consciousness outstrips the senses. They claim that we can be conscious of cognitive states that are not reducible to sensory or even verbal imagery. If they are right, theories of consciousness that have been developed to explain how perceptual states become conscious may not be adequate for explaining all aspects of consciousness. This would be a major setback for those of us who have invested in theories of perceptual consciousness with the hope that these theories can explain consciousness in general. If cognitive phenomenology outstrips perception, the AIR theory is incomplete, since it locates consciousness within perceptual hierarchies. This concern would be abated if it could be shown that cognitive phenomenology has a sensory basis. That is what I attempt to do here.

I will begin by clarifying the distinction between theories that restrict consciousness to perceptual states (restrictivism) and those that are more inclusive (expansionism). Then I will explore ways in which restrictivists can rebut leading arguments for expansionism. I will argue not that cognition cannot be conscious but rather that the felt qualities of our thoughts can be completely accommodated by appeal to concomitant sensory imagery.

1. Restrictivism and Expansionism

It was once widely assumed that every mental state is conscious. It's obvious to see why this was so: unconscious mental states simply went unnoticed. By the beginning of the twentieth century, people were increasingly recognizing the possibility of unconscious mental states. This shift was heavily influenced by Freud's theory of repressed desires and gained further traction from the failure of introspectionist psychology. In the early twentieth century, behaviorists railed against consciousness quite generally, and, in the mid-century, Chomsky argued that we comprehend language using unconscious rules. In the contemporary climate, it would be more than a bit eccentric to suggest that all mental states are conscious. But there remains considerable disagreement about which mental states are candidates for consciousness.

I will be defending the view that all consciousness is perceptual—what I'll call restrictivism. The contrasting view, expansionism, says that consciousness outstrips perception. These simple formulations are a good starting place for understanding the distinction, but there is an important clarification in order. As stated, the restrictive/expansive contrast implies a sharp separation between the perceptual and the nonperceptual, but there are distinguished philosophical traditions that deny any such distinction. Classical empiricists, such as Locke and Hume, claimed that all mentality is perceptually based: concepts are stored copies of percepts, and thoughts are combinations of concepts. On this view, thought is couched in a perceptual code. Thus, for a classical empiricist, the restrictive/expansive distinction seems to break down. Empiricists are technically restrictivists, in that they say all consciousness is perceptual, but there is nothing especially *restrictive* about this restrictivism, since, for them, all cognition is perceptual, too. Moreover, it would be misleading to say that empiricists cannot be expansionists simply by virtue of their perceptual theory of thinking. Imagine one empiricist who claims that only low-level perception is conscious and another who says that our most cognitively sophisticated thoughts can be conscious. Clearly, the latter is more expansive than the former, but by the definition above, neither qualifies as expansionist. I myself happen to think that classical empiricism is a plausible theory of the mind (Prinz, 2002), so I would prefer to define the restrictive/expansive distinction in a way that blocks a trivial inference from empiricism to restrictivism.

To provide such a definition, it will be helpful to distinguish vehicles, content, and qualities. *Vehicles* are the token particulars that have representational content. The vehicles in this sentence are orthographic marks on a page, and the vehicles in the head are mental representations. Empiricism is essentially a thesis about vehicles; it says that the vehicles used in thought are copies of the ones used in perceptual systems. The *content* of a vehicle, as I will use the term, is what that vehicle represents. For example, vehicles in the visual system may represent things such as shapes and colors. If empiricism is right, visual vehicles can represent other properties, too, such as objects or natural kinds or even highly abstract properties, such as numbers. The *quality* of a vehicle is how it feels when it is conscious—its phenomenal character. A red representation and a blue representation in the visual system have different content and different qualities; they feel different when they are conscious.

Now we need just one more piece of machinery to define restrictivism and expansionism. Let us say that the content of a vehicle is *sensory* just in case that vehicle represents some aspect of appearance. A content is *nonsensory* if it transcends appearance—that is, if there can be two things that are indistinguishable by the senses, one of which has the property and the other of which does not.

With these distinctions in hand, let's adopt the following definitions:

Restrictivism is true if and only if for every vehicle with qualitative character, there could be a qualitatively identical vehicle that has only sensory content.

Expansionism is true if and only if some vehicles with qualitative character are distinguishable from every vehicle that has only sensory content.

Notice two things about these definitions. First, I am not committing to the representationalist thesis that there is a one-to-one mapping between qualitative character and representational content. In chapter 1, I took issue with representationalism. These definitions apply only to states that represent (vehicles) and leave open the possibility that nonrepresentational states may have qualitative character. If restrictivism is true, there can also be states that are qualitatively alike but representationally different. Second, the definition of restrictivism is compatible with the view that perceptual states can represent things that are nonsensory. Restrictivism says only that having nonsensory content does not introduce phenomenal qualities absent from sensory representations. Put differently, restrictivism is the view that content that goes beyond appearance has no direct impact on quality.

Restrictivism has probably been a default position for many, until recently. Some authors have argued that we don't even experience external features of the world but only experience how the word affects our senses. Humphrey (1992) puts this in terms of Thomas Reid's sensation/perception distinction; he locates consciousness at the level of sensation and says that sensations represent "what is happening to me" rather than "what is happening out there." A somewhat more generous and typical view says that we experience *superficial* features of the external world, so that in vision, for example, we experience colors, shapes, and spatial relations (e.g., Peacocke, 1983; Dretske, 1995; Tye, 1995; Lormand, 1996). Some authors have also claimed that we can experience objects (Clark, 1993), and others have suggested that we experience action affordances (Gibson, 1979; Noë, 2005). The crucial thing about these views is that they deny, implicitly or explicitly, that the quality of experience goes beyond these aspects of appearance.

Expansionists say that consciousness is more encompassing. Siegel (2006) argues that we can experience natural-kind properties, even though being a natural kind goes beneath the surface. Pitt (2004) argues that for any thought that we can know we are thinking, there is a distinctive conscious quality, even though two distinct thoughts may represent states of affairs that look alike. Siewert (1998) has argued that there can be unverbalized, imageless thoughts. Expansionist views are also implied by Dennett (1991), whose cerebral celebrity theory of consciousness implies that just about anything in neocortex can become conscious, and Searle (1992), whose connection principle says that every mental state is potentially conscious. (Searle's view is a bit hard to interpret, since he defends the connection principle by arguing that many unconscious brain states do not qualify as mental, rather than arguing that every unconscious brain state can be conscious.)

When looking at this debate, it is easy to get the impression that the main issue is whether *concepts* or *thoughts* can be conscious. I have intentionally defined expansionism and restrictivism to avoid this impression. Restrictivists can allow conscious concepts and thoughts as long as they are encoded in sensory vehicles and have no qualities above and beyond their sensory qualities. Restrictivism is neutral about what can be *represented by* a conscious experience, but it is restrictive about what qualities our conscious experiences have. Some formulations in the literature are potentially misleading in this respect. Siegel (2006) presents the debate as turning on what is "represented in experience." This formulation is acceptable only if we define "representation in" (in contrast with "representation by") as a technical term for those aspects of content that have an impact on phenomenal qualities. Siewert (1998) presents the debate as turning on whether "phenomenal character extends to conceptual activity." This is acceptable only if "extends to" means that conceptual activity has phenomenal character above and beyond sensory activity. The debate I am interested in is not about whether conceptual activity can feel like something to a subject but whether it feels different from sensory activity. For this reason, I've resisted adopting Siewert's (2009) terms *exclusivism* and *inclusivism*, which are defined in a way that blurs this distinction. That said, I think Siewert's excellent arguments clearly pertain to restrictivism and expansionism as I have defined these terms, and I will turn to them below.

2. Resisting Expansion

Let me now briefly sketch the brand of restrictivism that I will be defending. In chapter 2, I presented empirical arguments for a theory of perceptual consciousness that builds on the work of Jackendoff (1987). In particular, I endorsed Jackendoff's conjecture that consciousness arises at the intermediate level. In vision, we experience stimuli as bounded wholes from a specific vantage point, occupying a specific size and position within the visual field (what Marr, 1982, calls the 2.5-D sketch). If the intermediate-level theory is right, the neural correlates of perceptual consciousness are restricted to those brain areas that implement perceptual processing at a level of abstraction that lies between local feature detectors and the abstract representations that play an active role in object recognition. This claim is highly specific about where consciousness arises and contrasts with more permissive views, which say that any state within our perceptual systems can be conscious. My goal here and in the next two chapters is to defend the claim that all consciousness is perceptual and hence located at the intermediate level of our perceptual systems. Thus, if concepts or thoughts can have an impact on experience, it is only by altering these relatively rudimentary perceptual representations (see also Prinz, 2007a).

In sharp contrast, expansionists claim that cognition contributes something to phenomenology over and above perception. More formally, I defined the view as entailing that there can be cognitive mental states that have phenomenal qualities that differ from every possible state that has purely sensory content. Expansionists try to make their case by devising examples in which cognitive phenomenology seems to outstrip anything sensory. I will survey putative examples here and offer restrictivist reconstruals.

2.1. CONCEPTUAL CONSCIOUSNESS

The question of whether concepts can contribute to phenomenology depends, of course, on what concepts are, and that is a big question, beyond the scope of this chapter. I will begin by offering a few remarks about what I take concepts to be and then turn to conceptual consciousness. My own views about concepts are not universally shared in philosophy (far from it), but they are ostensibly conducive to expansionism, so, assuming that I am right about concepts, I may be biasing the case in favor of expansionism and against restrictivism, rather than conversely. Since I will defend restrictivism, I am, in effect, making my own chore harder. Moreover, the strategies I offer to block expansionist theories of conceptual consciousness can be adapted to any other theory of concepts.

As already noted, I am partial to concept empiricism, according to which concepts are acquired by storing records of percepts (Prinz, 2002). This alone does not entail that concepts can be consciously experienced. There is good reason to think that we store high-level perceptual representations in long-term memory, not intermediate-level representations (chapter 3). That would explain why our powers of discrimination are far greater than our powers of recall (Raffman, 1995). If concepts are acquired by storing percepts, then concepts may be encoded in a high-level perceptual format that is not consciously accessible, if the intermediate-level theory is right. But I think that concepts *can* be conscious, because in occurrent acts of conceptualization, we use the high-level representations that are stored in long-term memory to construct temporary mental images of what our concepts represent (Martin, 2007). These temporary images can be conscious because imagery can be generated using intermediate-level representations (Slotnick, Thompson, and Kosslyn, 2005). I think we should regard images generated from long-term conceptual memory as occurrent tokens of the stored concepts used to generate them. Thus, I think that concepts can be conscious, and in this sense, there is such a thing as cognitive phenomenology. But it doesn't necessarily follow that expansionism is true, because it doesn't follow that conceptually generated images are qualitatively different from purely sensory images.

I think that the images generated from stored concepts inherit semantic properties from those concepts (Prinz, 2006a). So an image of a walrus represents that natural kind, and an image of an electron circling a proton represents these particles. But I think that these images also retain their sensory content. I endorse a Lockean notion of *double reference* according to which images represent *both* "real" natural kinds with unobservable essences and their "nominal" appearances (Prinz, 2000a). Put simply, images refer to their conceptual contents *by means of* representing sensory contents. A mental image represents walruses by representing how they look, and an image represents subatomic particles by depicting swirling circles. Thus, the brand of restrictivism that I favor says that the phenomenal qualities of an image derive entirely from its nominal content, not its real content. A little reflection (homework for the reader) will show that this formulation is a special case of restrictivism as defined earlier. That earlier definition is defined more generally so as to avoid any commitment to the doctrine of double reference.

To refute this story, the expansionists would need to show that real content contributes phenomenal qualities that are not already associated with the nominal content of an image. For example, the expansionist might try to show that my image of a walrus differs phenomenologically from a perceptual experience that someone might have the first time she sees a walrus, not knowing what it is. Siegel (2006) implies that this is the case when she proposes that we can experience natural kinds as such, but I am highly doubtful. I don't think we *experience* natural-kind properties when we apply concepts to what we are perceiving.

As a preliminary, it's worth noting that perception is not normally dependent on conceptualization. The phenomenology of object perception can remain undisturbed after incurring profound deficits in conceptual knowledge. Research on semantic dementia, associated with degeneration of the anterior temporal lobe, shows that individuals can continue to perceive normally once they have lost category memory (Patterson, Nestor, and Rogers, 2007). For example, when shown a picture of a duck, a semantic dementia patient won't be able to recognize it, and when asked to reproduce the picture from memory, she might produce a bizarre chimera with ducklike features and four legs. But the same patient would have no difficulty matching the duck picture with a duplicate or even matching it with pictures of the same duck at different orientations. This suggests that perception and conceptualization are somewhat autonomous activities.

In response, expansionists will hasten to note that conceptualization *can* influence perceptual experience. Consider the phenomenon of seeing-as. When we interpret ambiguous figures, they seem to transform experientially. The most famous case is Jastrow's duck-rabbit (for a version, see figure 13). Does

FIGURE 13 A duck-rabbit. Try to see it as one or the other, and then study it closely, trying to visualize it with your preferred interpretation. Don't switch.

the experience change when we see the duck-rabbit as a duck and then switch to seeing it as a rabbit? Introspectively, the answer seems to be yes, and this might be taken as evidence for the existence of cognitive phenomenology that goes above and beyond sensory phenomenology (see also Bayne, 2009, on associative agnosia).

In such cases, it is tempting to say that our concepts add something above and beyond our visual states. But the shift in experience can easily be explained in other ways. For one thing, concepts can alter sensory imagery. When we interpret an image as being of a duck, we gain access to duck knowledge stored unconsciously in long-term memory, and some of this knowledge may bubble forth in the form of mental imagery. It is possible, for example, that when construing the duck-rabbit as a duck, viewers faintly imagine a duck's body and other features. Research has shown that black-and-white images of familiar objects are misperceived as being faintly colored in appropriate ways (Hansen, Olkkonen, and Walter, 2006), and animal names prime auditory imagery of animal sounds (Orgs et al., 2006). And of course, picture recognition generates the production of verbal labels, so when seeing a duck-rabbit as a duck, the word "duck" is probably heard in the mind's ear. In addition, conceptualization can lead to perceptual distortions that make the object look prototypical or easier to discriminate from others (Goldstone, 2004). Linguistic labels can also have that effect: labeled ambiguous pictures are recalled as having label-consistent disambiguating features (Carmichael, Hogan, and Walter, 1932), and labeled ambiguous facial expressions cause label-consistent unambiguous emotional contagion (Halberstadt et al., 2009). Conceptualization can also affect the allocation of attention to the features most relevant to the operative interpretation (Aha and Goldstone, 1992).

The case of the duck-rabbit can be explained along these lines. When you see a duck-rabbit as a duck, you focus on the duck's face, and the rest of the image fades, and conversely when you see the figure as a rabbit. When this happens, the intermediate-level representation loses resolution in the regions that are not relevant to the interpretation. Experimental evidence is consistent with this interpretation. Chambers and Reisberg (1985) asked subjects to memorize a picture of a duck-rabbit without telling them that it was an ambiguous figure. They then asked subjects to identify the picture they had seen from an array of three choices: one was the original, one had been altered in the region of the rabbit's face, and the other had been altered in the region of the duck's face (see figure 14). Subjects who had interpreted the picture as a duck immediately ruled out the image that had been altered in the duck's face but were at chance in deciding between the other two, and conversely for those who had construed the picture as a rabbit. This suggests that subjects stored an intermediate-level representation that was altered by attention. When we interpret a duck-rabbit, we focus on the facial features corresponding to our interpretation, and the rest fades away.

These findings show that conceptualization can influence perception in dramatic ways: there are shifts toward prototypicality, verbal labeling, generation of associated images, and allocation of attention to category-relevant features. This may look like evidence for expansionism, but that would be a bad inference. Crucially, none of these effects requires postulation of distinctively cognitive phenomenology. In principle, someone who had no concept of ducks could, with careful contrivance, have a perceptual experience akin to the one that we have when we interpret a duck-rabbit as a duck. The top-down effects all involve the imposition of further sensory information or an allocation of attention to sensory features. There is nothing essentially cognitive in the resulting unambiguous image. Thus, we can fully account for the phenomenology of placing an ambiguous image under a concept without assuming that conceptualization introduces nonsensory features.

2.2. IMAGELESS THOUGHTS

Let's move now from concepts to thoughts. In some ways, this step should be trivial, since thoughts are said to be combinations of concepts. I have claimed that concepts can be conscious by means of sensory images that have no distinctively cognitive phenomenal qualities. If so, the same may be true of thoughts. We can render a thought conscious by forming an image

FIGURE 14 Test your memory. Which one of these is the one in figure 13? How many can you rule out easily? (Adapted from Chambers and Reisberg, 1995, with permission.)

of what it represents. I think that such images have no distinctively cognitive phenomenal qualities. Expansionists demur. They claim that the phenomenology of thought outstrips the sensory. One way to argue for this is to find thoughts that lack associated imagery but are nevertheless available to consciousness.

A century ago, imageless thoughts were a major topic of debate in psychology. Introspectionists such as Wilhelm Wundt and Edward Titchener claimed that all thoughts were imagistic and that psychological science should consist of eliciting subjective reports about the images that occur during cognitive tasks. This view was challenged by Oswald Külpe in Würzburg, who claimed that thought could be imageless. He based this conclusion on studies by his colleague Karl Marbe in which subjects were asked to assess which of two weights was heavier. Marbe's subjects often reported having what he called *Bewusstseinslage*, or conscious attitudes—feelings such as vacillation, hesitation, and doubt—but no images. Titchener quickly challenged the results, saying that his subjects reported kinesthetic images when he tried to replicate the study, and the accompanying epistemic attitudes, as we will see below, can be explained in emotional terms.

The debate did not end there, however. The issue was taken up again by George Stout, one of the early editors of *Mind*, who coined the term *imageless thought* but later denied that such things can exist (see Angell, 1911). The greatest champion of imageless thoughts was R. S. Woodworth of Columbia University, whose arguments anticipate much of the contemporary discussion. Woodworth acknowledged the limitations of Külpe's arguments and tried to improve on them. In his experiments, he would ask people to answer questions and then report on any images they formed. For example: Which is more delightful, the smell of a rose or its appearance? What is the difference between similarity and congruity? What substances are more costly than gold? Many people reported that they were arriving at answers without use of imagery. For example, in response to the question about what costs more than gold, one woman answered, "Diamonds," and said, "I had no visual image of the diamond; the thought of diamonds was there before the sound of the word" (Woodworth, 1906: 704).

These Woodworth experiments will not move the restrictivist. It's easy to suppose that his subjects are simply wrong about their own mental states. The woman may well have visualized diamonds, despite her insistence to the contrary. Indeed, the failure of introspection in cases just like this led to the end of introspectionist psychology. Titchener's subjects always reported images, and Woodworth's did not, suggesting that introspectionist results could not be replicated in a way that science demands. Modern measurement techniques now suggest that Titchener's subjects were more likely right. The mere reading of a word spontaneously prompts mental imagery (Chao et al., 1999), so the woman who claimed that she thought "Diamonds" without imaging them was probably mistaken.

Woodworth may have realized this, and he did not rest his case entirely on introspection. He has other arguments for imageless thoughts. One of these anticipated an argument in Dennett (1969) by sixty years. In 1907, Woodworth's colleague Edward Thorndike had asked students to visualize the front of Columbia's library, but even those who reported having vivid images were unable to report simple facts such as the number of columns. Woodworth (1915) suggests that people may be wrong to think that their images are copies of experiences, and he hints that maybe when people take themselves to be using images, they are actually relying on stored descriptions, which leave out details that would be apparent in any genuine picture. The argument threatens those who claim that conscious thoughts are always imagistic, by showing that even when people are instructed to use imagery and report using imagery, they may be relying on something else entirely. But opponents of imageless thought need not give in so easily. They can explain the uncountable columns in several ways: images may be blurry, they may omit details just as vision does, and they may fade too rapidly to report accurately. Forming an image is often easier than inspecting it; if you look at a cage, you may see it vividly but have difficulty counting the bars.

Woodworth (1906: 707) suggests another argument for imageless thought when he notes, "The thought of the object is not the image, for the image may change while the same object is thought of." This is a bit like Descartes's argument that we can be aware that an object is the same piece of wax even as it is melted and deformed, suggesting that we have an idea of wax that goes beyond imagery. Woodworth takes this a step further, adding that the idea of an object "is as substantial an element of thought as the image, and there is no absurdity in the notion that it may be present alone." Once we grant that ideas transcend images, we should suppose that they can exist without images.

This is an ingenious argument, but it can be rejected. First, the connective tissue that helps us recognize that successive images are images of the same object may be entirely unconscious. Reflecting on Descartes's example, it's far from clear that there is anything in consciousness that can qualify as a representation of wax as such as we watch a piece transform. Moreover, we don't need to postulate a single object representation that unites the successive images of wax. We can just as easily suppose that the mind tracks the object by its continuous spatiotemporal trajectory—something that infants readily do with no regard to structural continuity (Xu and Carey, 1996). By tracking objects in this way, we store knowledge of how they change, and we can use memory traces of object transformations to recognize two things as the same, even if they look different. We do not need some constant mental item to recognize that successive images correspond to one object; rather, observers can use knowledge of permissible transformations to treat successive images as belonging together.

Woodworth's most powerful argument for imageless thought draws attention to the fact that some thoughts represent facts that are difficult to represent imagistically. As an example, he offers his own recollection that a speaker at a meeting was exaggerating and that the speaker was acting in his capacity as chair of a committee (Woodworth, 1915). Since these features have no characteristic appearance, Woodworth concludes that the memories are not entirely imagistic. But this claim neglects the possibility that the relevant features were present in the form of verbal imagery. We might say to ourselves in silent speech that the speaker was exaggerating or serving as chair.

I suspect that verbal imagery can explain every instance of conscious thought that cannot be accounted for by appeal to images of the contents of our thoughts (what I will sometimes call simulations). Inner speech is incessant and implicated in many aspects of cognition (Hurlburt, 1990; Carruthers, 2002a; Morin, 2005). It is also known to be underwritten by the brain mechanisms involved in speech production and perception (Shergill et al., 2001). Given the conspicuous presence of silent speech in the stream of consciousness, it seems likely that we often come to know what we are thinking by hearing inner statements of the sentences that we would use to express our thoughts.

I don't mean to suggest that words alone constitute *understanding*. Comprehending that someone is the chair of a committee, for example, involves a complex set of norms and expectations, such as the expectation that the chair will lead the discussion and a granting of permission to do so. These things may affect phenomenology. For example, if someone who isn't chair tries to take control, witnesses may feel annoyed or outraged. But the totality of these complex expectations and norms will not be brought fully into consciousness at each moment. The verbal label ("that person is chair") can serve as a mental shorthand, consolidating a complex concept into a single sound ("chair"). Words serve as placeholders for ideas that cannot be experienced all at once, and through habit, inner speech becomes a way of registering complex thoughts in consciousness. Thus, the claim here is not that verbal imagery constitutes thought comprehension but only that, as a matter of fact, verbal images are often the way thoughts present themselves to us in consciousness, as a kind of shorthand.

This commonsense suggestion is effective against some recent arguments for expansionism. One of the most ambitious recent arguments comes from David Pitt (2004). He notes that we often have conscious access to what we are thinking. We know the content of our thoughts, and we can distinguish one thought from another and from noncognitive mental states. Pitt uses these claims to infer that thoughts must have a characteristic phenomenology. He thinks that this phenomenology outstrips mere imagistic simulations (because, e.g., thoughts often have contents that are more fine-grained or abstract than the images that might happen to co-occur with them). The argument is clever, but there is a natural reply: we know what we are thinking by means of verbal imagery. The impression that we can distinguish one thought from another and from other mental states can be easily explained based on the assumption that we identify thoughts by inner speech. Sentences can be distinguished from other forms of imagery, and distinct thoughts can be distinguished verbally, even when they might be visualized in similar ways (compare "The cat is on the mat" and "The mat is under the cat"). The claim, again, is not that words constitute comprehension but that they are handy bookkeepers that tell us what we are thinking under conditions when imagining thought contents in some other way might be difficult or inefficient. Pitt, of course, anticipates this verbal-imagery reply and offers a rejoinder, which I will take up in the next section. For now, let us settle on the conclusion that alleged examples of *imageless* thoughts either rest on dubious appeals to introspection or can be explained by supposing that cognitive phenomenology often takes the form of verbal imagery. The proponent of expansionism must show that verbal images are not up to the task.

2.3. LANGUAGELESS THOUGHTS

I have just been suggesting that some seemingly imageless thoughts may actually be cases in which we lack imagistic simulations of what our thoughts represent but have verbal imagery of the words that we would use to express them. Expansionists doubt this claim. In this section, I want to consider several arguments that they have levied against efforts to equate cognitive phenomenology with inner speech.

The first argument that I will consider comes from Pitt (2004). As we just saw, he argues for expansionism by noting that people have conscious awareness of what they are thinking. Conceding this, I suggested that such awareness characteristically takes the form of verbally imagery. Pitt is not convinced. He notes, first, that we have immediate acquaintance with our thoughts in a noninferential way. We don't need to extrapolate what we are thinking by experiencing something else. Pitt then notes that thoughts cannot be *constituted* by sentences. After all, words have their meanings arbitrarily (see also Woodworth, 1906: 706). If consciousness of thoughts is direct, and sentences aren't thoughts, then it follows that the conscious experience of thoughts can't be an experience of sentences.

Both premises in Pitt's reply can be challenged. The claim that we have noninferential access to our thoughts is surely right at some level: phenomenologically, it doesn't seem that we figure out what we are thinking by an act of inference. But it doesn't follow that we are directly acquainted with our thoughts. We might be directly acquainted with sentences and simply treat them as if they are thoughts without trying to infer what they mean. On this suggestion, sentences *stand in for* thoughts, and we are so habituated to this that we feel as if we are experiencing thoughts themselves. Alternatively, one can challenge Pitt's second premise and say that sentences do not merely stand in for thoughts but actually constitute thoughts. When we produce sentences in silent speech, they issue forth from unconscious representations that correspond to what those sentences mean (these are perceptual representations if empiricism is true). Sentences inherit their truth conditions from the unconscious ideas that generate them. So produced, these sentences are not arbitrary marks but rather meaningful symbols. If we define a thought as a mental state that represents a proposition, then mental sentences qualify as thoughts (see also Carruthers, 2002b).

Expansionists sometimes resist the equation of thoughts and inner speech by arguing that under some circumstances, we become conscious of a thought before becoming conscious of a corresponding sentence. Woodworth (1906: 704) makes this case by appeal to the phenomenology of conversation, in which, he claims, we become aware of our thoughts before we find the words to express them. A modern version of this argument has been put forward by Siewert (1998), who draws attention to the fact that thoughts sometimes suddenly occur to us in a way that doesn't seem like the inner rehearsal of words or construction of images. His favorite example is the sudden realization while driving to work that he left his briefcase at home.

Woodworth and Siewert want us to believe that we experience such thoughts in an immediate way prior to any images or sentences. They both call on examples in which thoughts come unbidden and quickly: the steady flow of conversation, a sudden realization. But these examples will not convince restrictivists. First of all, from introspection alone, it's far from obvious that there is any conscious thought prior to the sentences we utter in rapid conversation. We simply hear ourselves replying to our interlocutors. And in the case of sudden realizations, it's far from obvious that the phenomenology outstrips imagery and inner speech. While driving to the office, one might anticipate, with faint dread, a day of grading papers; this involves formation of an imagined scenario, in which one retrieves papers from a briefcase; that simulation triggers a recalled image of the briefcase standing by the front door at home; a panicked glance confirms that the briefcase is not in the car; this prompts the expletive, "Damn! I left my suitcase." I don't think Siewert has identified a clear case of a thought that appears unbidden in consciousness without accompanying imagery.

Unsurprisingly, Siewert does not rest his case for expansionism on introspective intuitions about a forgotten briefcase. He offers a battery of powerful arguments against the allegation that inner speech can explain the phenomenology of thought. The arguments all have a similar form: he generates cases in which we change our interpretation of a word or phrase and suggests that when this happens, there is a corresponding change in phenomenal qualities (Siewert, 1998; Siewert, 2009; see also Pitt, 2004; Siegel, 2006). For example, Siewert invites readers to repeat a word until it becomes meaningless, suggesting that this will alter the phenomenology. Or consider the change that occurs after learning the meaning of a word in a foreign language; *Eichhörnchen* is just a funny sound until we know it's the German word for squirrel. Siewert also treats us to lovely examples of lexical ambiguities, as in "I hope the food's not too hot for you," which we might interpret as a warning about temperature before realizing that the meal is very spicy. There are also cases of syntactic ambiguities or sentences that are difficult to parse. Pitt (2004) gives us the garden-path sentence, "The boat sailed down the river sank," which seems un-grammatical at first but then gets resolved by treating "sailed" as a noun modifier rather than a main verb. In each of these cases, the very same words give rise to distinct phenomenology, suggesting that phenomenology cannot be exhausted by inner speech.

This is a clever argumentative strategy, and the introspective intuitions are robust. But committed restrictivists need not surrender. In each of these cases, changes in interpretation may be accompanied by changes in associated im-agery. When we repeat a word, we go from imagining what the word represents to focusing on the way the word sounds. When we learn the meaning of a for-eign word, we can imagine its referent, along with sentences that we might utter in response to that word. When we shift from one meaning of an ambiguous sentence to another, we alter images and action plans (it's useless to blow on spicy food). When we hear garden-path sentences, we experience confusion, and then, on parsing them, there can be a change in imagery. When "sailed" is construed as a main verb in "The boat sailed down the river sank," we might visualize a boat that first glides down a river and then sinks; but when "sailed" is interpreted as part of the noun phrase, we might omit the gliding part and just imagine a boat sinking.

The examples fail because they do not rule out the possibility of changes in nonverbal imagery. They would be effective only against the person who claimed that verbal imagery *exhausts* cognitive phenomenology. But that posi-tion is not plausible. Evidence from short-lived episodes of aphasia clearly demonstrates that conscious thought continues in the absence of speech. For example, Lecours and Joanette (1980) describe a patient who was able to locate a hotel and order food at a restaurant during an episode of transient aphasia. There is also little reason to deny that some infraverbal animals have conscious thoughts, as when a chimpanzee figures out how to pull termites out of a hole using a slender stick. On any plausible restrictivist view, the phenomenology of thought is underwritten by both verbal and nonverbal imagery. Thus, expan-sionists face the difficult challenge of having to find cases in which the phenom-enal character of a thought transcends both of these rich sources.

That challenge is very difficult to meet. I can think of no examples that are even plausible. For any pair of thoughts that differ phenomenologically, there always seem be sensory features that distinguish the two. If you doubt this claim, try the following exercise. Visualize a baseball bat while saying the word "bat" in silent speech. Now, try as hard as you can to interpret that word as representing the flying mammals. It's not easy, and if you are like me, success comes only by visualizing one of the animals alongside the baseball bat and binding the word in attention to that image. If you suppress imagery of the animal (or associated verbal descriptions), your inner utterance of the word "bat" cannot take on any phenomenal character that would lead you to experience it as denoting anything other than the vividly visualized piece of sporting equipment. Consistent with this, Lee and Federmeier (2006) measured brain activity as they presented subjects with ambiguous words, such as "duck," which can be interpreted as a noun or a verb. When primed to interpret "duck" as a noun, activity was posterior, and visual areas were detected, and when interpreted as a verb, there were frontal activations consistent with motor commands. Here imagery, including felt images of the body in motion, may be recruited to disambiguate words, just as earlier we saw how words might disambiguate imagery (e.g., "The mat is under the cat").

If this picture is right, inner speech and nonverbal imagery are mutually supporting resources that can each pick up for the other's limitations. Words can help us experience very abstract thoughts or thoughts that arise too quickly to simulate in imagination. They can also disambiguate images, allowing us to think of Tweedledee when entertaining a visual image that equally resembles Tweedledum. Nonverbal images help us disambiguate words and simulate what our words represent. For most of us, both elements are constant components of conscious thought.

2.4 ATTITUDE DIFFERENTIATION

I have been suggesting that cognitive phenomenology can be exhaustively accommodated by the phenomenology of inner speech and sensory simulations of what our thoughts represent. These resources provide a powerful mix, but there is still one thing that they leave out. Inner speech and simulations give phenomenal coloring to the *contents* of our thoughts, but they do not encompass the *manner* of our thoughts. They reveal what we are thinking but not how. In philosophical parlance, thoughts are propositional attitudes, and we can have different attitudes toward the same content. We can believe that something is the case, desire it, doubt it, or fear it. These attitudes are often distinguishable in consciousness. When asked whether a particular candidate will win an upcoming election, we can immediately recognize whether we are confident, doubtful, or terrified. In all cases, the inner speech and associated visualization may be the same, but the attitude differs in palpable ways.

In the late nineteenth century, members of the Würzburg school of psychology regarded this as evidence for an imageless component in conscious thought. Attitudes correspond to Marbe's *Bewusstseinslage*. Recently, Peacocke (2007) has also suggested that attitude differentiation raises trouble for the view that all consciousness is perceptual. But restrictivists have an obvious resource for explaining the phenomenology of conscious attitudes: they can appeal to accompanying emotions.

In some cases, it's quite obvious that emotions contribute to the phenomenology of attitudes. Take fearing. The thespian who feels that she will forget her lines certainly experiences an emotion, and that emotion is (as suggested earlier) clearly felt in the body. Stagefright is manifest through butterflies in the stomach, shallow breathing, perspiration, and a racing heart. Likewise for other emotional attitudes, as when we are elated, annoyed, or sad that something is the case.

Emotions may also explain the phenomenology of desire. This is most obvious in the case of basic drives such as hunger and lust. When I desire that dinner be served soon, I may feel a hollow hankering in my gut. But even more cognitive desires may be accompanied by felt emotions. If I want it to be the case that my candidate wins, I will feel nervous anticipation, and the thought of victory will instill delight, while the thought of defeat will usher in waves of despair. On experiencing any of these fluctuating feelings, I may report that I desire a victory. There is no one feeling of desire but rather a family of anticipatory emotions.

Belief might seem a hard case. It's not obvious that it feels like anything to believe that grass is green above and beyond the visualization of that proposition. But I actually think that many beliefs come along with attitudinal feels. We can feel confident or certain. It feels like something to have a hunch or to suspect that something is the case. There are also emotions of doubt: uncertainty, incredulity, hostile dismissal. My suspicion, though highly speculative, is that all of these states are felt as emotions, which, like other emotions, are constituted by bodily expressions. We knit our brows in doubt and pound our fists in confidence. Further evidence for this proposal comes from the simple fact that doxastic attitudes can be expressed through intonation; we can vocalize the difference between an assertion, an interrogative, and even a tentative speculation. These speech sounds exemplify differences in bodily states.

Doxastic feelings belong to a larger category of epistemic emotions (Prinz, 2007a). They belong to a class that includes curiosity, interest, awe, wonder, familiarity, novelty, puzzlement, confusion, and surprise—all of which can give rise to corresponding propositional attitudes. With the exception of surprise, these have been woefully neglected in recent research, although they were once widely discussed. For example, Descartes (1649/1988) lists wonder as a basic emotion. In contemporary psychology, epistemic emotions are largely ignored, but there is a growing literature on one interesting example: the feeling of knowing (Hart, 1965). Memory researchers have noted that sometimes people clearly recall a prior stimulus, and sometimes they can't recall experiencing it, but they have a feeling of knowing that it was there. This is sometimes called metamemory—a memory that something is in memory. The feeling of knowing is a sense of assurance that arises without vivid recall. I conjecture that the feeling of knowing is an emotion. If so, it may be implemented, as other emotions are, in brain circuits that are involved in body perception (see Woody and Szechtman, 2002). There has been no empirical exploration of the link between the feeling of knowing and bodily perception, but fMRI studies reveal that it is associated with action in the ventromedial prefrontal cortex, which is a main player in embodied emotional responses (Schnyer, Nicholls, and Verfaellie, 2005).

In making these claims, I am not trying to suggest that attitudes are nothing but emotions. Each attitude may correspond to a complex functional role, making distinctive contributions to decision making. Their subtle workings may unfold in time outside the spotlight of consciousness. My claim is only that we may be able to distinguish some of these attitudes phenomenologically by virtue of accompanying emotions. Those who claim that attitude differentiation is incompatible with restrictivism must show that attitudes can be distinguished without felt emotions, which, I have suggested, can be characterized as perceptions of bodily states. This is largely uncharted territory, but the emotional account of felt attitudes has enough initial plausibility to defuse the objection from *Bewusstseinslage*.

3. Restrictivists' Revenge

3.1. EXPANSION AS ILLUSION

The vast majority of consciousness research has focused on perceptual experience and, even more narrowly, on vision. In recent years, that has started to change. There has been a welcome tide of interest in the phenomenology of thought. That interest has spawned an outbreak of expansionism. Restrictivists might try to stave off expansion by denying that cognition has any phenomenology, but that's an unpromising course, because there are both theoretical reasons for thinking that we have conscious thoughts (deriving from empiricism) and strong introspective evidence. I have been arguing that restrictivists should resist expansion in another way. We should try to explain the phenomenology of thought by appealing to inner speech, simulations of what thoughts represent, and emotions. These resources can all be characterized as forms of sensory imagery, and they are rich enough, I've argued, to accommodate introspective evidence for conscious thoughts.

In making this case, I have been on the defensive, blocking expansionist arguments for distinctively cognitive phenomenology. By way of conclusion, I want to go on the offensive by offering a diagnosis of expansionism and some reasons for being skeptical about the expansionist program.

First, the diagnosis. Those who still think that phenomenology outstrips the sensory may be subject to a family of introspective illusions. We often think that introspective access to our conscious states is perfectly accurate, but this is not the case. Having an experience and reporting what it's like are two different things, and the latter can be prone to errors. We saw some examples of these kinds of errors in chapter 2. People who think that perceptual consciousness resides at a high level may be mistaking experiences that represent such properties (an elliptical experience represents roundness) for experiences that have corresponding phenomenal quality (a round experience). People who think we are conscious of certain constancies (such as vertical lines) are mistaking unconscious identification of permissible transformations for a constancy in experience.

I think that the same kinds of errors may lie behind the impression that there is distinctively cognitive phenomenology. When Siegel says that we can have experiences corresponding to natural-kind properties, she may be mistaking experiences that represent such properties for experiences that have corresponding phenomenal quality. When Woodworth says that consciousness of an object can remain constant as our image of the object changes, he may be mistaking unconscious identification of permissible transformations for a constancy in experience. When Siewert says that the experience of a word changes when we shift interpretations, he may be mistaking one kind of experience (associated imagery) for another (alleged cognitive phenomenology). When Peacocke says that we experience propositional attitude types, he may be mistaking the effects of those attitudes (emotions) for their causes (functional roles). When Pitt says that we can't distinguish thoughts by inner speech, he may be misinterpreting mental states that constitute thoughts (silent sentences) as mere effects.

Of course, these authors provide arguments for expansionism. I am not trying to say that they are simply confused. I am merely suggesting that there are introspective illusions that may bolster the intuitive plausibility of expansionism. For some people, expansionism seems *obvious*, and that fact needs to be explained. The explanation on offer here is that introspection is subject to certain kinds of illusions, which lead us to posit features in experience that are not actually there. If we guard against these illusions, the impression that phenomenology outstrips the sensory may subside.

3.2. THE CASE AGAINST EXPANSION

The battle between restrictivists and expansionists often collapses into a clash of introspective intuitions. Restrictivists give their strategies for explaining alleged cases of cognitive phenomenology, and expansionists object that these strategies do not do justice to what their experiences are like. In this debate, expansionists are usually on the offensive, with restrictivists working defensively to accommodate hard cases. In this section, I will try to break the stalemate and provide restrictivists with some ammunition against expansion. There are at least five reasons for thinking that restrictivism is preferable even if introspection does not settle the debate.

The first argument was already intimated above. To make a convincing case for cognitive phenomenology, expansionists should find an example in which the only difference between two phenomenologically distinct cases is a cognitive difference. But so far, no clear, uncontroversial case has been identified. This is a striking failure given the ease with which we can find clear cases of sensory qualities. If every phenomenal difference has a plausible candidate for an attendant sensory difference, the simplest theory would say that sensory qualities, which everyone agrees exist, exhaust phenomenology.

The second argument points to the fact that alleged cognitive qualities differ profoundly from sensory qualities in that the latter can be isolated in imagination. If I see an ultramarine sky, I can focus on the nature of that hue and imagine it filling my entire field with no other phenomenology. Even in cases in which we experience one sensory quale among others, we can bring it into focal attention and marvel at its characteristic qualities. In contrast, it seems impossible to isolate our thoughts. For example, it doesn't seem possible to think about the fact that the economy is in decline without any words or other sensory imagery. If other qualia can be isolated, why not cognitive qualia? Siewert (2009) tries to resist this commitment, saying that the proponent of distinctively cognitive phenomenology need not deny that all conscious thoughts have imagistic components. But this may be cheating. Shapes, sounds, and smells can all be recombined and, when conditions are right, experienced without other conscious qualities. There are also selective deficits in which one sensory system is destroyed, leaving others intact, but there is no known case of global sensory disruption that leaves cognitive phenomenology intact. Given this, it is ad hoc to presume that cognitive qualities cannot be experienced in isolation. The elusiveness of purely cognitive qualities suggests that cognitive phenomenology is an illusion.

Third, as noted in chapter 1, it is axiomatic in psychology that we have poor access to cognitive processes. For example, when comparing three identical objects, people prefer the one on the right, but they don't realize it (Nisbett and Wilson, 1977). What we experience consciously is, at best, the outcome, a hedonic preference for the rightmost object, together perhaps with some confabulated justifications of the choice, which may be experienced through inner speech. Given the fact that cognitive processes are characteristically inaccessible, the claim that we can be conscious of our thoughts is perplexing. The perplexity is compounded by the fact that many cognitive processes are presumed to involve multiple representational steps, as when we reason our way to a conclusion. But we are notoriously bad at retracing these steps. This suggests that higher cognition is an unconscious affair and that we gain knowledge of our thoughts only when they cast a dim shadow on our perceptual systems in the form of imagery and verbal narratives.

A fourth argument follows on this one. The incessant use of inner speech is puzzling if we have conscious access to our thoughts. Why bother putting all of this into words when we are merely thinking to ourselves without any intention to communicate our thoughts to others? I suspect that language is a major boon precisely because it can compensate for the fact that thinking is unconscious. It converts cognition into sensory imagery and allows us to take the reins.

Finally, expansionism seems to dash hopes for a unified theory of consciousness. If only one kind of mental state can be conscious—intermediate-level perceptions—then there is hope of finding a single mechanism of consciousness. I think that mechanism has been identified; I have argued that perception is conscious when and only when we attend. But there is little reason to think that a single mechanism could explain how both perception and thought can be conscious, if cognitive phenomenology is not reducible to perception. This is especially clear if the mechanism is attention. There is no empirical evidence for the view that we can attend to our thoughts. There are no clear cognitive analogues of pop-out, cuing, resolution enhancement, fading, multiobject monitoring, or inhibition of return. Thoughts can direct attention, but we can't attend to them. Or, rather, thoughts become objects of attention only when they are converted into images, words, and emotions. When we encode a thought in working memory, it is by means of these sensory analogues. Expansionists might explain the fact that thinking does not show the patterns characteristic of attention by proposing that thoughts and sensations attain consciousness in different ways; they might adopt the AIR theory for sensations and another account for conscious thoughts. But if different mechanisms are involved, it's not clear what it means to say that both thoughts and sensations can be conscious. Disunity threatens to make expansionism look like an unwitting pun.

I conclude that the evidence for expansionism is at best inconclusive and that the evidence against it is considerable. Efforts to identify clear cases of cognitive phenomenology are open to alternative interpretations. There is also some sensory event that can be credited with our impression that we are conscious of thoughts. The very fact that it is difficult to find a clear case is telling. There is little room for skepticism about sensory phenomenology. To deny the qualitative experience of perceptual states would be about as radical a claim as one can make in philosophy. But there is nothing radical about denying cognitive phenomenology. This marked contrast in the extent to which sensory and alleged cognitive phenomenology are manifest provides reason for doubting the latter. This, together with the other arguments that I have just sketched, casts doubt on the expansionist program. It suggests that all consciousness may be contained within perceptual systems. In the next two chapters, we will see two more threats to the restrictivist program, but I will argue that neither succeeds.

6

Why Are We Conscious? Action without Enaction

According to the AIR theory, all conscious states are attentionally modulated intermediate-level perceptual representations. But why? What is special about these states? Do they serve any specific function? Does possession of consciousness do anything for us? These questions about function become more tractable with the AIR theory in hand. We can discover what consciousness is for by investigating the functions of intermediate-level representations and attention or, better yet, their conjunction. What benefits are conferred by having attention applied at this level of representation?

To anticipate, my answer to this question involves action. Consciousness is, in some sense, for acting in the world. This conjecture, which I will refine and defend below, can be situated between two more extreme views about the relationship between consciousness and action. On the one hand, there are theories that make the relationship *more* intimate. Such theories say that consciousness is not just for acting; conscious episodes are motoric in nature—they are realizations of sensory motor skills. One might express this extreme view with the slogan "Consciousness *is* action." Defenders of this "enactive" approach express this as a thesis about the nature of consciousness, rather than its function, but it relates to our function question insofar as it asserts that consciousness and action are inseparable. In probing the question about function, it will be important to see whether enactivism is true. On the other hand, there are theories that make the relationship between consciousness and action *less* intimate. These theories say that consciousness serves a function unrelated to action, and action is controlled by processes that are not available for consciousness. In a slogan, this extreme view says, "Consciousness *sidesteps* action." The most influential recent version of this approach centers around the hypothesis that vision divides into two streams, dorsal and ventral, which underwrite visually guided action and consciousness respectively and independently. I will call this the inactive theory of consciousness. A major goal of this chapter is to offer a critical assessment of these two extremes.

I will start with the extreme views: enactive theories and inactive theories. I will then offer a positive account of the relationship between consciousness and action, and I will argue that this account can provide an answer to the question of what consciousness is for.

1. Does Consciousness Depend on Action?

1.1. EVIDENCE FOR ENACTIVE THEORIES

Cognitive science has traditionally assumed a tripartite division of the mind. First, there are input systems, or perception; then there are central systems, where thinking takes place; and finally, there are output systems, which control motor responses or actions. Susan Hurley (1998) called this the "classical sandwich" model of the mind, with thought nestled between perception and action. Each layer is presumed to be independent of the others. Over the last quarter-century, there have been various efforts to reconfigure this traditional picture. For example, concept empiricists have argued that thought is not independent of perception and action but rather involves the offline redeployment of perceptual and motor representations in the form of imagery (Barsalou, 1999; Prinz, 2002). Situated roboticists have argued that the mind is made up of numerous simple input-output systems rather than one sandwich (Brooks, 1991). Members of the enactive perception movement have focused on the boundary between inputs and outputs, arguing that action and perception are inextricably bound.

This basic idea behind the enactive perception movement has been around for some time. It has adherents in cybernetics (MacKay, 1962), behaviorist-tinged philosophy (Ryle, 1949), embodied phenomenology (Merleau-Ponty, 1962), and ecological psychology (Gibson, 1979). Gibson's suggestion that we literally see the motoric affordances of objections can be read as a precursor to the enactive view, but the movement really got off the ground with the work of Francisco Varela and his collaborators, who argue that Gibson does not go far enough (Maturana and Varela, 1973; Varela, Thompson, and Rosch, 1991; Thompson, 1995). Gibson emphasized invariant features of the optical array as a starting place for vision, implying that the environment has a pregiven structure that is picked up by the organism. Varela (1991) coined the term *enactive perception* to suggest, in contrast, that organism and environment are cocreatures. The features of the environment to which an organism responds depend on the ongoing activity in the organism. Vision is principally concerned not with recovering objects as they exist in external reality but with "bringing forth" objects in a context-sensitive way. Varela's term *enaction* is meant to stress organism/environment codetermination, and it contrasts with the idea that vision represents ("re-presents") reality. But the term also incorporates the idea that vision involves physical activity, or action. This theme has been echoed in other work (e.g., Ballard, 1991; Cotterill, 1998; Hurley, 1998; and Mandik, 1999). Here I want to focus on the work of Noë (2005) and O'Regan and Noë (2001), whose version of the enactive approach is among the most developed and influential in current discussions of perception and consciousness.

Noë adopts the term *enaction*, although he does not take over the entire Varela program, and sometimes refers to his own approach as an "actionist" or "sensorimotor" theory of vision (Noë, 2010; see also Taraborelli and Mossio, 2008). I will follow Noë (2005) in using the term *enactive perception* to refer to any theory that says that perception is partially constituted by motor responses, that is, movements or neural states that orchestrate movements. O'Regan and Noë (2001) offer an especially lucid exposition and defense. The central concept in their theory is sensorimotor knowledge or, more specifically, knowledge of sensorimotor contingencies. Organisms have nonpropositional knowledge of the way movement alters sensory states—either the moments of the perceived object or movements of the perceiving body. For example, we know that a round plate will become increasingly elliptical in shape as its orientation becomes more orthogonal to our eyes. O'Regan and Noë argue that seeing a plate requires active exercise of such sensorimotor knowledge. They say that "experience of vision is actually constituted by a mode of exploring the environment" and that "skillful activity (consisting of behavior and sensory stimulation) is the experience" (2001: 946).

Notice that in these passages, O'Regan and Noë use the word *experience*, implying that the sensorimotor view is a theory of consciousness. That's a bit misleading. When they explicitly remark on how consciousness arises, their theory is actually similar to the one I've been defending. They say that consciousness arises when perception is used "for the purposes of thought and planning" (2001: 944). They even suggest that it arises by means of attention. This sounds very much like an attention-to-working-memory view, although they may think that consciousness requires encoding in working memory rather than mere accessibility. The key point is that O'Regan and Noë's enactive approach is not a theory of how we become conscious but a theory of what we are conscious of—a theory of conscious contents. They argue that we are visually conscious of sensorimotor contingencies. This contrasts with the part of the AIR theory that says that we are conscious only of intermediate-level perceptual representations, which implies that motor representations are not conscious.

I should note that O'Regan and Noë also depart from the spirit of the AIR theory in another way: they argue that conscious states cannot be mapped onto neural correlates. They propose that consciousness supervenes on both mind and world. I will not discuss this radical claim here (see Prinz, 2006b; 2008). Suffice it to say that the effort to map contents of experience onto brain states has been tremendously successful. Every aspect of experience that we look for, from illusory contours to motion aftereffects and color constancy, can be correlated with brain activity, and there is to date no known case of two qualitatively different visual states that correspond to the same brain state. As far as we can tell, every difference in experience corresponds to a measurable difference in neural activity, and there can be rich experiences in the absence of sensory inputs, as when we dream or undergo direct brain stimulation. Moreover, the time course of consciousness differs from the external events that we perceive, occurring with a slight delay, confirming that brain states, not world states, ground experience. Let me put this radical aspect of the O'Regan and Noë program to one side and focus on the claim that contents of visual experience are constituted, in part, by motor responses.

It's important to see that the enactive view does not state that motor responses simply influence visual experience. Rather, it states that such responses are prerequisites for experience. Absent such responses, Noë (2005) says that we would be experientially blind. That is a very strong claim. Call it *strong enactivism*. Weaker enactive views are, of course, also possible. One might hold the view that motor responses are not necessary for visual experience in general but that they are necessary for certain aspects of ordinary visual experience. Call this *weak enactivism*. Most enactivists are strong enactivists, and when they advance evidence for the view, they hope to establish that conscious perception is *always* constituted by sensorimotor knowledge. I will present that evidence now. A complete review would take too long, so I'll focus on what I take to be the best empirical arguments for strong enactivism.

I will begin with four lines of evidence from O'Regan and Noë's (2001) seminal defense. First, standard theories of vision have difficulty explaining why the world around us seems stationary. On the standard picture, we visually sample bits of the world as our eyes shift, and we compile the results into a panoramic inner image. The problem with this is that the visual system is not very accurate at registering the speed and location of eye movements, so it is not clear how we would successfully place bits of information in the panoramic view. The enactive approach avoids the problem by proposing that the experience of stationarity is constituted by knowledge of how movements will affect sensations, rather than by an inner model. The world looks stationary because we know how sensations will change in a stationary world; for example, we expect certain sensory changes when our eyes move.

Second, enactivism offers an attractive explanation of change blindness. As we saw in chapter 3, change blindness is the common phenomenon of failing to notice even dramatic changes in the visual scene. Experiments show that if pictures are altered during saccades or between brief flickers, people can fail to notice even dramatic changes, such as objects that shrink, disappear, swap locations, or undergo color inversions. This is surprising, because traditional theories of perception suppose that visual experience involves the construction of richly detailed mental images. If such images exist, dramatic changes in visual inputs should be detectable. Enactivists avoid this puzzle by offering a different explanation of the experience of richness. The world looks rich to us because we can visually sample a richly detailed visual world. Experiential richness consists in our ability to shift gaze and perceive these details at will. The know-how that allows us to do this constitutes an experience of richness, even if, at any given moment, we've stored only sparse information about the perceived scene. By locating experience in sensorimotor knowledge rather than inner images, enactivists can accommodate the intuition that experience is rich without making change blindness mysterious.

Third, enactivists have been impressed by how people adapt to inverting lenses (Stratton, 1897). After several days of wearing lenses that make everything look upside down, people begin to see the world as if it were right-side up again. This is hard to explain with traditional theories of perception, because the lenses continue to produce inverted retinal images after adaptation; if experience were based on sensory images alone, the world should continue to look peculiar. But during adaptation, people learn new sensorimotor contingencies, reaching upward, for example, to touch a stimulus that would have appeared downward when the lenses were first put on. Mastery of these new contingencies could explain why experience changes over adaptation.

Fourth, enactivists have also sought support in research on tactile visual substitution systems (TVSS), which are used to help blind people navigate the world. These systems convert video signals into tactile sensations, generated by a small pad of pins, which press against some part of the body (Bach-y-Rita, 1972). When blind people wear eyeglasses affixed with a video-to-tactile converter, they can learn to discriminate some objects and avoid obstacles. Some report that it is as if they were seeing those objects and obstacles. This suggests that touch takes on visual qualities when we learn motor responses that allow it to function in a visual way.

The studies mentioned so far suggest that motor responses can influence visual experience and even generate visual qualities in the absence of visual inputs. If so, learning how to respond physically to the world can alter how it visually appears and may even be sufficient for having visual experiences. Other research suggests that motor responses are necessary. Perhaps the most often cited research is an old study by Held and Hein (1963), which examined the effects of inaction on the visual abilities of kittens (Hurley, 1998; Cotterill, 1998; Mandik, 1999). Held and Hein took two kittens that had not yet had experience with vision and attached them to an apparatus that allowed one to explore the world physically, while the other was placed in a cradle that prevented exploration. The kitten in the cradle was attached to the other, so it moved when the other did, but it could not move on its own and thus failed to learn how self-initiated movements affect the visual input. After some time in the apparatus, the mobile kitten developed normal visual abilities, but the inactive kitten did not, suggesting that animals cannot learn to see if they are not able to act. This is just what strong enactivism predicts.

There is also neuroscientific evidence for the enactive approach. Much of this is summarized by Hurley (1998), along with the foregoing behavioral evidence. Hurley points out that some of the cells in the brain that respond to visual stimuli also play a role in the control of action. The most studied examples are mirror neurons, which fire when viewing a manual action, such as grasping, and also when performing that action (Rizzolatti and Craighero, 2004). These cells challenge the traditional division between input systems and output systems and raise the possibility that brain states underlying visual experience may also code for action. Hurley also discusses a patient who suffers from paralysis of the eye muscles (Gallistel, 1980). When this person tries to shift his gaze to the left, his eyes won't move, but objects in front of him seem to jump to the right. Hurley suggests that the mere motor command must be causing this change in visual experience, since the input to his eyes remains constant. Hurley also discusses a patient who has undergone a commissurotomy, separating the two hemispheres of the brain. When the patient uses the right hemisphere to initiate an action in response to an object that has been perceived by the left hemisphere, the object suddenly disappears (Trevarthen, 1984). In Hurley's interpretation, this shows that visual consciousness is directly affected by motor commands; when a command is initiated by the hemisphere that has not seen the stimulus, the visual state in that hemisphere overrides the other hemisphere, causing the object to blink out of existence.

Enactivists claim that their account provides the best explanation of the empirical evidence summarized here. Collectively, these findings suggest that the relationship between perception and action is more intimate than has been assumed. Motor responses (such as intentions to act) affect what we see, and that suggests that such responses might be partially constitutive of visual experience. If motor responses are partially constitutive, it might turn out that they are necessary for some aspects of visual experience. Pushing this further, enactivists invite us to believe that without motor responses, it would not be possible to see, as the Held and Hein results suggest.

1.2. THE CASE AGAINST STRONG ENACTIVISM

Although it is impressive in breadth, the evidence that the enactivists present fails to provide a compelling case for their view, and there are good reasons to think that the view is untenable. I will begin this section with a critical assessment of the empirical findings just surveyed and then offer some reasons for doubting that visual experience of any kind depends on action.

Let's begin with the suggestion that sensorimotor knowledge provides our impression of a stationary world. To support the enactive view, it would have to be the case that motor responses make some kind of constitutive or necessary contribution to the visual experience of spatial stability. That seems unlikely. For one thing, it's far from obvious that we do, in fact, visually experience the world as stable or stationary. Visual qualia seem to change constantly, with every shift of gaze. A movie showing what it's like to see would not contain any prolonged stills. So the impression of stability is, arguably, not part of visual experience but determined instead by unconscious processes. Chief among those unconscious processes are those by which we detect constancies, ways in which the world remains constant despite changes in the retinal input. Enactivists sometimes imply that we need motor responses to register such constancies, but in fact, much of this work can be achieved within the visual system. There are cells in the visual pathway whose responses change as our eyes move and others that remain constant. Among those that remain constant, some retain information about objective location in space, such as cells in the high-level visual area LOC. Others are indifferent to spatial changes, such as cells in left fusiform gyrus (McKyton and Zohary, 2007; Vuilleumier et al., 2002). There is no reason to believe that these cells depend on motor activity to extract spatial constancies. The judgment that an object is stable can, in many cases, simply derive from the unconscious visual responses that remain constant despite the ephemeral visual changes that we experience.

This is not to say that there is no interaction between bodily responses and the ability to tell that objects are stable. The judgment that a visually perceived object is vertical with respect to the surface of the earth can be influenced by the vestibular system. When one moves from a standing position to a lying position, the vestibular system can help confirm that objects retain their orientation; floor lamps continue to seem vertical relative to the earth, even when the tilt in our heads makes them retinally horizontal, and this is because the vestibular system can register that the pole of the lamp remains perpendicular to the gravitational pull of the earth. Notice two things, however. First, the phenomenal experience of verticality may be somatic rather than visual—a vertical line viewed while lying down looks the way a horizontal line would when standing up, even though it *feels* vertical. Second, the vestibular system is not a motor system, so its contributions do not support the conjecture that motor responses are needed to perceive that the world is stable.

Admittedly, motor responses can make one important contribution to the perception of stability. In some cases, we use motor responses to determine whether a changing visual experience results from a change in the perceived stimulus or merely a change in our vantage point. If a visual change co-occurs with a motor response, we infer that the change comes from the body, not from the world. But it does not follow from this that motor responses contribute to visual phenomenology. It may be that we distinguish self-motion from object-motion by *unconscious prediction*: when we initiate motion, we unconsciously anticipate how external objects will change appearance, and when that prediction comes true, we interpret the change as self-caused, whereas we fail to form such precise prediction when changes are caused by movements in external objects. If this alternative is right, then perceived changes are actually experienced ambiguously, and unconscious inferences help us locate their source. This conjecture is borne out by the fact that people can easily make errors about the source of visual change. These errors are especially common when inner changes become unexpected (such as the movement of an afterimage) or when outer changes are expected (such as mistaking a still train for a moving one because you correctly anticipate its displacement). The unconscious-prediction explanation also implies that it is not motor responses per se that allow us to perceive self-motion but rather anticipation of sensory changes. If that's right, motor commands are not making a constitutive contribution to self-motion detection, even unconsciously. Moreover, even if they were contributing in a constitutive way on some occasions (e.g., even if we determined self-motion by directly monitoring motor commands rather than predicting the sensory changes that they bring about), motor commands would make that contribution only contingently. Changes in vestibular perception and proprioception along with distinctive patterns in the optic flow are often sufficient for determining whether a visual change is caused by self-motion or object-motion. Thus, a creature that spent a lifetime without ever initiating a motor command could still learn to distinguish cases in which a visual change was caused by the movement of its body (e.g., while in a moving car) and the movement of external objects.

The second line of evidence for enactivism appeals to change blindness. According to the argument, change blindness proves that visual inputs are not rich, even though they seem to be; thus, the sense of richness must have another source, namely our ability to explore the richly detailed world. The first premise of this argument turns out to be empirically false. Change blindness does not result from a failure to perceive rich details but rather from a failure to store those details in a way that makes them available for identifying changes. This can be demonstrated by priming studies. Silverman and Mack (2001) used arrays of letters in a change-blindness paradigm and found that letters whose disappearance went undetected nevertheless facilitated performance in a subsequent task in which subjects had to identify fragmented letters. Mitroff, Simons, and Levin (2005) obtained a similar result using arrays of objects; people often failed to notice when one object was switched for another one, but they could guess which object had disappeared when given a subsequent forced-choice task. In these studies, each object in a complex scene is perceived and primes semantic networks, even though few of the objects get encoded in working memory, which explains why people don't recognize when scenes change. Nevertheless, these objects may be *available* to working memory, which would explain why vision seems rich, even when memory is poor. There is no need here to appeal to sensorimotor knowledge. Indeed, it's not clear why the mere ability to sample the world would engender a sense of richness in the absence of rich sensory representations. The fact that I can open an opaque cookie jar does not make the jar look full.

The evidence from inverting lenses is also unconvincing. There is a natural explanation for the fact that after adaptation, people who wear inverting lenses come to report that the world seems right-side up. The "seeming" here is not visual. The world may look inverted, but relearning motor skills makes it possible to behave as if things had their standard orientation. Compare what happens when you become adept at combing your hair in a mirror. You learn to move your hand backward to reach the back of your head even though the mirror reflection suggests that you should move your arm forward, since the reflected back of your head is in front of you. When you master this skill, the mirror doesn't appear inverted. Likewise, it's natural to say that some things in the mirror's reflection look as if they are behind you, but that doesn't mean that you experience what it's like to see out of the back of your head; it just means that you know from the reflection that they are located to your rear. Phenomenologically, the main impact of this knowledge is proprioceptive, not visual; you learn to automatically pull your hand backward to comb hair that appears farther forward in the mirror. Harris (1965) has argued in detail that proprioceptive adaptation can fully explain experimental results with distorting lenses. For example, after adapting to lenses that shift the visual input to the right, people will point slightly to the left when asked to point straight ahead, even when blindfolded. After adapting to left-right-inverting lenses, blindfolded people will write letters in the wrong direction. In a more recent study, Linden et al. (1999) found that people wearing inverting lenses quickly adapt with respect to motor performance but show no indication of a corresponding visual transformation. The experimenters exploit the fact that ordinary viewers extrapolate shape from shading in a way that presupposes an overhead light source. Shaded polygons that are intrinsically ambiguous regarding whether they are convex or concave are experienced as nonambiguous because we are accustomed to light coming from above. Consider figure 15; in the array on the right, there appear to be three concave forms and one convex form, and the opposite is true of the array on the right, but this is actually the same array reversed. When inverting lenses are worn, such polygons shift from convex to concave, and conversely. If lens adaptation altered vision, this reversal should eventually wane. That does not seem to happen. This suggests that it is the body that has changed during adaptation, not vision. Linden et al. confirmed this interpretation using neuroimaging; after ten days of lens adaptation, they found no inversion of the topography in the visual cortex.

Enactivists resist such arguments; they think that adaptation to inverting lenses alters visual phenomenology. Noë (2005) points out that people experience perceptual distortions as they undergo adaptation. But this can be explained without assuming that the visual image is inverting. In the course of ordinary vision, we often use anticipatory mental imagery to predict how the objects we see will change. This ability can be compromised with inverting lenses. For example, if a person with inverting lenses raises her arm, she might expect it to rise in her visual field, when, in fact, it lowers. The interaction between what she sees and what she visually anticipates might result in distortions. Visual anticipation

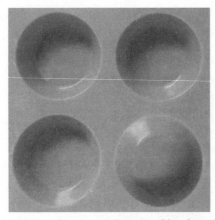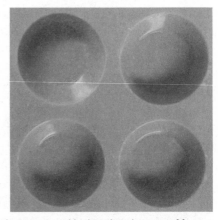

FIGURE 15 In one array, three out of four forms look concave, and in the other, three out of four look convex. The second array is the same as the first, but inverted.

can also explain an anecdote recounted by Hurley (1998). In one case report, a person with left-right-inverting lenses was looking at a chair that was in contact with the right side of his body; the lenses made the chair appear on the left, but the physical contact resulted in a ghostlike double image of the chair on the right. This may be explained by noticing that we use mental imagery to supplement ordinary perception, and the physical contact with the chair might have caused this particular individual (a rare case in the literature) to imagine a chair on the right. If images are literally inverted, such reports should be commonplace, and people should experience vivid doubling rather than ghostlike images. Hurley also notes that during adaptation, the visual world can seem *partially* reversed. For example, words take a longer time to look normal than other objects, suggesting that visual experience is being transformed during adaptation in a piecemeal way. But this example is unsurprising. Most objects are symmetrical and hence easily recognized when mirror-reversed, but words are not symmetrical, so mirror-reading requires strenuous mental effort. It's a difference in ease, not visual features, that makes some reversed objects seem "normal" more rapidly than others.

In short, it is possible to explain lens adaptation without assuming that the newly acquired motor skills have any impact on visual phenomenology. That said, opponents of enactivism need not deny that the acquisition of motor skills can have an impact on vision. It would be quite surprising if this never happened, given that there is widespread causal interaction between psychological subsystems: desire for money can increase the perceived size of a coin (Bruner and Goodman, 1947); observing lip movements can alter which vocalizations are heard (McGurk and MacDonald, 1976); listening to multiple tones can make a single tap on the hand feel like several (Hötting and Röder, 2004). Each of these interactions can be explained by supposing that one subsystem affects processing in another, without supposing that the resulting sensations are *constituted* by activity in two subsystems. The fact that vision can influence what we hear does not entail an "envisual" theory of sound. To argue for a constitutive connection, one would need to show that motor responses can have a visual impact without changing processes in the visual system. This has not been established. If inverting lenses ever have an impact on visual experience, it could be by altering processes in the visual system, and there is some evidence that this can occur (Sugita, 1996; but see Linden et al., 1999; Luauté et al., 2009). More often, though, vision dominates motor responses, which is another reason that proprioceptive explanations of lens adaptation are most plausible. And of course, the fact that vision can affect how we move does not entail that movement is partially constituted by seeing.

The enactivist appeal to tactile visual substitution systems (TVSS) can be dealt with even more easily. First of all, it's far from obvious that blind people trained on such systems come to experience visual qualities. They typically report that their tactile sensations are *like* vision in that they give them information about objects at a distance, but they are quick to clarify that these systems do not literally allow them to see. Of course, tactile recognition of familiar objects could generate visual imagery by association. If you feel a ball in your hands while blindfolded, you might visualize it. Likewise, if you discern a circle using TVSS, you might form a visual image. This can even occur in the congenitally blind, because of innate associations between the senses. In a neuroimaging study, Ptito et al. (2005) found that the congenitally blind show activations in the visual system when using a tactile-to-vision substitution device. Far from confirming enactivism, such results suggest that any reports of visual qualities are the result of ordinary visual states; there is no evidence that motor responses to distal stimuli can produce visual qualities if the visual system is not engaged.

One of the most important lines of evidence for enactivism comes from the Held and Hein kitten study. Of all of the studies surveyed, this one most directly tests the strong claim that creatures would be blind without knowledge of sensorimotor contingencies. On closer analysis, however, this study provides no evidence for that thesis and actually counts against it. Held and Hein report that the kitten that was not permitted to explore the world freely showed impairments in its ability to reach with its paws and was not afraid of visual cliffs. This might look like evidence for the conclusion that the kitten was blind, but in fact, once the kitten was released from its harness, it was actually quite successful at walking around (albeit clumsily) and avoiding obstacles. The reported deficits both indicate problems with sensorimotor associations, rather than vision itself. The kitten couldn't reach well because it hadn't practiced controlling its limbs in response to perceived stimuli, and it did not fear cliffs because it hadn't learned that walking over holes causes the body to fall. Nothing in this evidence establishes that vision is in any way abnormal; it shows only that when deprived of mobility, kittens don't fully learn paw-eye coordination and the physical affordances of objects. That is totally unsurprising on any theory of vision.

Let's turn, finally, to the neuroscientific evidence for enactivism presented by Hurley (1998). Enactivism may seem to find direct support in the existence of mirror neurons, cells that activate during manual actions and visual perceptions of the same actions. There are two problems with this appeal (see also Brincker, 2010, for a careful critique of the mirror-neuron literature). First, mirror neurons may be misinterpreted in the literature as both sensory and motor; it is possible that they are purely dedicated to motor control but happen to be triggered by visual inputs through associative learning. They are located in the motor system, and they are never directly activated by visual inputs but depend instead on prior activation in the visual stream. This suggests that they are not visual at all, but experience teaches us to imagine performing those actions that we perceive. As this interpretation would predict, studies show that mirror neurons can be reconditioned to fire in response to actions that are *opposite* to those they control (Catmur, Walsh, and Heyes, 2007). Second, mirror neurons are the exception, not the rule. Most cells within the motor system do not have visual receptive fields, and most cells in vision do not affect movements. Enactivists conjecture that there is a high degree of dynamic coupling between visual cells and motor-control cells, but little evidence for such coupling is offered. Even if visual and motor cells were dynamically coupled (i.e., even if activity in one causally depended on the other), it would not follow that they are both substrates of visual experience. Components in coupled systems can retain independent identities. For example, a heat-seeking missile can be coupled with the plane it is tracking, but we have no temptation to say that the missile and the plane are one object.

Hurley's next example is the person with eye paralysis who experiences sudden jumps in the visual world when he forms the intention to shift gaze even though his retinal inputs remain fixed. This looks like a case in which visual experience transforms when paired with a motor plan, but there is another explanation. The intention to shift gaze is an orienting response. As we saw in chapter 3, orienting involves not just overt changes in bodily position but also covert changes within the nervous system, including, most notably, a shrinking of receptive fields in the visual cells responsive to the target location. As a result, any objects in that location effectively grow in proportion to the visual field; they cause a greater number of cells to fire than they did before the shift. In healthy individuals, the sudden increase in size is usually followed by a shift in gaze and interpreted as a result of self-motion, not object-motion. When the eye muscles are paralyzed, however, the sudden increase in perceived size cannot be interpreted by unconscious processes as the result of self-movement, because movement in impaired. As a result, the increase is most naturally interpreted as a result in object motion; the augmented stimuli are moving more directly into the line of sight. An absence of motor feedback contributes to the illusion, but the actual visual experience in question—a shift in perceived size and position of objects—can be explained by a change in the visual response.

The final example that I culled from Hurley was a commissurotomy case reported in Trevarthen (1984). When a split-brain patient perceived an object with his left hemisphere and then initiated a motor response to it with the right hemisphere, the object disappeared. Does this prove that motor responses make a direct contribution to visual experience? I don't think so. There is a better explanation involving attention. After the surgery, split-brain patients are, quite remarkably, able to allocate attention independently in the two hemispheres, carrying out divergent visual searches, for example (Luck et al., 1989). But attention across the hemispheres is also known to interact when conflicts arise. For example, during dichotic listening, in which different words are played in each ear, split-brain patients cannot report what they hear in their left hemispheres (Sidtis, 1988). It is not clear why the right hemisphere trumps the left, but it may have to do with the fact that the right hemisphere is capable of attending to both sides, so it can exert a unilateral inhibitory force, whereas the left cannot. In any case, the dichotic-listening results mesh nicely with the Trevarthen case. When the right hemisphere chooses to act in response to a visual stimulus, it may selectively attend to the visual information available in that hemisphere, and attention may be withdrawn from the other hemisphere. This results in inattentional blindness for the suppressed stimulus, and the patient reports that the stimulus has disappeared. Motor responses are not directly responsible for this effect but merely play an indirect role by engaging selective attention.

Although my survey here is incomplete, I hope to have shown that some of the best-known empirical arguments for enactivism are far from decisive. It is noteworthy that there is no powerful direct evidence for the view. That is, there is no evidence showing that each visual experience is accompanied by a motor response, that distinct motor responses can alter the visual qualities of the same activation pattern within the visual system, or that damage to motor systems leads to blindness. None of these claims is empirically plausible. Consider the last of these predictions: if enactivism is true, damage to motor systems should impair seeing. Evidence suggests quite the contrary. When muscles of the body atrophy, even early in development, vision is unimpaired (Rivière and Lécuyer, 2002). When mirror neurons are damaged, as they may be in Broca's aphasia, action perception is not affected. When basal ganglia degenerate in Parkinson's disease, saccadic eye movements are impaired, but blindness does not ensue (Mosimann et al., 2005). The most profound counterevidence comes from amyotrophic lateral sclerosis. In this condition, there is a progressive degeneration of motor neurons in motor cortex, premotor cortex, and those connecting the brain stem and the spinal cord. But there is no correlative destruction in visual experience (Kandell, Schwartz, and Jessel, 2000). The only clinical condition that I am aware of linking motor control to visual experience is frontal neglect, caused by damage to the frontal eye fields (FEF), which contribute to eye movement. This shows that people who cannot easily look to the left stop perceiving on the left. Moreover, FEF cells that control saccades are interspersed with cells that control attention, so the deficit in vision may not relate to the motor deficit at all.

All of this suggests that the cells traditionally associated with motor responses do not contribute to visual phenomenology. Indeed, cells in the brain's motor systems may not have *any* associated phenomenology. They may not even engender motor phenomenology, much less visual phenomenology. It is difficult to obtain any evidence that we directly experience motor commands. Moving our bodies intentionally activates motor and premotor cortex, but there are also activations in parietal areas, which may correspond to the perception of bodily changes rather than their production. It is possible that the experience of action always involves an experience of sensory changes in the body rather than motor activity, inputs rather than outputs (Desmurget and Sirigu, 2009). Introspectively, it is plausible that the intention to move is felt as an anticipated change in how the movement would feel. This is consistent with leading models of motor control, which suggest that motor plans generate anticipatory imagery corresponding to what our actions will feel like (Blakemore, Wolpert, and Frith, 2002). Further support for this possibility comes from the fact that people with injuries in parietal areas associated with body perception can lose their ability to recognize motor intentions from within (Sirigu et al., 2003). Desmurget et al. (2009) found that electric stimulation to parietal areas causes people to experience motor intentions and even to believe that they have carried out those intentions, but no actions are actually generated; in contrast, stimulation to motor areas cause movements but no experience of intentions. The evidence is not decisive, but it should lead us to be cautious about the conjecture that there is motor phenomenology. In summary, activity in motor areas of the brain may make no direct contribution to visual phenomenology *or any other* phenomenology.

Enactivists might reply in two ways. First, they might drop the claim that visual phenomenology is partially grounded in motor responses and say instead that it is grounded in motor *knowledge*, that is, representations of movements and their visual consequences. But this requires an account of where such knowledge is stored, and it seems highly plausible that representations of motor knowledge are contained within motor systems. The fact that visual experience seems to depend on responses in the visual system alone casts doubt on the claim that visual experience involves a representation of action.

This brings us to a second reply that enactivists might offer. They might complain that my line of critique presupposes an overly orthodox view about the location of motor activity in the brain. Rather than focusing on traditional motor areas, one might look for motor responses within the visual system itself. After all, it is the basic tenet of enactivism that vision works by making use of such responses. Might there not be specialized systems dedicated to action as it pertains to vision? The answer may be affirmative, but it only raises further doubts about the enactivist program. The received view about systems dedicated to visually guided action is that they operate outside of consciousness. In an influential body of work, Milner and Goodale (1995) have argued that the visual system divides into two streams originating in occipital cortex. The ventral stream runs into temporal cortex and is primarily dedicated to object recognition. The dorsal stream runs into parietal cortex and is primarily concerned with visually guided action. Milner and Goodale argue that visual consciousness is located in the dorsal stream rather than the ventral stream. Later I will take issue with some features of this account, but I accept two points that are pertinent here: the only components within the visual system that have been directly implicated in action control are located in the dorsal stream, and activity in these components is not a correlate of visual consciousness. The main evidence for this comes from research on a patient called DF, who has lesions in her ventral stream but not in her dorsal stream. DF claims not to experience shape visually (she has apperceptive agnosia), but she can guide her hand movements to grasp visually presented objects accurately. Thus, the visual centers most implicated in action control lie outside of consciousness. Enactivism would seem to predict the opposite (Block, 2005; Clark, 2001).

O'Regan and Noë (2001) make two claims in response to this worry. First, they suggest that patients with ventral lesions such as DF are, contrary to their reports, aware of shapes. Second, they say that ventral representations, which Milner and Goodale classify as conscious, are, in fact, related to action. O'Regan and Noë propose that these representations encode sensorimotor contingencies related to the objective shapes of perceived objects, whereas dorsal representations encode egocentric features related to object manipulation. Both of these claims are implausible. The claim that DF is aware of shapes is ad hoc, given that she insists that she is blind to this aspect of the visual world. Methodologically, it is risky to posit consciousness where it is denied unless there are strong theory-neutral reasons for doubting subjective reports (e.g., evidence for a delusional disorder). As for the claim that the ventral stream encodes sensorimotor knowledge, there is simply no evidence. Cells in the ventral stream do not correlate with motor outputs, and damage to the cells does not produce known deficits in motor control. Therefore, the received view about the organization of the visual system remains a serious embarrassment for enactivism.

The foregoing discussion suggests that the empirical evidence for enactivism is not decisive, and the empirical evidence against it is considerable. There are also a priori reasons for thinking that the theory is unpromising. Concerns arise as soon as we try to get more precise about what the theory actually amounts to. Enactivists claim that visual experiences are constituted by the application of sensorimotor knowledge. Sensorimotor knowledge is then characterized as knowledge of how perceived objects change when we act. So characterized, this implies that sensorimotor knowledge consists in sets of conditional expectations of the form "if I perform action A, the object that is currently giving rise to an experience of type E1 will give rise to an experience of type E2." But on this formulation, sensorimotor knowledge is defined *in terms of* experiences, which implies that experiences cannot depend on such knowledge. Enactivists might rebut by saying that this formulation is overly propositional; it presents sensorimotor knowledge as knowledge of what will happen when we act, rather than as a kind of know-how or skill. But enactivists then owe us an account of skills that can escape the present objection. As with propositional knowledge, one might think of sensorimotor skills, such as bike riding, as input-output rules: when you feel gravity pulling to the right, you shift your body weight to the left. Motor skills may involve dynamic coupling between inputs and outputs, but, as already remarked, coupling is a causal relation, and the fact that a sensory input is coupled with a motor output does not mean that the input is *identical* to the output.

The most promising solution for the enactivist is to admit that inputs and outputs are distinct psychological states while insisting that phenomenal experience arises only when both are coactivated—that is, when the conditional rules that constitute a skill are put into practice. Of course, enactivists must concede that we sometimes see without acting, so the view has to be that visual phenomenology arises when we form motor plans, and these produce expectations about how sensory inputs will change. This gets around the initial conceptual difficulties, but it runs into the empirical problems I've been discussing (the evidence that we can have visual experiences without motor responses). It also faces an engineering problem. If experiencing a visual quality (e.g., a particular shade of red) requires forming motor plans, a question arises about which of these plans matter. There are an unbounded number of possible movements we could make; if we planned them all, it would overwhelm our motor-control systems. Enactivists might shift to a dispositional view at this point, saying that we are disposed to act in every way, but it is not clear how mere dispositions would give rise to experience (Block, 2005). The best option is to say that we select a finite subset of motor plans when we see a stimulus, and this subset determines what the stimulus is like. This suggests that the same stimulus will look different depending on which action plans we happen to form. But that often isn't the case. Red traffic signals do not change appearance when we choose to cross against the light rather than waiting. So enactivists face a trilemma: if motor plans are components of phenomenology, then the experience of a particular red must involve a deployment of either (1) all possible motor plans, which would overwhelm our motor systems; or (2) a mere disposition to act, which would raise questions about how mere possibilities affect actual experiences; or (3) some small set of plans, resulting in the odd conclusion that the red would change appearance if our plans happened to change. None of these alternatives is attractive. So, in addition to the empirical worries about enactivism, there are armchair reasons for thinking that the view is unlikely to succeed.

1.3. THE CASE AGAINST WEAK ENACTIVISM

At this point, enactivists could opt for a partial retreat. They might concede that visual phenomenology does not, in general, depend on sensorimotor skills, while insisting that certain aspects of visual phenomenology do. This would trade in strong enactivism for a weaker form. To assess weak enactivism, let me briefly consider three aspects of vision that have been said to require action.

First, consider what Noë (2005) calls the sense of "presence in absence." When you see a cow behind a wooden fence, you are in some sense aware of the whole cow, despite the fact that it is partially occluded. Vision scientists call this amodal completion, and Noë offers an enactive explanation. We are aware of the whole cow insofar as we form the sensorimotor expectation that were we to move, occluded parts would come into view.

Second, enactivists sometimes claim that action is required to see the objective or intrinsic structure of objects. When we encounter a round plate, we usually experience an elliptical shape, but we nevertheless see that the plate is round. O'Regan and Noë (2001) suggest that this ability depends on our knowledge of how the plate would change were we to move around it (see also Schellenberg, 2007, for a thesis that requires only the knowledge that action dispositions would change were we to change our location).

Third, enactivists ask us to suppose that sensorimotor knowledge is needed to represent objects as located in space (Noë, 2005: 87). When we see something as located to the left or just in front of us or as farther away than another object, we possess knowledge of how to interact physically with these objects. We know how to shift our eyes, to grasp, and to reorient our bodies in the direction of objects. This suggests that sensorimotor knowledge is required to see objects as located somewhere in space.

I want to reject all of these proposals, beginning with the first. The suggestion that action is needed for amodal completion is plainly at odds with the received view in vision science. There, the consensus is that we represent occluded parts of objects using the standard mechanisms of visual object recognition. Visible portions of occluded objects are used to extrapolate their hidden parts. This does not require the capacity for movement. Rather, gaps in interrupted lines are visually filled in. Neuroimaging studies confirm that the visual system is responsible for this process, not motor systems (Murray et al., 2002; Weigelt, Singer, and Muckli, 2007). For this reason, the term *amodal completion* is actually a misnomer; occluded objects are completed using the mechanisms comparable to those that allow the visual system to introduce illusory lines (sometimes called modal completion) or fill in the eyes' blind spots. In all of these cases, visual features surrounding an absent part are used to generate visual representations of what's missing. Noë (2005: 67) has entertained the view that illusory contours and filling in depend on action rather than visual completion, but this is hard to square with the evidence. We know, for example, that blind spots and illusory contours generate visual afterimages (Shimojo, Kamitani, and Nishida, 2001), and we know that neurons in relatively low-level visual areas function as if absent elements were present in the stimulus (Komatsu, Kinoshita, and Murakami, 2000). Given the availability of visual explanations for these phenomena and the mass of empirical support for those explanations, it would be extravagant to assume that motor responses play any role.

What about the claim that action allows us to perceive objects as having objective properties? We always experience objects from a particular vantage point, yet we recognize that they have intrinsic structure. It is tempting to suppose that this recognition depends on knowledge of the fact that any given object can be perceived from multiple vantage points and that knowledge might involve the ability to move around an object or the recognition of such an ability (for a careful argument along these lines, see Schellenberg, 2007). This explanation would have more appeal if scientists had not established the visual system's capacity to extract allocentric representations from egocentric ones. The point here just echoes the previous remarks on amodal completion and the earlier discussion of perceived stability. There are well-established models of how the visual system extracts the intrinsic geometry of objects from specific views (e.g., Biederman, 1987). For example, when we see a cube, most of its sides appear like parallelograms rather than squares, but the visual system uses depth cues and prior knowledge to derive a representation that faithfully captures its structure. There is extensive evidence that the extrapolation of intrinsic structure occurs within the visual system. For example, some cells in inferotemporal cortex fire differently when the form of an object is altered but invariantly when the object is rotated in space, even when spatial rotation results in a larger change in the retinal input (Kayaert, Biederman, and Vogels, 2003). This suggests that the visual system is capable of tracking objective forms, not just visual appearances.

Enactivists might reply that the visual extrapolation of intrinsic forms cannot fully explain the phenomenology of objectivity. When we see objects as objective, we see them as out there in the world, not inside our minds. The mere extrapolation of invariant form does not explain this. Viewpoint invariant representations in the visual system do not locate objects in the world and therefore lack an essential aspect of objectivity. It is tempting to suppose that action is required to see objects as spatially located. Perhaps I experience a plate as being in front of me because I recognize that I could reach out and touch it. This was the third example on the list of features that allegedly become visible only when we possess sensorimotor knowledge.

Our felt capacity to grasp undoubtedly constitutes one way of perceiving objects as located in space, but it is not the only way. The visual system can locate objects in space without motor involvement. Indeed, there are six different senses in which vision can be said to provide information about spatial location. First, purely visual features covary with spatial features and have the function of doing so; thus, on leading naturalized approaches to psychosemantics (Dretske, 1995), visual features *represent* spatial features. This point is supported by the fact that there are spatial maps within the visual system whose cells fire as a function of stimulus locations, regardless of stimulus shape (Sereno, Pitzalis, and Martinez, 2001). Second, cells in visual areas are often retinotopically or topographically arranged, which means that spatial relations in the world are *recapitulated* in the brain. Research on mental imagery suggests that we exploit this fact by "mentally scanning" mental images to estimate distances (Kosslyn, 1994). Third, visual states have a characteristic spatial *phenomenology*. If you look at a 3-D image using a stereoscope or 3-D glasses, some objects appear closer and some farther away. Stereoscopic vision, feature overlap, fading in the distance, and other visible features give us an experience of depth. Fourth, visual information can be used to make *judgments* about spatial locations. These judgments are not always accurate, but the inaccuracies often result from the fact that eye movements distort the visual input, suggesting that action can detract from the spatial accuracy of vision (Ehrenstein, 1977). Fifth, vision obeys spatial *rules*, such as the rules of perspective. Violations of such rules, as in an Escher etching or impossible figure, are jarring, and this can be explained without appeal to motor responses. Finally, visual features allow us to make spatial *predictions* about how objects will change as they move through space. If we watch a train move along tracks that converge toward a horizon, we expect the train to get smaller. This does not require motor predictions. Of course, we can make motor predictions (what Gibson calls "affordances") on the basis of visual inputs; when we see a hammer, we know that we can grasp it (Tucker and Ellis, 1998). But our knowledge of affordances often depends on prior possession of purely visual information about space. Seeing the plate tells us where to aim the fork, not conversely. In cases of brain injury, we can lose the ability to grasp accurately while retaining a visual sense of where objects are located (see below).

The enactivist might protest by insisting that the visual sense of space is not really spatial at all. What meaning can we give to "out there," the objection might go, if we can't relate the objects of experience with a felt sense of our bodies? The idea is that we locate objects in space by relating them to an embodied (and perhaps motoric) sense of self. This objection begs the question against the evidence that vision provides information about space. Indeed, the perspectival nature of vision even provides information about the location of the viewing eye and thus presents objects as out there relative to some vantage point. Of course, we need bodily senses to experience this vantage point as physically embodied, but this does not mean that the visual experience of space depends on bodily senses. A person who lost all feeling in the body would not suffer corresponding bouts of spatial blindness—the world would not look visually flat. This is confirmed by the case of Ian Waterman, who lacks proprioception, kinesthesia, and somatosensory responses but navigates his environment successfully using vision (Cole, 1995).

In conclusion, there is no evidence that motor responses make a constitutive contribution to visual phenomenology. Such responses are not needed to experience any visual features of the world, contrary to even weak enactivism.

2. Does Consciousness Sidestep Action?

2.1. EVIDENCE FOR INACTIVE THEORIES

If the foregoing considerations are right, there is no constitutive link between visual consciousness and the processes that control action. Seeing and acting are dissociable. This might be taken to imply that consciousness has little to do with action; perhaps theories of consciousness can be developed without emphasis on or even mention of how behavior is produced. In practice, this is exactly how theory construction normally proceeds in this area. Leading philosophical theories of consciousness (see chapter 1) make little or no mention of the relationship to action. Such theories nicely illustrate Hurley's metaphor of the classical sandwich. Consciousness is seen as an input system, which feeds, perhaps in interesting ways, to cognition (central systems) but does not relate directly to output systems. The AIR theory of consciousness also fits this pattern. I have argued that all consciousness is perceptual, and I've just been suggesting that perception does not depend on action. This might be taken to imply that consciousness is *inactive*. In this section, I will reexamine that assumption and argue that the inactive approach goes too far. To make that case, I will critically examine the most explicit arguments in the neuroscientific literature for a dissociation between consciousness and action.

The most influential recent defense of inactivism has already been touched on above. It owes to Milner and Goodale (1995), who argue that the visual system divides into two pathways: an unconscious dorsal stream that guides action and a conscious ventral stream that does not (see also Goodale and Milner, 1992 and 2005). This division is depicted in figure 16. Milner and Goodale often characterize the two streams in functional terms. They say that the dorsal stream is *for* action, and the ventral stream is *for* perception (Goodale and Milner, 2005: 45). More specifically, the ventral stream, which is the seat of consciousness, is for object recognition. It tells us what we are seeing, while the dorsal stream helps us physically interact with what we are seeing. Thus, according to Milner and Goodale, consciousness is inactive in two senses: it is not constituted by processes that control action, and it does not have the function of guiding action.

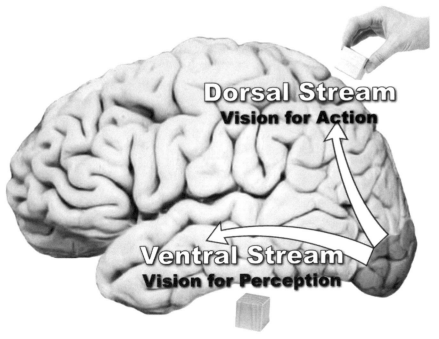

FIGURE 16 The dorsal and ventral streams as interpreted by Milner and Goodale.

Some of the main evidence has already been summarized. Recall Milner and Goodale's work with the patient DF, who sustained damage to her ventral stream from carbon-monoxide poisoning. As a result, she is unable to experience consciously the shapes of visually perceived objects, but she is nevertheless able to perform shape-sensitive actions. For example, she was able to slide a rectangular card accurately into a narrow slot, a task that requires sensitivity to the card's shape and orientation. Astoundingly, she cannot report the orientation of the slot, even though she can successfully orient her hands to slide the card into it. In other words, she can use vision to act, even though she cannot visually recognize objects. Milner and Goodale attribute DF's success in the "posting" task to her intact dorsal stream, and they attribute her inability to report on object shapes to the lesions in her ventral stream. By her own account, DF cannot consciously see shapes, so consciousness seems to go with recognition, not with action.

The dissociation between conscious perception and unconscious perception for action has also been investigated in healthy individuals. Pellisson et al. (1986) designed a task in which participants had to saccade and reach toward a target. In some trials, the target shifted slightly during the saccade. These shifts were often invisible to consciousness, because of the fact that the visual system suppresses signals during saccades, but reaching movements nevertheless made adjustments that compensated for the shifts. Thus, people can be unaware of visual changes while aware of the movements made in response to those changes (see also Johnson and Haggard, 2005).

An even more striking dissociation was reported by Aglioti, DeSouza, and Goodale (1995), involving the Ebbinghaus (or Titchener) illusion. In that illusion, two identical circles are presented, but one is surrounded by smaller circles, and the other is surrounded by larger circles; under these conditions, the circle surrounded by little circles looks larger than the circle surrounded by large circles, even though they are the same size. The Aglioti investigators wanted to know whether the dorsal system is susceptible to this illusion of size, so they replaced the central circles in the illusion with disks that could be grasped. Then they measured the aperture between the fingers as people reached down to pick up the disks. They reported that when subjects grasped, their hands opened to the same width for both disks, regardless of whether the surrounding circles differed in size. They concluded that visually guided actions seem to be immune to the illusion. This finding adds further support to Milner and Goodale's claim that action and recognition are dissociable and that the visual representations used for action are not accessible to consciousness.

Milner and Goodale's research on the dorsal/ventral distinction is perhaps the most direct effort to establish that vision is inactive, but another widely discussed research program can be interpreted as adding further support. In influential experiments, Libet et al. (1983) investigated the experience of conscious will. They asked people to move their fingers at a moment of their choice while watching a clock. They were asked to report the exact moment that they formed the intention to move. The investigators also measured electrical activity emanating from the premotor cortex while subjects performed this task. The startling result was that motor-readiness potentials, which preceded the finger movement, occurred several hundred milliseconds before the time at which people reported experiencing a conscious intention to move. One interpretation of these results goes as follows. Motor commands are generated unconsciously and cannot be experienced, but just after they are formed, a predictive signal is sent to brain centers that perceive body movements. These signals result in the experience of conscious intentions, which are really anticipated sensations of movements. The motor commands also cause the body to move, which takes slightly longer, and the sensations caused by the actual movement are compared, perhaps unconsciously, to the anticipated movements. If this interpretation is right, it supports a conjecture advanced above: we are not directly aware of motor commands. It can also be taken as evidence for a stronger claim: the sense that we have conscious control of our actions is an illusion. Conscious experience of intentions is a by-product of the unconscious intentions, which are sufficient for action control. Libet et al. are tempted by this conclusion, but they do think that we can consciously veto actions that have been initiated by the motor cortex; we lack free will but have "free won't" (Libet, 1999). But if decisions to act begin outside of consciousness, there is little reason to think that decisions to stop acting originate within consciousness. In fact, there is empirical evidence that we are bad at consciously assessing when the capacity to veto an action has been brought to bear (Kühn and Brass, 2009). Our impression that we can consciously initiate and stop actions may be an illusion.

The idea that conscious will is an illusion has been pushed even further by Wegner (2002). He has performed numerous experiments that are designed to show that we are prone to gross errors about our control over actions and outcomes. For example, if people hear the name of an object in a pair of headphones just before their hands are moved to a picture of that object by another person, they feel as if they moved their hands to the picture voluntarily (Wegner and Wheatley, 1999; see also Moore et al., 2009). The effect size in this study was small, but it is suggestive. It raises the possibility that people do not directly experience their control over actions but merely interpret actions as controlled when they occur in close temporal succession to related thoughts. More accurately, Wegner says that we interpret an action as under our control when it is consistent with a prior thought, close in time, and not readily explained by some salient alternative cause. Wegner concludes that we have no direct experience of the mental states that actually cause our actions.

Wegner and Libet are not explicitly defending the inactivist program, but their work can be enlisted for that end. If we don't directly experience our efficacious motor plans, then such plans are not constituents of consciousness more broadly. The idea that perceptual experience depends on motor responses seems unlikely. The critique of conscious will also casts doubt on the hypothesis that the function of consciousness is to guide action, as Rosenthal (2008) explicitly argues. Were that the case, we might expect those states that most directly control action to enter into experience, and we might expect a higher degree of accuracy in assessing when we are in control. This research seems to suggest that consciousness exists for some other purpose—perhaps for perception—and only conveys information about action indirectly and imperfectly, by providing sensory impressions of real and anticipated movements.

Together with the evidence that motor responses are not implicated in visual consciousness (reviewed in criticizing enactivism), the research under consideration here points toward an inactive theory of consciousness. The view advanced by Milner and Goodale can be dubbed *dual-stream inactivism*, and the view derived from Libet and Wegner can be called *volitional inactivism*. One emphasizes a dissociation between conscious visual processing and processing that serves action, and the other emphasizes a more general dissociation between consciousness and motor commands. In both views, action is said to be guided by processes that lie outside of consciousness. Both count against the functional thesis that consciousness is for action. Should we join inactivists in abandoning that thesis? Perhaps not.

2.2. THE CASE AGAINST DUAL-STREAM INACTIVISM

I agree with inactivists that motor responses make no constitutive contribution to visual phenomenology, but I want to challenge the functional thesis that consciousness is for perceiving rather than acting. I will begin by reexamining the work of Milner and Goodale, who have advanced this thesis most explicitly.

Milner and Goodale argue that vision divides into two separate streams with different functions. I think that this way of dividing things is potentially misleading. In order to make this case, I will proceed in three steps: I will challenge the claim that vision has two independent streams, I will argue that some dorsal processes are conscious, and I will raise some doubts about the claim that ventral processes are unimportant for action.

Talk of two visual streams has long been popular in visual science (Ungerleider and Mishkin, 1982). Other authors have argued that vision contains a third stream. For example, Husain and Nachev (2007) posit a pathway that registers visual salience, nestled anatomically between dorsal and ventral. But all such divisions begin to look like gross simplifications when one considers connectional anatomy within the visual system. In their influential map of the macaque visual brain, Felleman and Van Essen (1991) identified thirty-two visual areas and a complex subway-like pattern of interconnectivity among them (figure 17). To illustrate, area V1 (primary visual cortex), which is supposed to feed into both dorsal and ventral streams, actually has four outputs in the Felleman and Van Essen map. Should we conclude that there are four streams? Things get even messier when we consider secondary visual cortices. V4, which is part of the ventral stream, has eleven outputs, and V3A, which is regarded as dorsal, has nine. What's more, these dorsal and ventral structures talk to each other. The degree of connectivity between the so-called dorsal and ventral streams may reduce as one moves deeper into parietal and temporal cortex, but the fact remains that there is considerable cross-talk between visual areas all the way up. Presented with this picture, talk of two streams begins to look like a distortion. It's hard to know how to individuate visual streams; anatomically, there are dozens of criss-crossing paths from V1 to the farthest reaches of visual, and functionally, there is no simple bipartite division. For example, MT, which codes motion information, is considered dorsal, but motion can contribute to both object recognition and action affordances, which makes it impossible to decide which stream MT belongs to on the basis of function. MT has seven outputs, according to Felleman and Van Essen, which include both temporal and parietal structures.

Given this morass, one might say that there aren't two streams in vision but uncountably many. I think an even better way of putting it, however, is that there is one stream in vision: a complex branching delta whose interweaving tributaries can be characterized as progressing from primary visual areas deeper

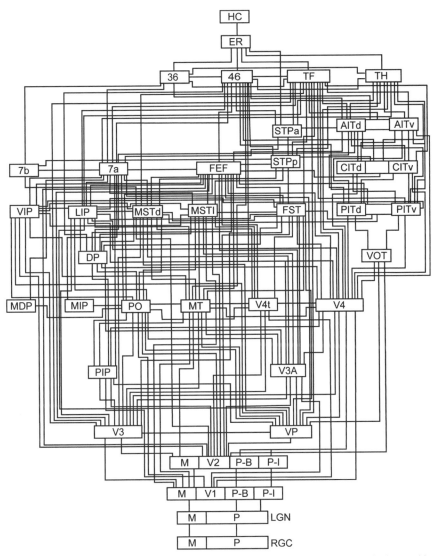

FIGURE 17 Felleman and Van Essen's (1991) connectivity map of the visual system (redrawn with permission).

into the brain. We can measure synaptic distance forward from V1, but given the massive cross-talk, it is not especially helpful to think about these parallel branches as separate pathways.

Against this, Milner and Goodale might argue that the dual-system view is supported by behavioral dissociations. Recall the claim from Aglioti, DeSouza, and Goodale (1995) that the dorsal stream is not susceptible to certain optical illusions, and the evidence from Pellisson et al. (1986) that the dorsal stream registers shifts in stimulus location that are invisible to the ventral stream.

Doesn't this suggest that the brain has two independent networks for processing visual information?

In rejecting the dual-stream view, I am not suggesting that visual subsystems are always transparent to one another. Subsystems are functionally specialized, and consequently, some may register information that others do not. We get into trouble, however, when we reify two streams as opposed to a large number of mechanisms working in parallel. Moreover, some of the evidence for the autonomy of these mechanism has to be regarded with caution. Franz et al. (2001) discovered a design flaw in the Aglioti study: in the visual-judgment task, subjects were asked to compare the sizes of two circles, and they reported an illusory contrast, but in the grasping task, these two circles were presented individually. When Franz et al. reran the study making the two tasks more similar, the illusion appeared in both, suggesting that both dorsal and ventral processes use a shared representation of size. The Pellisson study is also inadequate for establishing a strong duality. The main finding is that the brain mechanisms involved in reaching do not lose track of position information during saccades. But once again, this only establishes that some dorsal structures register things that other ventral structures miss. One can make the same point *within* the ventral steam. In cases of change blindness, for example, some ventral structures fail to detect changes that others detect. Thus, there are numerous structures in both regions operating somewhat independently, rather than two regions that are independent of each other but internally consistent. There is one highly complex, parallel process stream.

Notice that this way of putting it does not undermine the claim that vision is hierarchical. The visual hierarchy can be measured both anatomically by distance from primary areas and functionally by an increase in abstraction. One can even parcel the hierarchy into three stages, even though there may be more than three anatomical loci between V1 and the highest visual areas. The trick is to use the Marr/Jackendoff distinction between disunified, local feature detectors (low-level vision), viewpoint representations (intermediate-level vision), and representations that abstract away from vantage points (high-level vision). So the complexity that casts doubt on dual-pathway talk is perfectly consistent with talk of a three-level hierarchy. If we want to locate consciousness, the strategy of finding a privileged level in the hierarchy is, therefore, more promising than the strategy of finding the privileged pathway.

That brings me to the second worry about Milner and Goodale's picture. They insist that consciousness is located in the ventral stream, rather than the dorsal stream. This is unlikely if I am right that these two streams cannot be neatly distinguished. Moreover, if the AIR theory is correct, consciousness is located at the intermediate level of the abstraction hierarchy, and that division crosscuts any division into streams. In other words, both ventral and dorsal areas may contain abstraction hierarchies, and the AIR theory predicts that intermediate areas can contribute to consciousness regardless of whether they are ventral or dorsal.

There is strong evidence in support of this conclusion. To find out which dorsal areas are intermediate-level, one needs to determine which ones are viewpoint-specific. One method for doing this is to measure whether brain areas adapt to images as they change in size and orientation; viewpoint-specific areas should not adapt to such changes in position, whereas high-level areas should. Using this technique, Konen and Kastner (2008) found that dorsal areas MT, V3A, and V7 (a parietal structure with no monkey homologue) are viewpoint-specific. The AIR theory predicts that each of these dorsal areas can contribute to consciousness, and there is empirical support for that conclusion. In chapter 2, I characterized MT as an intermediate-level motion detector and argued that it contributes to the conscious experience of motion. MT activity correlates with both real and illusory motion, and MT lesions cause motion blindness (Zeki, 1991). There is also evidence pertaining to the other intermediate dorsal areas. The experience of stereoscopic depth is associated with activity in V3A and V7 (Tsao et al., 2003), and activity in V3A has also been credited with the conscious detection of velocity (McKeefry et al., 2008).

Milner and Goodale base their conclusion that the dorsal stream is unconscious on their work with the patient DF, who claims to be blind to the shapes of visual presented objects. But DF is not completely blind; she has some visual phenomenology. Goodale and Milner report that DF can perceive motion (2005: 10) and stereoscopic depth (2005: 92). In a case study of a similar patient, SB, Milner and his collaborators report that ventral lesions preserve the ability to perceive velocity (Lê et al., 2002: 68). This is just what one would expect if intermediate-level dorsal structures contribute to phenomenology.

If I am right, consciousness arises in both dorsal and ventral streams at the intermediate level of processing. Thus, the caricature of the dorsal stream as a zombie action system, which might be inferred from a reading of Milner and Goodale, is best avoided. Closer reading of their work actually provides evidence, just mentioned, that the dorsal stream contributes to experience. Let's now turn to the claim that the ventral stream is for perception, rather than action. Milner and Goodale gloss things this way, but on reflection, there is something obviously wrong with it. Perception—that is to say, object recognition—is clearly important for action, so it cannot be their view that the ventral stream is unimportant for action. They are happy to grant that the ventral stream matters for deciding what to do. Their main point is that the dorsal stream contains structures that are directly implicated in the guidance of motor responses, and the dorsal stream does not. So, for them, the ventral stream contributes to action indirectly. Its function is object recognition, and recognition, in turn, may contribute to practical decisions. One might clarify by saying that the ventral stream is not *primarily* for action, even though it is extremely important for action, whereas some structures in the dorsal stream seem to have action guidance as their primary function.

To assess these claims, one might delve into philosophical theories of what "functions" are. Such an exercise is unlikely to favor Milner and Goodale.

Despite considerable controversy about the details, the term *function* is used in two basic ways: teleological and causal. Let's look at these in turn. Teleological theories are usually Darwinian: the teleological function of a mechanism depends on what it was selected for during evolution—that is, its contribution to fitness (e.g., Millikan, 1984). Object recognition has little value in itself and is likely to have been selected for its role in helping organisms respond effectively to the stimuli they encounter. From this perspective, the ventral stream's raison d'être is action.

Causal theories of functions emphasize the impact of a mechanism or process as it currently operates within a complex system (e.g., Cummins, 1985). Milner and Goodale might insist that the ventral stream does not causally contribute to action because it doesn't directly control movements. They will insist that it contributes to object recognition. But the story gets complicated when we focus on *conscious processes* in the ventral stream, rather than all ventral-stream activity. If the AIR theory is right, then much ventral activity is unconscious, including those high-level processes that are most centrally implicated in object recognition. Thus, the claim that *consciousness* is causally contributing to recognition is a stretch. Intermediate-level representations contribute to high-level recognition only indirectly, and in subliminal perception, they make that contribution without being conscious. This suggests that the main causal contribution of conscious activity in the ventral stream is not recognition, contrary to Milner and Goodale's thesis.

One might make progress in determining the function of consciousness (in both senses of "function") by asking what happens when consciousness is absent. What happens, for example, when a person cannot consciously experience shapes? Milner and Goodale emphasize the fact that such an individual cannot recognize objects, but it is equally evident that such a person no longer spontaneously reacts to objects. Absent consciousness, people become nonresponsive. Aim a gun at DF, and she won't run.

This simple observation has been made in the context of blindsight (Weiskrantz, 1986). People who have residual visual abilities but no visual consciousness act as if the objects in front of them aren't there. GY, the famous blindsight patient, can point to objects when cued but won't do so spontaneously. The same can be observed in healthy individuals. When presented with visual stimuli below the threshold of awareness, priming occurs, but people do not electively act in response to what they have unconsciously seen. In these cases, we know that object recognition is taking place, so recognition on its own is not sufficient for action. Consciousness seems to be crucial. Thus, if visual consciousness includes activity in the ventral stream, we have an initial reason to believe that the ventral stream contributes to action. Moreover, the ventral stream may be more important for action than the dorsal stream. DF uses her dorsal stream to guide her movements visually, but she would not move in response to objects if she were not prompted by the experimenters. One might even venture to say that the dorsal areas are for movement, not action. A movement can be defined as any change caused by motor responses within an organism, whereas an action is a movement or complex sequence of movements initiated by an intention. A case might be made for the conclusion that ventral processes are at least as important as dorsal processes for actions so defined. Ventral processes contribute to the decision *to act*, in addition to decisions about what to do, while the dorsal processes implicated by Milner and Goodale are more involved in decisions about how to perform actions, once they've been selected. The most important point for now is that consciousness, including conscious events in ventral structures, seem to be crucial for action. I will develop this point below.

2.3. THE CASE AGAINST VOLITIONAL INACTIVISM

Dual-stream inactivists try to show that visual consciousness is anatomically and functionally dissociable from the visual control of action. Volitional inactivists place emphasis elsewhere; they argue that the processes that initiate our actions are not conscious. This is sometimes taken as a threat to free will, since some theories of free will stipulate that freedom requires conscious initiation, but I will not take up that issue here. As far as I'm concerned, robust forms of free will were refuted long ago, and anemic compatibilist successors to that concept need not make any commitment to conscious initiation, and the discovery that actions can originate unconsciously is granted by compatibilists from the outset. The question that concerns me is whether the empirical results supporting volitional inactivism can be used to argue that action is not central to the function of consciousness.

Consider the experiments of Libet et al. (1983). Their main finding is that electrical potentials arise in the motor cortex prior to the conscious experience of a decision to move. There are some methodological concerns with this study. First, Libet et al. asked people to move when they felt the urge, but urges are arguably not voluntary actions but involuntary impulses, so the study sheds no light on the question of whether consciousness contributes to actions that seem more controlled (Mele, 2009). Second, it takes time to read a hand on a clock, and that means that the time that people report as the moment of decision will actually be slightly later than the decision itself; therefore, the conscious decision may actually coincide with the readiness potential rather than the reported clock time (Dennett, 2003). Third, even if Libet's results show that the decision to perform some action or other precedes consciousness, it is possible that consciousness plays a role in deciding which specific action to make. Consistent with this, Haggard and Eimer (1999) distinguished two readiness potentials—one that corresponds to general excitation in motor systems and another that corresponds to specific movements—and found that the timing of the latter coincides temporally with subjective reports of intentions.

These objections cast doubt on Libet's initial results, but they don't cut ice against subsequent replications. Haggard and Eimer (1999) address the worry about "urges" by instructing subjects to "decide of their own free will" when to act. Soon et al. (2008) address the worry that it takes time to read a clock. In their replication, subjects report the timing of an intention by noting which letter was visible in a rapid stream of letters, rather than reading and reporting the location of a second hand. Strikingly, they found motor-readiness potentials up to ten seconds before the conscious intention. In any case, Libet's method of clock reading may be less problematic than it appears, because it is just as likely that people read the clock before deciding to act, rather than the other way around. A person who waits for the clock to pass a certain point and then consciously elects to act may actually overestimate the onset of the conscious intention, locating it at the clock time rather than a moment later. That error should diminish the temporal gap between readiness potentials and the reported timing of conscious decisions, but a gap still remains.

The Haggard and Eimer findings offer the most direct evidence in favor of consciousness coinciding with neural control of action, but it is important to note that, like Libet, they rely on memory reports. The fact that people recall forming an intention at the time that their brain was preparing an action does not entail that these events actually coincided. Other evidence suggests that such memory reports are reconstructions, rather than perfect records of what occurred. Using a version of Libet's paradigm, Lau, Rogers, and Passingham (2007) applied transcranial magnetic stimulation to the motor cortex just after people performed an action. This led to systematic distortions in their judgments about when they formed the intention to act (pushing it farther back in time) and when the action took place (pushing it forward in time). This suggests that our impression of when an intention was formed is not based on an accurate memory but rather is constructed after an action takes place. The fact that under certain conditions (e.g., Haggard and Eimer's study), we recall having experienced an intention at the time when the brain was preparing to act suggests that these memory reconstructions sometimes locate conscious intentions at the moment when actions are initiated, but it doesn't follow that our conscious intentions actually arose at that time. Perhaps there is an unconscious decision made when the clock hits a certain point, and that unconscious decision generates a false memory of the conscious intention arising at that point, when, in fact, the intention may come significantly later.

The Lau, Rogers, and Passingham findings suggest that the disconnection between consciousness and action may be even more extreme than Libet realized. For all we know, conscious decisions do not only arise after readiness potentials; they may arise after actions have taken place and then get erroneously backdated to earlier points in time. If so, then conscious decisions aren't even a causal step en route to action.

This possibility might seem to support inactionism. But that conclusion may be premature. Let's suppose that conscious intentions occur after actions and that the commonsense ordering is just an illusion. Does it follow that consciousness is not involved in the guidance of action? Absolutely not. We should distinguish between two ways in which consciousness can guide action. On the one hand, we might be conscious of our decisions and use those decisions to guide action. On the other hand, we might be conscious of the *inputs* to our decisions, and those inputs may guide our action. The first possibility says that action is controlled by the conscious experience of the mind, and the second says that action is controlled by the conscious experience of the world. On reflection, there is something peculiar about the first view. If a decision has been made, it will cause us to act. Being conscious of that decision before the action will do nothing for us, because the decision already sets the action into motion. The second view makes much more sense from a functional perspective. Consciousness of inputs can help us make decisions. So conscious control benefits more from awareness of the world than from awareness of the mind. Of course, once an action has been performed, it is an event in the world, and it helps to know what that action is. So it helps that we become aware of our actions once we perform them. If consciousness of decisions is really consciousness of our bodies in actions, then such consciousness is useful. Such consciousness does not allow us to revise a decision that has already been made, but it can serve as a perceived input for the next decision. Thus, even in the most dire interpretation of the Lau results, there may be an important link between consciousness and action. Those results say nothing about whether we are conscious of the worldly inputs into decision making.

This point applies equally to Wegner's claim that conscious will is an illusion. Wegner may be right, but his studies actually reveal something important about the relationship between consciousness and action. Wegner shows that we make erroneous judgments about control when we are conscious of an input that is temporally contiguous and relevant to a subsequent movement in our bodies. This suggests that we are ordinarily aware of the inputs that drive us to act and that such inputs are perceived as instigators of action. In other words, illusions of will establish that we regard conscious experiences of inputs as action-guiding. Thus, these results don't establish the irrelevance of consciousness to action, as inactivists might propose, but rather provide fodder for the view that consciousness is in the business of telling us what to do. Wegner's studies help to confirm that decision processes are unconscious, but they do not cast doubt on the claim that we are conscious of the inputs that contribute to our decisions.

In summary, I don't wish to reject the conclusions of Libet and Wegner. I concur that we are not directly aware of action decisions, and to that extent, conscious will is an illusion. But it would be a mistake to enlist these results in the service of inactivism more generally. Neither Libet nor Wegner would argue that consciousness does not contribute to action, although it is tempting to infer that conclusion from their work. The temptation should be resisted. Libet and Wegner help confirm that consciousness is directed outward, not inward, and attributions of inner states tend to be inferential. That fact impels us to look for the function of consciousness in its capacity to provide information about inputs. This might lead us to follow Milner and Goodale in saying that consciousness is for perception and not action, but I have already cautioned against that deduction. It remains an open possibility that consciousness contributes to action *by* contributing to perception. That is the possibility I will turn to now.

3. Action Guidance and Consciousness

3.1. AIR, ACTION, AND FUNCTION

We can summarize the interim conclusions as follows. There is no compelling evidence demonstrating that motor responses are essential for conscious experience. In fact, such responses may never be conscious. We may also have no direct consciousness of the decisions that cause us to act. Instead, we are just conscious of our bodies in motion and the external stimuli toward which our actions may be directed. This might be taken to imply a profound dissociation between consciousness and action. On the other hand, consciousness seems to be a precondition for elective behavior. We don't spontaneously react to a stimulus unless we experience it. We are left, then, with a question: if action and action control are unconscious, why is consciousness a precondition for action? To answer this question, we need to investigate the function of consciousness.

Questions about the function of consciousness cannot be fully answered without a theory of consciousness in hand. Competing views about how consciousness arises suggest competing theories of what consciousness is for. I have been defending the AIR theory of consciousness, and it is against the background of that theory that I will advance a proposal about function.

According to the AIR theory, conscious states are attended intermediate-level representations. Thus, consciousness requires two things: a viewpoint-specific representation and attentional modulation. Attention, I have argued, is a process by which information becomes available to working memory. In defending the AIR theory, I have essentially ignored questions of function. I have not said why viewpoint-specific representations are useful, and I have not said what availability to working memory does for an organism. Nor have I said why this combination—viewpoint specificity and availability—might be something worth having. One can develop a theory of when consciousness arises without considering why it arises. Much work on consciousness proceeds that way. But there is something unsatisfying about this oversight. One wants to know what, if anything, conscious states are good for.

To address this question, I want to look at the two parts of the AIR theory in turn. But first, let me note that some specific details of AIR may not matter for the question at hand. Some authors might not like the equation of consciousness with attended intermediate-level representations, but there is a more general formulation of the theory that has broad appeal: consciousness states are perspectival and accessible. One might deny that the intermediate level is the best explanation of the perspectival nature of consciousness or that attention is the best account of accessibility, while accepting the general formulation. Thus, the speculations about function that follow could be embraced by those who reject particular commitments of the AIR theory.

Let's begin with the perspectival character of consciousness. Why might an organism have perceptual states that represent the world from a particular point of view? Notice that perspectival perceptual representations could turn out to be an accidental by-product of how information gets into our sensory systems. For example, the retina can only pick up light from one surface of an object, so it will inevitably deliver information in a viewpoint-specific way. But a moment's reflection confirms that viewpoint specificity is useful. Viewpoint specificity is a relational property: it concerns how an external object is situated in relation to the viewer. There are many contexts in which this information might be valuable. If there is a predator present, it's helpful to know in which direction it's facing and how close it is. If you are hoping to pull an apple off a branch, you need to know whether the branch is within reach. If you are climbing up a rocky surface, you need to know where to find a toehold and which jutting edge would afford a solid grip. If you want to kiss someone, you'd better be able to locate that person's lips. Perspectival representations preserve the information required for these kinds of decisions. If we had to rely on high-level or allocentric representations, we'd be at a loss. We might know that a predator is present, but we wouldn't know which way or even whether to run. We might know that an apple is in view, but we'd grope blindly if we tried to obtain it. Low-level representations would also be insufficient for guiding action. Detecting an edge might help with fine-grained motor responses, but we need whole contours, situated in three-dimensional space, to coordinate our actions with objects.

Now, consider accessibility. According to the AIR theory, consciousness requires attention, and attention makes information available to working memory. Working memory is a temporary storage capacity, but, unlike long-term storage, it is not a dormant warehouse of knowledge. As the term *working* implies, working memory is a form of storage that allows information to be actively used by an organism. It is the mind's scratchpad, where information is recorded for making decisions here and now. An organism without working memory would be able to react to its environment, but it wouldn't be able to deliberate about what to do. It would have to reply with automatic responses that were either innate or conditioned. Working memory is the seat of "executive" or "controlled" responses. Such terms are misleading, insofar as they imply choice when in reality, all mental operations are likely to unfold mechanically, without any homunculus to call the shots. But executive processes exhibit a distinctive kind of flexibility. An organism with executive control can bring the past to bear on the present in a context-sensitive way, so that the decision arrived at is not simply a repetition of past responses but potentially something new.

Working memory is clearly useful. In fact, increases in working-memory capacity may be the major factor behind phylogenetic advances in behavioral complexity (Coolidge and Wynn, 2009). But it is important not to attribute the functions of working memory to consciousness. I have argued that consciousness requires not actual encoding in working memory but mere availability. The actual computations that take place within working memory are largely inaccessible to us. We are notoriously bad at recounting how we solve problems (Nisbett and Wilson, 1977). Ironically, we can report what's available to working memory but not the processes that take place within it. And of course, much of what is available never gets encoded. So the question at hand is, what purpose does availability serve?

An analogy might help. Consider menus. At a restaurant, you order only a small number of items, but the menu presents you with a variety of different choices. But the menu doesn't include every possible dish. The range of options is constrained by you, in some sense, because you chose the restaurant, but it is also dictated by factors you can't control, namely the dictates of the chef. Menus vary in size, but most offer more than anyone could eat in one sitting. A choice has to be made, and if you don't choose, there will be nothing to do but sit there waiting. We can ask, what good are menus? The obvious answer is that we like having a choice about what we eat. We can select those things that we enjoy most or those that satisfy any number of other preferences, such as nutritional value, budgetary considerations, moral concerns, and so on. Some items on the menu pop out in an irresistible way, and some are found after a careful search. Availability to working memory is like a menu in this respect. Only those items that are available can be selected. The range of things on the menu depends on what's in our environment and on the allocation of attention. And these items can vary in salience because of their perceivable qualities (bottom-up) or our goals (top-down). Having such a menu is helpful because it reduces environmental complexity. At any given time, there can be an enormous number of objects around us. Simpler creatures, such as insects, cope with this complexity by having sensory transducers that perceive only a very limited range of inputs. We cope with complexity by choosing which inputs to act on. The capacity for choice makes us much more flexible than insects. But choices can be overwhelming when there are too many options. Attention serves as a filter that greatly reduces the choice space.

We can now put the two pieces of this story together. Perspectival representations provide relational information that is especially important for decisions about how to interact with objects in the environment. Availability to working memory provides us with a menu of options for deliberation. So available perspectival representations provide a menu for decisions about interactions. More succinctly, such representations provide a menu for action.

If this story about what perspectival representations and availability do for us is correct, it follows that consciousness is fundamentally related to action. Consciousness provides the range of things that can be selected for practical decision making. I would venture to say that this is the function of consciousness, in both the teleological and the causal sense (for a related conjecture, see Ramachandran and Hirstein, 1997). Consciousness makes information available for decisions about what to do, and it exists for that purpose. That is to say, the reason we evolved to have processes that make perspectival representations available to working memory is that such availability allows for selection from a range of inputs that encode information pertinent to action. If survival didn't benefit from selective choices about behavioral interactions, this capacity might not have been selected for. Even without getting embroiled in technical debates about biological functions, we can see that there is reason to think that consciousness is causally implicated in action. The fact that we are conscious of perspectival representations and that they are available to working memory suggests that they play a causal role in the selection of behavioral responses. If consciousness were for theoretical reasoning, we might be conscious of more abstract representations and of representations that are already encoded in working memory. Attended intermediate-level representations are ideally suited for action.

This suggestion contrasts with the views surveyed earlier in this chapter. Unlike enactivists, I deny that action is a constitutive part of consciousness, and unlike inactivists, I insist that consciousness is nevertheless for action. Moreover, unlike Milner and Goodale, I think that it is misleading to say that consciousness is for perception, defined as object recognition. Object recognition tends to rely on high-level representations, which are unconscious. Consciousness presents objects in a precategorical way that preserves their action-relevant relations to the organisms that perceive them. Put differently, consciousness does not furnish us with information about what objects are present, so much as information about how the objects in our surrounding are situated in relation to us. It does not follow from this that we are conscious of our practical decisions or action plans. These, I have suggested, are usually unconscious when they occur. Consciousness is not in the business of telling us what we are thinking or deciding; rather, it reveals the objects in the world as they are positioned relative to us and is thus a precondition for decision rather than a mechanism of decision.

This last point helps explain why consciousness is necessary for elective actions. If we did not have access to the objects around us and their relationship to us, we would not be in a position to choose what to do. If we could know that a predator exists in the environment, without knowing where it is in relation to us, we would not be able to select an appropriate response. The unconscious mechanisms that make choices for us require inputs. Without inputs, they remain idle. Consciousness provides the range of possible inputs. We might be able to perform some automatic actions in response to unconscious stimuli, but actions that involve deliberation depend on consciousness. Once again, if consciousness occurred at another level, if it weren't an input to action, the fact that we do not act without consciousness would be harder to explain. The present proposal shows how the AIR theory directly bears on this otherwise puzzling fact.

3.2. SOME OBJECTIONS

I have been arguing that the function of consciousness is to provide a menu for action. In this section, I will consider several objections. Most of these concern specific features of the proposal on offer, but the final objection raises a more general worry about the very idea that consciousness has a function.

The first objection takes issue with my use of the singular article in talking about *the* function of consciousness. Might consciousness have many functions? Why focus on action to the exclusion of other contributions that consciousness makes to information processing? In principle, I accept the spirit of this objection and would happily concede that consciousness has many functions. Certainly, if we think about what consciousness does for us in the causal sense rather than in the teleological sense, it seems likely that it is a highly versatile tool (see Baars, 1988: chap. 10). This objection can't be fully addressed without considering specific proposals about alternative functions. I think such alternatives are either unconvincing or special applications of the action link emphasized in my proposal. Let me illustrate with some examples.

Consider first the suggestion that consciousness is for planning. Responding to Milner and Goodale's dual-steam view, Glover and Dixon (2001) argue that conscious states allow us to plan actions, whereas unconscious dorsal processes allow fine-grained motor control. They base this distinction on studies that involve grasping toward optical illusions, like the Ebbinghaus case described above. As we have seen, the evidence for a grasping dissociation has been challenged (Franz et al., 2001), but the proposal about planning does not hang on these experimental results. Whatever one concludes about the dorsal/ventral distinction, it remains plausible that consciousness contributes to planning. Gaining access to viewpoint-specific representations helps us plan our next move. Notice, however, that this is just an application of the menu-for-action idea. Planning is a deliberative action that involves forethought. In providing a menu for action, consciousness lets us plan. But it also lets us react in ways that do not involve much forethought, especially when fast reactions are required. A kick boxer might do some planning as she combats her opponent, but some responses will occur without the benefit of forethought. These will nevertheless depend on conscious perception of her opponent's moves. The point is, planning may be too narrow a construct to explain how consciousness contributes to action, even if action planning is among the things it is good for.

Another suggestion is that consciousness allows us to form episodic memories. Many kinds of memory do not depend on consciousness. Procedural knowledge, associative learning, various forms of conditioning, category learning, and other kinds of semantic information can be encoded unconsciously. But there is evidence that we don't lay down episodic memories without consciously experiencing the episodes. That is a fascinating fact, and it might add further support to the AIR theory, because episodic memory encoding depends on prior availability to working memory (Fletcher and Henson, 2001). Should we infer from this fact that it is a function of consciousness to allow episodic memory? I think that would be an overstatement. The brain mechanisms most centrally involved in episodic memory formation are located in the para-hippocampal region, and these can be impaired without any impact on consciousness. Consciousness is a precondition but is not centrally implicated in memory formation itself. Moreover, the relationship between consciousness and episodic memory may be illuminated by the conjecture that consciousness concerns action. In a provocative treatment of the topic, de Brigard (2011) argues that episodic memory is not primarily in the business of recording the past as much as planning the future. Recollection is a constructive process, highly prone to systematic errors, and de Brigard argues that these facts are best explained on the assumption that we use episodic memories to plan for the future, not to relive the past. The errors we make facilitate planning. With this framework in hand, we can ask why episodic memories require consciousness. The answer that suggests itself is that episodic memories store information in a viewer-centered way, because such representations are most useful for guiding action. Thus, episodic memories require consciousness because consciousness is ideally suited for action. Consciousness is not for memory, but it allows for memories that operate in the service of deliberative action.

Some researchers have argued that consciousness has functions that are more fundamentally cognitive than practical. Some of these proposals come out of the global workspace tradition, which emphasizes the idea of information integration: consciousness arises when inputs from multiple sources come together. In this spirit, Morsella (2005) has proposed that consciousness is for "supermodular" integration. The basic idea is that at any given time, there are multiple parallel processes across our sensory systems vying for control; consciousness arises at a higher level, allowing cross-talk and resolving conflicts among these modules. I am reluctant to accept this proposal, however, because I think that consciousness arises *within* each sense modality, rather than in a global workspace. Consciousness is not a high-level phenomenon, even though it allows for availability to control structures that could be described as super-modular. I think the supermodular idea should be rejected, but we need not abandon Morsella's emphasis on parallel inputs vying for control. The claim that consciousness provides a menu for action is consistent with this. Each item on the menu vies for control. Consciousness does not resolve these conflicts, but it presents us with a range of options and ranks them according to their salience. Then unconscious processes (including unconscious goal rankings, priming, and other context effects) are used to select among these.

My claim that consciousness is not high-level and that it is primarily re-lated to action might look implausible to those who are impressed by the role of consciousness in thought. Surely, they will say, consciousness is for thinking, as much as it is for acting. Our most sophisticated intellectual achievements, such as science, literature, and—yes—philosophy, seem to depend on con-sciousness. Why not suppose that a central function of consciousness is to allow these extraordinary cognitive achievements? The problem with this pro-posal is that we have very little conscious access to how we solve problems (Nisbett and Wilson, 1977). More recent research has shown that, when we try to exercise conscious control over decisions, we are often dissatisfied with the choices (Dijksterhuis et al., 2006; see also Rosenthal, 2008). I don't mean to imply that consciousness makes no contribution to thinking. Consciousness can help us learn abstract rules, carry out logical deductions, and engage in philosophical reflection. But it is possible that these contributions of con-sciousness are parasitic on its role as a tool for action. Here is a conjecture.

As I discussed in chapter 5, we become conscious of our thoughts through sensory imagery and language. Sensory imagery is perspectival, of course, and arguably, the ability to think using imagery is a special application of the ability to plan. Planning involves offline simulations of what it would be like to encoun-ter specific situations, and the conscious imagery used as we plan is tailored for practical decisions. When we use imagery to think, we exploit the same resources that we use in planning, even if we have no practical objectives. For example, when scientists use imagery to think about physical laws, it makes sense to say that they are tapping into practical reasoning capacities and using them for practical ends. I think a similar story is available for language. Words are per-ceivable entities, and we experience words in a perspectival way: at a particular volume, intonation, and location. Our ordinary perceptual encounters with words are social; we hear the speech of others and use it to determine what they are thinking. Words are, in this sense, thoughts rendered perceivable. In conver-sational contexts, words help us act. The speed, volume, location, and, of course, lexical content of what is said all play a role in the verbal and other behavioral responses that we select. Words afford actions, including principally verbal ac-tion. Correspondingly, I'd like to suggest that the use of language in thought, like the use of imagery more broadly, involves the simulation of sensory states in an action-conducive format. When we speak to ourselves, we generate sensory inputs of the kind that we might encounter in conversation, and these inputs allow unconscious mechanisms to generate appropriate responses in the form of further inner speech. A linguistically encoded inference in the mind's ear is a verbal action triggered by an imagined verbal input. What makes language so extraordinary is that linguistic actions are actions on representations, and these representations can represent things that are highly abstract and unrelated to any object in one's local environment. Language allows us to engage in theoretical reflection using a psychological resource, consciousness, that evolved in order to facilitate practical decisions about objects here and now.

In summary, consciousness is more than a menu for action, if action is defined as an immediate response to sensory inputs. But its ability to take us beyond the present in planning, memory, and thought piggybacks on its role in practical deliberation. One might say that the primary function of consciousness is to serve as a menu for action. This is probably what consciousness evolved for, and its current functioning uses representations that are ideally suited for action selection. But we have also evolved and devised ways of translating problems that are hypothetical, retrospective, and theoretical into a practical format. The highest forms of thought are just behavioral responses that have been internalized and symbolically encoded.

Let me turn now to another objection. In defending the claim that consciousness is a menu for action, I've suggested that we would not act without consciousness (excluding automatic reactions and responses prompted by experimenters). In support, I mentioned that people with blindsight do not spontaneously respond to stimuli that they unconsciously perceive. But the claim that people don't respond (nonautomatically) to unconscious stimuli can be challenged. For example, consider a clinical condition dubbed "inverse Anton's syndrome" (Hartmann et al., 1991). Anton's syndrome is a condition in which people who are cortically blind claim to see. In inverse Anton's syndrome, patients with intact visual abilities claim to be blind. The Hartmann et al. case study is striking. They describe a patient who insists that he has no visual experience but successfully reads, names colors, and rates the familiarity of objects when presented in one small region of his visual field; he is able to cook for himself and conducts a relatively self-sufficient life, suggesting that he spontaneously and accurately responds to the visual world, despite a lack of visual experience. This pattern of symptoms is a counterexample to the proposal that consciousness is needed for nonautomatic action and also to the AIR theory itself: if visual information can be reported without experience, then access to working memory is not a sufficient condition for consciousness.

It is risky to invest too much credence in a single case study. The patient described by Hartmann et al. has several large brain lesions, which leave his symptoms difficult to interpret. One lesion has extensively damaged his right occipital cortex, and another affects part of his left occipital cortex, as well as extensive parietal areas. The left parietal lesion is analogous to the right-hemisphere lesions that usually result in neglect. Left parietal lesions, however, usually leave experience intact, so this case is puzzling. I offer the following tentative explanation. It is important to distinguish the capacity to consciously see and the capacity to know that you are consciously seeing, although usually these occur together. In chapter 10, I will argue that knowing what your visual experiences are like involves a process of *maintaining* them in working memory. The relevant kind of maintenance is not a matter of storing a perceptual item in some memory buffer but rather of maintaining the perceptual state in the sensory areas of the brain. To know that you are seeing something requires holding that experience in place. As it turns out, there is strong evidence that such maintenance recruits the left parietal cortex (Smith et al., 1995; Finke, Bublak, and Zihl, 2006). One possibility, then, is that the left parietal injuries in the inverse Anton's patient prevent him from maintaining his visual states. The problem may be exacerbated by the fact that he has only a small island of residual visual acuity and by the fact that this island is in the left hemisphere, where his parietal attention mechanisms are impaired. Another factor is that his injuries prevent him from distinguishing dark and light, which may entail that he experiences darkness when he senses shapes, making his shape experiences very unlike normal visual percepts. The patient claims to feel "something" when he sees; he just denies that it is visual, and this suggests that he may have visual phenomenology but of a very unusual sort. These are mere speculations, of course, but they offer enough reason to think that inverse Anton's syndrome could involve a failure to identify conscious states rather than a failure of consciousness.

I want to consider one final technical worry about the claim that consciousness is a menu for action, which relates to the fact that working memory does not actually encode intermediate-level representations. Working memory encodes information in a more abstract format, perhaps the format of high-level representations. It is these representations, then, that factor into deliberations about what to do. In fact, high-level representations are needed for practical deliberation, because they carry information about the identity of the objects we perceive. When deciding whether to run from a predator, one must first recognize that it is a creature of a certain kind. Thus, high-level representations are the representations that are most relevant to action. Therefore, the claim that the intermediate level serves an action-guiding role is unmotivated.

This objection stems from a failure to appreciate that action, like perception, is hierarchically organized. As already intimated, it is useful to distinguish high, intermediate, and low levels of action control. At the high level, an organism uses semantic knowledge, memory, and goals to decide what to do. The high level is, itself, hierarchically organized according to the complexity of these decisions (Fuster, 2004). Koechlin and Summerfield (2007) distinguish three grades of complexity and map these onto increasingly cascading regions of the lateral prefrontal cortex (LPFC). Contextual control (posterior LPFC) refers to decisions that bring context to bear—for example, don't drink more wine if you are tipsy. Episodic control (anterior LPFC) refers to decisions that deviate from familiar contextual rule—drink when tipsy if it's a special celebration. Branching control (polar LPFC) refers to temporary exceptions—postpone the next drunken sip until the host of the celebration has finished her toast. Decisions of these kinds require categorical knowledge of the current situation—you need to know that there are drinks present—but they do not necessarily utilize viewpoint-specific information. This is high-level action control. But there is also intermediate-level action control, and viewpoint-specific information is crucial for that. The intermediate level plays two crucial roles, in fact. It invites us to make high-level decisions and helps us determine how those decisions should be carried out. The decision about whether to drink might be preceded by seeing a bottle nearby, and the execution of that decision requires tracking the changing position of the bottle. High-level decisions about categories of objects and molar behaviors (should I drink alcohol?) depend on relational information (there is a shiny cylindrical object in front of me). Intermediate-level representations are needed to act on our plans. Such representations are fed to the premotor cortex, which lies at the base of the lateral prefrontal hierarchy and serves as a common denominator for the higher areas. Premotor cortex uses perspectival representations to orchestrate actions and thus corresponds to an intermediate level in action control. There is also a low level. Once one begins to execute an action, fine-grained movements need to be carried out. These don't require deliberation, because they can be driven by perceived stimuli as an action is performed.

If this story is right, the intermediate level of vision is implicated at the intermediate level of action control, even if higher-level visual representations play a more important role in deciding what to do. Of all of the levels in the action hierarchy, the folk term *action* may actually apply most naturally to the intermediate level. The high level corresponds to decision making, and the low level corresponds to movement. The intermediate level corresponds to the performance of a behavior in accordance with a decision. Intermediate-level visual representations are crucial for actions so defined. Notice that high-level decisions, like high-level visual representations, remain invariant across many transformations. As your body's position changes in relation to a bottle of alcohol, your decision to drink and your high-level bottle detectors may remain constant, but your intermediate-level visual representations undergo changes from moment to moment. Tracking these changes is crucial for the performance of actions. We don't need to store the changes, but we need to experience them so that our decisions can be updated. Experience is not necessary to execute stimulus-driven behavioral response (as the case of DF shows), but experience is needed if ongoing changes are to inform deliberative processes. In the drinking scenario, we must choose how high to fill our glass, where to place the bottle on completion, and how gingerly to lift the full glass. Unless our drinking skills have become so rehearsed as to be automatic, these decisions benefit from ongoing conscious inputs.

The objections thus far consider specific details of my story about the function of consciousness. I want to end with a more general objection. The claim that consciousness has a function is sometimes rejected out of hand because it seems possible, in principle, that anything we achieve with our conscious states could also be done unconsciously. There could always be unconscious organisms, for example, that deliberate about how to act. In a word, there could be zombies. As long as this is the case, it will be hard to defend the claim that consciousness itself has any function. Consciousness seems to be epiphenomenal. It plays no more role in guiding action than black and white pentagons play in guiding the trajectory of a soccer ball.

I think that this objection rests on an ambiguity in questions about function. When asking what consciousness is for, we might be asking two different things: what is the functional advantage of our conscious states, or what is the functional advantage of having consciousness in the first place? The first question assumes that some of our mental states are conscious and asks what those states do for us. This is the question that I have been trying to address. It is a scientifically tractable question and can lead to informative theories about the nature of consciousness. The second question, concerning the advantage of having consciousness, can be read as a question about zombies: does consciousness per se give us abilities that couldn't be had without it?

To address this issue, let's distinguish between zombies in the strict sense, which are physical and functional duplicates of us but lack phenomenal consciousness, and zombies in the loose sense, which also lack phenomenal consciousness but are mere behavioral duplicates of us rather than physical duplicates. Does either kind of zombie threaten the thesis that consciousness has a function?

On the face of it, the claim that consciousness has a function is not threatened by loose zombies. The claim that we use consciousness to make deliberative decisions does not entail that all creatures who make deliberative decisions are conscious. By analogy, the fact that fly swatters are used to kill flies does not entail that they are the only way to kill flies. To pursue the objection, one would need to argue that the specific functional or physical processes that constitute consciousness in us are not causally implicated in our ability to deliberate. An objection of that kind would no longer have much to do with zombies; it would require an empirical challenge to some detail of the account that I've been defending. Most likely, it would end up with an alternative account of the role that consciousness plays rather than an epiphenomenalist view. If consciousness has a material basis, then presumably it has a causal function, at least insofar as it has a causal impact on psychology. Consciousness is sometimes said to lack a teleological function (see Rosenthal, 2008), but that conclusion is unlikely if consciousness is the process by which perspectival representations become available to working memory. That process is the linchpin for practical flexibility.

What about strict zombies? If there could be creatures exactly like us functionally and physically but lacking consciousness, would it follow that consciousness is epiphenomenal? This depends on your theory of causation. On a simple counterfactual theory, zombies may seem to threaten epiphenomenalism, because causal efficacy would be measured by seeing what would change if consciousness were removed. But this may not be the most promising way to think about causation. We might think of this as a case of causal over-determination: consciousness could have a causal role even if there are other mechanisms in place with the same role (compare: each bullet fired by a firing squad has the causal effect of killing the prisoner, even if no individual bullet is necessary across counterfactual scenarios in which there was one gun fewer).

These are controversial matters in the philosophy of causation, and I don't intend to settle them here. The real problem with zombie arguments, of course, is that strict zombies are impossible. If materialism is true, consciousness is identical with a functional or physical process, and if that identity obtains, there cannot be duplicates of us without consciousness. Those who believe that zombies are possible are dualists. Like most materialists, I think that the best way to defeat dualism is to explain why we seem to be able to conceive of zombies when, in fact, they are impossible. In other words, we need to explain why conceivability does not entail possibility in this domain. I take up this challenge in chapter 10. I don't focus on zombies there, but what I say can be easily put to use in blocking zombie arguments. My reply to the worry about epiphenomenalism can be extrapolated as a homework assignment.

Let me conclude by registering a gripe. It is tempting to derail the honest toil that goes into investigating the causal role of consciousness by raising questions about how something like consciousness could possibly belong to the causal order. Such "how possibly" questions are interesting, but they consume a disproportionate amount of intellectual energy within philosophy. If it can be shown that consciousness correlates with material properties that play a particular causal role, questions about whether it's really consciousness that does the causal work distract from the causal proposals that should be the focus of critical assessment. If one were to concede that consciousness is epiphenomenal, there would still be an interesting question about which causal processes co-occur with consciousness, and proposals about the function of consciousness could be rephrased as questions about the function of the correlate of consciousness. So described, theories of function are no less interesting, because they identify the capacities that come into play when we are conscious, and knowing what we can do when we are conscious is a matter of considerable theoretical and practical concern.

In this chapter, I tried to steer a course between enactivism and inactivism. Consciousness is not constituted by action, but it is for action. The relationship between consciousness and action is functional, not metaphysical. If I am right, then consciousness can arise without action but not conversely, because action—when not automatic—depends on a menu of conscious inputs. This proposal builds on the central tenets of the AIR theory, but it also provides a further argument for that theory. The fact that people don't spontaneously act without consciousness can be explained by assuming that consciousness arises when actionable representations become available to systems of deliberative control.

7

Whose Consciousness? The Illusory Self

1. Hume's Thesis

In one of his most famous passages, Hume writes:

> [W]hen I enter most intimately into what I call myself, I always stumble on some particular perception or other, of heat or cold, light or shade, love or hatred, pain or pleasure. I never can catch myself at any time without a perception, and never can observe any thing but the perception. (1739: 252)

This remark admits of various interpretations: metaphysical and phenomenal, strong and weak. Here I want to defend a strong phenomenal version of Hume's view. I want to argue that there is no phenomenal quality corresponding to the subject of experience, no phenomenal I.

This topic has been much discussed by philosophers, and, like Hume, most tend to rely on intuitions, introspective reports, and contestable transcendental arguments. My review will begin with a brief historical survey of the philosophical terrain. But I will be more interested in assessing lines of research that treat the phenomenal I as a topic for empirical enquiry. There have been a number of recent attempts to identify a subject of experience using the techniques of contemporary brain science. I will consider some of the more promising proposals and argue that they come up short in important ways.

Let me begin with some clarifications. Hume offers his introspective report in a discussion of personal identity, which is traditionally regarded as a metaphysical issue. Thus, one can interpret him as addressing the question of what it is to be a self and how a single self can endure through changes over time. Hume's "bundle theory" identifies the self with collections of perceptions, and elsewhere, Hume despairs of ever finding an adequate theory of endurance if this is right (1739: 635). My concern here is not metaphysical. Perhaps selves exist, and perhaps they endure. My concern is with the phenomenal thesis that Hume advances in the course of addressing the metaphysical question.

I take the phenomenal thesis to be this: among the various phenomenal qualities that make up an experience, there is none that can be characterized as an experience of the self or subject in addition to the qualities found in perceived features of the world, sensations, and emotions. Although we might convey the content of our experience using a sentence of the form "I am experiencing X," the actual qualities that make up the experience can be exhaustively surveyed by enumerating the qualities that constitute the experience of X. There is no remainder corresponding to the word *I* in the subject position of the sentence.

This interpretation remains ambiguous on a crucial point, however. The claim that there are no I-qualia *in addition* to the qualities of perception, sensation, and emotion might be understood in two ways. On a weak reading, there are qualia corresponding to the I, but these are nothing above and beyond the qualities of perception, sensation, and emotion. That is to say, I-qualia exist but are reducible to other kinds of qualia. I feel myself *as* a bundle of perceptions. When I say, "I experience X," there is an experience of the I, but it is to be found in the experience of X. Call this the reductive reading of Hume's thesis. On a stronger reading, Hume's thesis says that there are no I-qualia, whether reducible or not. On this reading, we cannot save the phenomenal I by equating it with the qualia that correspond to something that the I would be described as experiencing. Call this the eliminativist reading of Hume's thesis. I will be defending a version of this stronger interpretation.

It is important to get a little clearer about what the eliminativist is denying. There is an obvious sense in which conscious experience of a self is incontrovertible. Many of my experiences are experiences of things that take place inside my body. A sensation on my skin or an emotion is in me. If the body is part of the self, then surely I can experience myself. So the eliminativist about the phenomenal I cannot deny that the self (or part of the self) can be an *object* of conscious experience. There is a phenomenal *me*. The issue concerns the subject of conscious experience. When I experience a sensation in my body, there is an experience of me, but is there also an I, a subject who is having that experience? Is there any experience that corresponds to the I when I say, "I am experiencing X"? The eliminativist will say no. One might put this by saying that the eliminativist denies any consciousness of a self *as a self*, that is, serving as the subject of an experience, thought, or action. More precisely, the eliminativist says there is no component of an experience that has a special claim to being the experience of self such that *that* component is playing something like a subject role for the experience. There is nothing phenomenal that corresponds to the I in states that we would express using that word.

Those who believe in the phenomenal I, whether reductive or not, claim otherwise. They claim that we can find an I in experience. Reductionists claim that the I is there in Hume's bundle, and nonreductionists say that the I is something above and beyond the bundle. Some believers say that the I comes and goes, and others say it is always there in every experience. I reject both claims.

To be clear, the eliminativist about the phenomenal I need not be an eliminativist about the I in a metaphysical sense. The eliminativist is not necessarily what P. F. Strawson calls a no-subject theorist or a defender of Wittgenstein and Anscombe's semantic thesis that *I* is not a referring expression. Perhaps *I* refers. Nor is the eliminativist committed to the view that we cannot find anything in experience on the basis of which an I can be inferred. Perhaps we are indirectly or inferentially aware of an I. Indeed, there may be an implicit I in every experience. In the concluding section, I will discuss several ways in which this might be true.

2. Nonreductive Theories of the Phenomenal Self

2.1. THE CARTESIAN I

Philosophical thinking about self-consciousness got a major boost when Descartes formulated his *cogito*. In saying "I think" in the first person and declaring that this is indubitable, Descartes implies that there is an I, which is directly accessed in consciousness. He then went on to speculate on the nature of this I, noting that it can be accessed with greater certainty than any thing in the physical world and also implying that it exists independently from any existing thought. I am a thing that thinks, he concluded, a *res cogitans*.

Descartes's account is a paradigm case of a nonreductive theory of the phenomenal self, because it implies that the self is present in experience but not reducible to anything else. Unfortunately, however, Descartes does not say much to back up this claim, and he has been accused, most famously by Lichtenberg (1765–1799: 190), of smuggling in the I. It may be indubitable that there is thought, quips Lichtenberg, but not that there is a thinker. The I is not given in the experience of thought; we just experience whatever it is that we are thinking about.

Lichtenberg's critique is damaging if we interpret Descartes's *cogito* as a deductive argument. If Descartes thinks that the existence of thought logically entails a thinker, he is mistaken. Or, rather, the logical entailment here is just an empty fact about grammar. It's true that Latin requires verb conjugation and English requires a grammatical subject. So sentences using the verb *to think* will always allow quantification into the subject position. But this point of logic does not carry ontological weight. We could always swap out verbs for nouns and say, "An episode of thinking is occurring now."

A Cartesian might try avoid this reliance on grammar by appeal to introspection. Perhaps we find an I in experience whenever we think. This strategy is unpromising. To see why, consider the kinds of thoughts that lead up to Descartes's *cogito*. Consider the thought that we might express as "I doubt that the table in front of me really exists." In consciousness, this thought might present itself as a combination of verbal imagery (saying "This table may be a dream"), visual imagery (seeing the table and perhaps imagining it vanishing suddenly), and emotions (a feeling of uncertainty or withered confidence). Now the question for

Descartes is, can we find a phenomenal I in this conscious episode? If so, it certainly isn't obvious. It seems that I can have all of these experiences without any experience of an I.

One might think that the I appears when introspection turns inward, and I recognize my own doubt. I move from doubting the reality of the table to judging that I have such a doubt. But this shift can be explained without bringing in any phenomenal I. To recognize my own attitude toward the table, I need only have a capacity to notice and label my feeling of doubt. Imagine that this is achieved the way ordinary perceptual object recognition is achieved: I match a current experience against stored, labeled records of prior states. When I turn inward, I am able to classify my feelings of uncertainty as such. In so doing, I don't seem to require any kind of conscious experience of a self. I just need to experience an emotional state. Indeed, phenomenologically, the experience of doubting that a table is real and the experience of recognizing such a doubt in myself may be extremely similar. In both cases, there is an experience of an emotion, some verbal narrative, and a table. An inward focus on the emotion may lead to an intensification of that feeling, which is what happens when we focus on any perceived feature, and the verbal narrative might change from "The table may not be real" to "I am having doubts about the table's reality." But these changes, including the addition of the word *I* in my subvocal report, do not bring in an experience of a subject; just the doubt itself, a particular feeling, comes into sharper view.

I don't intend this introspective sketch as a powerful argument. My point, on the contrary, is that introspection is not especially reliable here. The Cartesian who is certain that there is an experience of a thinker as an add-on to every thought will clash with Lichtenberg, who introspects and finds no such thing. Given the clash in introspective reports, it seems that the debate is at best a stalemate.

Concerns about the limits of introspection are not limited to Descartes. We find contemporary thinkers falling into the same trap. One example is Kriegel (2005), who claims that it is introspectively apparent that every phenomenal experience contains an element of me-ness. It's usually not the focus of experience, he concedes, but it is there in the periphery, in the way that one might be aware of a canvas while looking at what a painting depicts. He uses this introspective intuition to ground a self-referential theory of consciousness according to which consciousness arises when mental states represent themselves. Self-referential states have the requisite duality, according to Kriegel: they represent features of the world, and they represent representing, which imparts a sense of me-ness (notice that this theory is reductive, unlike Descartes's).

There are some problems with Kriegel's account, which I will only flag here. One issue concerns the biological plausibility of the claim that perceptual states represent themselves. Neurons are said to represent perceptual features by virtue of their response profiles: edge detectors fire when edges are present.

There is nothing about these neurons by virtue of which we should say that they also represent themselves: they don't cause themselves to fire, and when perceptual cells fire unconsciously, they don't change their dynamics in any way that could be plausibly interpreted as a loss of a self-representing function. Another issue concerns the claim that self-reference would impart a sense of me-ness. Self-reference is cheap. The word *word* refers to itself; this sentence refers to itself; a concave mirror represents itself infinitely. None of these things can be said to have a sense of me-ness as a result. It's not clear why a perceptual state that also represents itself would give rise to a phenomenal I. Finally, and most important, Kriegel's theory rests on an introspective datum that might be challenged. When I introspect, I don't find the me-ness that Kriegel describes. I find only the world. Which one of us is introspecting more accurately? Who knows? Clashing reports of this kind are notoriously difficult to resolve. That is precisely why introspectionist psychology failed.

In summary, the long and distinguished tradition of arguing for a phenomenal I by appeal to intuition may be a blind alley. Of course, Hume's argument also rests on introspection. He says that he finds no I when he looks inward. But Hume is at a slight advantage. He does find other things that most people believe to exist: perceptual, sensory, and emotional qualia. Given the obviousness of these, one might wonder why the phenomenal I is not obvious to everyone. That asymmetry gets his position off the ground. But it doesn't settle the case, because there is always a chance that Hume and his followers are not introspecting well. So we need to look for other kinds of evidence.

In making these remarks, I don't mean to be suggesting that we should do without introspection entirely. Studies of consciousness often depend heavily on first-person reports. Rather, the claim is that introspection on its own may not suffice. Those who claim to find an I in experience would do well to find some nonintrospective convergent evidence. Perhaps a substantive theory of what the phenomenal I consists in, backed up by nonintrospective evidence for whatever the theory postulates, can help the Humeans see that there is an I in experience, after all.

2.2. THE KANTIAN I

One might try to escape the pitfalls of introspection by devising an a priori argument for a phenomenal I. Why rely on observation when we can make discoveries through the light of reason? A version of this approach has been famously pursued by Kant in the "Transcendental Deduction" chapter of his first *Critique* (1781). This is not the place to get embroiled in a scholarly debate on what Kant is doing in this difficult section of the first *Critique* (see Brook, 1994; Patricia Kitcher, 1982; and Strawson, 1966, for different readings). But it will be instructive to see one highly simplified version of Kant's strategy, because the limitations found therein will likely generalize to more detailed renditions of his argument. Whatever Kant may succeed in showing in his transcendental deduction, I don't think he provides compelling reason to postulate a phenomenal I.

Here, then, is a very stripped-down version of the Kantian argument. Suppose you are looking at a glass of wine. The visual state you are in has multiple parts, corresponding to different portions of the glass's contour, the color of the wine, the reflected light, and so on. When you lift the wine for a sip, the shape changes, and you become aware of other sensations: the cool glass on your fingertips, the bouquet, the feel of the wine swishing into your mouth, the puckering caused by the tannins, and, of course, the taste. Again, there are multiple components to the perceptual episode, and these are extended in time and in space. Yet despite this multiplicity, you experience all of these components as part of a single object. They are all features of the glass of wine. To see it as a glass of wine, you need to place it under a concept. Indeed, for Kant, your perceptual experience would be "blind"—or meaningless—in the absence of a corresponding concept; representation requires conceptualization. But how, one might wonder, can the concept be applied if the various components of the percept do not get bound together? Consciousness of an object requires conceptualization, which, in turn, requires unification of the sensory manifold in space and time. But what can perform this unity? Kant's answer is the transcendental unity of apperception, which is, on his view, a kind of self. Intuitively, there must be an I that exists from moment to moment, and for each component of the image, the I must recognize that all of these components are experiences of that single I. In Kant's idiom, they must be part of a single consciousness.

Kant calls this unifying self transcendental because it is not an item found in the sensory manifold. Rather, it is a precondition for perceiving objects in the first place. He distinguishes the transcendental unity from the "empirical self," which is a self that we might look for in the sensory manifold; the empirical self is an object of experience rather than a subject of experience, and in seeking the empirical self, Kant often sounds a bit like Hume, implying that there is no single thing there beyond the bundle of experience. But the transcendental unity remains constant across sensory episodes. Moreover, the transcendental unity is not recognized by discovering any of its features. Like the Cartesian I, it is a kind of pure, simple ego, although Kant does not go so far as to call it a substance.

There is a thorny exegetical question about whether Kant's transcendental self is supposed to present itself somehow in the quality of experience. Since we do not know this self by description, it might be that there can be no feature of experience, no quale, that corresponds to it. On the other hand, Kant does imply that the quality of experience overall depends very much on this self (compare Kriegel, whose me-ness inheres in each feature of experience, because all sensory qualities are self-referential). In particular, it is a feature of conscious experience that it is unified, and Kant's transcendental self is that by virtue of which the unity is achieved. Thus, one might say that the phenomenal I, for

Kant, is the felt unity of experience. Notice that this is a nonreductive theory, because the I is something above and beyond the sensory items that we happen to be experiencing: it is their felt unity.

Kant's argument, as rendered here, is interesting for two reasons. First, it offers an account of what the phenomenal I consists in, and second, it presents reasons for thinking that a phenomenal self, so conceived, is a precondition for consciousness. The I is not only felt; it is necessary for feeling. This provides a powerful strategy for responding to Hume, whose skepticism about self-awareness may have provoked some of Kant's discussion (see Kitcher, 1982).

The defender of Hume's thesis must address Kant's argument, and there are various places where one might wage a Humean counterattack. One issue is Kant's highly contentious claim that perception without conception is blind. This claim is rejected by those who believe in nonconceptual contents, and I think they are right (e.g., Bermúdez, 1995; Crane, 1992; Evans, 1982). Most naturalistic theories of representation explain mental content by appeal to mind-world relations such as causal relations between inner states and features of the world, and these can exist without the involvement of concepts (e.g., a perceptual edge detector can represent edges by virtue of causally covarying with edges). Arguably, Kant's case for the self hangs on his claim about the conceptual basis of unity. Kant believes that concepts differ from percepts by virtue of being "spontaneous" as opposed to "receptive"; that is, they can be applied by act of will by an agent rather than depending on stimulation of the sense organs. Spontaneity, so understood, is agentic; it requires an acting, norm-sensitive subject. So it is in spontaneity that the self comes in. Kant's claim that experience involves a subject is directly linked to his view about concepts and his conjecture that perception is always conceptual.

This is not the place to settle the debate about nonconceptual content. Rather than taking on that contentious topic directly, I want to focus on another point of vulnerability in Kant's argument. Whether or not concepts are necessarily applied to percepts, one can ask whether concepts, or, for that matter, anything like a unified subject, are necessary to explain the unity of experience. If unity has an alternative explanation, then when we experience unity, we are not experiencing something that deserves to be called the self. The Kantian effort to identify the phenomenal I in unity would be thus undermined.

There are popular accounts of unity available that do not appeal to a self. I will not outline a positive proposal here, because that is the main task of chapter 8. But let me simply point out for now that there are numerous proposals in the empirical literature to explain how components of experience get bound together, and few of these presuppose anything like a subject. Four representative approaches illustrate this. There are object file accounts, according to which unity is achieved through causal links to mental maps (Treisman and Gelade, 1980); there are global workspace theories, according to which unity arises with broadcasting to functionally integrated central systems (Baars, 1988);

there are conjunctive unit theories, according to which distributed features get linked to shared nodes in neural networks (O'Reilly, Busby, and Soto, 2003); and there are temporal binding accounts, according to which unity derives from synchronized neural activity (an approach that I will defend in chapter 8). Each of these accounts is different, but they share one crucial attribute: none supposes that there is any sense in which the mechanism or process of integration qualifies as a self. Mental maps, global broadcasting, neural oscillations, and conjunctive nodes would all be pathetic neural correlates for the subject of experience. If any such mechanism can explain unity, then the Kantian conjecture is unmotivated.

At this point, committed Kantians might try to bring the I back in by arguing that these approaches to unity are inadequate. Neural accounts are intended to explain how the components of an experience get bound together, but that is not enough. A Kantian might say that an adequate theory of unity must also specify that it is I, the subject, who is experiencing all of these components. Suppose that I see a glass of wine and then choose to take a sip. The seeing and the sipping are not just bound to each other in time, as subject-less events, but they depend crucially on the fact that I see the glass and I desire wine, and I know that sipping it will satisfy that desire. The I who sees, lifts, and sips must be the same for the sequence to make any sense.

Perhaps this is right. Ordinarily, there is integration among beliefs, desires, and actions over time. As one moves from premise to conclusion in a practical syllogism, the subject must remain constant, or the syllogism would be invalid. But this does not require a conscious or phenomenal subject. Consciously, I may experience nothing but a glass of wine and a subsequent sip. Unconscious unity is needed for that transition, but there need be no felt self, however minimal, that carries over from one event to the next. Indeed, I don't think that Kant's transcendental subject could provide such unity. The transcendental subject is not descriptive but consists merely in the binding. But notice that bindings change from moment to moment. The features that get bound vary, and the mechanisms that achieve the binding, such as object maps, are themselves ephemeral. If some kind of continuity is needed to explain practical deliberation, it is unlikely that they will be found in conscious binding. It is more likely that continuity depends on unconscious mechanisms of control, planning, and memory.

In summary, I see little in Kant that should lead us to postulate a phenomenal I.

2.3. SELF, LOST AND FOUND

Descartes and Kant suppose that the I is always present. There is no experience without an experiencer. For some, this does not ring true phenomenologically. There is a common phenomenon that we refer to as "losing yourself" in experience. Sometimes we become so absorbed in an activity that we seem to lose awareness of everything else, including, it is said, one's own self. Taken at face value, this phenomenon would be hard to square with the Cartesian and Kantian perspectives on the topic. When we lose our selves, we don't stop thinking, as a Cartesian might suppose, and we don't lose conscious unity. More important, the phenomenon suggests that the consciously experienced self can come and go. If that's right, there is a clear strategy for trying to find out what the conscious self consists in: we can compare what happens when we lose ourselves to what happens when the self reappears.

This is exactly the strategy that has been pursued by a group of researchers in contemporary neuroscience. Goldberg, Harel, and Malach (2006) used fMRI to test brain activation as subjects listened to brief musical recordings or looked at pictures. In one condition, they had to say whether the pictures depicted animals and whether the recordings contained a trumpet. They were given ample time to reflect on their choices. In another condition, they had the same instructions, but the recordings and pictures were presented very quickly. The authors reasoned that when subjects were forced to answer quickly, they would tend to lose themselves in the task. Finally, there was a condition in which subjects were asked to decide whether they liked recordings and pictures, a task that requires introspection and is thus maximally self-involving. They found that the introspection condition showed greater activation in the superior frontal gyrus (SFG) than the other two conditions, and SFG was actually suppressed in the rapid task, suggesting that self-awareness was actively being suppressed. In another pair of studies, they also found that SFG was highly active when people read a word list and decided whether each word was true of themselves, as compared with when people read a word list and decide whether each word is a noun or a verb. The words included a wide range of objects and activities, which are not especially emotional in nature, unlike the picture-preference task (e.g., study, run, coffee, and bus). Here again, SFG seems to correlate with the degree of self-involvement. One of the authors of this work was also involved in a further study that showed minimal SFG activation (along with other frontal structures) during passive watching of a movie, suggesting that viewers lose themselves in the film. All of this evidence suggests that SFG is active in a self-related task and inactive when people lose themselves. The authors conclude that it is a neural correlate of self-awareness.

Interestingly, the authors imply that SFG corresponds to an experience of the self in some sui generis sense, rather than reducing the self to some other aspect of experience. SFG activity arises when we perceive sounds and images or feel emotions, but the authors do not think that it is a center of perception and feeling. Rather, it is a common denominator across different cases in which we attribute states to our selves, and this might be taken to suggest that it is the neural correlate of the self as such. In this respect, the work differs from research that will be summarized below, which attempts to reduce self-experience to some kind of bodily experience.

To assess this research, it is important to have some perspective on SFG. We cannot conclude that this is the neural correlate of the self without knowing what other roles it might play in cognition. This is tricky because the label SFG is often used to cover a large region, with subcomponents that vary in function. But it is revealing to notice that SFG has been implicated in working memory, especially when working-memory tasks are highly demanding (du Boisgueheneuc et al., 2006). If SFG is involved in working memory, we can explain the Goldberg, Harel, and Malach results without assuming that it is a correlate of self-awareness. In order to decide whether a picture or a song is appealing, one has to focus attention on that stimulus *in addition to* one's reactions to it. Holding two things in mind at once requires more use of working memory than mere perceptual classification. And searching memory to see whether words apply to one's self requires more working-memory effort than deciding whether they are nouns or verbs. In both cases, the authors are comparing a relatively passive bottom-up classification task to one that requires reflection. The increase in brain activity may reflect this change in cognitive demands, rather than consciousness of the self.

Against this interpretation, Goldberg, Harel, and Malach might point out that in their study, SFG activity diminishes when they increase task difficulty (i.e., in the high-speed condition). Working-memory structures usually increase in activity when tasks become harder, so the decrease reported by Goldberg, Harel, and Malach counts against the hypothesis that SFG is a working-memory center. But this objection can be rejected. It is a mistake to assume that the high-speed condition increases working-memory demands. When speed is required, reflection slows down performance, so working memory must be inhibited. The reduction in SFG activity is predicted by the working-memory interpretation. A reduction in SFG activity is also predicted in the study when people watch movies; in passive movie viewing, we usually absorb the content without reflecting. Thus, all of the results are consistent with the view that SFG is a structure whose function is to play a role in demanding forms of working memory. There is little pressure to say that it is the neural seat of the self.

Goldberg, Harel, and Malach might object that this deflationary reading is ad hoc. After all, they explicitly ask subjects to introspect by giving them questions about their preferences and traits. Isn't it obvious that the tasks require self-awareness? I don't think so. Or, rather, I don't think that the tasks require any special phenomenal character that corresponds to the experience of oneself as a subject. The picture/music preference task involves emotional responses to stimuli. These emotions exist within the minds of the experimental participants, of course, but there is a difference between feeling an emotion and feeling a phenomenal I. If you introspect and discover delight in a piece of music, your experience contains delight and the music. You might describe it by saying, "I like this music," but you could equally well say, "There is a delight response happening along with the music," without using a first-person pronoun. Likewise, when you decide whether a word applies to you ("Do I run?" "Do I take a bus?"), you may call up memories of your morning jog or your morning commute, but there need be no experience of a self in these. The recollection may be relived from a particular point of view (running from this perspective), but points of view need have nothing especially selflike. Notice that a movie camera presents the world from a point of view. To assume that such *memories* involve a phenomenal I begs the question against those who think that the recalled activities do not involve a phenomenal I. When I board a bus, I experience the bus but not a subject of that experience.

Goldberg, Harel, and Malach might still object. They might say that the phenomenon of "losing yourself" is commonplace and that it is clearly a case of losing a phenomenal experience of one's self as a subject of experience. We may be misled by language here. The phrase "losing yourself" implies that there is an experience of one's self that comes and goes. But in reality, that phrase is characteristically used to refer to situations in which we focus attention narrowly on an activity and stop experiencing other things, whether they are self-involving or not. If you lose yourself watching a movie, that means that you stopped thinking about the day's events, that overdue paper you need to get done, and perhaps even the people sitting in the theater all around you. Losing yourself is just temporal absorption. It's true that when you stop thinking about your to-do list, you have thereby stopped thinking about yourself in some sense, but that is only because the items on the list are things that *you* need to do. Phenomenologically, your experience does not lose an explicit sense of me-ness; it just loses the usual rumination about activities or events that happen to involve you.

These lines of reply might be summarized by saying that the Goldberg study can at best be regarded as an investigation of the self as object, rather than the self as subject. In their tasks, we report things about ourselves, but in so doing, we are treating the self as just another thing in the world with certain describable features. We are not experiencing ourselves acting as the subject of thought or experience. This is not the elusive self as I. They do not establish that some thoughts have a qualitative component that occupies the position that the word *I* occupies in self-ascriptions, such as "I like this music." As Lichtenberg might say, they establish the liking, not the liker.

3. Reductive Theories of the Phenomenal Self

3.1. FEELINGS

The theories I've been considering are nonreductive. They suppose that the phenomenal I is something above and beyond the things experienced by that I. Such theories incur a heavy burden, because it is difficult to find anything in experience above and beyond the items delivered to our senses. All contents of consciousness seem to be perceptual. If we were to list each perceptual feature that we were experiencing at a given moment, including sensations of our own bodies, mental imagery, and subvocal speech, there would seem to be no remainder. This is the central insight behind Hume's thesis, and it is very hard to deny. We've just seen three efforts to locate a self that transcends mere perceptual qualia, but none is convincing. This suggests that Hume was right. But recall that Hume's thesis has two versions. The weaker version says that there is no self *over and above* the items we perceive. The stronger version says that there is no phenomenal self at all. One could try to challenge the stronger version by offering a reductive account, on which the phenomenal I gets equated with some subset of the many things we happen to be perceiving in any given moment. Some privileged subset of conscious perceptions may qualify as the perceiver, the subject of experience. As Damasio (1999) puts it, the I may not be the viewer of an internal movie but rather an object in the movie. This is the kind of approach I want to consider now, and Damasio will be the first example.

Damasio came into widespread recognition because of his (1994) work on the emotions. Here he resuscitated a theory that originated with William James and the Danish physician Carl Lange. On the James-Lange theory, emotions are not the things that cause us to laugh or cry or flee or fight. Rather, they are perceptions of patterned bodily changes that include such characteristic responses. When an emotionally significant stimulus is encountered, it triggers a bodily change that prepares us for a behavioral response, and then the mind perceives this change, and our experience of that bodily perception is the emotion. Damasio argues that contemporary research in psychology and neuroscience (including his own field, neurology) supports the James-Lange theory, and I have argued at great length elsewhere that he is right (Prinz, 2004b). But Damasio also thinks that this story can help provide an account of self-consciousness, and here we part company.

Damasio's (1999) story goes like this. Emotions are short-lived events that arise in response to specific elicitors, but emotions are not the only mental events in which we perceive changes in our bodies. In reality, we are perceiving our bodies all the time, and emotions are just one special case of this broader phenomenon. Damasio (1994) calls such perceptions "background feelings," and despite the term, he thinks that these can go on unconsciously. In his (1999) book, he says that we can think of these background feelings as a "proto-self" for reasons that will become clear below. Background feelings are not constant over time but rather change incessantly as objects in our environment impinge on our senses. When we see something or hear something or smell something, the body reacts. Damasio speculates that the nervous system must keep track of these changes; it must monitor how the world is affecting the body at all times. To do this, there must be "second-order maps," representations of the first-order body representations as they undergo changes. Damasio thinks that these second-order representations are conscious, and he thinks that they constitute a basic form of self-consciousness shared by humans and other animals. To experience the feelings constituted by fluctuations in your body is, according to Damasio, to experience yourself. Damasio calls this the "core-self," and he distinguishes it from the "autobiographical self," which involves the reliving of episodic memories. The autobiographical self is not found in all animals and can be absent in people with anterograde amnesia. Its status as a form of self-consciousness depends, in part, on the fact that when we relive memories, we experience the core-self acting in events from the past. The core-self is essential for self-experience. As I understand him, Damasio thinks that the core-self is necessary and sufficient for having an experience of one's self as a subject.

Damasio's account of self-consciousness echoes themes in William James's discussion of that topic. James is interested in how we feel like the same self from moment to moment—the qualitative counterpart of personal identity— and he suggests that continuity of bodily experiences plays an important role: "*Resemblance among the parts of a continuum of feelings* (especially bodily feelings) experienced along with things widely different in all other regards, *thus constitutes the real and verifiable 'personal identity' which we feel*" (James, 1890: 336).

The bodily feelings proposal has some intuitive plausibility. First, the body is part of the person, so an experience of the body, unlike an experience of some object out there in the environment, is an experience of the self, in some sense. Second, changes in the body reflect a person's subjective responses to the world, including emotional responses, and the numerous unnamed responses we have to everything we encounter. Everything makes us feel some way, and tracking those feelings is, to that extent, tracking subjectivity. Third, there may be repeatable or predictable bodily responses that correspond to enduring aspects of the self such as values and personality traits, which are part of personal identity. The way my body reacts reflects something about who I am as a person, and I can recognize those reactions as such. I can also notice that on some days, I do not "feel myself" because my reactions are different from what they normally are. Here again, we find something very selflike in the experience of the body.

Given all of this, it is very tempting to adopt the Damasio-James approach and identify the phenomenal I with the experience of bodily feelings, associated with second-order bodily maps in the brain. But I think that this temptation should be resisted. The experience of our bodily feelings is neither necessary nor sufficient for a phenomenal experience of one's self as a subject.

Let's begin with necessity. The intuition that bodily feeling contribute to self-awareness is strongest when we imagine encounters with physical objects that matter to us. If a loud noise startles me, for instance, I will feel a strong sudden response in my body. Attention is drawn inward as I feel myself reacting to the sound. But there are many other cases in which the experience of the body is less pronounced without any loss in the impression that I am the subject of my experiences. Consider intellectual exercises such as reflecting on philosophy, solving a crossword puzzle, or performing calculations in your head. Such activities might engage the body, but intuitively, they need not. To take one simple case, imagine counting backward from one hundred. It seems very plausible that while doing this, one periodically loses conscious experience of the body for brief moments. Indeed, there is evidence that tasks involving working memory tend to suppress activity in brain structures associated with emotion and bodily experience (Yun, Krystal, and Mathalon, 2010). But when that happens, the task seems no less agentic, no less self-involving. I am not claiming that there is some phenomenal I present in counting backward, which is preserved when we stop experiencing the body. I think that there is no experience of an I in either case. My point here is that Damasio's theory predicts that a phenomenal I should disappear when body awareness does, but there seems to be no subjective sense of I that comes and goes with bodily experience. There is no sense of I as subject at all, but there certainly doesn't seem to be one that depends on the body.

Nor does body awareness seem sufficient for a sense of self. To see this, consider the phenomenon of emotional contagion (Hatfield, Cacioppo, and Rapson, 1993). Emotions are catching. If I see you grimace in anger, I will undergo the corresponding bodily change and feel a flash of anger, too. It turns out that this capacity may play a crucial role in emotion attribution. My ability to know what you are feeling depends to some degree on my ability to catch your emotions. We use our own bodily switchboard to attribute feelings to others. This is confirmed in many neuroimaging studies, showing that the same brain structures are used both to experience emotions and to recognize them in others, and injuries to these structures result in deficits of both experience and attribution (Adolphs, 2002). Now, imagine a case in which I recognize an emotion in you. Perhaps I see that you are angry. The science suggests that I do this by first mirroring your bodily expression in my own body and then feeling that change in me. Still, there is no temptation for me to say, "I am angry." I might not be. I feel anger, but I don't feel as if it's mine. The anger I feel is, in some sense, yours. I feel through myself; but it doesn't feel like myself that I am feeling. There is no subjective ownership of the felt state. This suggests to me that we can feel patterns of change in our own bodies without that feeling constituting a phenomenal I. This may sound paradoxical (how can I feel my body as you?), but perplexity subsides when you recall that a body feeling is just an inner state that registers basic physiological facts: a heart is racing, muscles are tensed, breathing is constrained, and so on. It seems plausible that one could become aware of those facts without thereby experiencing them as facts about me. For example, if my brain could get wired to your heart, I could feel your heartbeat, just as I do when I put a stethoscope to your chest.

Finally, if bodily feelings were the basis of self-consciousness, we should find a correlation between these feelings and the degree to which one experiences a sense of self. But that does not seem to be the case. The sense of self neither increases nor decreases with felt bodily changes. For example, consider very intense emotions. These don't seem to engender a greater phenomenal sense of self than mild emotions. Terror after hearing an intruder enter your house does not feel more selflike than mild delight while strolling on the beach. Indeed, with intense emotions, focus is often more outward than inward: the terror makes you forget yourself for a moment and focus intensely on the sounds coming from the intruder. Conversely, a sense of self can increase without a change in the intensity of bodily experience. Emotions, again, can illustrate. Consider a familiar contrast between shame and guilt. With guilt, we focus on some offending act, and with shame, we focus on the self. When ashamed, one feels like a bad person. Both emotions can be equally intense, and hence the bodily feelings are equally vivid, but one seems to involve a greater degree of self-awareness. I am not suggesting that there is a phenomenal I in either of these emotions (I am skeptical about the phenomenal I), but if there is anything at all to the idea that experiences can relate to the self, shame seems to be a better case than guilt. The difference may involve the thoughts and actions that come to mind when shame is experienced: there is a desire to conceal one's self, a feeling of being impure, and a self-conceptualization as a bad person. These specific contents, not the degree of bodily involvement, add up to a pattern of behavior and judgment that can be characterized as self-focused. The intuition that some mental states involve a greater degree of self-awareness seems to track the degree to which those states lead us to think about ourselves, not anything about their bodily character.

This leaves us with just one question. Why do we use locutions such as "I do not feel like myself today" when our bodily responses depart from their usual pattern? Doesn't this suggest that feeling like one's self is a matter of feeling one's body? I don't think so. When one says, "I don't feel like myself today," one is comparing a current experience to the past. It doesn't require a selflike feeling but rather the knowledge that certain feelings are typical for me and the judgment that those typical feelings are not arising in the present. Recognizing variation in feelings is no more self-involving than recognition of variation in behavioral performance. Suppose I am a good ping-pong player and have an off day. I can say, "I am not playing like myself today." And in saying this, I am not implying that there is subjective feeling of self-ness present on most days but absent on this one. I am saying that my response patterns are diverting from the statistical norm. By analogy, if I am normally giddy but feel depressed today, I might say, "I don't have those feelings I usually feel." In saying this, I am not saying that I've lost my phenomenal I. Perhaps there was never one to lose.

3.2. OWNERSHIP

One difficulty with identifying the phenomenal I with feelings and emotions is that there seems to be nothing paradoxical about an unfeeling self. Another difficulty is that the mere presence of feelings does not yet decide between self and other; we need a story about what makes feelings count as mine. Both of these concerns are addressed by another approach to the phenomenal I, which has been gaining momentum in cognitive science. It is the view that the experience of a self can be reduced to a feeling of bodily ownership. The phenomenal I emerges when we feel our own bodies and feel them as belonging to ourselves.

This view bears a resemblance to the view advocated by James and Damasio, because it places emphasis on the body, but it shifts from inner feelings and emotions, which are associated primarily with visceral changes, and focuses on bodily position and location. Here, the most relevant sensory qualities are proprioception and kinesthesia, which help us determine the configuration of our limbs and torso in space. By shifting away from the viscera, the view avoids an implausible commitment to the view that emotions and feelings are essential to the experience of selfhood. Perception of body position can be present even when experience of emotions and feelings is not.

That said, a mere feeling of a body in space is not sufficient for a sense of selfhood. Just as you can feel emotions without feeling them as yours, you can feel a body without feeling it as yours, even if it happens to be your own body. This may seem paradoxical, but the possibility is brought out clearly in some pathological cases. Consider, for example, alien hand syndrome, in which a person comes to believe that one of his own hands belongs to someone else. For example, Moro, Zampini, and Aglioti (2004) describe patients with right-brain injuries who suffer from a lack of feeling in their left arms (a syndrome often comorbid with unilateral visual neglect); when these patients cross their arms, some feeling is restored, but they continue to insist that the affected limbs do not belong to them. Healthy people may also be capable of experiencing bodily sensations without feeling a sense of self. Indeed, this may be commonplace in social cognition. Just as we use our own emotion systems when perceiving emotions in others, we use our own capacity for bodily sensation when perceiving the bodies of others. For example, Keysers et al. (2004) found activation in somatosensory cortex when individuals watched another person's leg being touched. Thus, any theory that identifies the phenomenal I with perception of bodily position needs a further element: an account of how my body feels as if it is mine. This is often called a sense of ownership.

Body ownership has been intensively studied in recent cognitive neuroscience. One popular strategy is to investigate cases in which the ordinary sense of ownership breaks down. Consider out-of-body experiences, in which one seems to occupy a ghostly imaginary body that hovers in the air or stands beside one's real body. This may sound dubiously mystical, but such experiences are actually relatively common. Moreover, they can be induced in the laboratory, and they can also arise with high prevalence after certain brain injuries. Blanke and Metzinger (2009) review this literature, and they argue that research on out-of-body experiences can help us identify brain structures associated with body ownership. Normally, people feel as if they own their real bodies, but in these exotic cases, ownership shifts to a new imagined body. Blanke and Metzinger reason that the underlying mechanism may be the neural correlate of felt body ownership, which they regard as a minimal form of the phenomenal self. (More elaborate forms of phenomenal selfhood arise when this minimal self is integrated into a global workspace.) To find the mechanism, we can look for the brain area that is active when people have out-of-body experiences and that leads to such experiences when damaged. Here, all signs point to the right temporoparietal juncture (de Ridder et al., 2007). This, Blanke and Metzinger surmise, is the neural correlate of the phenomenal I.

There is a problem with this inference, however, and it has to do with what we know about the right temporoparietal junction. This region is also known to be active in mental-state attribution (Saxe and Powell, 2006) and when subjects imagine another person performing an action (Ruby and Decety, 2001). Such findings suggest that the region has more to do with a sense of the other than with a sense of the self. And indeed, this makes sense in the case of out-of-body experiences. Such experiences typically involve seeing one's real body (or sometimes the imaginary body) as if it were another person. So the temporoparietal junction may not be the seat of bodily ownership after all. To find the mechanism, we must consult other research.

The most promising line of investigation involves a class of perceptual illusions that are, in a way, the inverse of out-of-body experiences. When people have out-of-body experiences, they can see their real bodies without a sense of ownership. But there are also cases in which people experience artificial bodies or body parts as their own. Under certain conditions, we can be made to feel as if we are located in the body of a mannequin, a virtual avatar, or even a block of wood. The most studied demonstration of this phenomenon is the rubber-hand illusion (Botvinick and Cohen, 1998). Here, a rubber hand is placed in front of a person while that person's real hand is hidden from view. Then both the real and the rubber hand are stroked using a brush at the same time (figure 18). After a short time, many people begin to experience the rubber hand as if it were their own. They even misremember the location of their real hand after the procedure is finished, locating it closer to the rubber hand than it actually was. The rubber-hand illusion is well suited to study the sense of bodily ownership because it involves both a feeling of the body in space and an impression that the body belongs to the self.

Tsakiris (2010) set out to identify the neural correlates of body ownership by inducing the rubber-hand illusion inside an fMRI scanner. In comparison with a control condition in which the rubber hand and the real hand are stroked

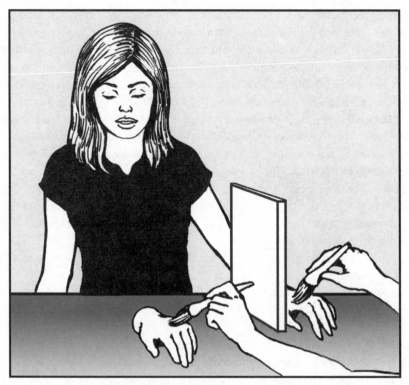

FIGURE 18 Setup to generate the rubber-hand illusion.

out of sync, the illusory sense of ownership was associated with activity in the right posterior insula and the right frontal operculum. The frontal operculum has been associated with motor planning in a TMS study (Tunik, Lo, and Adamovich, 2008), and the insula is associated with body perception and control (Critchley et al., 2004). Indeed, the right posterior insula has been directly implicated in other research as a basis of ownership. Farrer et al. (2003) found that activation in this region correlates with a sense of control in a task involving a virtual hand. Karnath, Baier, and Nagele (2005) found that injuries here are associated with anosognosia for paralyzed limbs, suggesting that an inability to monitor limb ownership results in a failure to recognize when an owned limb is not responsive.

To understand the role of the right posterior insula, it is helpful to understand how the rubber-hand illusion works. We can experience our bodies using a number of senses: we can see a limb, feel something touching a limb, and experience position through proprioception. Normally, such experiences converge on a single location in space, but in illusory cases, that fails to happen. Seeing a rubber hand while feeling a paintbrush shifts the proprioceptive sense of location into the region occupied by the rubber hand. The visual representation of location dominates the proprioceptive, causing the shift. Against this background, it is reasonable to speculate that the right posterior insula plays a role in sensory integration. It brings the different sources of information together and facilitates the proprioceptive shift. The feeling of ownership may arise when senses are brought together. This is a bit like the Kantian suggestion that selfhood emerges with binding, but the thesis here focuses more narrowly on the integration of multiple body representations. I can feel a hand without it feeling like mine (as in alien hand syndrome), but if the hand I feel is integrated with the hand I see in the right way, then it feels like me.

The results of the Tsakiris experiment may seem somewhat puzzling at first. The authors found *more* activation in the right posterior insula when subjects experienced the rubber hand illusion than in the control condition when there was no illusion. But in both conditions, subjects presumably had a sense of ownership; the difference concerns only the accuracy of that sense. Moreover, in the control condition, there was greater activation in somatosensory cortex than in the illusion condition, even though both conditions involved a tactile feeling on the hand. Perhaps what's going on here is a shift in attention. In the control condition, subjects might be focused on the sensation in the hand, and then in the illusion condition, they focused on the sense of ownership because they were surprised to feel the rubber hand as their own. In addition, the increased insula activation may reflect the extra neural work that is involved in forcing visual and proprioceptive information to come into alignment, despite the initial mismatch.

In summary, then, it does seem that the right posterior insula is playing a role in sensory integration and that integration of body representations supports judgments of ownership. Tsakiris and his collaborators regard this as a kind of self-consciousness, and surely, in some sense, they are right. When I experience a body (real or otherwise) as mine, I am experiencing something as related to myself. But things get a little bit thorny when we try to unpack that relation. Ownership is normally thought of as a two-place relation. Body ownership is a relation between a body and a self. It can't be, however, that the phenomenal experience of body ownership involves two relata: a feeling of the body and a feeling of a self. Those interested in the feeling of ownership want to explain the latter in terms of the former. Thus, the feeling of ownership has to be understood in a nonrelational way, if that makes any sense. Or rather, it is experienced in the integration of multiple experiences as of a body. Thus, there is an *n*-place relation here, but no component is privileged as owner of the other components.

Once we see this, we can see a problem for any attempt to explain the phenomenal I in terms of bodily ownership. For the question arises, where is the I in experience? The I cannot be identified with any part, because each bodily perception on its own can be had without a sense of it belonging to the self. So the I must be experienced in the relation or, more plausibly, in the various components as they are related to one another. But what is it to experience two bodily perceptions as related in this way? It won't do to say that we experience them as belonging to the same self, because we need to experience a separate self to which they are related. Instead, we must just experience them as bound together like two features of an object. Perhaps we achieve this by using a map strategy of the kind I mentioned in my discussion of the unity of consciousness. Perhaps visual, tactile, and proprioceptive experiences can be linked to a shared unconscious body map. This analysis treats bodily unity in the same way that unity is explained more broadly. Body perceptions are bound together in the way color is bound to shape. If this is right, it may cast doubt on the view that the experience of bodily ownership can be accurately described as a phenomenal experience of the self. Instead, it seems to be an experience of a bound whole, with no more claim to being me than my polysensory experience of your body when I simultaneously see you and shake your hand. In other words, what begins as a theory of ownership turns out to be no such thing. It's just another case of polysensory binding and does nothing to bring anything especially self-like into experience.

A critic might object that, when I unify the sensory components of my own body, it feels more like myself than when I unify the sensory components of someone else's body. After all, I don't confuse myself for you. True enough, but this objection only serves to highlight the deeper concern. The question is, why don't I confuse myself for you? One might think that the answer has to do with the specific qualities that get bound together. Proprioceptive and tactile sensations, in particular, seem to be uniquely self-involving. But this possibility has already been rejected. I can experience these qualities without experiencing them as me. Indeed, it may well be that when I form an integrated representation of someone else's body, I do so by generating an integrated mental image using my own proprioceptive and tactile mechanisms. I may simulate what it's like to be the other. If so, when I encounter another, I may have two tactile-proprioceptive unities in mind, and there may be nothing in those polysensory bundles as such that determines which one is me. This problem comes out all too vividly in the case of out-of-body experiences. The person who drifts outside of her own body will experience two polysensory somatic bundles. The fact that they are unified is not what makes her identify with one of these bundles as opposed to the other. She might feel both bundles simultaneously but only identify with one. Thus, identification cannot simply be a matter of sensory integration. Something else must be going on.

I am arguing, in effect, that the phenomenal sense of ownership cannot simply be a matter of integrating multiple body representations. More pointedly, I think it is misleading ever to talk about phenomenal ownership of the body, because there is nothing like an experience of an owner bearing a relation to bodily perceptions. I am not denying that we can form *judgments* about ownership. I know that my limbs belong to me. But there may be no *experience* of ownership. There may be an experience on the basis of which we *infer* ownership, but the experience must involve more than an integrated body representation. Such a representation is not sufficient.

Moreover, even if an integrated bundle of bodily perceptions were sufficient for a sense of ownership, it's far from obvious that it would be sufficient for having a sense of one's self as a subject, as opposed to an object. If I feel a pain in a foot, I might be able to perceive that the affected foot is mine, but it doesn't follow that I experience the foot as a subject of thought, experience, and action. The foot does not correspond to the *I* in the ascription "I have a pain in my foot." There is a gulf between *my* and *I*. The thesis of this chapter is that there is no phenomenal I, and integrated bodily representations do not allay that skepticism. If there were a phenomenal sense of ownership (which I doubt), it would not qualify as a phenomenal experience of being a subject.

I would add that having integrated body representations also isn't necessary for having a sense of self. It seems perfectly possible to have one kind of bodily perception in the absence of others. An anesthetized person may lose the sense of touch, a severely dizzy person may lose coherent proprioceptive information, and a blind person will have no visual experiences of the body. Yet none of these conditions prevents a person from using the intact faculties to identify the self. This point is poignantly illustrated in the case of Ian Waterman, who lacks proprioception and touch (Cole, 1995). Waterman locates his body using vision and has as much claim to knowing where he is and how his body is positioned as someone with a more diverse sensory repertoire. He faces challenges in the dark, of course, but when vision is available, he can recognize that his limbs are his own.

In summary, I see several serious hurdles for those who want to find the phenomenal I in the experience of body ownership. First, a sense of ownership would not be sufficient for a sense of self as subject. Second, the leading theory of body ownership—integration of bodily perceptions—is not sufficient for explaining how we judge that felt states of my body are mine. Third, integration of bodily perceptions is not necessary for making such judgments. Fourth, there may not even be such a thing as the phenomenology of ownership.

3.3. AUTHORSHIP

The notion of ownership has been contrasted in cognitive neuroscience with the notion of authorship. Ownership is the feeling associated with a mental state belonging to me. Authorship, also called agency, is the feeling associated with being the author of physical and mental acts. It is identified with a feeling of control. I experience some thoughts and actions as issuing from me. Like ownership, agency involves a kind of possession: the acts I control are mine. But it is an active form of possession, and this, one might think, introduces an entry point for the self. With passive perception, the world can pass by the senses without any sense of being a subject, but with active agency, the self seems to come in essentially. Perhaps the phenomenal I is an experience of oneself as the author.

This proposal overcomes the four problems adduced in response to the suggestion that the phenomenal I derives from a sense of ownership. First, I said that ownership is not sufficient for a sense of oneself as subject, but, as just intimated, authorship is a form of subjectivity par excellence; to experience oneself as author is to experience oneself as the subject of an act—as the I, as opposed to the me. Second, I said that the leading theory of ownership cannot explain how a bundle of experiences feels as if they are mine. Authorship may provide the solution. If I experience two separate bundles of bodily perceptions, I can figure out which one is me by figuring out which one I control. A sense of control can provide a greater sense of mine-ness than mere *sensory* integration because it brings in a motor element that provides for a robust sense of possession; my body is the one that obeys my intentions in predictable ways. The element of control may help explain why the frontal operculum, a motor control structure, is active in the rubber-hand studies. We imagine owning the rubber hand, in part, by preparing to issue action commands. Third, I said that sensory integration is too demanding, because people with just one bodily sense have no difficulty judging which body is theirs. Authorship handles this easily, because one can recognize one's control over a single dimension of bodily perception without reference to any others. Ian Waterman can confirm his bodily control using vision to see that his limbs obey his movements. Finally, I raised doubts about whether there even can be a phenomenology of ownership, because ownership requires an owner. With authorship, things are easier, because there is a functional and anatomical separation between the intentions or commands we issue and their subsequent effects.

One might try to argue against this approach by contending that authorship is never directly experienced but only inferred. One such argument can be distilled from Wegner's (2002) critique of the conscious will, which was discussed in the previous chapter. Wegner argues that we derive a sense of control when we experience a conscious intention that meets three conditions: it occurs just before an observed effect (priority), it is consistent with the observed effect (consistency), and it is the only salient event that meets these first two conditions (exclusivity). Wegner's main point is that the sense of control can be an illusion, because these three conditions can occur even when there is no causal link between intention and effect. Suppose, for example, that my limbs are controlled by unconscious motor commands, but those commands also generate conscious intentions to move, intentions that dangle idly without having any impact on my behavior. The intentions occur before the movement, are consistent with it, and are the only conscious precursor, so I conclude that my intentions are efficacious. Wegner's theory can also be adapted to raise a skeptical worry about the phenomenology of authorship. If he is right, control might not be something we experience; it may be something that we simply infer from conscious intentions and conscious bodily movements. This would spell trouble for defenders of the phenomenal I, because one can surely experience an intention or a movement without feeling any quality that corresponds to being a subject. Indeed, as Wegner points out, in some cases, we experience intentions and actions without inferring control because alternative explanations become available. In one experiment, he asks subjects to press "true" or "false" on a keyboard in response to questions, but subjects are instructed to provide answers on behalf of another person by feeling minute muscle movements in that person's hand, rather than providing their own answers. In actuality, the other person can't even hear the questions, so the answers derive entirely from the subjects, but they nevertheless believe that the other person is selecting the answers. Intention and action are both experienced, but subjects infer a lack of control (Wegner and Wheatley, 1999). Thus, control is not part of the phenomenology but is only inferred by an argument to the best explanation.

The Wegner story gives us reason to be cautious in assuming that there is a phenomenal experience corresponding to authorship. It is possible that in many cases, authorship is merely inferred. But Wegner's theory is not the only game in town. In cognitive neuroscience, there has been an active campaign to find the neural correlates of authorship, and the people conducting this research think that authorship can be phenomenologically experienced, and they even have an explanation of how this occurs. The leading story stems from research on motor control. According to prevailing theories of motor control, intentional action begins when an intention is converted into a motor command by a mechanism called a "controller" (or sometimes an "inverse model"). Controllers output motor commands, but they also send "efference copies" of those commands to a mechanism called a "forward model," which uses the copy of a command to generate a prediction of how the body will move when the command is carried out. Meanwhile, the body carries out the command, and sensory transducers register the resultant changes, which are called reafferent signals. The reafferent signals are compared with the predicted outcomes by means of a comparator, a mechanism that determines whether predicted and actual movements are alike (figure 19). This account has been adapted to explain the phenomenology of authorship (Wolpert, Ghahramani, and Jordan, 1995; Blakemore, Wolpert, and Frith, 2002). We experience actions as our own when a predicted action and a perceived action match. If our bodies move in unpredictable ways, we lose the sense of agency. This happens, for example, when something pushes into us, causing the body to move without a prior motor command.

The comparator model explains a number of interesting phenomena. It explains why it is so hard to tickle yourself (Blakemore, Wolpert, and Frith, 2000). Tickling seems to depend crucially on unpredictability. If you try to tickle yourself, your motor system will accurately predict the hand movements, and you will lose the crucial element of surprise. The comparator model also

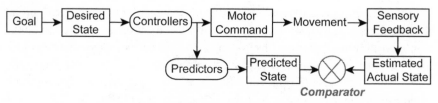

FIGURE 19 The comparator model (simplified from Blakemore, Wolpert, and Frith, 2002).

explains some striking pathologies in the phenomenology of agency. There are cases of alien and anarchic hand syndrome in which patients feel that an appendage is not in their control even though they can feel its movements (Biran and Chatterjee, 2004). These patients characteristically describe the disobedient hand in the third person, as if it did not belong to them. The syndrome is typically associated with damage to the corpus callosum, which allows for communication between the hemispheres. That damage may prevent one hemisphere from predicting actions controlled by the other, giving rise to the experience of alien control.

So far, the cases I have been discussing involve motor behavior. A nice feature of the comparator model is that it can also be adapted to explain the experience of authorship in cognitive processes (Frith, Blakemore, and Wolpert, 2000; Hohwy, 2007; but see Vosgerau and Newen, 2007). One can explain the sense that a thought is my own by supposing that prior to generating a conscious experience of the thought, we anticipate what that experience will be like. The two are then compared, and if the thought is as predicted, it seems to belong to us. If not, it seems to come unbidden. Frith, Blakemore, and Wolpert (2000) use this model to explain the experience of thought insertion in schizophrenia. A thought that comes without being predicted may seem to come from some external source, as if it's been planted in the head. People with schizophrenia may experience their own thoughts this way because of a malfunction in their comparator mechanisms (but see Campbell, 1999, for doubts).

The extension of the comparator account to thought is a big advantage. One problem with the ownership theory discussed in the last section, and also with Damasio's account of self-awareness in terms of feelings, is that they place too much emphasis on the body. If there is a phenomenal I, it would be extremely surprising that it could manifest itself only through the body (see also Strawson, 1999). After all, we are subjects of thought just as much as we are subjects of physical actions. There may even be conditions under which all bodily phenomenology is lost (sensory deprivation tanks? locked-in syndrome?), but there is no reason to think that such conditions essentially involve any less sense of selfhood than we find in the case of physical actions. For those who think that the body is inessential to the sense of selfhood, the comparator model is surely attractive.

In sum, the comparator model provides an elegant and unified account of authorship. It locates the experience of authorship in a process that is well motivated by theories of motor control, and it extends nicely to cases of cognitive ownership. It also offers a tidy explanation of cases in which authorship seems to be lost. All of this is very good news for those who want a reductive account of the phenomenal I. In authorship, unlike mere ownership, the self functions as the subject of a thought or act. Thus, authorship gives us an I rather than a mere me. It is therefore tempting to equate the phenomenal I with the phenomenology of authorship, which, in turn, can be equated with the experience of a successful matching process in an output/input comparator.

This account of agency differs from Wegner's in that it treats authorship as an experience, rather than as a mere inference. But it can be easily reconciled with Wegner's experimental findings and his skeptical hypothesis about free will (see also Bayne, 2006). The comparator model does not presuppose the causal efficacy of conscious intentions, because it is consistent with the view that motor commands are initiated unconsciously. Wegner may be right that conscious intentions lack efficacy and are linked to actions through an inferential, rather than phenomenological, process. Wegner's experiments on erroneous lack of control may appear to conflict with the comparator model, but this appearance can be explained away by a more careful look at the findings. In Wegner's true-or-false study, subjects judged that they did not choose which answer to type into the keyboard, but if asked, they probably wouldn't deny feeling a sense of control when pressing the keys. They felt as if the initial choice of which key to press had an external source, but once that choice was registered, the subjects pressed the keys themselves and might experience a sense of authorship in doing so. In other words, these studies do not show that authorship is inferential rather than phenomenal; they merely show that we can have false beliefs about the factors that lead us to carry out the controlled actions that we experience.

It may look as if we have found the phenomenal I at last. Appearances, however, can be deceiving. The comparator model does offer a plausible theory of the processes by which we recognize agency and disruptions to agency, but it does not give us the coveted I-qualia. I have two reasons for this disheartening assessment. First, the comparator model cannot, in the end, give us a phenomenology of subjectivity in the required sense; it continues to present the self as object rather than subject. To see this, we need to consider the neural correlates of the comparison process (focusing here on the case of physical actions, as opposed to thoughts). One might think that comparison involves a conscious experience of a motor command being matched against a perceived movement. This would be something like an experience of authorship, because one would be experiencing the command *that created* an action together with the action caused. The command could stand proxy for the self, in an act of agentic control. But in reality, the experience cannot be an experience of a motor command.

For one thing, as argued in chapter 6, there is no evidence that we have motor phenomenology. The best theories of phenomenology are theories of sensory phenomenology, and every experience associated with motor response can be chalked up to a sensory experience of the corresponding movements. For another thing, the motor command cannot be directly matched against a perceived action, because motor commands and action perceptions are couched in a different neural code; to make a match, we need to generate an anticipatory image of what the action will feel like perceptually and then compare that with the actual perception. And finally, neuroscientific research on comparator models using fMRI and cell recordings in animals suggests that the comparison takes place in posterior parietal cortex—a somatosensory area—rather than motor cortex. If this is right, the feelings associated with authorship are really not experiences of an author and an authored act; rather, they are experiences of an anticipated act and a real act. To experience the body acting, whether through perception or anticipatory imagination, is to experience the self as object rather than subject. Such an experience is not a phenomenal correlate of the *I* in first-person reports. It is a correlate of the *me*. When I say, "I feel myself act," what I report is an action, not an actor. Put more pointedly, there is no experience of authorship. To suppose otherwise is to mistake a feeling of bodily changes that occur when we are the authors of our actions for a feeling of authorship itself. It is to mistake the effect for the cause. When we use the experience generated by the comparator to judge that we are in control, the judgment is inferential, rather than a direct report of the phenomenology.

The second complaint against the comparator theory of phenomenal authorship is that its defenders sometimes give the erroneous impression that the comparison process itself has a phenomenal character. If authorship had a phenomenology and the comparator theory of that phenomenology were true, then we might expect to find, in controlled action, a phenomenal experience of an anticipatory image being compared with a perceptual input from the body. But when we act, we find no such thing. We experience only our bodies in action (see also Pacherie, 2001). There is one experience, not two, a single unified perceptual experience of action, not a comparison between image and percept. Likewise for the phenomenology of thought. When we experience subvocal speech, for example, we do not experience an anticipation of this silent narrative followed by the narrative itself—much less a matching between two verbal streams. We just experience one stream of speech. This suggests either that the comparison process is entirely unconscious or that the anticipated act and the experienced act blend into each other seamlessly in experience. Either way, there is no hook to hang the self hat on. There is no item or process in experience that we can label the I. There is an experience of the action but not the actor.

Against this deflationary reading, one might object that we *must* be able to experience ourselves as actors, because otherwise, we would not be able consciously to distinguish cases of control from cases where others act upon us. It does seem that we can tell the difference between lifting an arm and having an arm lifted by another, but if my arguments succeed, both should be alike; in both, we just experience the movement. It won't help here to say that our own actions are accompanied by feelings of effort and that externally caused actions come accompanied by resistance, for some self-controlled actions are effortless, and some other-controlled actions meet with no resistance. The puzzle can be put like this: the distinction between internally and externally generated actions seems to be phenomenologically available, and the comparator model offers a good explanation, but on my account of the phenomenology of the comparator model, internally and externally generated actions should be phenomenologically alike, because the matching process is unconscious.

The puzzle can be solved by considering what happens when the unconscious comparison process fails to find a match between anticipated acts and perceived acts. Presumably, the experience of an uncaused action sets off a kind of alarm signal that tells the body that it has come under external influence. To cope with this fact effectively, the source of that influence must be identified. If your body moves in an unpredictable way, you mind goes searching for the cause. You may find the cause; perhaps something or someone is forcing your body to move. And you may not; perhaps you had a spasm or a twitch. Either way, there may be a conscious experience associated with the recognition that an external source caused a movement. And there is no special puzzle about having a phenomenal experience of external causes. You can experience someone or something acting on you, even if you cannot experience yourself acting. Thus, there is a fundamental asymmetry here. We cannot be conscious of ourselves as agents, but we can be conscious of others as agents. There is no phenomenology of being a controller, but there is a phenomenology of being controlled. Ironically, we can feel the absence of the self (or, rather, the presence of some external cause) but not the presence of the self.

4. Coda: is Experience Selfless?

The foregoing has been an extended defense of Hume's thesis against recent developments in cognitive neuroscience. Hume says that when he looks for a self in the flow of experience, he doesn't find one. He can find perceptions of the world and the body but no subject. On a weak reading, Hume thinks that there is no subject above and beyond the flow of perceptions, and on a strong reading, he thinks that none of our perceptions qualifies as an experience of one's self as a subject. Both of these assertions have been challenged, and recent work in cognitive neuroscience has offered several theories, both reductive and nonreductive, of the phenomenal I. It has been my contention that these theories fail. Some of them may point to ways we can experience ourselves as objects, but that we can do so has never been in dispute. Some may also provide some of the mechanisms and experiences on the basis of which we can infer that we are acting as subjects of our actions and thoughts, but they do not bring the self-qua-subject into phenomenal view. Thus, Hume seems to be right, even on a strong reading. There is no phenomenal I. If I wait for myself to appear in experience, I will never arrive. I might believe that I exist as a subject through inference and philosophical speculation, but I have never been acquainted with myself. I see indirect signs or, more strikingly, recognize my own agency at just those moments when agency is lost.

Fortunately, we don't need to end on this gloomy note. Even if the search for the self is a pointless exercise, there is a sense in which the I is present *by virtue of* its absence. To see this, consider three ways in which the self enters implicitly into experience. First, the self is present in the fact that we always experience the world from a perspective. As I argued in chapter 2, conscious states are presented from a point of view. The self is not depicted within consciousness, but it is implicit in the fact that we experience things from the location that we, as thinking and acting organisms, occupy in space. Second, consciousness cannot present what lies beyond our senses; the sensory field has boundaries. Those boundaries presuppose a sensing self. Third, the qualities of experience are dependent on our sensory apparatus. Colors arguably are projections of our minds onto the world. Even shapes reflect our size and position; the surfaces that feel so solid under our feet are really swarms of atoms. So the senses do not simply pick up the world as it is; they impose order that would be invisible if we were different kinds of beings. Our goals, interests, and histories can contribute to this process of construction; we see a world imbued with value. Thus, the contents of experience are not a transparent window onto the mind-external world but are always filtered through the self. In these three ways, the self is always present in the perceptions given to us in consciousness. It is present not as an item of experience but as a kind of constraint. To echo Wittgenstein, echoing Schopenhauer, the self is the limit. I cannot see my own eyes, but seeing is constrained by my sensory systems and is thus bounded and rendered by me. For this reason, consciousness is not selfless; it is thoroughly permeated by the self. The self is absent if we look for it but always already there in each act of looking.

PART THREE

Metaphysical Puzzles of Consciousness

8

Whence the Unity of Consciousness?
Attentional Resonance

The last three chapters have each told us something about what consciousness is not. Each of those chapters identifies a limitation: we have no direct conscious experiences of our thoughts, of our motor responses, and of our selves. We will now turn back to questions about what consciousness is. The main contours of the positive story were already presented in chapters 2 and 3, with a discussion of neural correlates in chapter 4. But that account left some metaphysical questions unanswered. The next two chapters take up the mind/body problem: is consciousness physical in nature, and, if so, what sort of physical thing is it? Another metaphysical puzzle concerns the unity of consciousness. That will be my focus here.

At any given moment, we are conscious of many different things. We see multiple objects at once, and their many features, and we see them as located against often complex backgrounds. Plus, we hear things, smell things, and feel things at the same time, and all of these senses seem to coalesce into a coherent experience. Unity also has a temporal dimension. We don't experience a series of rich sensory stills but rather one moment flowing into the other, forming a coherent stream of consciousness. This raises a question: how do all of the parts form a whole? The puzzle is especially vexing if the AIR theory is true. The AIR theory says that conscious states arise when intermediate-level representations are modulated by attention. But such attentional modulation is a local affair. Each perceptual representation can be attentionally modulated independently of others. Indeed, attention is often selective, and it seems to make items of experience available to working memory by separating one thing from another. If consciousness is unified, the AIR theory, as stated so far, seems to leave this fact unexplained.

In this chapter, I will begin by saying something about what unity is supposed to consist in and how we should try to tackle it. Then I will advance a proposal about how unity is achieved across the senses and through time. One consequence of this proposal is that consciousness is somewhat less unified than we might have thought. In the final section, I will describe how the account of unity that I am offering applies to the AIR theory. What initially appears as a liability for that account may turn out to be an asset.

1. Approaching Unity

1.1. THE PROBLEMS OF UNITY

It is widely believed that consciousness is unified. In this section, I will try to clarify what unity is supposed to consist in and why explaining unity is often seen as a difficult challenge.

Historically, discussions of unity often revolved around Descartes's idea that there is a single indivisible soul that remains constant across changes in the contents of conscious experience. In this vein, William James (1890: 337) discusses the unity of consciousness by analogy with a herdsman who keeps his cows (the contents of experience) in line. But contemporary discussions move away from this idea of a unified subject of experience and focus instead on the unified contents of experience. Positing a unified subject is, as we will see, one explanation of unified contents but not the only one.

What does it mean to say that the contents of experience are unified? This is not an easy idea to articulate, although it may seem like an obvious phenomenological fact. In one of the most useful discussions of unity, Bayne and Chalmers (2003) say that two conscious states are unified "if there is something it is like for a subject to be in both states simultaneously." This is a good first stab, but there is a residue of Cartesianism, which we would do better to exorcise. Unlike Descartes's, this formulation does not attribute unity to the experiencing subject, but it does define unity relative to a subject; this might presuppose unity of the subject or imply that the existence of a subject plays a role in achieving unity. That, again, would be a substantive theory of unity, rather than the phenomenon that a theory of unity should seek to explain. A better formulation comes out later in Bayne and Chalmers's discussion. They say that for some pairs of conscious states, there is also a conscious state corresponding to their conjunction. For example, there seems to be a conscious state that makes up both the visual experience of seeing lips move and the auditory experience of hearing speech. Phenomenologically, this seems like one state rather than two, even though it certainly has two parts. It would be satisfying if a theory of consciousness could provide an account of conscious-state individuation that explained this impression of unity.

Bayne and Chalmers also articulate what they call the total conjunctive unity thesis. According to this thesis, "If C is the conjunction of all of a subject's phenomenal states at a time, then C is itself a phenomenal state." This formulation involves the subject again, but there is an easy fix. We can restate the thesis as a claim about the conjunction of all of the phenomenal states "in an organism" rather than "of a subject." The claim that all of an organism's conscious states are united at any given time is obviously much stronger than the thesis that some states can be united. I think that the weaker thesis is the main phenomenological datum that a theory of unity must explain. The total conjunctive unity thesis requires further consideration, and I will ultimately argue that it is false. If it seems obviously true, that may be because of the sneaky word *subject*. If we think of a subject as the one who enjoys conscious experiences, then it may seem that a single subject cannot enjoy two experiences at the same time without having an experience of their conjunction. That may be a result of the Cartesian tendency to think of the subject as a unity. If we avoid talk of subjects and retain the organism formulation, the total conjunctive unity thesis looks less obvious. When we ask whether two conscious states can co-occur within an organism without being unified into a single state, the answer is unclear.

For now, let's focus on the claim that *some* conscious states are unified. Why think this is true? To begin with, consider the experience of a square. I take it as phenomenologically incontrovertible that there can be a unified visual experience of a square. But notice that squares have parts. The lines that make up a square are experienced, and they could be experienced separately. On some occasions, they are experienced together. The square may also have a color, which is experienced as being located within its boundaries. One cannot experience a square without experiencing the space around it, the background against which it is presented. That, too, is part of the experience. All of these different parts belong to a single experience. If the square were vibrating, you would experience it as moving, and if it were ringing whenever it vibrated, you would experience it as ringing. These attributes seem like parts of a single experience. There is also unity over time, as the vibrating case makes clear. Vibration is a change in time, so we can experience vibration or any other movement if we can unify adjacent time points together as part of a single experience.

Notice that the unity under consideration goes beyond mere binding. When you experience the background and foreground together, they are not bound. You might also see a square next to a circle and have an experience of them as aligned next to each other. Suppose the circle rolls into the square, in which case you would experience the temporal event of one object hitting another. The moment of contact is an experience of two things interacting, not of one thing bound. Or suppose you look at a square while hearing a sound and wonder if the square emitted the sound; both sensations are experienced as coexisting, while the question of their binding remains unsettled. Thus, there seems to be some sense of phenomenal unity that transcends binding. That is the sense of unity that I want to investigate.

These appeals to phenomenology suffice, I hope, for making the idea of conscious unity seem intelligible and plausible. Unity is easy enough to illustrate, but it is hard to explain, especially when we consider how the physical correlates of consciousness are organized. Consider first what I will refer to as *synchronic* unity: the unity of two conscious states at a single time, such as a square and its color. The difficulty is that there is no actual location where distinct features come together. There is no blue square in the brain when we look at a blue square, and the cells that process color are often separate from cells that process form. The problem is even more obvious when we consider unity across the senses, because some sensory pathways are in entirely different brain regions. When smelling a glass of wine, olfactory information is processed in frontal cortex, visual informational is processed in temporal and occipital areas, and the feel of the glass is processed in parietal areas. Clearly, we need an explanation of how widely distributed brain areas can be functionally integrated.

The problem of *diachronic* unity is slightly different, since two temporally unified instants might have neural correlates in the same area of the brain, even the same population of cells. But the neural activations that underlie the experience are separated in time. The challenge is exacerbated by the fact that some temporally extended brain events are not experienced as unified in the relevant sense. If I listen to a song, the final note is not part of the same experience as the first, although two consecutive notes may be experienced as a unity. This must be accounted for.

Synchronic and diachronic unity raise different challenges, but they are related. Both concern the question of how to individuate experiences, and both, I will argue, can be explained in similar ways.

1.2. APPROACHES TO UNITY

There are various approaches that one might take to explaining unity. Before moving on to the approach that I favor, I want to consider briefly some alternatives that I regard as less promising (for useful review, see Bayne 2004).

One approach has already been touched on, and that is the denial of unity. I take this to be a desperate move that flies in the face of simple phenomenological facts of the kind adduced above (experiences of colored moving shapes). I am not entirely unsympathetic to the no-unity view. Below, I will argue that unity claims have been exaggerated. But wholesale denial of unity is implausible.

Another approach denies that unity is a problem, because conscious states have no parts that need to be united. Call this the no-parts view. It is widely assumed that experience is atomic: there are little separable bits that need to be strung together. But one could challenge this assumption and argue that perception gives us a unified stream, and any separable parts must be extracted from that stream (see Tye, 2003, and classic work in Gestalt psychology). This is an appealing view, but I think it is empirically false. As noted, the neural correlates of conscious perception are widely distributed in the brain, and they are also all dissociable. One can lose vision, or even one aspect of vision, without

loss of hearing or touch. Tye would reply that this claim about neurophysiological disunity simply confuses levels of analysis: a part-less experience might be
constituted by brain states that have parts, just as a single bar of gold might be
made up of many molecules. True enough, but this just pushes the problem
back a level; we need an account of how these physical parts are bound together
to form one experience. Moreover, even at the phenomenal level, I find it hard
to make sense of the no-parts view. Surely we can focus attention on one part
of an experience or have one part remain constant as others change. Phenomenally, our experiences are complex. To say that these many parts make up a
whole simply by virtue of the fact that they feel united is not an explanation. It
simply labels the problem that we are trying to solve. How can things that are
phenomenally distinct simultaneously feel like parts of a unity? One cannot
explain how a skyscraper holds together by pointing out that it is a single object.
No one denies that singularity, but one wants to know how a multitude of materials can combine as a unit.

Another approach, which can be called subjective unity, was alluded to
earlier. One might think that experiences are united by virtue of belonging to
a single subject (recall James, 1890). In chapter 7, I argued that there is no
conscious self. If that's right, the subjective unity thesis must be understood
as involving a relationship to an unconscious self. I am agnostic about
whether any such entity exists, but I do doubt that there is a notion of the self
that can be useful in explaining the unity of consciousness. One difficulty is
that some of the best candidates for the self are not good candidates for
explaining how two conscious states can feel like one. For example, selves
have been said to be constituted by interlinked memories, narratives, character traits, and self-concepts. None of these things seems capable of explaining
unity, since they are either distributed in time (memory chains), dispositional
(character traits), or not active during every episode of consciousness (narratives, self-concepts). One can define a self as a bundle of experiences, as
Hume did, but that presupposes an account of unity, because we need an
account of how experiences bundle together. Moreover, as we saw in discussing Kant, there need be nothing especially selflike about bound collectives of
experience.

One could stipulate that the self is a subject of experience (Strawson, 2009),
but without appealing to any of the constructs just mentioned, this notion is
rather mysterious. Why think that experiences have subjects, as opposed to
merely being possessed by persons (constituted by memories, narratives, etc.)?
What are such subjects above and beyond the experiences that happen to occur
within an organism? And more to the point, by virtue of what do they link experiences together? If we think of the subject of experience as an inner homunculus, we will end up with a regress: how do the self's inner experiences get
unified? There is also a subtler regress that arises whenever the unity between
two things is explained by appeal to a third. If two experiences are unified by

being linked to the same self, what does that link consist in? Perhaps there is a further entity connecting the self to each item in experience, and so on (see Hurley, 1998, for this line of critique). Finally, it seems that being experienced by the same self would not guarantee unity. This point is sometimes made by appeal to split-brain patients, who arguably have singular selves but lack unified experiences (Marks, 1980). Bayne and Chalmers (2003) argue that split-brain patients might, for all we know, have a unified phenomenal field and divided access to that field, rather than divided consciousness, but this possibility wouldn't help the defender of subject unity, because positing an inaccessible phenomenal field would imply a phenomenal field that is inaccessible to the self.

The subject unity thesis is vulnerable, in part, because it is not clear why sharing a self would make two experiences into one. Another proposal, which I will call representational unity, does better on this score. One might say that two conscious states are unified when they are represented as being part of the same state (e.g., Rosenthal, 2005). Representation looks like a promising avenue to explore, because representation has the power to unify. For example, if you point to three cookies and say, "Those look delicious," the word *those* serves to refer to the three cookies as a single collective. But the suggestion that consciousness is representationally unified faces some objections. First, it seems to depend on a higher-order-representation theory of consciousness, and I suspect that such theories are false (chapter 1). There is little empirical evidence for higher-order representations playing a role in consciousness and even less for the view that conscious states are accompanied by representations that re-represent every item that is unified in experience. Remember, most conscious experiences are unified, so the representational approach must stipulate that such joint representations are automatically generated all the time. This move exacerbates the already exorbitant computational price tag of higher-order theories and lacks empirical support. It's also not clear why we would represent all of the unified items in experience as a single unit. The most natural role for unifying representations in cognition is to group together sets of objects, as in the cookie example. But items that do not constitute a natural set are also unified in consciousness, such as an object and the background against which it is situated. Why would we form a single representation of figure and ground, rather than representing them separately?

Finally, there is a technical difficulty, which stems from the fact that higher-order-representation theories say that consciousness is conferred by representational states that follow immediately upon their first-order targets. It's possible that seeing a square sometimes immediately induces a representation of the seeing of that square, and hearing a tone sometimes immediately induces a representation of the hearing. But when one sees a square that is emitting a tone, it seems unlikely that one could recognize this joint fact without first representing the seeing and the hearing as two separate facts. If that were the case, the representation of the seeing-plus-hearing would be indirect, and it's hard to see why an indirect higher-order representation would have the same impact with respect to conferring consciousness as a representation that occurred immediately.

Let's consider another approach, which can be termed broadcast unity. On this view, conscious states are unified when they are broadcast to a common receiver. Put in computational terms, the idea is that two experiences are unified when they stand in an access relation to the same psychological subsystem. This idea would fit naturally with a global workspace theory and might also look like a promising option for the AIR theory. Both of these theories assume that consciousness involves access, or at least accessibility to working memory. Perhaps unity derives from the fact that separate sensory systems project to a single memory store. The problem is that this supposition is probably empirically false. Working memory is not a single subsystem but a family of functionally analogous subsystems, corresponding to different modalities (Baddeley, 2007). In fact, there may be multiple working-memory systems for different kinds of information within a single modality. In vision, for example, there is evidence for a separation between working memory for object identity and object place.

One might try to get around this difficulty by shifting from the mechanisms that receive conscious broadcasts to the mechanisms that cause broadcasts to be transmitted. According to the AIR theory, broadcasting is achieved via attention, and one might hope to find unity in the mechanisms that regulate how attention is allocated. The problem is that attention is regulated by a variety of different control structures. Attention can be top-down or bottom-up, focal or diffuse, spatial or object-based. There is no anatomical or functional uniformity in attentional control. Thus, the hope that we can find unity in broadcasting is thwarted at every level. In conscious broadcasting, there is no unity in the perceptual senders of information, the working-memory receivers, or the attentional channels that allow for transmission.

With the exception of the no-parts view, all of the approaches mentioned thus far share a feature in common: they try to explain how two experiences get unified, if at all, by positing some third thing to which they are related. Approaches of this kind don't seem to succeed. There is little evidence for psychological or biological entities that serve to bring the components of our unified experiences together. Somehow, then, the parts seem to come together without a unifier to help them. An adequate explanation of unity should honor this constraint. In a word, we need to posit *unmediated* unity. This brings us back to the definition of unity advanced at the outset. Following Bayne and Chalmers (2003), I said that two experiences are unified when they are parts of the same experience. This mereological definition of unity invites an unmediated account of how unity is achieved. Consider an ordinary physical object, such as a chair. Chairs are not unified extrinsically. Some chairs are held together by screws, others have legs and seats that interlink without screws, and some are hewn or cast from a single piece of material. In all of these cases, it is chair parts that do the unifying. By analogy, one might think that experiences are also bound by their parts. The mereological definition of unity does not entail an unmediated approach, but many of the most familiar mereological unities are unmediated, so this is a natural option to explore. The no-parts view is unmediated but also unmotivated; there is empirical and phenomenological evidence against it. We need an account that grants the componential structure of experience without supposing that unity is externally imposed. Fortunately, such an account is available.

2. Synchronic and Diachronic Resonance

2.1. INDIVIDUATING EXPERIENCES

The crucial question for a theory of unity is what makes two conscious states part of the same state? In other words, we need a way of individuating experiences. In this section, I will offer a proposal. I begin by considering cases of synchronic unity and extend the story to diachronic unity in the next section.

In tackling the individuation question, it's helpful to remember the obvious fact that no organism can experience states that are in another organism's head. I can't experience your experiences. What special relation do two experiences in my head have that an experience in my head lacks with respect to an experience in yours? One flat-footed answer is that they are both mine. This is an obvious point of contrast, but as an account of unity, it faces the problems already adduced against subjective theories.

A second answer that can be quickly discarded is that unity can be explained by appeal to a binding relation. It's true that my conscious states are mental representations, and they represent some features that are bound together, but it is a mistake to equate binding and unity. Features that are bound together—for example, perceived as inhering in a single object—are unified in consciousness, but binding is not a necessary condition for unity. As noted above, objects are perceived as unified with their backgrounds but not bound. In addition, we might experience two objects together as part of one experience without perceiving them as a single object. Disorders such as agnosia can disrupt binding without corresponding deficits in unity; when an agnosic experiences a visual object as a disconnected jumble, that experience is presumably unified. In fact, we don't need to look at pathological cases to understand what this is like. Consider the case of hearing a cell phone ring in a crowded room. The ring is heard, and the crowd is seen, but it can be very difficult to determine where the ring is coming from. When this happens, one is clearly relating the ring to the visual experience of the crowd, actively looking for a culprit. In this sense, the ring is unified with vision, even when not yet bound.

Clearly, we need another account of what two conscious experiences share when they are unified in a single mind. At this point, one tempting move is to say that two items of experience are unified if they occur at the same time. This would make sense of the agnosia case, because even when two lines are disconnected, they can be experienced concurrently. Likewise for the ringing phone and the crowd. But simultaneity faces two objections, one of which may be superable, the other not.

The first objection is that many of the things that we experience as unified are perceived at different speeds. For example, there is evidence that the nervous system can detect motion faster than color (Schmolesky et al., 1998). Thus, when we see a tennis ball fly across the sky, its trajectory is processed before its hue, but we don't experience it that way. In experience, color and motion are often bound and unified. Similarly, light travels much faster than sounds, so light can reach the nervous system at the same time as a simultaneously produced sound only from certain distances (Pöppel, 1988b). We nevertheless have synchronized experiences of sound and light across distances far outside that range. If *experienced* synchrony is indicative of unity, then *objective* synchrony may not be the basis of unity, because the components of a unified percept may not be objectively synchronized. We might say that unity involves experiential synchrony, but without an account of that, we're back at square one.

This objection can be answered in two compatible ways. First, the discrepancies in physical and neural transmission may actually show up phenomenologically. There is evidence that different sensory dimensions are experienced slightly out of sync. For example, Zeki and Moutoussis (1997) show that simultaneous color and motion are experienced as offset, and Dixon and Spitz (1980) show that sound and vision appear simultaneous only when offset. These asynchronies are usually too small to *notice* in experience, but given these laboratory findings, it is plausible that the phenomenal experience actually presents different stimulus dimensions as minutely out of sync. Second, the nervous system has ways of compensating for temporal discrepancies, albeit imperfectly. There is no consensus about how this is done, but one possibility is that sensory inputs along different dimensions are briefly stored and then unconsciously compared before they are consciously experienced. If so, the representations generated by this comparison process might be synchronized in objective time, despite asynchronies in the input. On this view, experiential synchrony would be objective synchrony; phenomenal time would coincide with brain time. In support of this model, there is ample evidence that experience is preceded by an unconscious comparison process. This can be seen by the fact that the brain compensates when external stimuli are presented out of sync. One example of this is temporal ventriloquism. In ordinary ventriloquism, people perceive a sound as coming from a location other than its actual origin because of visual stimulation in the other location. This is evidence for the view that there is unconscious recalibration in space prior to experience. In temporal ventriloquism, sound and sight are recalibrated in time. In one demonstration, Vroomen and De Gelder (2004) played a clicking sound either just before or just after a flash. When offsets were small but significant, the two stimuli were experienced as simultaneous. This proves that the brain can realign discrepant sensory inputs, even when the offset is artificially imposed by experimenters. It is plausible, then, that the brain compensates even more effectively for offsets that occur naturally as a result of discrepancies in neural and physical transmission time.

The upshot is that experienced simultaneity may actually coincide with simultaneity in the brain. The brain may replay offset input in sync, and when it fails to do so, the offsets may be phenomenally detectable. If phenomenal simultaneity correlates with phenomenal unity, then simultaneity of processing may be a mechanism by which unity is achieved.

There is, however, another objection, which shows that this proposal is insufficient as it stands. Recall that we were looking for a relation that exists between two experiences in one person's mind that does not obtain between experiences located in two different minds. Simultaneity does not satisfy this requirement. An experience in my head might occur at the exact same time as an experience in yours, yet they won't be unified.

Fortunately, there is an obvious fix. When my experiences occur at the same time as yours, it is just a coincidence. There is no causal mechanism linking them. What we need is a kind of nonaccidental simultaneity. As a first stab, then, we can say that two experiences are synchronically unified if they co-occur simultaneously and if *one would not have occurred had it not been for the occurrence of the other*.

This proposal faces an immediate objection. It is not clear how one event can depend on another if they are simultaneous. The definition seems to imply that a cause can come into existence with its effect, rather than preceding it. The objection can be averted, however, by noticing that the dependency between two experiences need not be explained by a causal relationship between them. Rather, both experiences could be under causal control of some other process. If two experiences are under control of the same regulatory processes, then one might occur only if the other does.

This raises an even more pressing objection. On the face of it, the claim that concurrent perceptual experiences are under common regulatory control seems implausible. Given the anatomical and functional independence of the senses, there is no obvious reason to suppose that visual experiences should depend on smell or hearing, for example. Even within a given modality, there is considerable anatomical and functional differentiation. For example, shape and color are processed independently to some degree. A person with focal brain injuries can lose the capacity to perceive one of these dimensions of sight without the other. If unity depends on interdependent processes, then we should find that consciousness is completely disunified!

To address this worry, it is crucial to recall something that was already noted in discussing judgments of simultaneity: what we experience depends on unconscious calibration processes. In temporal ventriloquism, two stimuli are experienced as simultaneous even if they were offset in time. Ordinary ventriloquism functions similarly; experience corrects spatial offsets. Both cases illustrate a pervasive feature of sensory systems: they interact. The contents of experience are informed by unconscious calibration processes that allow one sense modality to influence another. There are many other dramatic examples: the appearance of lip movements influences the speech sounds we hear (McGurk and MacDonald, 1976); coloring can influence the flavor, intensity, and pleasantness of beverages (Zellner, Bartoli, and Eckard, 1991); a single flash is seen as two if accompanied by two beeps (Shams, Kamitani, and Shimojo, 2000); and adaptation to visual motion causes tactile motion aftereffects and conversely (Konkle et al., 2009). Far from anomalous, such phenomena show that the senses are in constant dialogue. What we experience in one sense depends on what's happening in the others. This doesn't contradict the anatomical observation that senses are dissociable (but see Shimojo and Shams, 2001), but it proves that in practice, the senses interact extensively. Had your last glass of white wine been colored red, you would have experienced flavors characteristic of red wine (Morrot, Brochet, and Dubourdieu, 2001).

In response, one might argue that such cross-sensory effects are necessary only when the senses are responding to the same object and delivering discrepant information. This would entail, ironically, that experience is unified only when senses conflict. I think that entailment can be blocked. Sensory interaction is often most pronounced in conflict cases, but in order for conflicts to be detected, there must be constant, automatic, cross-sensory (and intersensory) comparison. Presumably, there are fast unconscious processes that use prior associations to search for discrepancies between sensory inputs, sometimes correcting for these when conflicts are found. When no conflicts are found, no corrections are necessary, but comparison has still taken place, and that might be a basis for unity.

Cases without conflict may still pose a problem for the first-stab formulation above. I suggested that experiences are unified if one would not have occurred had it not been for the occurrence of the other. Now consider the case of drinking white wine that has its normal color. Here, the taste that occurs might be just what it would have been had the color not been seen (or so we can suppose for illustration). Does it follow that the color and taste are not part of a unified experience? To avoid this consequence, we need to take a second stab at characterizing the relevant dependency. The needed amendment will require a detour into the brain.

Let's consider how the brain gets one sense to bear on another. There are both direct connections between the senses and sensory convergence zones that detect coincident activity between two or more modalities. These connections allow the senses to communicate actively during perception. One frequent finding is that sensory integration results in increased neural activity. Using implanted electrodes, Ghazanfar et al. (2005) found that cells in monkeys' auditory cortex that respond to vocalizations show enhanced activity if the monkeys also view vocalizing faces. Using scalp electrodes, Senkowski et al. (2007) found increases in both auditory and visual signals when sounds and shapes were presented together as opposed to alone. Using fMRI, Caplovitz et al. (2008) found that neural activity corresponding to one part of the visual field increases when objects presented there are perceived as grouped with objects presented in other parts of the visual field; this pattern was found across multiple retinotopic areas.

Such findings firmly establish that the senses and sensory subsystems regularly modulate each other's activity, and they do so even when (in fact, especially when) there is no conflict. But what is the nature of these modulations? The answer to this question is still under active investigation, but one possibility is that the observed increases in neural activity reflect increased neural coordination. The idea is that during intersensory integration, the firing pattern in one area conforms in some way to the firing pattern in another, such that cellular dynamics become correlated across distant areas of the brain. One form of correlation is synchronization: cells may fire at the same time. But perfect synchrony is not the only form of correlation; the main idea is that the pattern in one place depends on the pattern in another. Think of two dancers who move their bodies differently but in a coordinated way. Researchers who study intersensory integration sometimes measure "phase coherence." Neurons oscillate, which means that their levels of activity go up and down at various rates. Two populations are phase-coherent when there is a constant relationship between their oscillation phases (Senkowski et al., 2008). I will use the term *resonance* to refer to phase coherence or any other pattern of causal dependency between neural populations. The way one population of neurons fires can be said to resonate with another if and only if the pattern of activity in one depends on the pattern in the other.

The notion of resonance gives us the tool we need to characterize the dependency underlying synchronic unity. It isn't always true of our simultaneous sensory experiences that one would not have occurred had it not been for the occurrence of the other. That formulation needs improvement. I'd like to suggest that the neurons underlying a given sensory experience typically resonate with the neurons underlying concurrent sensory experiences. Thus, I propose that two experiences are synchronically unified if they co-occur simultaneously and they are realized by resonant populations of neurons. More succinctly, unity is neural resonance.

There is a growing body of evidence for intermodal resonance during perception. One form of resonance, neural synchrony, has frequently been observed within individual sensory systems. For example, neural synchrony in visual pathways increases during perception of natural scenes in comparison with blank screens (Maldonado et al., 2008); synchrony is higher when viewed stimuli are coherent (Lima et al., 2010); and cells with nonoverlapping receptive fields show high levels of synchrony when responding to the same contour (Samonds et al., 2006). When measuring cellular responses across sensory systems, precise synchrony may decrease, but there are often, nevertheless, high levels of correlation in neuronal activity. Von Stein et al. (1999) found greater coherence across multiple cortical sites during visual perception as compared with rest. Maier, Chandrasekaran, and Ghazanfar (2008) found high correlations between visual and auditory areas when they presented participants with audiovisual experiences of looming objects; correlations went up when looming sounds matched looming images. Kanayama, Sato, and Ohira (2007) found intermodal correlations when subjects experienced the rubber-hand illusion, suggesting again that sensory integration increases resonance.

The hypothesis that resonance is unity might be challenged by pointing out that these studies link resonance to sensory *coherence*, but we can have perfectly unified experiences that lack coherence. For example, one can have the joint experience of listening to Bach while looking at a sunset. In reply, it's important to be clear about what the studies show. The main finding is not that coherence is necessary for resonance; recall from the discussion of temporal binding in chapter 1 that cells responding to a figure and its background can be neurally synchronized. Rather, coherence increases resonance, and this, I submit, is consistent with the phenomenology of unity. When the objects of perception are coherent, we are more likely to have a unified conscious experience. With unrelated inputs, consciousness sometimes alternates between sensory features, such as attending to the sound of the Bach cantata at one moment and then focusing on the sunset in the next. And sometimes with unrelated inputs, we focus exclusively on one input and suppress the rest, as when filtering out background sounds during a lecture.

Of course, the lack of coherence between two inputs is sometimes so jarring that we can't alternate or filter between them. On these occasions, we vividly experience both at once. We have a unified experience of a disunified input. Thus, one strong test for the resonance hypothesis concerns stimuli that are jarringly out of alignment. If resonance is merely a correlate of coherence, it should decrease markedly with such inputs, but if it is a correlate of unity, it should increase. Doesburg et al. (2008) found evidence for the latter. When presenting subjects with visual and auditory speech streams that were out of sync, correlations increased across auditory and visual areas of the brain. As they put it, synchrony registers asynchrony in this case. This is just what the resonance-as-unity hypothesis would predict.

We can now put all of these pieces together. Phenomenologically, unity occurs when two states are experienced as parts of one experience. Computationally, this occurs after sensory inputs have undergone a rapid, unconscious calibration process designed to minimize discrepancies between the senses. Neurobiologically, the result of this process is a widely distributed pattern of resonant neural activity. When the unconscious calibration processes produce a coherent input, resonance is likely to increase, because we tend to filter out inputs that don't cohere. But sometimes unconscious calibration processes identify failures of coherence that are profound enough to capture attention; when that happens, resonance also increases.

We can think of resonance as a principle of neural-state individuation. Neural populations in different sensory pathways constitute a single state if they resonate together. This principle of individuation is attractive because it can also be applied at the local level. Cells corresponding to two adjacent edges in a perceived object might be said to be part of a single representation by virtue of resonating together. Resonance is a matter not of spatial contiguity but of coordinated activity. The main proposal here is that this account of neural-state individuation can also provide an account of conscious-state individuation. Two sensory experiences are part of one experience if their underlying neural activities are part of one neural state. If unity can be defined, following Bayne and Chalmers, as the property of being parts of the same experience, then resonance offers an elegant explanation at the neural level.

This approach to unity leaves several questions unanswered. Does resonance come in degrees? Are all concurrently conscious states resonant? Does resonance occur when two senses get inputs that are simultaneous but unrelated? I will come back to these questions in the final section. Now I want to see how the general proposal could be extended to account for unity across time.

2.2. HOW LONG IS THE MOMENT?

The hypothesis that unity is neural resonance is attractive because resonance seems like a promising construct for pursuing a theory of neural-state individuation. If neural states are resonant neural populations and unified experiences are experiences that are parts of a single state, then it's natural to suppose that unified states are resonant populations. The empirical evidence for long-distance resonance adds further reason for taking the proposal seriously. But it is not yet clear whether resonance could provide a general theory of conscious unity, because it is not immediately obvious how the idea can be applied to unity across time. Diachronically unified states are, by definition, not synchronic, whereas the kinds of resonance described so far involve populations of neurons that are active at the same time. So we must determine whether resonance has a temporal counterpart. Before that can be done, however, we need a better purchase on the idea of temporal unity. Can the idea of a single experience make sense when applied temporally? Can two moments in time really be part of a single experience? To answer that question, we need to consider the nature of moments. We need to visit a classic question about whether moments have temporal duration.

In this section, I will argue that moments can be quantified in at least three different ways, and one of these ways corresponds best to the phenomenology of diachronically unified experience. I will then apply resonance theories to moments of this kind.

There are at least three divergent approaches for quantifying the conscious moment. One is to find a minimal unit of conscious experience. Another is to find the maximal breadth at which things can be consciously integrated in time. A third approach, which can be regarded as a compromise between these two, seeks the minimal unit at which temporal integration takes place, a minimal duration. All three approaches arrive at different temporal estimates. Rather than deciding which of these really deserves to be called the conscious moment, I think we should count each as a kind of moment. To distinguish them, I will stipulatively use three different words from ordinary language. The minimal conscious unit I will call the *instant*. The minimal duration I will call the *now*. And the maximal duration I will call the *present*. I will argue that the now has a special status, vis-à-vis unity, which the instant and the present lack. Before making that case, let's consider how these different moments are measured.

One way to measure the instant is to determine the minimal time that a stimulus must appear in order to be consciously perceived. Strictly speaking, this method only directly reveals a temporal detection threshold—the speed at which we can register a stimulus—not the time course of the stimulus once it is perceived. But these two things might be related. Failure to perceive a stimulus that is too fast may reflect the fact that conscious instants have a certain length, and anything shorter than that length in presentation time results in a brain activation that is, correlatively, too short to extend the full length of a conscious instant. One way to qualify the instant is to use backward masking. For example, Szczepanowski and Pessoa (2007) briefly flashed a photograph of an angry face followed by a neutral face of longer duration. When the angry face was presented for 17 milliseconds, subjects were not confident that they had seen anything but performed above chance on a forced-choice test, suggesting that it was perceived subliminally. But if the angry face was presented for 25 milliseconds, subjects were confident that they had seen it, suggesting that this is the threshold for subjective awareness. This is comparable to threshold for flicker detection on a computer monitor or television. Typical monitors refresh at rates of 60 Hz or 16.7 milliseconds, but when the rate drops to about half of that, flickers can become visible. This suggests that, for vision at least, conscious instants may be about 25 to 30 milliseconds long.

Interestingly, instants may lack temporal breadth. Long ago, Wertheimer (1912) conducted a study in which subjects observed sequential flashes and had to determine whether they were viewing one object or two. When flashes were spaced 30 milliseconds apart, they were perceived as simultaneous. This might be interpreted as showing that when two stimuli of perceivable duration occur within the time window of the conscious instant, they will be perceived as occurring together, even if they are consecutive. At slightly longer intervals, something quite surprising happens. People can perceive that there are two stimuli, but they cannot tell the order of occurrence. This may suggest that the experience lacks temporal order or that the order is present in the experience but cannot be recalled after the fact. In any case, such temporal smearing might go some way to explain why time seems continuous. Instants blend into instants such that two adjacent instants are, paradoxically, both temporally distinguishable and not.

After this interval, which might be described as the time of "overlapping instants," one begins to be able to discern an ordering. It is at this point that experience has an unambiguous duration; it becomes truly temporal. Wertheimer found clear orderings of successive stimuli at interstimulus intervals of 60 milliseconds (although under some conditions, ordering errors can still be made at this duration; Eagleman and Sejnowski, 2000). If stimuli are placed close enough together and are similar enough in form, then an interesting thing happens when they are presented at 60-millisecond intervals: we experience apparent motion. Under these conditions, there is clear temporal ordering, because the stimuli appear consecutively, but they look like consecutive appearances of the same object, moving from one location to another. Wertheimer calls this illusion of movement the "phi phenomenon." There are also closely related illusions of movement at longer intervals, such as 100 milliseconds. The brain seems to fill in the gap between stimuli spaced at these short intervals. This can be demonstrated by showing that when two consecutive stimuli appear to be one object in motion, stimuli presented in the spatiotemporal gap between them are harder to detect, as if they were occluded by the moving object (Yantis and Nakama, 1998). In order to do this filling in, the brain must process the two stimuli unconsciously before projecting the result into consciousness with interposed transition points between them. Dennett and Kinsbourne (1995) call this a Stalinesque theory of consciousness, in which the brain edits information before making it public, and they contrast it with Orwellian theories, according to which we consciously experience the stimuli as separate and then replay them in consciousness as connected, forgetting the original experience the way memories are erased in Orwell's *1984*. Dennett and Kinsbourne say that there is no way to decide between these possibilities, and there may be no fact of the matter that is right. But this conclusion seems extravagant. There is no positive reason to think that we experience the stimuli separately and then forget them; such experiences would be profoundly and ineluctably inaccessible, so there is little reason to take the Orwellian view seriously. Moreover, if consciousness requires attention and attention takes time to engage, then there is independent reason to think that some stimulus processing can take place prior to consciousness. Experience of temporally extended events is, in this Stalinesque approach, like experiences of the simultaneous events described in the previous section. Both are actually experiences of memories: they are replayed from stored and modified records of events that were first detected some milli-seconds earlier (see Rao, Eagleman, and Sejnowski, 2001). Consistent with this, there is evidence of a brief memory capacity in the visual system (Harrison and Tong, 2009; Nikolić et al., 2009; Serences et al., 2009), which should not be confused with working memory, because it is automatic and inaccessible to executive systems.

I'm not so concerned here with illusory motion. What's more important for present purposes is that between 60 and 100 milliseconds, stimuli are perceived as temporally ordered. In my terminology, this is the duration of the now, a minimally ordered event. This time window crops up frequently in studies of events that are ordered but integrated. It is the maximum interstimulus interval for short-distance motion perception (Braddick, 1973) and a suitable stimulus duration for judgments of direction and velocity (De Bruyn and Orban, 1988). Within this window, we can also perceive an event as causal, while at longer intervals, the experience of causation tapers off precipitously (Michotte, 1963). In addition, this time window coincides with the average length of syllables in naturally occurring speech (Greenberg et al., 2003). Syllables have an inter-esting property from a phenomenological perspective. They are clearly ordered (e.g., /top/sounds different from /pot/), but they are also experienced as units. They are, as it were, both successive and simultaneous. All of these examples have the interesting property of being both integrated and temporally extended. They are experiential units with duration.

The 100-millisecond time window is not the only temporal expanse in which we perceive events as integrated in some way. There can also be inte-gration at time scales in the neighborhood of two to three seconds. This is the interval that I will call the present. The evidence for a psychologically signif-icant interval of this length is varied and extensive (for a review, see Pöppel, 2009). Pöppel (1971) found that people are highly accurate at repeating sound patterns, but performance drops off precipitously after three seconds. Pöppel (1988a) also found that units in music tend to be about this length, and Turner and Pöppel (1988) found similar durations for metered poetry. Szelag (1997) found that people can impose rhythmic structure on metronome clicks by subjectively accentuating beats at regular intervals, but subjective experi-ence of structure is lost when the gap between clicks exceeds three seconds. Moving beyond sound, Pöppel (1988b) found that three seconds is the average time for spontaneous reversal while looking at ambiguous visual im-ages. Burr and Santoro (2001) found that global motion patterns take three seconds to integrate and perceive. Lipps (2002) reports that this is the average time that people look through a camera before snapping a picture. Years ear-lier, Köhler (1923) showed that successive visual stimuli can be accurately compared in their intensity only if they are presented within about three sec-onds of each other. This also turns out to be the median duration for many repetitive actions. In a cross-cultural study, Schleidt and Kien (1997) found that activities such as stacking, rowing, scratching, hammering, gathering, and shoveling tend to divide into three-second "action units." Similar action units have also been found across a range of mammalian species (Gerstner and Fazio, 1995).

Phenomenologically, three-second intervals do not feel as if they are happening all at once. In this respect, the present is unlike the now and the instant. But events taking place within three seconds do have a palpable sense of temporal immediacy. To test this, stop what you are doing at any moment and see how vividly you can travel back in time, retracing what you were experiencing for the prior two or three seconds. See how far you can go. If you are like me, the immediate past presents itself as available in a way that moments slightly earlier do not. For example, the words in a spoken sentence disappear one by one as a sentence unfolds, and this makes them unlike the sounds in a syllable, which are experienced all at once, but the words nevertheless retain a psychological reality that differs from those in sentences heard just moments earlier. This phenomenological intuition may be what James (1890: 609) referred to as "the specious present," following E. R. Clay. For James and Clay, the past—even the recent past—has a psychological unreality akin to the future. It seems to be gone from us in a profound way. But the immediate past seems to be part of a moving window in time, a sense of the present. James estimated this window to be about twelve seconds long, which greatly exceeds the three-second duration emphasized by Pöppel and others. This overestimate may simply reflect a failure of introspection in measuring temporal boundaries. The key idea is that very recent events endure and give rise to a sense that the present has a temporal extension that greatly exceeds the infinitesimal units of physical time and even the fleeting moments, which I termed instants.

These three kinds of moments are summarized in figure 20. We can now ask which of them are phenomenally unified and how that unity is achieved.

The Instant:
25-30 milliseconds

The Now:
60-100 milliseconds

The Present:
2-3 seconds

FIGURE 20 Three kinds of conscious moment: the instant (e.g., the duration a monitor flicker would have to be to become visible); the now (e.g., the duration required to experience an ordered event sequence); the present (e.g., the duration of a spontaneous endogenous change in the experience of a bistable figure).

Recall that states are phenomenally unified when they are part of a single experience. We can ask which of these three kinds of moments can be thought of as experiential wholes with component parts. For the reasons just given, I think that the present is not best construed as an experiential whole; points making up the present do not feel like a single experience. The words at the start of a spoken sentence are not experienced together with the words at the end. The present is too long to be a single experience. Instants qualify as whole experiences, but they lack temporal breadth. If instants have unity, it is synchronic, not diachronic. Only the now deserves to be called diachronically unified. The now is experienced as a whole with duration. I submit that any account of diachronic unity should be an account of the phenomenal unity of the now.

I explained synchronic unity in terms of resonance. This construct can be extended to explain diachronic unity, too. At first, this proposal might look completely untenable. Within the nervous system, resonance is canonically regarded as a synchronic property. Consider again the notion of phase coherence: two neural populations cohere if there is constant relationship between their oscillations. One example of this would be oscillatory synchrony. But synchrony clearly can't apply to neural events that are diachronic. One neural event cannot synchronize with an event that succeeds it. Fortunately, the notion of resonance is not restricted to synchrony. One neural event resonates with another if its constitutive pattern of activity depends on the other. This could occur in two ways. One even might directly cause another, or both events may be regulated by a common cause.

In the case of synchronic unity, I gestured toward a common-cause explanation. I said that intersensory integration depends on unconscious comparisons between concurrent stimuli and that consciousness is a kind of replay that takes place after such comparisons are made. One can think of the resonance between neural populations as resulting from whatever mechanisms implement these comparisons. Much the same story can be told about diachronic resonance. We have learned from studies of apparent motion, such as the beta phenomenon, that temporal episodes often involve filling in time steps that are not present in the stimulus. Sensory systems presumably accomplish this by unconscious comparison and editing. The results become conscious after comparisons have been made. Whatever does the comparing may also serve to keep groups of successive instants in resonance. The neural pattern of one instant may depend on a prior instant in that both are regulated by this common source. For example, if each instant is a neural oscillation, a succession of instants may be caused to occur at a rhythmic frequency. The succession of instants that arise under common regulatory control can be said to resonate. And because they resonate, they might also be described as belonging to a single temporally extended state.

This picture is attractive because it offers a uniform account of diachronic and synchronic unity. But it also raises a puzzle. If diachronic unity is explained by resonance in time, then why does the now have a more or less fixed and minute duration? Why don't the mechanisms that coordinate neural dynamics in time cause long successions of instants to be experienced as unified wholes? What explains the exact duration of the now?

The answer to this question may depend on physical properties of the nervous system, which will be sketched somewhat tentatively in the next chapter. But without the details, one can see how the story would have to go. Suppose again that instants are individual oscillations, and successive instants are unified when they occur in rhythm. Now suppose that rhythmic oscillations are regulated by some external source. The best way to explain the temporal duration of the now would be to assume that whatever regulated these rhythms has a rhythmic cycle of its own. If that were the case, then the duration of the now could be explained as the number of instants occurring within a cycle of the regulatory mechanisms. A series of rapid beats are nested within slower beats. By analogy, think of the rotations of a bicycle wheel, which depend on the slower rotations of the pedal. The now might be equivalent to the number of rotations caused by a single rotation of the pedal.

It's a consequence of this view that time is parceled into discrete units. This is an old and controversial conclusion (see, e.g., Di Lollo, 1980; Kline and Eagleman, 2008), but it has contemporary adherents (see VanRullen and Koch, 2003). One might be tempted to resist discreteness on phenomenological grounds; time seems to flow continuously. I have already offered an explanation of this: immediately consecutive instants cannot be ordered. It's also worth noting that the discreteness of time does not entail that time flows at an irregular rate. Again, think of the bicycle wheel, which may rotate at a constant velocity even if it depends on pedal rotations. Discreteness may, however, result in fluctuations that are detectable in our behavior. The unitizing of language and action are examples of this. There may be corresponding fluctuations in perception. Mathewson et al. (2009) show that stimulus detectability varies over 100-millisecond intervals. We may miss briefly presented stimuli when they coincide with the boundaries between moments that make up conscious experience. This provides evidence for the discreteness hypothesis and, even more strikingly, for the specific proposal about the duration of the now. Although it is controversial, this gives us further reason to take the suggestions advanced here seriously.

3. Unity and Attention

3.1. RESONANCE AND SYNCHRONIC ATTENTION

At the start of this chapter, I noted that the unity of consciousness presents a problem for the AIR theory. If conscious states are attended intermediate-level representations, then it seems that each conscious state becomes conscious separately, and the unity between any two is a mystery. I have now sketched a theory of conscious unity that goes some way toward alleviating this worry, because we can see that the brain actively works to calibrate synchronic and diachronic states. This suggests that perceptual representations do not arise autonomously but rather interact, giving rise to resonance. But there is still a question about how this account of unity relates to the AIR theory. Resonance might seem like an add-on, going beyond the resources already implicated in AIR. It might look as if I have implicitly endorsed a RAIR theory, according to which conscious states are resonant attended intermediate-level representations. In this section, I want to suggest that resonance is not an add-on but actually falls out of the AIR theory, suggesting that the theory, unlike some others in the literature, has built-in resources for explaining the unity of consciousness. It will also turn out, however, that AIR entails certain limitations on unity, which I will discuss below.

The key to linking resonance and AIR is to realize that attention might be the source of resonance. This would entail that resonance arises with attention or, more accurately, with what I will call co-attention. In principle, one could attend to a single feature in one sense modality without attending to others, but in practice, we always attend to more than one feature. As we will see below, it might be possible to divide attention in such a way that two streams of information are not attended in an integrated way, but much of the time, we seem to attend to things together. I will say that two items are co-attended if they are modulated by the same attention-allocating process. My conjecture is that the resonance that constitutes conscious unity arises with co-attention.

To pursue this claim, I want to begin by revisiting the topic of intersensory integration, which framed the discussion of synchronic unity. As we have seen, intersensory integration arises after an unconscious process of calibration, in which activity in one sense is modulated by another. One might think that such calibration can arise in the absence of attention, and indeed, there is evidence for such a dissociation. For example, De Gelder et al. (2005) presented blindsight patients with facial expressions in their blind field, followed by consciously experienced audio recordings of words. They found that the unconscious, and presumably unattended, faces influenced the emotional tone of words. Similarly, Vroomen, Driver, and De Gelder (2001) found that the emotional tone of speech is influenced in healthy subjects by facial expressions that are attentionally suppressed. There is also evidence that attention does not modulate the ventriloquism affect (Bertelson et al., 2000; Vroomen, Driver, and De Gelder, 2001). On the other hand, Tiippana, Andersen, and Sams (2004) found that attention can influence the McGurk effect.

These inconsistent results are difficult to interpret, but they suggest that attention will influence intersensory integration only for certain kinds of stimuli; ventriloquism may depend on a preattentive process (see Bertini et al., 2010). But that conclusion is consistent with the conjecture under consideration. The equation of resonance and co-attention hangs not on whether attention affects integration but on whether integration affects attention. The crucial prediction is that when unconscious calibration processes cause two stimuli to resonate, they do so by bringing both into attention together. The blindsight study doesn't bear on this prediction, because the visual stimulus is never attended, and the studies of ventriloquism would count against the prediction only if it could be shown that the auditory and visual streams that get spatially united are not co-attended. But ventriloquism does seem to cause co-attention. Busse et al. (2005) provide compelling evidence using fMRI and EEG that attention spreads from the visual stimulus to the auditory stimulus during the ventriloquism effect.

The notion of co-attention may seem obscure. It is not a standard construct in the attention literature. There is, however, a related construct. Studies of multisensory processing show that attention to one modality can sometimes influence performance in another. It has long been known that a stimulus in one modality can improve performance in response to a stimulus in another—the "intersensory facilitation effect" (Welch and Warren, 1986). Conversely, when people try to perform concurrent tasks that require use of two different modalities, there can be intersensory degradation. For example, Bonnel and Hafter (1998) show that auditory and visual identification can interfere with each other when done in parallel, and Pizzighello and Bressan (2008) were able to induce inattentional blindness in vision by having subjects listen to verbal material. Such findings do not directly support the idea of co-attention, but they suggest two things. First, the allocation of attention may depend, in some cases, on a process of intersensory comparison. Second, such comparisons can lead to cases in which stimuli across two senses can both be attended at the same time or to cases in which one interferes with the other. This suggests a model that works as follows. When two stimuli are presented, an unconscious decision is made about whether they are congruent. If they are, then attention may be increased for both, and if not, attention may be disproportionately apportioned. It is a small step from this notion of correlated changes in attention to co-attention. Attending causes a change in the way a sensory representation is processed. Intersensory comparison allocates attention and does so by causing this change to occur in appropriate proportion to two or more sensory representations. In this way, the attentional modulation in one modality depends on the modulation in another.

One can also elucidate this notion of co-attention by thinking about it in neural terms, and this will actually bring us to the strongest empirical evidence for the foregoing approach to unity. In chapter 3, I investigated the neural correlates of attention and proposed that attention is implemented by neural synchrony within the gamma range. If attention is neural synchrony, then co-attention occurs when two populations of neurons are synchronized together. Or, more carefully, we might define co-attention in terms of states that are phase-locked, which is to say causally coordinated in time, even if not completely coincident. Perfect synchrony across brain areas may be difficult to broker, but this slightly weaker construct allows us to capture the idea that, at a neural level, attention involves the imposition of temporal coordination. This is just what the resonance story postulates. The fact that attention involves temporal coordination of neurons entails that co-attention involves neural resonance. If co-attention is the best account of unity, given the idea that unified states are co-conscious, it follows that neural resonance is the best account of co-attention, given that attention involves gamma synchrony.

Thus, the resonance approach to unity coheres perfectly with the neural correlates of attention proposed, on independent grounds, in chapter 3. Indeed, there is direct evidence supporting this equation of unity and synchrony. A large body of research links gamma to intersensory integration (e.g., Bhattacharya, Shams, and Shimojo, 2002; Kanayama, Sato, and Ohira, 2009; and for a review, Senkowski et al., 2008). This is very satisfying, because we arrived at the neural-resonance story independently, via the construct of co-attention. The intersensory integration literature does not focus on attention but leads to the neural correlate of attention. This suggests that attention is involved in intersensory integration and provides convergent evidence for the attentional approach to unity.

This account could also explain one aspect of the phenomenology of synchronic unity that I have yet to mention. When two items are unified in consciousness, they also seem to be relatable. That is to say, one item can be related along some dimension to the other. Within vision, we can try to assess whether two items in consciousness are adjacent, proximate, parallel, or perpendicular; equal in size, color, form, or intensity; capable of fitting together; and so on. Across modalities, we can compare duration, direction of motion, location, and numerosity. It is an important feature of consciousness that such comparisons are possible only for items that are unified. I cannot relate the conscious items in my head to items in your head, to unconscious items, or to items that are conscious at significantly different times.

The claim that unity is co-attention offers an explanation of this important fact. As we saw in chapter 3, attention allows access to working memory. Working memory is presumably necessary to make explicit comparisons of the kind I have just been referring to. These comparisons involve executive processes, which are believed to depend on working memory. The fact that the unity of consciousness is necessary and sufficient for relatability can be explained on the assumption that unified experiences are co-attended. Co-attended items are made available together to working memory. If resonance were not linked to attention, the hypothesis that unity is resonance would leave relatability unexplained. The present story fits all of these pieces together. Preattentive processes calibrate sensory inputs and then cause the resulting states to resonate. Resonance makes these states relatable, and it does so because resonance is, in this instance, an implementation of co-attention.

3.2. RESONANCE AND DIACHRONIC ATTENTION

My emphasis so far has been on synchronic unity, but much the same story can be told about unity across time. The account of synchronic unity began with the observation that unconscious processes coordinate concurrent sensory events. Temporal events also require unconscious coordination. It's not far-fetched to suppose that these unconscious processes regulate attention and that attention accounts for the unity of consciousness in time.

Let's begin with a classic case of temporal integration: apparent motion. Some evidence suggests that attention is involved in the generation of apparent motion across long distances (Horowitz and Treisman, 1994), but the proposal that I want to make does not depend on this. The crucial claim is that once two events are recognized as time slices of a single object in motion, attention is temporally spread, in a resonant way, across the whole. It is known that apparent motion can capture attention (Bonneh, Cooperman, and Sagi, 2001). When this occurs, we can think of attention as being allocated to an event, not just an object. At the level of implementation, this might mean that the neural processes underlying attention to one instant would not have occurred the way they do were it not for their allocation an instant earlier. The proposal is not restricted to motion. I want to suggest that attention is generally extended through time in this way, with successive moments in resonance. This is speculative, but it finds strong support in the fact that conscious neural dynamics tend to be rhythmic, suggesting that attention is not allocated by independent processes from instant to instant but is rather allocated in an orderly way across time.

This story is incomplete on its own. We also need to explain why consciousness is temporally discrete. Why would temporal integration of attention parcel into 100-millisecond units? The answer, sketched above, is that neural processes may need to be refreshed at regular intervals. In terms of attention, this means that the neural processes by which we attend have a regular refresh rate of about 100 milliseconds. This may sound like a wild conjecture, but there is actually evidence based on both psychophysics (VanRullen, Reddy, and Koch, 2005) and EEG recordings (van Dijk et al., 2008). In terms of time, this means that certain temporal illusions will increase in likelihood when stimuli have a time course that coincides with the attentional refresh rate, which is precisely what VanRullen, Reddy, and Koch found.

Whether or not 100 milliseconds is a refresh rate, there is other evidence suggesting that this interval is psychologically real and important for the allocation of attention in time. Rohenkohl and Nobre (2010) found that temporal expectations increase neural oscillations in the 100-millisecond range, which suggests that temporal units of that size are used top-down to search for specific moments in time (see also Verstraten, Cavanagh, and Labianca, 2000, for a slightly lower estimate). Oscillations at this frequency also reflect attentional anticipation (Foxe, Simpson, and Ahlfors, 1998), and interruptions at this frequency interfere with conscious detection (Romei, Gross, and Thut, 2010). The emerging picture suggests that conscious attention is organized both temporally and spatially and that 100-millisecond units are used to sample ongoing perceptual activity. This is consistent with my hypothesis that the conscious now has a 100-millisecond duration. Crucially, for the present context, the evidence suggests that this is an interval in which neural activity is both organized and attentionally modulated. That bolsters the conjecture that attention is implemented by neural processes that resonate temporally.

Attention may also play a role in explaining duration of the instant, which lasts about 25 milliseconds. This duration may sound arbitrary, but it looks far less surprising once we equate attention with gamma-band activity. The gamma oscillations associated with attention often average around 40 hertz, and 40 hertz means 40 times per second. Thus, 25 milliseconds is the duration of a single gamma beat. It may be that a stimulus needs to be present for 25 milliseconds because it needs to endure long enough for a complete gamma beat to complete. When two successive stimuli are too close in time, overlapping in the same gamma beat, they may be impossible to discern or order, but when they fall on different gamma beats, ordering becomes possible. This can explain the duration of the instant and why more than one instant is needed for the brain to do the bookkeeping required to sequence events in the world. If so, the instant is intimately tied to gamma.

This gamma conjecture would also help relate the instant to the now. As we just saw, the duration of the now may be related to an attention refresh rate. That refresh rate, 100 milliseconds, coincides with a well-known frequency of brain oscillations, the alpha band. Alpha beats tend to be 100 milliseconds long. The reason temporal experience seems to be parceled in units of this length could stem from the fact that gamma is regulated by alpha. Alpha beats may be needed to keep gamma going, and each alpha beat may serve to recharge the gamma cycle or, in some cases in which new objects are perceived, to reset it.

The neural story is less clear when it comes to the present, but there is strong evidence linking this time span to attention. The present is about three seconds long, and that is the duration typically found in studies of a phenomenon called inhibition of return (Bao, Zhou, and Fu, 2004). After attending to a stimulus, attention for that stimulus location is briefly inhibited. As mentioned earlier, this is also the time that needs to elapse before spontaneous reversals of ambiguous figures. Pöppel (1994) suggests that every three seconds or so, the brain asks, "What's new?" This may be regarded as a kind of attentional dwell time. The brain keeps track of what is attended to or what it is attending to for approximately three seconds, before some kind of resetting occurs. One explanation for this involves working memory. According to the theory of attention in chapter 3, attention is availability to working memory. Some authors have suggested that working memory has a natural decay rate, such that it will lose its contents at that rate if it does not actively maintain them. Decay rates have been estimated at between two and four seconds (Mueller and Krawitz, 2009). It is possible, then, that the duration of the present reflects the temporal properties of working-memory decay. An alternative explanation is that the three-second delay reflects the duration of iconic memory, an automatic storage of information within sensory systems, which does not depend on working-memory encodings. Studies of iconic memory suggest a temporal duration within this time range (e.g., Lamme, 2010), although some estimates are much lower. In any case, Lamme's research on poststimulus cuing suggests that a record of visual stimuli can be retained for a few seconds after presentation, when subjects are required to recall what they've seen. Once a stimulus is removed, it is no longer conscious, so it is not directly available for working memory. The memory trace can still be reactivated by attention, however, rendering its contents available. One might say that these traces are available for availability. As I interpret these findings, attention makes stimuli available, and then the sensory record can be reactivated by attention, making recent stimuli available again. The time course of the present reflects the window in which attention can operate on a memory trace. It is a kind of mnemonic availability.

To summarize, I think that the duration of the conscious moment depends fundamentally on attention. Instants reflect the minimal time for a neural process of attention to occur, the now is a succession of instants parceled together by the rhythmic processes that regulate attention, and the present is a period in which attention can be reallocated to a memory trace of a very recent event. One perennial question that has been raised by recent research on temporal experience concerns the plasticity of time. Can moments shrink and expand? If the duration of the moment is determined by attention, then one might expect temporal expansion or contraction under conditions in which attention is intensified or relaxed. Consistent with this, there is a considerable body of evidence linking attention to perceived duration. Tse et al. (2004) used an oddball paradigm in which a moving black disk occurred in a series of still black disks. Oddballs are known to attract attention, and Tse et al. found that they also show a dramatic increase in perceived duration. Correlatively, time seems to shrink when attention is withdrawn. Using a dual-task paradigm, Cicchini and Morrone (2009) showed that estimates of temporal intervals were compressed when subjects were attending to a primary task. Time also shrinks during saccades, which reflect correlated changes in attention (Binda et al., 2009).

The claim that time shrinks and expands with attention has not gone unchallenged. Stetson, Fiesta, and Eagleman (2007) measured the resolution of temporal perception using rapidly flickering numbers as subjects fell from a great height at an amusement-park ride. Falling induces fear, and fear increases attention. It turns out, however, that fear does not increase temporal resolution; numbers that flickered just below the perceivable threshold did not become visible as subjects fell. However, subjects did overestimate the durations of their falls. The authors conclude that overestimations result from a memory distortion rather than a change in temporal experience; when we are afraid, we encode more information, but temporal experience does not actually slow down.

One problem with the Stetson, Fiesta, and Eagleman study, in addition to the challenge of getting people to read during a free fall, is that it does not distinguish different kinds of moments. If the instant is determined by the time it takes for attentional processes to take place in the nervous system, there may be no way to slow their duration significantly. But this would not rule out the possibility of stretching the present or the now. Instead of concluding that temporal dilation is a memory distortion, one might explore the possibility that changes in attention affect the number of instants in the now or the decay rate of the present.

There is an intriguing finding from the aforementioned oddball study that may bear on this. Recall the main result of Tse et al. (2004): when a moving disk is placed in a series of still disks, it appears to last longer. Curiously, however, Tse et al. did not show this dilation effect for moving disks that appear for 75 milliseconds. Of all of the durations tested, 75 milliseconds was the only one that fell within the usual length of the conscious now. One possible explanation is that a stimulus of this duration is too fast to reset the time scale of the now, so it doesn't benefit from the temporal-expansion effect. If the now has an average duration of 100 milliseconds, items within that duration can exert an influence on that duration of the now only at the next time step, which means that their impact on time comes too late. Attentionally alluring items that last longer than 100 milliseconds can reset time while they are still visible and thereby benefit from the perceived expansion. It's hard to see how this kind of idiosyncratic effect could be explained by a memory distortion.

However these disputes about temporal dilation get resolved, the main claim that I want to make here remains plausible: time is unified by means of attentional resonance. This story echoes the account of synchronic unity and coheres with a body of literature linking key temporal durations to psychometric properties associated with attention. The upshot is a tidy theory of unity that relates directly to the AIR theory of consciousness. Where other theories may need auxiliary machinery to explain unity, the AIR theory has a built-in explanation. If consciousness arises with attention and the processes underlying attention resonate, then attention may be the basis of experienced unity.

3.3. HOW UNIFIED IS EXPERIENCE?

In the first section of the chapter, I accepted the thesis that consciousness is unified on phenomenological grounds. Like many others, I find it evident from introspection that different conscious experiences can cohere together as one.

This is also evident functionally, in that different experiences can be related to each other in various ways. But I postponed the question of whether all of the concurrent and consecutive conscious experiences in a given individual are unified. This is what Bayne and Chalmers (2003) call the total conjunctive unity thesis. The resonance account gives us reason to think that this thesis is false. Here I want to spell out why and see whether this implication threatens the account or supports it.

I have suggested that there are principled reasons to expect a fair degree of resonance among conscious sensory states. The nervous system actively calibrates the contents of perception both synchronically and diachronically, and it is plausible that this process results in coordinated attentional modulation. But nothing guarantees that every pair of attentionally modulated states will resonate. In principle, attention can also be applied in a piecemeal way. For example, if two sustained sensory inputs are uncorrelated and unrelated, attention might start to respond to them independently. Consider the hum of cars passing and the taste of your cocktail when you sit at an urban café. One might consciously experience both sensory states without co-attending them. The result would be simultaneous streams of consciousness without resonance. Likewise, one might attend to two temporal events, such as a song on the radio and a fly crossing the room, without relating the two. Under such conditions, resonance might not occur. Resonance might also be graded: high for related stimuli in one sense modality and lower for less related inputs in different senses. This could lead to violations of transitivity, such that the degree of resonance between one pair of experiences, A and B, and another, B and C, is greater than the resonance between A and C. Resonance might also fluctuate. It might increase when one notices an object slowly encroaching on another, and it might undergo Gestalt shifts, as when we see a forest and then focus on an individual tree.

It is not easy to find direct evidence for these possibilities, but there are reasons to believe that they occur. Some models of multiobject attention assume that each attended object is attended at a different temporal frequency (Kazanovich and Borisyuk, 2006). There is also evidence that we can successfully detect inputs in sound and sight, without attention to one stream degrading performance in the other (Bonnel and Hafter, 1998). We can even keep track of the course of two concurrent sequences without making the same duration estimation for each, suggesting that time consciousness can divide into separate streams (Kawamura, 1998).

One might think that this is a strike against the resonance theory of unity. Some people think that it is obvious from introspection that all of our conscious experiences are unified, even when they don't relate to one another. But two replies are available to those who make this objection. First, disunity may be quite common in ordinary experience. Consider the phenomenon of focusing intensely on an activity, such as watching a movie, while also having certain bodily sensations, such as the feeling of your legs being crossed. It's natural to say that you experience both of those things at once, but it is not phenomenologically obvious that they are unified as a single state of consciousness. The relationship that these two experiences bear to each other seems quite different from the relationship between sound and sight in the movie.

Second, the impression that all conscious states are unified might be an illusion caused by the fact that unity arises when we look for it. Suppose you are wondering whether two items in experience are part of a single experience. To find out, you will make an executive decision to attend to both. That very act will bring about co-attention. There will be a single control state allocating attention to two experiences, and they will resonate together as a result. Thus, when you look for unity, you find it, even if it wasn't there before you looked. This is a little bit like the refrigerator-light illusion, in which you mistakenly think that the light is always on because it is on whenever you look. A better analogy: when the teacher of a rowdy class turns away, the children behave wildly, but they return to order when the teacher turns to face them. The search for order imposes order. Thus, we cannot find disunity by looking for it.

The resonance account is attractive because it can explain the vague impression of disunity, as in the movie case, while also explaining why unity is always found when sought. The account also ensures that unity will be common, because calibration is common, while allowing for gradations. Our firmest impressions of unity concern stimuli that are clearly related, such as two edges on the same contour. The AIR theory explains unity without any added mechanisms. Unity just is co-attention. The prevalence of unity is given by the facts of calibration. So unity does not require any ad hoc assumptions. AIR also offers a unified theory of unity: the principles of state individuation that apply locally to a pair of visually represented edges also apply cross-modally and across successive moments in time. Most important, the AIR theory explains unity without appeal to a unified subject of experience or a place where all conscious states come together. It avoids the pitfalls of other accounts by locating unity in the unified experiences themselves.

9

What Is Consciousness? Neurofunctionalism

In part I of this book, I presented a theory of consciousness, which included both a psychological characterization and a neural characterization. One might put this in terms of correlates. The psychological correlates of consciousness (PCCs) can be expressed in terms that echo the way the AIR theory was formulated in chapter 3: conscious states are attended intermediate-level representations (AIRs). The neural correlates of consciousness (NCCs) are the neural realizers of AIRs. In chapter 4, I proposed that these are gamma vectorwaves. But this leaves us with a question. If conscious states have both psychological and neural correlates, which of these constitutes their material basis? Is one essential and the other merely contingent? This brings us to the metaphysical question that has been at the heart of the mind-body problem in twentieth-century analytic philosophy. Once we assume that some form of materialism is true, we are left asking: At which level of analysis in the material world should we specify the identity conditions of conscious mental states? What sort of physical things are conscious states? Are they brain events or something that can be characterized more abstractly?

To provide an answer, we must first look at the leading forms of physicalism, which divide on the question of whether consciousness is a psychological or a neurobiological phenomenon. I will ultimately argue that it is both. When philosophers assume that we must choose between these alternatives, they are making a mistake. That mistake lies in a long-standing debate between psychophysical identity theorists and functionalists. I will review some standard moves in that debate, and I will conclude that it ends in a stalemate. Then I will offer a way out.

1. The Psychophysical Identity Theory

1.1. THE THEORY INTRODUCED

Throughout this discussion, I will assume that physicalism (which I defined in chapter 1) is true. The goal here is to decide between physicalist theories; dualism will be addressed in the next chapter. Physicalist theories have a long history in philosophy (consider Democritus, Hobbes, La Mettrie, and Diderot), but the prevailing contemporary forms emerged in the 1950s and '60s. The first form of physicalism to earn a wide following within that period was the psychophysical identity theory of Place (1956), Feigl (1958), and Smart (1959). The central idea behind this theory is that there is a type identity between mental and physical states. A type identity is one that can be specified between types, or kinds, such that every instance of a kind specified in psychological terms is identical to an instance of a neutrally specified kind. The most frequent example given in the literature is the putative identity between pain (a type of mental state) and c-fiber stimulation (a type of brain process). This example is unfortunate, because it is wildly implausible. C-fibers are nociceptive cells in the peripheral nervous system, and they are only associated with the transduction of dull pains. Within the central nervous system, pain has two components, sensory and affective, which are processed in several brain areas (SI, SII, insula, anterior cingulate, etc.) as different cellular responses within these areas convey information about the location, intensity, quality, source (e.g., heat versus pressure), aversiveness, and coping responses. Given this, type-type reductions for pain are likely to be fine-grained. For example, the sensory component of burning pains might be a particular kind of neural activation in the upper posterior insula (Ostrowsky et al., 2000). But for short, we can say that identity theorists believe that pain is a certain kind of neural response. The defenders of this view have disagreed about whether this *is* a relation of identity or of constitution (e.g., Place favors the latter), and they have disagreed about whether the relation is necessary or contingent (e.g., Smart refers to contingent identities, but Kripke, 1980, convinced many philosophers that identity statements between singular terms are necessary). These details won't matter for the present discussion.

The pioneers of the psychophysical identity theory often spend more time defending it against objections than providing positive evidence, but it is possible to reconstruct some arguments. Let's focus on Place. He begins with the assumption that neuroscience has established correlations between mental-state types and brain-state types, but he recognizes that mere correlation is not enough. The lunar cycle correlates with the tides, but we have no temptation to equate the two. How, then, do we move from correlation to identity? At this point, Place offers something puzzling. He says that the correlation in the lunar cycle is not explanatory, and he elucidates this idea by saying that the moon does not directly cause our observations of the tides, so the correlation between moon and tide must be causal. He contrasts this with the case of electrical discharge and lightning, saying that the former directly causes our observations of the latter. But the contrast is unhelpful, because pursuing the lightning analogy in this way, Place would be forced to say that neural events cause our observations of mental events. But such causal talk implies that neural events are separate from mental events, which is just what the physicalist wants to deny.

Moreover, it has become a commonplace in consciousness studies to point out that neural correlates never fully explain phenomenal qualities. Why does a particular neural pattern get experienced as red rather than blue? This is what Levine (1983) calls an explanatory gap, which some (though not Levine) have used to argue for dualism.

Place's intuition is that the moon case, unlike the lightning case, involves an explanatory mechanism (the moon) that is clearly separable from the thing it explains (the tide). But dualists will insist that brain states are separable from mental states. To counter this worry, Place needs to deploy another argument. Dualism is a nonstarter, he says, because it violates strictures on parsimony: if mental states are nonphysical and all brain states have identifiable neural causes, then mental states are causally inert (they are "nomological danglers"); we shouldn't posit nomological danglers unless we are forced to; in the case of mental states, we are not forced to, because mental talk can be restated in language that is neutral about whether the entities in question are mental or physical; therefore, we shouldn't posit irreducibly mental entities. Thus, unlike the tide case, where we have reason to posit both moon and sea, psychophysical correlations are best explained by positing one entity rather than two.

On this reconstruction, Place's argument has two parts: an appeal to correlations and an argument against dualist interpretations of those correlations, which would render them indirect. To counter this parsimony, dualists need some reason for thinking that mental states and brain states, like tide and sea, are distinct. Correlations are evidence for identity, when no such reason is given. In chapter 10, I will consider one of the most influential recent arguments for dualism, which could be construed as a reply to Place. In this chapter, I am assuming that physicalism is true, so I will assume that Place's parsimony argument can hold up to more recent replies. The question for now is whether Place is right about type-type correlations between mental and physical events. Most physicalists who reject the identity theory focus on this premise.

1.2. OBJECTIONS AND REPLIES

The most famous objection to the identity theory originates with Putnam (1967). He argues that mental-state types are "multiply realized" by brain-state types, thereby breaking the correlation needed by Place. For example, octopus brains are very different from human brains, yet they seem to exhibit pain. This suggests that the mapping between fear and brain states is one to many. In other words, Putnam presents Place with a dilemma: he must either deny that biologically different creatures can have mental states that are type-identical to ours, or he must deny that pain is a single type of brain state. Putman considers the first option less palatable, and that means that any token-level equation of mental and physical states is doomed to fail.

There are two standard replies to the argument from multiple realizability. The first response is to relativize (Kim, 1972; Hooker, 1981; Enç, 1983; Churchland, 1986; see also Lewis, 1980). Pain for humans might be identified with one kind of neural state, while pain for octopuses is identified with another. Proponents of this relativizing move can then either deny that there is any overarching category, pain, or they can concede that pain exists in some functional sense while insisting that this does not preclude type identities within a species. Following this latter strategy might force the psychophysical identity theorist to trade in identity talk for constitution talk. If pain were identical to c-fiber stimulation in humans and to a different neural state in octopuses, then pain would identical to two nonidentical states, which is a contradiction. Talk of constitution gets around the worry, because the same type of thing can be constituted by different stuff. Thus, this version of the relativizing move departs from the letter of psychophysical identity theory, but it preserves the spirit: it justifies the search for neural correlates in a given species and allows us to say that for humans, pain is such-and-such brain state.

The other standard reply to Putnam's objection is to deny that octopuses have pain. This assumption is based on the observation that octopuses exhibit withdrawal behaviors in responses to stimuli that would cause pain in us. But that inference is problematic for two reasons. First, octopus withdrawal behaviors are actually quite different from ours. If you pinch an octopus, it will squirt a cloud of black ink, contract its legs, and jet away, until it finds a hard surface, at which point it will either squeeze into a hole or camouflage its body by adopting the texture and color of the place on which it has perched. Should we call this pain behavior? It might be safer to say that the octopus avoids tissue damage without assuming that it has pain. As Shapiro (2000) points out, multiple realizability is really a dogma in philosophy. Only behaviors described in extremely coarse terms (such as avoidance) are implemented by multiple mechanisms; once we move to terms that interest consciousness researchers (such as pain, anxiety, or seeing red), claims about multiple realization lose their intuitive foothold.

Second, even if octopus behavior were just like ours, we could not safely infer that they have pain (Polger, 2004). This point is most obvious if we switch from talk of "having" pain to "experiencing" pain. We cannot infer similarities in experience from similarities in behavior; similar behaviors could occur in creatures with radically different phenomenology or even no phenomenology. To determine whether another creature has conscious experiences like ours, we should figure out the correlate of experience in us and then see whether the other creature has those correlates. If conscious qualities correlate with neural states in us, then we should resist granting comparable experiences to creatures whose neural states differ from ours. If octopuses have different neurophysiology, that can be taken as evidence for the conclusion that they don't experience pain.

The claim that octopuses lack pain does not entail that pain is a uniquely human experience. If we consider mammals instead of cephalopods, we find that there is actually extraordinary continuity across species. As Bechtel and Mundale (1999) have observed, the basic organization of mammalian brains is very similar. Brodmann's early brain maps, based on the structure and organizations of cells, which are still widely used in neuroscience today, established striking commonalities across species. The commonalities are even greater when we consider cell types and neurotransmitters. In fact, the chemical composition of neurotransmitters in human beings is similar to functionally similar neurotransmitters in insects, suggesting that claims about multiple realization are greatly exaggerated. Putnam's argument can even be turned on its head. The level of similarity between octopuses and human beings may be very low when it comes to behavior, as noted above, but at the physiological level, there may be greater similarities (Zangwill, 1992). Thus, the identity theory may be in a better position than rival theories to establish mentality in other critters.

These two replies can be integrated into one decisive reply to the multiple-realizability objection. Mental states can be individuated at different levels of abstraction, and some mental-state words pick out phenomena at higher levels than others. We grant that there is a notion of pain that is identified with a broad class of avoidance behaviors, while also insisting that the characteristic feelings of, say, dull burning pains correlate better with neurophysiological states than with anything manifest in behavior. Likewise, we can distinguish color perception from the experience of a particular shade of red as it is for human beings. The former may be attributed to any species that can differentiate wavelengths, whereas the latter might be restricted to creatures whose brains process colors in just the way ours do. Similarly, fear conditioning might depend on having a physiologically implemented freezing response, because fear may be reducible to perceptions of specific kinds of bodily states (Prinz, 2004b), but learning, more generally, may not require any specific type of physical realization. Desire may depend on a specific neural realizer (Schroeder, 2004), even if appetitive states are multiply realized.

One might sum this up by saying that the psychophysical identity theory is plausible for mental states individuated finely, even if it is false for states individuated more coarsely. This conclusion looks like a partial defeat, but it is actually a moral victory. Opponents of the identity theory tend to argue that neural reductions undermine scientific psychology because they prevent robust generalizations (Fodor, 1974). But this move may be self-defeating. Generalizations at the most abstract level of mental-state individuation tend to be boring or even nominal (Shapiro, 2000). Learning, when defined as stimulus-shaped behavior, is not a projectable construct. It covers so many heterogeneous cases that nothing can be learned about learning in general by studying any specific instance. So the main generalization we can make about learning, as such, is that it involves shaping of behavior, but that just restates the definition. If we consider fear conditioning, in contrast, we can do real science, empirically discovering extinction rates, delay thresholds, and so on. Novel generalizations can be empirically discovered by observing individual cases. The mental kinds that map onto neural mechanisms are the most likely to have rich inductive potential and natural, as opposed to nominal, laws. There may be some levels of individuation between these extremes, but opponents of identity theory owe us examples. Would the replicable reports of error rates and reaction times that fill our psychology journals be possible if the phenomena they studied had radically different realizations?

Present-day identity theorists drive this point home by drawing attention to the remarkable success of reductive programs in neurobiology (Churchland, 1986; Bickle, 1998; Bechtel and McCauley, 1999). Neuroscience can be used to generate and confirm predictions about phenomenology, and it can identify mechanisms that account for observed phenomena. Neuroscience may not explain why red feels the way it does, but it can account for highly specific features of visual experience. For example, the existence of negative afterimages and their temporal duration can be accounted for by appeal to adaptation and decay rates in specific kinds of color-sensitive cells (Suzuki and Grabowecky, 2003). Properties of visual cells can also account for optical illusions such as the Hermann grid illusion, in which black smudges seem to appear at the intersections of black squares arranged in a grid. The illusion diminishes if the grid is rotated at an angle, if the squares have serrated edges, if the squares are not vertically aligned, and if the square-to-gap ratio is too small, and each of these facts can be attributed to the response profiles of neurons in visual cortex (Schiller and Carvey, 2005). There is a neat mapping from observed features onto neural mechanisms, just as the identity theorists conjectured a half-century ago.

In summary, the argument from multiple realizability is unsuccessful. Some mental states have behavioral identity conditions, but the states that we are most interested in as consciousness researchers tend to map onto neural mechanisms. When it comes to phenomenal states, there is little reason to assume similarity across biologically divergent species.

The psychophysical identity theory can rebut the most publicized objection, at least when it comes to phenomenal states, but there is another problem for the view as it has been traditionally conceived. It concerns the idea of "physical" here and the contrast it implies. The main alternative to psychophysical is functionalism, which we will turn to below. When philosophers say that mental states are identical to physical states, they imply that mental states are not functional. But what are we to make of this physical/functional contrast? One possibility is that physical means structural, but this is problematic. It's not clear that the physical structure of neurons is implicated in any empirically supported neurobiological reduction. A neuron lying inertly in a petri dish cannot be identified with any mental state. In discussing the neural correlates of consciousness, I appealed to synchronized firing and activation vectorwaves. These are functional characterizations, and functional characterizations go all the way down. In this sense, the identity theory is just a special case of functionalism (Lycan, 1987: chap. 4).

Identity theorists might not be embarrassed by this, but there is a deeper worry lurking here. To have a defensible account of the mental, identity theorists are not only required to appeal to the way neurons function, as opposed to inert neurons, but they must also establish that the neurons in question play the right psychologically characterized functional role. For example, we began with a psychological account of attention and then found the realizer. It follows that the neural states that we identify with mental states are, *eo ipso*, states that play psychological roles, and having this property is what makes them candidates for being mental. Likewise, when identity theorists explain edge perception by appeal to edge detectors—cells that register oriented discontinuities in light—they are individuating neurons by their psychological role. This concession to functionalism calls the spirit of the identity theory into question, because it threatens the reductive ambitions of the program. The cells that detect edges can be characterized in nonpsychological terms, but if they ceased to play their psychological role, they would be bad candidates for the reduction. Thus, mental states are not to be identified with neural activations as such but with neurons playing certain psychological roles.

This may seem like a trivial point, but it is actually an important departure from the way identity theory is sometimes conceived. By emphasizing formulas such as "pain = c-fiber stimulation," identity theorists give the impression that psychological roles drop out of the picture. We might use a functional description of pain to *pick out* the phenomenon, but once we find the neural correlate, we can kick away that description as if it didn't matter. This implies that functional descriptions are merely contingent reference fixers. On this view, pain is just a feeling, and regardless of how it functions, that feeling is identical to a particular brain-state type. I'm suggesting that this is a mistake.

The point is most obvious with unconscious states. What sense does it make to explain edge perception by appeal to edge-sensitive cells in ocular dominance columns and then say that those cells would still be edge detectors if they didn't detect edges? Human edge perception is a functionally characterized psychological process. Even if the edge detectors can be type-identified with neural mechanisms, it doesn't follow that the functional characterization is merely contingent.

Applied to phenomenal states, the argument gets a little more complicated. Famously, phenomenal qualities are identified by how they feel, rather than how they function. This might suggest that the way they function is contingent—that something could feel just like pain if it didn't act like pain. But there is no reason to believe that this is the case. It's not an analytic truth that painful feeling must function in any given way, but it's empirically clear that feelings have some of their functional properties essentially. To illustrate, consider how the AIR theory handles color qualia. At the neural level, color qualia are gamma vectorwaves, and at the psychological level, they are attended intermediate-level representations. Now we can ask, would the gamma vectorwave for chartreuse remain the same if it were located in an animal that was not attentionally modulating representations of chartreuse stimuli? I think the answer is no. First, consider attention. On any given occasion, control structures that gate access to working memory determine whether an intermediate-level representation will fire in the gamma range. Were these control structures not doing any work—that is, if an organism were not attending—gamma would not arise. So, counterfactually speaking, removing attention removes gamma. Now, consider vectorwaves. Granted, tokens of the vectorwave that represents chartreuse could arise in the absence of chartreuse stimuli; this is what happens in cases of misperception. But consider the type. Here we need to ask whether the vectorwave that is normally caused by chartreuse could be normally produced by some other color. There is undoubtedly some jerry-rigged scenario in which this happens, but in the closest possible worlds where color inputs change, cell populations respond by changing their firing pattern. So, there is a counterfactual connection between colors and vectorwaves, such that the cells that produce a vectorwave in representing one color would produce another vectorwave if they were to represent another color.

The connection between vectorwaves and colors is not robust across all possible worlds (such as worlds in which infants are implanted with color-inverting lenses). Likewise, the link between gamma and attention could be broken in worlds where humans mutate so that they retain gamma but lose working memory. Thus, the link between gamma vectorwaves and attended intermediate-level representations is neither metaphysically nor nomologically necessary. But it is a counterfactual supporting connection. Were attention to wane or content to change, a given gamma vectorwave would stop firing at gamma and change its temporal geometry. We can call this kind of counterfactual supporting connection a natural necessity. One type of condition naturally necessitates the other if the removal of the other were to lead to the cessation of the first. Natural necessities are not transworld correlations; they are sustaining conditions in the actual world. I am suggesting that gamma vectorwaves are AIRs by natural necessity.

This thesis is borne out by research on neural plasticity. When one population of cells is taken over by another, the felt qualities sometimes remain the same and sometimes change (Hurley and Noë, 2003). They seem to stay the same when their overall role remains similar. For example, phantom-limb pain involves invasion by nearby functionally similar cells in the somatosensory cortex, which do not disrupt the effects of the invaded cells, such as directing ameliorative behavior toward a (now missing) limb (Ramachandran and Hirstein, 1998). In cases in which the invading cells have a very different function, however, the invaded cells often undergo more radical rewiring, resulting in a very different functional role and new phenomenal qualities. The use of visual cells for Braille reading may be a case in point (Sadato et al., 1996). Again, it doesn't follow that psychological function is strictly necessary for phenomenal character, where strict necessity means true in all possible worlds. But psychological functions may be "naturally" necessary. If a psychological function were to change, the neural realizer would change. Research on neural plasticity adds empirical confirmation.

Psychophysical identity theorists have given the impression that the brain states undergirding mentality have their functional properties contingently, and there is an important sense in which this is false. Brain states have their roles by natural necessity. If I am right about that, then the contrast between the identity theory and its archrival has been exaggerated in a way that is seriously misleading. Let's turn to that archrival now.

2. Functionalism

2.1. THE THEORIES INTRODUCED

Functionalists say that mental states can be identified with functional roles. Fear, for example, is associated with various causes and effects, both behavioral and mental; functionalists say that to be in a state of fear is to be in a state that has some subset of these causes and effects. This general approach comes in a variety of different forms. Here I will briefly review some varieties, specify the version that is most plausible, and indicate why it may still be inadequate as it stands.

The most influential taxonomy of functionalist theories comes from Block (1978). I will use this taxonomy here, although two further versions of functionalism will appear below. In Block's taxonomy, functionalists differ in two main ways: how they specify functional roles and where those roles come from. "Machine functionalists" specify these roles using the kinds of tables that computer scientists use to represent Turing machines; mental states are equated with machine states, which are defined by the input-output functions that can be extrapolated from machine tables (Putnam, 1967). "Ramsification functionalists" specify the functional role of a mental state by writing out a psychological theory as a long compound sentence and then replacing each occurrence of the mental-state term with a quantifier (Lewis, 1972). For "commonsense functionalists," the functional roles that constitute our mental states are culled from the platitudes that make up our folk-psychological theories, while "psychofunctionalists" appeal to the functional roles that are empirically discovered within scientific psychology.

I think that machine functionalism and commonsense functionalism can be rejected out of hand. Machine functionalism suffers from a simple technical difficulty: Turing machines are in only one state at any given time (Block and Fodor, 1972). None of the mental states that we have names for or investigate in psychology corresponds to such global states, so this approach will be unhelpful. The problem with commonsense functionalism is that our platitudes are often false ("emotions are irrational") or contradictory (we say both "absence makes the heart grow fonder" and "out of sight, out of mind"). Furthermore, there are many empirically discovered distinctions that are not recognized in folk psychology (episodic versus semantic memory; trace versus delay conditioning; prototype versus exemplar representations), and countless real psychological phenomena have gone unnoticed by the folk (iconic memory, inhibition of return, confirmation bias, and so on). Thus, even if platitudes could be used to define some psychological states and processes, others would be left out if we restricted the mental to folk theories. It is better to think of folk theories as reference fixers, which help us identify phenomena of interest, which can then be empirically studied. This is comparable to the role that folk theories are presumed to play in science and theories of reference more broadly, so the rejection of commonsense functionalism is in harmony with the rejection of folk physics or the rejection of descriptivist theories of reference.

Using Block's taxonomy, we are left with Ramsified psychofunctionalism. In this approach, we specify mental states by writing out empirically derived theories and then quantifying into them. For example, suppose attention is scientifically shown to allow working-memory access, guide saccades, increase acuity, select from complex scenes, allow for strategic search, be engaged by stimulus contrasts, and so on. The Ramsified psychofunctionalist will say that attention is whatever (an x that) plays that role. There is a subtle issue here about whether attention is the filler of the role or the role itself. Many functionalists are token-identity theorists and therefore happy to say that every particular instance of a mental state is the neural state that plays a mental role. But functionalists fiercely resist type identity, saying that roles can be occupied by different fillers while remaining psychologically equivalent.

One of the main arguments for Ramsified psychofunctionalism is that we allegedly do characterize mental states in this way. If we want to know what attention is, we point to some paradigm cases (that's where common sense comes in) and then study its causal profile. We don't treat attention as a chemical microstucture or cellular form that happens to play a certain role; we treat the role as the essence. In this respect, mental phenomena are like the phenomena in special sciences. Consider some economic kinds: inflation, unemployment, trade deficits, free markets. We don't think that the physical realizers of these things matter very much.

2.2. OBJECTIONS AND REPLIES

The most celebrated objection to functionalism also comes from Block (1978). In that paper, he argues that, while functionalism may be plausible for some mental states (e.g., beliefs or memories), it is not well suited for phenomenal qualities. To show this, Block devises thought experiments that are designed to show that qualia can be absent in systems that realize the functional roles that are characteristic of human psychology. The textbook example involves the population of China. Suppose that the people of China decide to enact a functional description of the human mind (Block has them carrying out the instructions on a Turing machine table description of the mind, but any functional description will do). Each person carries out some minute input-output function, and they communicate using walkie-talkies. We can imagine each person possessing large look-up tables and saying things such as "If walkie-talkie 391 calls, then call walkie-talkie 615." Some of the outputs are sent to a robot, causing changes in its movements and verbal outputs. The robot will act like a human being, because it computes the input-output functions that we do, but, Block says, the robot will not be conscious. When the robot is kicked, it will say "ouch," but it won't experience pain. Nor will there be any massive cloud of pain distributed across the millions of Chinese citizens who happen to be implementing the functions that guide the robot's behaviors. Or, as Block more carefully puts it, we have "prima facie doubt" (i.e., it seems intuitively dubious to us) that the population feels collective pain. Block notes that people also have prima facie doubts about whether pain can be generated by neural activity, but in our case, these doubts have little force, since we know that human brains are conscious. But in cases where we don't have an antecedent reason for believing that a system is conscious—systems that are physically different from us—these doubts are sufficient for skepticism. We should conclude that there is no collective pain in the China case, and thus, implementing the functional role associated with human pain is not sufficient for pain experience.

I find this kind of thought experiment wholly unconvincing, and Block might now concur. He has become a leading force behind the move to ground theories of consciousness in empirical science (see, e.g., Block, 2007). But in the 1970s, thought experiments were relied on more frequently, and at considerable peril. Our intuitions about what kinds of implementations can or cannot be conscious are simply irrelevant. Intuitions about what can be conscious have little basis in reality. Recent empirical work suggests that people will deny that human collectives can be conscious (Knobe and Prinz, 2008) and deny that robots can be conscious (Huebner, 2010), while allowing that a magically enchanted chair can be conscious (Knobe and Prinz, 2008). Gray et al. (2012) have recently shown that people are more likely to attribute phenomenal states to a naked woman than to a clothed woman. There is no reason to think that these intuitions track reality. The fan of intuitions might counter that these are merely untrained lay intuitions and that philosophers' intuitions are more reliable. This is a highly contested issue, which I will not weigh in on here; indeed, a sophisticated argument from intuition will be considered in the next chapter. But the present point is that the China argument is not sophisticated in the right way. Its proponents don't articulate why it is incoherent, conceptually problematic, or inconceivable that the Chinese population has collective pain when instantiating a functional description of the human mind. Rather, the argument turns on knee-jerk reactions to this case. Philosophical reflection might actually deliver the intuition that pain is possible in the example.

There is another fatal flaw in Block's prima facie doubt argument. He says that such doubts can be dismissed in cases in which we have good prior reason to think that a physical system can be conscious—cases in which human brains are involved. But why should the presence of a brain disqualify such doubts, while functional similarities do not? Remember, I am assuming that the population of China is implementing a set of instructions that would cause the robot to behave like us on any psychological test, and these instructions conform to the same algorithms that human minds use when producing these behaviors. To assume that brains matter for consciousness and that highly specific inner computations don't simply begs the question. I'm not suggesting that functional similarity is sufficient for attributing consciousness, only that it provides some evidence and that doubts based on material constitution cannot overrule that evidence without a prior argument for the conclusion that consciousness requires a brain.

In response, Block might point out that he intended the China example as an argument against commonsense functionalism (although he offers a parallel objection to psychofunctionalism involving the economy of Bolivia). Block's primary arguments against psychofunctionalism are no more convincing, however. Where commonsense functionalism is too liberal in Block's view (attributing consciousness to systems that lack it), psychofunctionalism is too chauvinistic (denying consciousness to things that may have it). He gives an example of Martians that behave like us, interact with us, and read our books but implement a different computational psychology. Psychofunctionalists are forced to say that these Martians lack mental states like ours, and Block finds this objectionable.

This argument underscores the pitfalls of armchair philosophy. First, is it really possible that creatures could behave just like us but be computationally different? That's an empirical question, and there is little reason to expect an affirmative answer. Computationally different creatures might behave very similarly, but it is implausible that they would have the same reaction times and error rates and the same responses to psychoactive drugs and the same limits on information processes (e.g., effects of cognitive load, exhaustion, distraction, task complexity, and so on). Second, if we found computational differences in intelligent space creatures, should we still insist that they have conscious mental states? Intuitions are useless here. People deny that robots are conscious, even if they are computationally like us, while insisting that Martians are conscious if they are computationally different. That suggests that we are biased toward attributing consciousness to biological systems. If Martians radically depart from our psychology at the algorithmic level, then denying that they are conscious may be empirically justified, if our best theories of consciousness find that algorithmic-level processes have an impact on conscious experience. As noted earlier, some mental states are individuated very abstractly, and these could be ascribed to Martians regardless of implementation (perhaps they have memory and perception), but there is no reason to say that they have memory like ours or sensations like ours if they are computationally different. Intuitions about chauvinism and liberalism are highly sensitive to the level of abstraction of the mental states we consider, and when we go down to the states that are more fine-grained, these intuitions have little value.

Block has one argument that does not rely on intuitions about chauvinism or liberalism. He tries to refute psychofunctionalism by appeal to the possibility of inverted spectra. We can imagine two people who have the same functionally characterized response to red but experience that color differently. This suggests that functional roles are not enough. But again, the fact that we can imagine this doesn't entail that it is possible. In fact, there is strong empirical reason to reject this possibility. It turns out that there are significant asymmetries in color space (see Hardin, 1988; Palmer, 1999); a color and its complement sometimes have very different functional roles. For example, orange is the complement of blue, but dark blue continues to look blue (navy), and dark orange looks brown, changing color categories (Hardin, 1997). There are also asymmetric differences in the relation between hue and perceived size; blue shapes look smaller than equal-size orange shapes. Thus, color inverts would probably behave differently.

This does not mean that functionalism is out of hot water. In responding to these objections, I have been assuming that conscious mental states should be equated with fine-grained functional states, if they can be equated with functional states at all. This assumption is motivated by the fact that psychofunctionalism derives functional descriptions from scientific psychology, and psychological research on conscious states suggests that they play subtle and complex functional roles. Psychology tells us that colors interact with perceived size, give rise to afterimages with particular decay rates, and fuse when flickered. These subtle features belong to a complete psychofunctional analysis of color. But once we get to this level of specificity, the gap between functional roles and neural realizers closes. It is possible that the full psychofunctional profile of colors can be filled only by neurons or something structurally analogous to neurons. Thus, those who raise the flag of functionalism to differentiate themselves from identity theorists may be guilty of false advertising.

Functionalists might try to get out of this corner by denying that the complete psychofunctional profile is essential for any given color. They might try to distinguish essential aspects of the color role from inessential ones and then suggest that the essential ones can be realized by entities other than neurons. But this is to get out of the frying pan and into the fire. First, there is the challenge of specifying which aspects of the color role are essential. That challenge is not easily met. If we are interested in explaining color perception in psychofunctional terms, there is no principled reason for excluding restricting the role, and if we don't restrict the role, the likelihood of unique realizers rises. In response, the functionalist might retreat from questions about color perception inclusively understood to questions about specific properties of color perception. In this context, the question that concerns us is whether the qualitative character of color perception has a physical essence. Focusing on this question may seem to help the functionalist, because there is no reason to suppose that qualitative character depends on every aspect of color perception. On the AIR theory, for example, a chartreuse experience is an attended intermediate-level representation of chartreuse. On the face of it, this formulation does not place strong restrictions on realization. On closer analysis, however, there are good reasons to think that realizers are restricted, even if the AIR theory is true.

Above, I argued that there is a natural necessity linking color representations to specific vectorwaves. If neurons were to change content, they would change vectorwave realization. The converse is also true. Normally, if the vectorwave in a person's brain at a given moment in time were to change to another, that would be tantamount to a change in representational content. Thus, there is a counterfactual relation between function and realizer such that a change in the realizer changes the function, even if the function itself is specified in a way that does not constrain realization.

Admittedly, natural necessities are not robust across possible worlds; there are possible visual systems that represent chartreuse using different waveforms. A functionalist might try to break the link between function and realization by appeal to such worlds, but this would be a risky move. There is no reason to think that chartreuse representations in these other possible worlds are qualitatively identical to our chartreuse representations. Functionalists sometimes endorse representationalism and argue that sensory states with different neural realizers would be qualitatively alike if they simply represented the same thing. I rejected this conjecture in chapter 1. Representational equivalence does not entail phenomenal equivalence across possible worlds. Representationalists and other functionalists who specify roles in a way that does not restrict realizers end up with theories that are untenable. Functionalists would be better off saying that qualitative mental states require both functional roles and specific kinds of neural realizations. In other words, we need a hybrid theory.

3. Beyond the Standard Dichotomy

3.1. NEUROFUNCTIONALISM

Philosophy of mind often looks like a wrestling match between the psycho-physical identity theory and functionalism. On the face of it, these two forms of materialism are radically different: the former identifies mental states with structural kinds, the latter with functional kinds. They are also methodologically different: the former implicitly advocates a heavy investment in neuroscience, and the latter places bets on psychology. And they ostensibly align with conflicting philosophies of science: reductionism and antireductionism. If the objections in the last two sections are right, these distinctions are confused, and the two competing theories should coalesce as one. Here I want to consider what the resulting hybrid might look like.

In section 1.2, I argued that the neural correlates of consciousness play functional roles that can be characterized psychologically, and a change in function would result in a qualitative change. In section 2.2, I argued that the functional roles that characterize our conscious mental states are so specific that they are likely to have unique neural realizers. Together, these two conclusion imply that PCCs and NCCs are both essential. Roles are needed, and realizers are needed.

To capture this conclusion, we must move beyond the old dichotomy and introduce an approach to the ontology of the mind that I call neurofunctionalism. A mental state is neurofunctional just in case it has identity conditions at both psychological and neurobiological levels of analysis. Its being the state that it is depends on its psychological role and its neural implementation. A neurofunctionalist might go further and say that these levels are not just jointly required but also interdependent. Function depends on realizer, and conversely. The levels hang together.

I think that conscious mental states are neurofunctional states. To be a conscious experience, a state must be a neural activation vectorwave firing within the gamma range, and that vectorwave must serve as a representation of a viewpoint-specific microfeature that is available to working memory. The word *must* here can be understood in terms of natural necessity. If an experience changed its psychological role or neural implementation, it would cease being the same experience and might stop being an experience entirely. The neural identity conditions of an experience are probably also necessary in a stronger sense: a given gamma vectorwave will be an experience in every possible world in which it occurs. But this should not lead us to adopt a psycho-physical identity theory at the expense of functionalism. Functional roles sustain gamma vectorwaves. They are the raison d'être and the sine qua non. Gamma vectorwaves are used by the brain because gamma allows for accessibility and vectorwaves serve as codes for communication. Thus, their very existence hinges on their psychological function.

If conscious mental states are neurofunctional, many of the traditional debates between materialists can be dissolved. The impression that we must choose between functional roles and physical realizers is based on a false dichotomy. Conscious mental states depend on both. Moreover, the two levels are interdependent. Neurofunctional states have their neural properties because those are the ones that play certain psychological roles, and they have those psychological roles by virtue of having their neural properties. Trying to decide which is the true essence is foolish.

Likewise, it is counterproductive to worry about whether we should be reductionists or antireductionists. Granted, there is something breathtaking about the descent from psychology to neural mechanisms. Our ability to find lower- and lower-level realizers of psychological phenomena bolsters the materialist precept that everything ultimately bottoms out in the same stuff and the same basic laws of nature. But reductionism as normally construed is a misguided research program. It assumes that lower levels are somehow more real, as if regularities at higher levels are illusions that beings like us are forced to live with because we are not small enough to see the true structure of the world. We need to get away from this mind-set. I advocate a "no explanatory priority" thesis. Neuroscientific facts can account for psychological observations, such as the illusory black smudges in the Hermann grid illusion. But psychological facts can also account for observations in neuroscience: edge-detecting cells function as they do because of their role in detecting edges. Likewise, I think that discoveries about psychological roles are as important and illuminating as neurobiological discoveries. Finding the PCCs is just as important as finding the NCCs, and indeed, we can't do one without the other; PCCs allow us to find NCCs, and NCCs must be understood in terms of their psychological role. If Nobel prizes were doled out for work in consciousness, Ray Jackendoff would be as good a candidate as Francis Crick.

This effort to move beyond the debate about reduction resonates with a recent program in philosophy of science, to which I alluded earlier: work on mechanisms (e.g., Machamer, Darden, and Carver, 2000). Mechanisms are spatially located entities, which have parts that undergo changes over time, in the service of some function. They can decompose into smaller parts, and these parts may also be mechanisms. Mechanistic decomposition bears similarities to reduction, but it differs in crucial respects. As Craver (2007) points out, reduction is usually seen as a relationship between two theories, whereas mechanistic decomposition involves specifying the relationship between parts of a specific entity. The ambition behind such decompositions is not to discharge the higher levels but to show how different levels can be integrated. Neurofunctionalism can be thought of as part of the effort to bring philosophy of mind in line with contemporary philosophy of science by moving away from simple reductive models and emphasizing interlevel interdependence (see Wimsatt, 1976). Defenders of the mechanistic program do not necessarily claim that some natural kinds have identity conditions at two levels (what we can refer to as two-levelism), but they make room for such an approach by offering an account of what levels are that makes sense of this possibility. If we think of levels as scientific theories rather than nested parts, two-levelism would be harder to get off the ground.

There is nothing anachronistic about saying that conscious mental states have identity conditions at two levels. Many things are individuated in this way. Consider artifacts. It is uncontroversial that artifacts have functional essences: a boat is a boat because it is a vehicle that floats on the surface of water. But psychological research has confirmed that people also take artifacts to have structural essences (Sloman and Malt, 2003). Some water vehicles are not regarded as boats because they have the wrong physical organization; consider rafts, inner tubes, and Jet Skis. So boats have two-level essences, and a similar story could be given for bicycles, umbrellas, violins, and countless other artifacts. Two-levelism is also common among natural kinds. Malt (2004) argues that people treat water as having both a physical essence (H_2O) and a functional essence (residing in rivers, slaking thirst, etc.). One might object that folk classification is irrelevant, given my resistance to folk intuitions. But the folk practice just illustrates a phenomenon that can also be found in scientific classifications. Consider photosynthesis, which can be characterized physically as a process that converts carbon dioxide using solar energy or functionally as a way in which algae, bacteria, and plants get energy from the sun. Even animal kinds may be said to have a dual essence. A mouse is not just a genotype; it is a genotype as implemented in a living organism with a particular organization of parts. Disembodied mouse DNA is not a mouse. If you put a mouse in a blender, you lose the mouse and get soup.

One might wonder why the individuation of conscious mental states should be restricted to two levels. Mechanisms can have many levels, and as we saw earlier, the mechanisms involved in consciousness can be analyzed from the level of large-scale neural systems down to molecules, with everything in between. Why not say that all of these levels matter? In principle, neurofunctionalism does not need to insist on the two-level picture; some mental states may have identity conditions at several levels of analysis. But as it happens, two-levelism may be a useful first approximation for conscious mental states. At least, I don't think there is reason to say that every level of analysis counts.

Here I depart from a view that I used to hold, called level-headed mysterianism (Prinz, 2003; see also Block, 2002). I used to think that there was no way to decide which levels of analysis matter when it comes to conscious states. The reason for the conclusion involved a replacement argument. Suppose we replaced neurons in a person's visual system with microchips that had comparable causal effects. That person's behavior would remain the same; she would avoid obstacles, and she would insist that she was visually conscious. But there would be no way to confirm that she was. If we moved above the level of neurons, replacing whole neural circuits with chips, behavior wouldn't be preserved, and she might report losing consciousness. So we have reason to believe that organization at the level of neurons is necessary for consciousness but no way of confirming whether, say, the biological materials out of which these neurons are built are necessary. I concluded that consciousness depends on neural processes, but we'll never know how far down.

I now think that my reasoning was based on a dubious methodological premise. I was abiding by the following principle: if tinkering with some level has an impact on what conscious experiences a person reports, then that level contributes to consciousness, but if tinkering at some level has no impact, then we can't know whether it contributes to consciousness. This principle is need-lessly conservative. It asymmetrically assumes that impact supports involvement and nonimpact supports agnosticism. Why not say that absent any evidence for the impact of low-level changes, we should assume that such changes don't matter? On this principle, we would assume that nothing contributes to consciousness unless we have positive evidence that it does (the color of neurons, quantum events in microtubules, the exact rate of oscillation, and so on). Granted, consciousness *might* depend on these things; someone *might* be wired so as to exhibit normal conscious experience in the absence of such experiences. I concede that such possibilities can't be ruled out, but agnosticism is not necessarily the appropriate response in the absence of evidence. In this case, I think that there is reason not to be agnostic. Suppose we can find a level of analysis that can account for every aspect of conscious experience, in the sense that every conscious difference can be mapped onto a difference on this level. Finding such a level would not give a complete explanation of consciousness, because there is always an explanatory gap between phenomenal experience and physical descriptions (a topic addressed in the next chapter), but no physical level would fill that gap. Finding a level that maps onto quality space without remainder would be the best candidate for the level at which consciousness is located. Assuming that arguments for dualism fail, it would be the level at which we should make identity claims, because it would be the one whose variations correspond to variations we encounter in experience. I have suggested here that there is a neural level that fits this bill: populations of neurons that fire in synchrony and register the presence of viewpoint-specific microfeatures. I have also argued that these neurons play psychological roles that are essential for consciousness. I see no positive reason for thinking that any other neural level matters.

The point can be underscored by considering a concrete case. In discussing the molecular correlate of attention, I said that gamma might be triggered by a process that involves a particular class of dopamine receptors. As the name implies, those receptors bond with dopamine. It so happens that they can also bond with serotonin (Kuznetsova and Deth, 2008). Thus, if this model is correct, then gamma can be induced by two different chemicals, which are both highly prevalent in the brain. It's safe to assume, then, that gamma induction is multiply realized. But there is no evidence that these chemical differences make a difference for the quality of experience. Does dopamine-induced gamma feel different from serotonin-induced gamma? That is something we might empirically test, but given the functional similarities with respect to gamma, we'd probably find no measurable difference between these two types of states. Should we conclude that all people might have two kinds of consciousness that alternate from moment to moment with fluctuating chemicals in the brain? I see no reason for taking this possibility very seriously.

In summary, I don't think that we should rule out the possibility that more than two levels are essential to conscious experience, but some levels are unlikely to contribute. Two-levelism can be read as shorthand for at-least-two-levelism, but we should resist the mysterian line, which says that there is no way to decide which levels matter.

3.2. OTHER LEVEL-HEADED VIEWS

I want to conclude by comparing neurofunctionalism to some related views. In section 2.2, I mentioned that there are forms of functionalism that I would postpone till later. Later is now. I am not the first functionalist to think that low levels are important to consciousness, so it will help to see how neurofunctionalism differs from three options that are already in wide circulation.

The first option, which seems to be Block's (1978) preference, is that some mental states can be individuated psychofunctionally, while others are type-identical to brain states. Call this the divide-and-conquer view. Other proponents include Shoemaker (1981), Philip Kitcher (1982), and Horgan (1984). I have some sympathy for this approach. As I've noted, some mental states seem to have very coarse-grained identity conditions, and these are unlikely to have neural identity conditions. I've also noted that some of our more abstract psychological categories (learning, memory, perception) are so general as to be scientifically uninteresting, so we might even expect commonsense functionalism to offer the most promising analyses of these. That makes me a divide-and-conqueror. But when it comes to fine-grained psychological states, especially conscious states, I am adamantly opposed to division. The whole idea of neurofunctionalism is that such states do not fall neatly on either side of the traditional debate.

Consider an example from Block (1978). He suggests there that we can explain pain by dividing and conquering its two components in different ways. Psychofunctionalism can handle the sensory part, while the identity theory is needed to explain the affective part. But this is untenable. Both components of pain have psychofunctional essences and, I would argue, neural essences. The sensory component is clearly phenomenal. It feels like something to have a burning sensation on your left pinky. These feelings remain when people take drugs such as morphine that quash the affective component of pain. Like visual perception, the sensations in pain have a complex psychophysical profile that can be mapped onto neural states. For example, there are errors in how we localize pain, which often stem from poor spatial resolution in c-fibers. The affective components of pain can also be mapped onto neural responses in the emotional circuitry of the brain, as Block would have predicted. But there is also a rich psychofunctional story to tell about these. Like other emotions, the negative feelings that arise when we are in pain have associated action tendencies, expressive behaviors, and psychological interactions; for example, pain negativity is increased by anxiety and promotes attention to the source of the injury. Thus, a neurofunctional story suggests itself for both components.

Neurofunctionalism shares a bit more in common with a kind of functionalism that was advocated at one point by David Lewis (1980). Lewis (1972) started out as a role-filler commonsense functionalist. He said that mental states are physical states that play the roles set out in our folk theories. In saying this, he assumed that those roles could be multiply realized across species. However, he also thought that there might be a standard physical realizer in each species, and he began to wonder what would happen if the standard filler played a nonstandard role. Lewis (1980) has us consider a madman who has the brain state that usually plays the pain role, but he exhibits none of the usual pain behaviors. He also considers a Martian who has a different kind of brain from ours but has a brain state that plays the same role that pain states normally play in us. To accommodate both cases, Lewis adopts a disjunctive view, according to which pains can be individuated by functional states or by their physical realizers. A physical realizer is sufficient, provided it's the realizer that standardly plays the pain role in your species.

This disjunctive account faces serious objections (see also Tye, 1983). First, it's odd to suppose that two beings can both be in pain even though they have nothing physically or functionally in common, but that is just what the madman/Martian contrast is supposed to allow. Second, the claim that madmen would experience pains if their brain states played none of the usual pain role is tenable only in a commonsense functionalist view, which emphasizes overt behavior. Once we consider the fine-grained roles that pains play according to psychological research, there is no reason to think that the usual brain state can come apart from the usual role. The madman case may be impossible. The Martian case is also dubious if we are to suppose that Martians experience pains just like ours. If their brains are totally different from ours (unlike, say, other mammals, which may have gamma vectorwaves), then all bets are off. These points should be familiar by now. I've already suggested that finely individuated mental states have essential properties at both the neural and psychofunctional levels, and this conclusion was based on the empirical conjecture that at this fine level, dissociations are impossible. Neurofunctionalism is not a disjunctive view like Lewis's but a denial that such dissociations are possible.

Let me turn finally to a theory that resembles neurofunctionalism quite closely: homuncular functionalism. The view owes in large part to Dennett (1978), who likened the mind to a large institutional bureaucracy, with multiple agencies and subagencies carrying out progressively simpler operations. Lycan (1987) coined the term *homuncular functionalism* or sometimes *homunctionalism* to advance a theory of mental states based on this analogy. The mind can be represented as a vast flow chart, with sub-flow charts and sub-sub flow charts at multiple levels of abstraction. For Lycan, mental states are identified with activity in one or more of the boxes making up these nested flow charts (1987: 41). The similarities to neurofunctionalism should be obvious. Like neurofunctionalism, homuncular functionalism begins with a broadly mechanistic view of the mind, according to which complex psychological abilities can be decomposed into increasingly simple abilities, all the way down to the lowest levels of analysis. Homuncular functionalists also deny that there is a principled difference between functionalism and the psychophysical identity theory (Lycan 1987: 58). Lycan even presages neurofunctionalism in saying, "It is simply an error to think . . . any single mental state must be localized entirely at one level."

I think that homuncular functionalism is the most promising of the leading theories of mind, and I would be happy to regard neurofunctionalism as a special case of it. But there are also some differences. First of all, despite the quotation, Lycan does not claim that phenomenal states have identity conditions at both a neural and a functional level. He actually endorses a fairly conventional psychofunctionalist theory of consciousness, which abstracts away from neural realization (see also Lycan, 1991). Lycan also endorses a teleological notion of function in his account. In response to Block's example of a robot controlled by the population of China, Lycan argues that there can be no pain, because the Chinese people have not evolved as a biological unity with the natural function of enacting the pain role on their walkie-talkies. I find this unconvincing. Whether or not a creature feels pain cannot hang entirely on its evolutionary history. Presumably, random mutations can cause new phenomenal experiences regardless of whether they are selected for. So, while I embrace the decompositional spirit of homunctionalism, neurofunctionalism introduces commitments not intrinsic to that approach (the two-level view) and avoids commitments that are intrinsic to it (teleology). Homunctionalism allows for two-levelism, but it does little to show that such a view would be attractive in the case of consciousness or to specify how psychological and neural mechanisms might relate.

In chapter 4, I argued that conscious states are implemented by gamma vectorwaves. That left open a metaphysical question. Are conscious states identical to these neural events, or should they be identified with something at a higher level of analysis? In this chapter, I have argued that standard objections to psychophysical identity fail, opening up the possibility that gamma vectorwaves are necessary for consciousness. But I resisted the conclusion that they are sufficient. Gamma vectorwaves are conscious and have the conscious qualities that they do by virtue of the psychological functions that they serve. Thus, they have identity conditions at two levels of analysis. The view can be expressed by offering a further and final unpacking of the AIR theory:

The AIR Theory of Consciousness (Fully Unpacked)

Consciousness arises when and only when vectorwaves that realize intermediate-level representations fire in the gamma range and thereby become available to working memory.

In other words, conscious states are gamma vectorwaves that realize AIRs. The formulation incorporates two levels. It uses the language of realization, but, unlike standard forms of functionalism, it does not imply that the realizers are contingent. And, unlike standard forms of the identity theory, it implies that the realizers must play a particular psychological role. The *must* here can be understood in terms of natural necessity: were gamma vectorwaves to change their psychological profile, they would cease being the conscious states that they are. In this way, the AIR theory circumvents the dichotomy that has divided the philosophy of mind for the last half-century and offers a neurofunctional alternative.

10

Could Consciousness Be Physical?
The Brain Maintained

From an outside perspective, the philosophical literature on consciousness may look a bit obsessive. A disproportionate amount of ink has been dedicated to Frank Jackson's (1982) "knowledge argument." On cursory analysis, the knowledge argument is patently unsound. It illicitly draws a metaphysical conclusion from an epistemological premise. It takes only one philosophy class to learn that such arguments are fallacious. Why have philosophers wasted so much energy on a howler? The answer, I suspect, is that the obvious (and often less than obvious) responses to the knowledge argument don't succeed. The argument is remarkably resilient, and addressing it is a very useful way to draw positive conclusions about the nature of consciousness. When philosophers advance responses that seem to undermine the argument, new puzzles for physicalism almost immediately arise. Responding to Jackson is like killing a worm with a big rock: it's easy enough to kill the initial worm, but when you lift the rock, you expose a writhing tangle of new worms. That's what makes the knowledge argument so good.

In this chapter, I will argue that prevailing responses to the knowledge argument do not succeed. For each response that I survey, I will identify a corresponding constraint that any theory of phenomenal knowledge must respect. These constraints can be regarded as guidelines for satisfying the phenomenal knowledge desideratum laid out in chapter 1, according to which an adequate theory of consciousness should provide an account of how we epistemically access phenomenal states that blocks standard arguments for dualism. After identifying the constraints, I will propose a new response to the knowledge argument, which appeals to neuroscientific resources deriving from the AIR theory. This response, which I dub the mental maintenance proposal, provides an empirically motivated explanation of the fact that knowledge of our phenomenal states does not reveal them to have physical nature. If this fact can be explained without abandoning physicalism, then the knowledge argument can be refuted.

An adequate explanation of why phenomenal knowledge does not reveal physical nature can function as a magic bullet in consciousness studies. Such an account could be used to answer the most publicized arguments for dualism, including Chalmers's (1996) zombie argument and Kripke's (1979) modal argument. Such an explanation would show that conceivability does not entail possibility in this domain. In that way, it would help establish that consciousness *could be* physical. In this chapter, I won't directly address modal arguments or zombie arguments, but readers should be able to imagine how my response to Jackson could be extended in these directions. The theory of phenomenal knowledge that I will offer can explain why our ability to conceive of dissociations between phenomenal states and their physical correlates cuts no metaphysical ice.

1. The Knowledge Argument

In its simplest form, the knowledge argument begins with the premise that a person can know all of the physical and functional facts correlated with a particular kind of phenomenal experience without knowing what it is like to have that experience. From this, it is inferred that the experience in question is neither physical nor functional. If experiences are neither physical nor functional, then physicalism is false. Broad and Feigl devised thought experiments along these lines decades ago (Güzeldere, 1997). Broad says that an archangel with microscopic vision would know the chemical structure of ammonia but not its smell. Feigl says that a Martian might attain perfect knowledge of human behavior without knowing the qualitative character of human senses or sentiments. Nagel is responsible for bringing these kinds of considerations into the center of contemporary debates about consciousness. In "What Is It Like to Be a Bat?" he says that we can learn all about the physiology of echolocation without knowing "what it's like" for a bat to echolocate (see also Farrell, 1950). Jackson (1982) added further refinements with two other cases. First, imagine Fred. He has four retinal color receptors rather than the usual three, and as a result, he sees two distinct primary colors in the spectral range that we label "red." We can't experientially distinguish these two reds, and we cannot know what they are like by learning about the physiology of Fred's visual system. Jackson's second case concerns a brilliant neuroscientist named Mary. She has become a celebrity in the consciousness literature, and her story is tediously familiar.

Mary has lived her entire life in a black-and-white room with no access to colors. Nevertheless, she learns everything there is to know about what happens physically during color perception. Filling out some of the details, we might imagine that Mary first learns about what causes color experience. Light is electromagnetic radiation within a range that is detectable by human eyes.

Wavelengths vary in size, and the perceived color of an opaque object is determined by the wavelengths that it reflects, rather than absorbs, when illuminated by white light. Transparent objects transmit light, and luminous objects emit light. The ordinary human retina has three kinds of cone cells that are maximally sensitive to three different wavelengths of light. The ratio of reflected light in these wavelengths is the primary determinant of perceived color. Retinal cells are stimulated in proportion to those ratios and send a signal via ganglion cells in the optic nerve to the dorsal lateral geniculate nucleus (dLGN) of the thalamus. Some ganglion cells (the magno cells) are fast and have low resolution; these are responsive to activity in retinal rod cells, which register light and dark but not color. The parvo cells are color-sensitive, are slow, and have high resolution. Magnocellular and parvocellular inputs arrive at different layers of the dLGN, which then feed forward to different layers of primary visual cortex (V1); color-sensitive parvo cells are localized to layers 2 and 3. The functional separation continues into V2, and then the parvocellular pathway feeds forward into various subregions of an area termed V4, in the extrastriate cortex. V4 is a likely locus of color experience (Zeki, 1993). There is a subregion of V4 on the middle third of the lingual gyrus. Cortical color blindness (achromatopsia) occurs when this region is damaged. Mary knows all of this. She also knows about population coding, and she masters computational models that precisely characterize the vectorwaves that become active during occurrent red experiences and the synchronized processing that makes them available to dorsolateral prefrontal cortex. More broadly, she knows about the neural processes associated with attention, orienting, and working memory in temporal, parietal, and frontal cortex. Convinced of the AIR theory of consciousness, she will infer that cellular responses in V4 become conscious when they send afferents to working-memory areas. Mary supplements this functional knowledge with further facts about the causal role of color experiences. For example, she learns that seeing red causes an increase in heart rate, breathing, and muscle tension. She masters color vocabulary (which terms go together) and the colors of familiar objects.

In short, Mary learns everything physical and functional about seeing red. No facts of this kind escape her. Nevertheless, Mary seems to be missing something. She does not know what it's like to see red (hereafter "WIL"). Upon her release from the room, she learns WIL; she sees roses, ripe tomatoes, strawberries, fire engines, splatter films, a torero's muleta, Maine lobsters, and a fetching glass of Chateneuf de Pape. She didn't know what these things were like before her release, and she didn't know what it was like for others to see the mysterious color they call "red." Now Mary knows what red is like. "Red looks like *that*," she says while looking up at a cardinal in the park. Since Mary didn't know this before her release, when she had merely physical knowledge of colors, WIL cannot be a physical fact. Phenomenal facts are evidently not physical, and therefore, Jackson concludes, physicalism is false.

Mary has been much more popular than Jackson's Fred case. Perhaps readers have found Fred too fanciful. In actuality, the Mary case is less realistic for two reasons. First, color-sensitive cells respond to black-and-white stimuli, so Mary would be able to imagine color after exposure to a black-and-white environment (even assuming that she never caught a glimpse of her tongue or inner eyelids). Second, color-sensitive cells may need to be triggered during a critical period of development to become active. If Mary were really prevented from seeing light in the red range, she might never develop the capacity. Despite these difficulties with the case, Mary has certain advantages over the Fred case (and Nagel's bats). Mary *can* ultimately overcome her ignorance of WIL without undergoing any unusual surgical procedure. Thus, she provides a useful way of posing the question of what's needed to transition from phenomenal ignorance into the glory of a Technicolor world. I will address that question below. But first, I want to summarize the argument and review standard strategies of response.

Here is a concise rendition of Jackson's argument:

P1. Before her release, Mary knows all of the physical facts about seeing red.
P2. Before her release, Mary does not know everything about seeing red. (She doesn't know what it's like to see red: WIL.)
P3. If knowledge of WIL is not derivable from physical facts, then WIL is not physical.
C. WIL is not physical, therefore physicalism is false.

The knowledge argument is irresistible to physicalists, because it is a bold attack that seems to rest on a simple mistake. But *which* mistake? Critics of the knowledge argument agree that it is fatally flawed, but they disagree about where that flaw lies.

Finding a flaw is challenging, because each premise seems very plausible. Almost everyone agrees that premise 1 is beyond reproach (but see Van Gulick, 1993). *Ex hypothesi*, Mary knows everything physical about seeing red. She could give a complete physical description of what goes on in the brain when red is perceived, along with the more abstract causal roles that the brain states in question play. The only room for dispute here concerns an ambiguity in "physical fact." Facts might be individuated by both sense (i.e., psychological concepts by which they are grasped) and reference (i.e., states of the world) or by reference alone (see Horgan, 1984). If individuation requires modes of presentation, and there are physical states of the world that can be grasped via phenomenological states, then Mary does not know all of the physical facts. This line of objection is unpromising, however, because the dualist can simply stipulate how the term *fact* is to be understood in the argument. Let a fact be a state of affairs, and let a physical fact be any state of affairs that can be described in the language of the completed physical science, using no phenomenological vocabulary (the assumption made by standard physicalists is that phenomenological properties will ultimately be reduced to some other properties). Let's presume that Mary knows all of *these* facts. P1 is secure.

Premise 2 also looks secure, although, as we will see, it has not gone unchallenged. After all, *something* seems to change for Mary psychologically when she leaves her room. Seeing a colored object for the first time would qualify as a new psychological state. What's more, once she has a color experience, she is clearly in a position to know what it is like. Granting that Mary learns something on leaving, this seems to be the best candidate for what she learns. She gains knowledge of what colors are like.

Premise 3 is perhaps the least obvious of the three, and it has garnered the most controversy, so it deserves a bit more attention. Jackson thinks that there is a principled argument in favor of P3. In particular, he has become a proponent of a doctrine called a priori physicalism (Jackson, 1998; see also Chalmers, 1999; Chalmers and Jackson, 2001). According to physicalism, there are no facts above and beyond physical facts. That means that the physicalist is committed to the following entailment: a complete description of the physical facts, stated in physical vocabulary, entails all facts stated in any vocabulary. According to a priori physicalism, if physicalism is true, then that entailment must be knowable a priori. If so, Mary must be able to deduce all phenomenal facts from her physical knowledge, as P3 insists.

Why think that a priori physicalism is true? After all, there are many physical identities that seem to be discovered empirically, such as the identity between water and H_2O. Doesn't this prove that some physical facts are known a posteriori? Isn't that precisely what we learned from Kripke (1980)? Ironically, Jackson thinks that Kripke himself is committed to a priori physicalism. To see why, consider the identity between water and H_2O. The ordinary water concept fixes reference by means of stereotypical properties. We conceive of water as a clear liquid that boils when heated. We know this stereotype a priori. Now, suppose that we supplement this a priori knowledge with complete knowledge of microphysics. We know about microphysics a posteriori, but with that knowledge in hand, we can use the water stereotype to deduce that water is H_2O from the armchair. Complete microphysical knowledge can be used to deduce logically that H_2O satisfies the water stereotype: it is a liquid at room temperature, it transmits light rather than reflecting it, and it bubbles upward when its kinetic energy rises. In summary, the identity between water and H_2O depends on empirically discovered physical knowledge, but the inference from that knowledge to the identity is a priori. Putting this into steps, we get:

1. A priori knowledge that water has watery properties.
2. A posteriori knowledge of all H_2O properties.
3. A priori inference that water is H_2O (from 1 and 2).

If this procedure generalizes to all physical identities, then Mary should be able to deduce knowledge of what red is like, if such knowledge corresponds to a physical fact. Thus, the argument for a priori physicalism can be used to support P3 of the knowledge argument. In response, one might try to challenge a priori physicalism. I think that such challenges are convincing and that a priori physicalism is false, but the most obvious challenge actually serves to underscore why P3 is plausible. Let's see why.

In using the water case to argue for a priori physicalism, Jackson assumes that we know a priori that water has certain stereotypical properties. It's a priori, says Jackson, that water is a clear liquid that boils, and physical knowledge can tell us which liquid has these properties. But this claim is based on an implausible account of stereotypes. Rather than thinking of stereotypes on the model of analytic truths, we should think of them as defensible folk theories acquired through observation and social inculcation. Stereotypes may even include features that are false. As Putnam pointed out, the gorilla stereotype includes the property of ferocity, even though they are the most docile apes. Moreover, research on how ordinary people think about water suggests that folk theories are not even committed to the claim that water is a natural kind (Malt, 1994). The decision to equate water with H_2O (as opposed to a broader category that includes heavy water and any tasteless clear liquid or a narrower category that excludes sea water or steam) is partially a matter of scientific fiat. Identity statements result from "satisficing," in which we try to map scientific theories onto folk theories as best we can, making stipulative decisions where necessary. In a series of steps:

1. A posteriori knowledge that water has watery properties.
2. A posteriori knowledge of all H_2O properties.
3. Satisficing inference that water is H_2O (from 1 and 2).

This captures the gist of the approach to theory construction that has been in vogue since Quine (1951). The idea that identities are discovered deductively flies in the face of everything Quine taught us about scientific practice and the semantics of ordinary terms. The argument for a priori physicalism is committed to an antiquated theory of scientific theory construction (for a more detailed and trenchant critique, see Block and Stalnaker, 1999). I think that the vast majority of theoretical identities by scientists are actually pragmatically and politically brokered decisions rather than discoveries. Water could have been identified with a larger class of clear liquids or a narrower class. The same is true for category classification in science: whales could have been fish, platypuses could have been birds, Pluto could have been a planet, isotopes could have been elements, electric shocks could have been miniature lightning bolts. Chalmers and Jackson (2001) reply that such cases are rare, but I suspect that they are nearly universal; every theoretical identification involves some degree of arbitrary decision. They also counter that such cases involve a change in meaning, so they do not undercut the claim that, fixed in time, there are a priori identities entailed from microphysical theories. They concede that prior to pragmatic decisions, these identities may be indeterminate, however, which presumably means that the microphysical facts are compatible with multiple macro-identities, none of which is uniquely or even fully entailed. But this concession renders their thesis about a priori derivation moot, because the theoretician's role is to move beyond such messy entailments to determinate and useful identity claims. I think that this is a fatal problem with a priori physicalism, because there is always a gap between the manifest and scientific image that must be bridged by fiat if we are to affirm any specific identities.

Unfortunately, this response to a priori physicalism does little to soften the blow of the knowledge argument. While they are wrong about a priori deduction in theory construction, Chalmers and Jackson may win a moral victory. The main reasons just given for thinking that theoretical identities are not generally derived a priori from microphysical knowledge do not apply when dealing with knowledge of what it's like. First of all, on a physicalist theory of consciousness, the mapping from brain states to phenomenal states is not supposed to be a matter of fiat. Pragmatic considerations may play a role in selecting among competing theories, but, unlike in the water case, we assume that scientists are not making an arbitrary choice when they select among possible neural correlates. Second, we do not know what red is like by means of defeasible folk theories. We know what red is like by its phenomenal character. This is related to Kripke's argument that we know what red experiences are like by means of its essence, but the point does not depend on that modal claim. Suppose that red experiences (or, if you prefer, red perceptions) can occur unconsciously and that when this happens, they lack phenomenal character. If so, phenomenal character would be a contingent property of the states that have that character. Still, it is a property of those states, and it is a property that we can know those states to have by merely introspecting them. Thus, qualitative character is fundamentally different from the features making up a stereotype, which can turn out not to apply to the categories that our stereotypes aim to represent. Putting these two points together, it's not obvious that psychophysical reduction will fit the Quinean satisficing model. If there is a mismatch between science and phenomenal qualities, we don't revise the manifest image but rather conclude that phenomenal qualities fall outside of science. This doesn't entail that psychophysical reduction is a priori if physicalism is true, but it does suggest that it will differ from other kinds of theoretical identities.

There is also a deeper worry that brings us right back to the third premise of the knowledge argument. Let's imagine a cousin of Mary, call her Arid Mary, who is locked up in a room without any water. Arid Mary knows everything about chemistry, and through careful reflection, she is able to derive many facts about how collections of H_2O molecules would behave. She determines that they would move around a lot at room temperature without becoming unbound; she would infer that these molecules would transmit far more light waves than they reflect; and she would infer that these molecules do not fit gustatory and olfactory receptors in the human nervous system. She labels these features liquidity$_1$, transparency$_1$, and tastelessness$_1$. She uses subscripts because she knows that corresponding to each of these properties, there are similar properties that H_2O would also exhibit. For example, corresponding to what she calls liquidity$_1$ is the property of looking like a liquid, a property that some granular solids would have. She calls this liquidity$_2$. She also knows that there are some other chemicals, such as H_2O isotopes, that would exhibit liquidity$_1$ and liquidity$_2$, and other properties that would resemble these at some level of analysis. Supposing that Arid Mary has never heard of water, she might nevertheless identify a family of concepts making up every combination of the macro properties that she would predict H_2O to have. It seems that one of these combinations would be just like our water stereotype. Of course, since these concepts would apply to multiple chemicals, Arid Mary would have to stipulate that this combination refers to H_2O, just as scientists stipulate that water is H_2O when they make a satisficing scientific reduction. She could decide by fiat, as we do, whether tears, tea, and the liquid in oceans belong under the same concept or not. The point is that Arid Mary could derive a concept that happens to coincide with the water concept exactly, a concept making up the same features and applied, however stipulatively, to the same substances. Thus, even if we grant that the identity between H_2O and water cannot be deduced a priori, because theoretical reductions involve stipulation, we can nevertheless grant that one can derive the features that make up our water stereotype from chemical knowledge. Arid Mary would have no way of knowing which feature combination we express by water, but one of the derived feature combinations would, by chance, coincide. The total set of concepts that Arid Mary can derive from microphysical knowledge would include a concept with the same features as our water stereotype. In this sense, knowledge of water can be derived from microphysical knowledge even if microphysical knowledge does not entail that water is H_2O.

The situation facing Arid Mary differs strikingly from Mary's situation. Arid Mary can acquire concepts that coincide with folk chemistry, but Mary cannot acquire knowledge of what red is like. When Arid Mary leaves the room, she will learn about our concept *water*, but this won't require acquisition of a new concept. Instead, she will learn which of the concepts she already possesses coincides with our water concept. She acquires no new knowledge of water beyond the social fact that her community tracks water using a particular stereotype, which she already possesses. Mary, in contrast, acquires new knowledge of red experiences, knowledge that she would gain prior to any further inference about how others understand their color terms. This brings us back to premise 3 in the knowledge argument. Given that Arid Mary can infer all of the features of water from her physical knowledge, there is prima facie reason to think that macrofeatures can be derived from microfeatures in the physical domain. If so, then physicalism gives us prima facie reason for thinking that Mary should be able to derive the features of what red is like. In other words, we have prima facie reason to think that P3 is true.

This argument for P3 falls short of a priori physicalism, but it echoes the contention in Chalmers and Jackson (2001) that micro-properties ordinarily have macro-entailments, albeit indeterminate ones. That helps us see why the knowledge argument is so powerful. All three of its premises are plausible, and that spells trouble for physicalism. In what follows, I will review some well-known replies. I will not consider challenges to P1, because the other two premises have been challenged more frequently.

2. The Mary Wars

2.1. IMAGINATION

Let's begin with P2, which asserts that Mary does not know what it's like to see red before her release. That seems extremely reasonable. Learning about the brain does not look like a sufficient way to attain phenomenological knowledge. But P2 has its critics.

One objection is advanced by Churchland (1985). He speculates that Mary might actually be able to imagine red before her release; by mastering neuroscience, Mary might learn to enter novel brain states by act of will. This is completely implausible, I think, and unhelpful to the physicalist. It is implausible because there is no special link between physiological knowledge and physiological control. We cannot digest our food better by learning about digestion. We know from the real-world case of Knut Nordby, a congenitally color-blind vision scientist, that encyclopedic knowledge of color vision does not suffice for imagining red (Sacks, 1996). Even if Mary could imagine red, she could not imagine what it is like for Fred, who has an extra rod cell. Nor could Mary know what it's like to be a bat. To know what the world is like for them, we would need new neural machinery, not willful control over the neural machinery already in place. Thus, Churchland's reply has no hope of addressing the knowledge argument in its other guises.

In any case, Churchland's suggestion would not help the physicalist (see Jackson, 1986). The crucial claim in the knowledge argument is that knowledge of physical facts does not *constitute* complete knowledge of what it's like. If that is the case, then there is prima facie reason to think that what it's like is not physical. Churchland's imagination argument does nothing to block this inference. He merely says that knowledge of physical facts might allow us to arrive at knowledge of what it's like through imagination. But this is consistent with the claim that the products of imagination are not physical. The physicalist must show that physical knowledge is, at least, knowledge of phenomenal qualities, not that it can be used to have phenomenal experiences. So Churchland's imagination argument won't suffice. In fairness, Churchland offers an alternative argument against Jackson, based on modes of presentation. I will raise worries about this strategy below.

Whatever its limitations, Churchland's imagination proposal draws attention to something very important. In saying that we can acquire knowledge of what something is like by imagining it and not merely by describing it, Churchland implies that we come to know what phenomenal states are like only by having them. This might be described as the have-it-to-know-it principle. The have-it-to-know-it principle is quite striking. Most knowledge doesn't require possession of what we know. I know what it is to be a billionaire without having a billion in the bank. Churchland draws attention to this special property, but he does not explain it. This gives us a first constraint:

> **Possessive Knowledge:** An adequate account of phenomenal knowledge should explain why you need to have a phenomenal state in order to know what it is like.

One might protest that phenomenal knowledge can occur without possession. Tim Bayne (personal communication) has pressed the point with regard to what Hume called the missing shade of blue. Having seen two shades of blue, one might gain knowledge of what an intervening shade looks like even if one has not possessed that phenomenal state. Isn't this a form of phenomenal knowledge? I think not. Or, rather, I think one doesn't know what the missing shade of blue is like until one has imagined it and thus possessed it. All phenomenal states have imaginable permutations, but we don't know what they are like until we actually imagine them. We can imagine familiar songs played in alternative keys, but we must imagine them to know what they are like. With missing shades, this may be easy to do, but the imaginative act is necessary. To see this, imagine that we surgically furnished Mary with a capacity to imagine red. If she had not exercised that capacity yet, she wouldn't know what red is like, and she would learn something new when she imagined red for the first time.

2.2. REPRESENTATIONALISM

The next response to the knowledge argument has actually been endorsed by Jackson himself. In the years since introducing the philosophical world to Mary, Jackson has had a change of heart (see Jackson, 2003). He now thinks that physicalism is defensible, but, for reasons we will examine below, he does not want to give up on P3 of the knowledge argument. Jackson thinks that the best hope for defending physicalism is to show that Mary's knowledge of physical facts is sufficient for knowing WIL. Unlike Churchland, Jackson does not think that physical facts merely allow Mary to imagine red; he conjectures that there are physical facts the understanding of which constitute knowledge of WIL.

Jackson's conjecture rests on two assumptions. The first is a thesis we encountered in chapter 1: representationalism. Representationalists claim that phenomenal facts are representational facts. More precisely, they think that every phenomenal quality of a mental state is constituted by representational properties of that state. Any two states that differ in their phenomenal qualities differ by virtue of representing different things. If phenomenal character can be understood in representational terms, then, says Jackson, there is hope for Mary. Jackson's second assumption is naturalism about representation. According to this thesis, representational properties are reducible to properties that can be specified in physical language. For example, representation may be explicable in terms of causal relations. In one popular naturalist story, a mental state represents whatever feature of the world caused it to be acquired. Another popular naturalist story says that mental states represent whatever reliably causes them to be tokened. There are numerous combinations, variants, and elaborations on these two ideas. Since causation is a physical process, causal theories of representation are physically specifiable.

Putting these two assumptions together, Jackson says that Mary is able to use physical knowledge to learn about all of the properties that our phenomenal states represent. Mary can learn what red experiences represent and how they come to represent those experiences. Mary might learn, for example, that the experiences we call red are reliably tokened by encounters with certain reflectance properties. A visual experience of a ripe strawberry represents its surface as reflecting a preponderance of wavelengths in the range of 600 to 700 nanometers. Mary also learns that color experiences have a variety of further representational and functional properties distinctive to sensory representations. Jackson thinks that five of these properties are especially important:

1. Color experiences are rich (color is represented along with extension, location, motion, orientation, and shape).
2. This richness is inextricable (you cannot prise the color apart from the shape, etc.).
3. The experience is immediate (we do not perceive colors by first experiencing something else).
4. There is a "causal element" in the experience (we represent colors as located where we see them).
5. Color experiences, like all perceptions, have a distinctive functional role (we use them to update our current beliefs).

Jackson supposes that this knowledge will be enough for Mary to know all of the phenomenal facts about seeing red. The phenomenal qualities of red are exhausted by these representational and functional properties (for a similar claim, see Dretske, 1995). In presenting this account, Jackson admits that Mary will learn *something* on her release. He says that she will acquire an ability to recognize, remember, and imagine colors (I will come to this proposal below). But he thinks that those abilities do not constitute knowledge of how colors feel. The representationalist story is supposed to explain that. But does it?

I think that Jackson's proposal doesn't pan out. First, his specific account of what sensory experiences are like is inadequate, and second, representationalism is not a promising account of sensory qualities. Jackson's assumption that colors have representational content is very contentious. Color antirealists deny this, and secondary quality theorists argue that colors must be explained with reference to color experiences, not the other way around. But suppose we grant that color experiences represent. Could their representational content really explain how they feel? Obviously, the representational content is not sufficient. A verbal description of the reflectance properties that red experiences register does not feel anything like a red experience, even though they represent the same property on Jackson's account. To explain the feel of red, Jackson must appeal to the five properties just enumerated. The problem is that these five properties are neither necessary nor sufficient for color experience.

Let's begin with Jackson's claims that color experiences are rich, inextricably so. This is often the case, but it's hardly necessary. When we stare at a large uniform color field, we see no shapes, orientation, or motion, and when groups of colored shapes are presented very briefly, we can see the colors, but we are not sure which shapes they belong to (Treisman and Schmidt, 1982). Consider also a patient named P.B., who sustained severe damage to his visual system as a result of an electric shock (Zeki et al., 1999). P.B. is essentially blind; he cannot discern shapes or locate features in space. But he can perceive and recognize colors. Clearly, those experiences are not rich in Jackson's sense. P.B. also suggests that color experience need not be causal in Jackson's sense. P.B. probably can't locate colors at a causal source of their origin. Neither can we locate colors when, for example, we produce a red experience by pressing down on our eyes. Colors induced by psychoactive drugs may also be free-floating in this way. Must color experiences be immediate? Probably not. Synesthetes experience colors when they see shapes, and ordinary perceivers can train themselves to imagine colors by association. Kosslyn et al. (2000) hypnotized subjects to experience colors when they looked at black-and-white images, and that resulted in activation of color centers in the brain. Presumably, these subjects were not seeing the colors immediately, but they were experiencing them. The final item on Jackson's list is the distinctive role that experiences have in belief updating. This strikes me as implausible. Experience can play many different roles with respect to belief; experiences can confirm, disconfirm, or be entirely ignored. There is no effect on belief that necessarily follows a red experience. Without spelling out the details, the functional-role criterion cannot do any explanatory work.

I conclude that Jackson's five features are not necessary for color experiences. They are also insufficient. One can have a rich, immediate, causally located, belief-influencing experience without any phenomenal qualities. For example, Heywood, Cowey, and Newcombe (1994) describe a patient, M.S., who can respond to color information, despite profound cortical achromatopsia (see Akins, 2001, for discussion). M.S. cannot recognize or, as far as we can tell, experience hues, but he can recognize and trace out the contours of shapes whose only difference from their backgrounds are chromatic. In other words, M.S. perceives color, and the color information is presumably immediate, rich, causally located, and capable of supporting spontaneous beliefs—but he has no color qualia.

The insufficiency of Jackson's five features can also be brought out in normal subjects. Consider unconscious priming. It seems plausible that we can have perceptual episodes that are rich, immediate, and so on, without awareness, when stimuli are rapidly presented and followed by a contrasting mask. There are even experimental demonstrations of unconscious color priming (Breitmeyer, Ogmen, and Chen, 2004). Stretching things just a little bit, we can imagine a variant on the Mary case, called Subliminal Mary. Before her release, Subliminal Mary is exposed to color patches but only in a masked priming paradigm. Presumably, she forms rich color representations during this procedure, but she still doesn't know what colors are like. Jackson's claim that Mary knows everything about colors prior to release seems grossly implausible.

These kinds of considerations underscore the limitations of representationalism, (for a more thorough critique, see chapter 1). That theory is, at best, an account of how we ordinarily individuate phenomenal experiences, not an account of what phenomenal qualities are. Representationalism can help provide a theory of *which* states we are conscious of but not a theory of *when* we become conscious. It is a mistake to think that a theory of which states we are conscious of is a theory of WIL. The qualitative character of experience is not exhausted by the representational content. Contents get their character by becoming conscious. What it's like to see red is a matter of red representations becoming conscious, not a matter of red representations as such. The case of Subliminal Mary shows this.

In fact, the point can be pushed even further. Arguably, it's not even sufficient that Mary's phenomenal state be conscious for her to know what it's like. Consider Clumsy Mary. One day, when Clumsy Mary is still in her colorless room, she trips and hits her head. This causes her to have a fleeting experience of high-saturated red. The experience is phenomenal, but because she is in pain, Mary doesn't notice it. In Ned Block's terms, she has phenomenal consciousness of red but never gains access. As a result, there is no moment of surprise and little temptation to credit Mary with learning anything new. To know what red is like, Mary has to *notice* the experience. Or, to use a term mentioned in chapter 3, she has to be *aware* of it.

This suggests that our first constraint, possessive knowledge, was not strong enough on its own. We need a second constraint:

Noticed Knowledge: An adequate account of phenomenal knowledge should explain why you need to be aware of a mental state in order to know what it is like.

On most theories of consciousness, noticed knowledge entails possessive knowledge; we cannot be conscious of states that we don't have. But there are theories that break this connection, allowing that we can be aware of states that do not exist, by simply representing them. Dennett's (1991) account may be an instance of this, and likewise, some higher-order thought theories allow that consciousness can arise when there is a HOT but no target of that HOT. Defenders of such views may opt for noticed knowledge in lieu of possessive knowledge, but as a skeptic about such views, I think that the former entails the latter, and hence we need both. I will keep both constraints on the roster, because they are dissociable on some theories.

2.3. ABILITIES

I have been focusing on premise 2 of Jackson's knowledge argument. Most commentators agree that the offending premise is P3. According to that premise, WIL must be derivable from physical knowledge if WIL is itself physical. There are several popular strategies for rejecting this premise.

The first strategy is to argue that knowledge of WIL is not factual knowledge; it is not knowing *that* something is the case. Instead, it is procedural knowledge, or knowledge of *how* to do certain things (Lewis, 1988; Nemirow, 1990). Know-how cannot be derived from knowledge *that*. We cannot learn how to ride a bike by reading about how legs move when riding; we must train our legs to move properly. Physicalism is fully compatible with the supposition that know-how requires experience. Like bike riding, Lewis and Nemirow suppose, knowing WIL is a form of know-how. In particular, knowing what red is like is constituted by the ability to imagine red, recall red, and recognize red.

This proposal is deeply implausible. First, the kind of know-how in question is not necessary for knowing WIL. Some people are very bad at forming mental images. For them, imagining colors may (we can suppose) be impossible. Yet they clearly know what it's like to see red. Similarly, a person may be incapable of encoding or retrieving memories of experiences (consider anterograde amnesia), yet they can know what an experience is like while they are having it. Recognition is also unnecessary for knowing WIL. It is well known that discrimination outstrips recognition. We can experience differences between two color patches, even when we cannot recognize, on a subsequent presentation of three color patches, which two patches we saw a moment earlier. As noted in chapter 3, Halsey and Chapanis (1951) estimated that we may be able to discriminate between one million different colors, but we can recognize only between eleven and sixteen.

The abilities in question are also insufficient for explaining knowledge of WIL. Recognition often takes place unconsciously, and there may be things that we recognize without ever having qualitative knowledge of, such as the character of a pheromone. Likewise, there is little reason to think that recollection is always conscious. Memory is the backbone of problem solving, and much problem solving takes place without consciousness. This suggests that the ability to recall does not guarantee phenomenal knowledge. Similarly, there is likely to be unconscious imagination. To imagine something is to form a mental image, and to form an image is to create a sensory state endogenously. There are widely accepted models of perception according to which we form mental images constantly to facilitate perception. These models postulate "predictive codes," which use perceptual inputs and stored knowledge to form a sensory prediction of what we will see in the next time step. These predictions help to filter out noise but, on some models, are not themselves conscious. Thus, imagination does not entail phenomenal knowledge. If these abilities are neither necessary nor sufficient for phenomenal knowledge, we should resist implicating them in a response to the knowledge argument.

This leaves us with a third constraint:

Ephemeral Knowledge: An adequate account of phenomenal knowledge should explain why you can know what a state is like while having it without retaining an ability to recall, recognize, or imagine it on another occasion.

We will see below that this constraint rules out a class of responses to the knowledge argument, known as the phenomenal concepts strategy.

2.4. FREGEAN MODES OF PRESENTATION

There is a second strategy for blocking P3, which is perhaps the most popular response to the knowledge argument. Many of Jackson's critics think he has made a simple blunder. We cannot derive knowledge of WIL from knowledge of physical facts, because WIL is grasped using modes of presentation that differ from the kind used in physical science (see, e.g., Churchland, 1985; Lycan, 1987; Loar, 1990; Tye, 1995; Hill, 1997; Papineau, 2002). As Frege showed a century ago, whenever we have two modes of presentation for the same thing, we can have informative identities. In discussions of the knowledge argument, this point is often put in terms of phenomenal concepts, which are posited as concepts that represent phenomenal states in a distinctively phenomenal way (the specifics of which vary from theory to theory). Proponents of phenomenal concepts say that phenomenal concepts, and hence phenomenal knowledge, cannot be derived from knowledge expressed in physical concepts, because these concepts differ. Both kinds of concepts can express the same facts, but they represent in different ways, and therefore we are surprised to learn that they are co-referential. By analogy, we cannot derive the identity between water and H_2O, because "water" and "H_2O" are grasped using different concepts. The identity seems to be discovered a posteriori. In assuming that WIL should be derivable from physical facts, if WIL is physical, Jackson is assuming that theoretical identities must be discoverable a priori. If we simply suppose that phenomenal concepts and neural concepts refer via different modes of presentation, we can explain why Mary's physical knowledge does not tell her what it's like to see red.

How could Jackson make such an elementary mistake? The answer is that this seemingly obvious response to the knowledge argument is deeply problematic on scrutiny. The troubles begin with a long-standing challenge to physicalism, which was influentially discussed by Smart (1959: n. 13), who attributed the objection to Max Black. The objection trades on a basic assumption about modes of presentation. Descendants of the Fregean tradition assume that modes of presentation are individuated by properties; a mode presents its referent by representing some property of its referent. Thus, two co-referential modes differ if they present via different properties, and they are otherwise the same. From this it follows that if there are two modes of representing the brain states that underlie conscious experience, they must represent those brain states via different properties. Neural descriptions quite obviously represent via neural properties. If, in addition to neural descriptions, we have phenomenal ways of representing phenomenal properties, which represent via different properties, then phenomenal states must have properties that are not neural. Thus, even if experiences are neural states, they must have nonphysical properties. Property dualism looms.

Smart's own reply is to argue that phenomenal modes of presentation represent in a topic-neutral way. He admits that they do not represent phenomenal states by explicitly describing their neural properties, but neither do they explicitly appeal to any properties that are mental. Rather, they present experiences to us by appeal to the role those experiences play: red is the kind of experience I have when I see strawberries or ripe tomatoes under good lighting conditions.

Smart's strategy faces an obvious objection. The topic-neutral properties that he mentions are functional role properties. His suggestion is that we pick out our phenomenal states by the roles they play. For example, we might pick out the quality red by describing it as that which we experience when we look at a cherry in good light. But this can't be the only way we pick out redness. A person can know what red experiences are like without having any idea about red objects. Recall, for example, the neurological patient who sees color but no form. A person born with this condition might have no idea which objects are red. In response, Smart might say that red experiences also have a subtler functional role, which is not linked to any particular object. Perhaps the role involves the wavelengths that cause red or the way red combines with other colors. Such subtle roles are not part of folk psychology; they must be identified scientifically. But this also seems inadequate for explaining our knowledge of what red is like. First, it is perfectly obvious what red is like, so it cannot be something that must be ascertained scientifically. Second, Mary could have a thorough description of the scientifically discoverable roles that red plays and still not know what red is like. Therefore, the property by which we know red cannot be equated with a functional role. Once we rule out the role strategy, Max Black's objection reappears. If the property by which we pick out phenomenal states is not neural or functional, then it must be irreducibly phenomenal.

In conclusion, the physicalist should resist the view that Mary learns a new Fregean mode of presentation. Fregean modes refer by means of properties, and since Mary knows all of the functional and neural correlates of red experiences before her release, physicalists cannot say that she learns a new property of red experience after her release. And that means that she cannot learn a new Fregean mode. Stated as a constraint, we get:

Unmediated Knowledge: An adequate account of phenomenal knowledge should not suppose that we know what a phenomenal state is like by representing some property of that state.

The Fregean approach makes phenomenal knowledge too indirect.

2.5. RUSSELLIAN MODES OF PRESENTATION

Fregean modes of presentation refer by presenting their bearers with reference-determining properties. I have just suggested that physicalists should not explain phenomenal knowledge by appeal to Fregean modes. But the Fregean approach to modes of presentation is not the only option. Russell famously departed from Frege's theory of linguistic meaning and argued that some terms refer directly without the benefit of mediating descriptions. One could express this idea by saying that some words have no modes of presentation. This way of putting it is slightly misleading when one moves from a theory of language to a theory of thought. It seems incoherent to suggest that an idea can be grasped without any mode of presentation, since this would imply that we grasp nothing when we grasp such an idea, and ideas are, by definition, things that we grasp. So we might express the Russellian view by saying that directly referring expressions have modes that are nondescriptive. Or, taking a page from Mill, we can say that such terms are grasped as mere labels. Similarly, we can imagine that there are ideas that have no descriptive content. They merely label what they represent. We can think of a Fregean mode of presentation as a mental description, and we can think of a Russellian mode as a mental label. If Mary acquires a new Russellian mode when she leaves her room, then the worries about modes raised above would not arise.

Loar's (1990) influential approach to phenomenal knowledge can be characterized as a theory of this kind. Loar's account centers on "recognitional concepts." Like Russellian labels, these concepts denote without describing. Recognitional concepts have neither meaningful semantic analyses nor any semantically interpretable mental states mediating between them and what they represent. Consequently, a recognitional concept cannot be deduced from any other concept that happens to refer to the same thing. It follows that identity conjectures containing recognitional concepts are a posteriori. But, unlike concepts in other nonobvious identity conjectures, recognitional concepts do not refer via contingent properties. They refer via direct causal links directly to the things that they are used to recognize.

Loar tried to save physicalism from the knowledge argument by proposing that we represent our phenomenal states by means of recognitional concepts. Suppose the phenomenal experience of redness is a brain state and that knowing what red is like consists in having a recognitional concept that can be used to detect when such an experience is occurring. Since recognitional concepts do not describe what they denote, knowledge of what it's like does not require ascription of any property, whether phenomenal or neural. Loar also uses this strategy to address the knowledge argument. Jackson assumes that if Mary cannot deduce knowledge of WIL from knowledge of brain states, then WIL is not a brain state. But in Loar's view, knowing WIL is a matter of having recognitional concepts. Since recognitional concepts are nondescriptive, the knowledge constituted by having recognitional concepts cannot be deduced from knowledge couched in other concepts. Therefore, there is a principled reason for thinking that we should not be able to deduce knowledge of WIL from knowledge of brain states that we grasp using scientific concepts. This inferential barrier poses no threat to the physicalist.

Loar's response has advantages over the first mode of presentation view considered above. He does not assume that we represent phenomenal states by means of their properties, and this insulates him against the Max Black objection. Still, Loar's response faces some objections. One worry has been put forward by Chalmers (2004a). He finds a tension between the two major components of Loar's account of phenomenal concepts. On the one hand, these concepts are supposed to be nondescriptive. They refer directly, not via any specific properties of the phenomenal states that they designate. Chalmers calls this neutrality. On the other hand, phenomenal concepts are supposed to be opaque; they cannot be freely replaced with co-referring concepts, even if those co-referring concepts refer via essential properties. Substitution with co-referring concepts changes cognitive significance. Mary can believe that "red experiences" are identical with V4 activations, without knowing that red experiences are like *that*, where *that* expresses a phenomenal concept. Normally, differences in cognitive significance between concepts are explained by presuming that those concepts refer via different properties. Opacity presupposes nonneutrality. Loar owes us an explanation, says Chalmers, of how a concept can be both neutral and opaque.

I think that this objection can be answered. Opacity does not require non-neutrality. In principle, there can be an informative identity claim made using any two representations that are not token identical, as Kripke's (1979) Paderewski case illustrates. In that example, someone fails to realize that Paderewski the statesman and Paderewski the musician are one and the same person; discovering that they are the same comes as a surprise, even though the very same name was used to think about Paderewski in both of these two roles. Indeed, there can be informative identities with two tokens of the same name even when no information is known about whom it designates. If I overheard the name Otis one day and then again the next, I can wonder whether Otis is Otis. Opacity is cheap. A label that tells us nothing about its referent provides us with no information about which we can derive identities using other labels. Neutrality yields an intractable form of opacity. There is no tension here at all.

But Loar is not off the hook. For one thing, recognitional concepts run afoul of a constraint that has already been adduced. In considering the Lewis/Nemirow position, we saw that a person can have phenomenal knowledge ephemerally, without acquiring any ability to recognize a quality on a future occasion. If that's right, phenomenal knowledge cannot consist in the acquisition of a mental representation that can be used for recognition.

Loar also gets into trouble because of his neutrality assumption. Phenomenal concepts are supposed to be radically neutral; they are inner labels that tell us nothing about the phenomenal states that they designate. This is implausible for three reasons. First, when we say, "That's red," we are not reporting that a neutral label has switched on in our heads; we are reporting that we recognize a specific phenomenal quality, redness. If phenomenal concepts were neutral labels, then we couldn't use them to draw substantive conclusions about our phenomenal states, such as the conclusion that orange is more like red than it is like blue. Second, if phenomenal concepts were neutral labels, then one should be able to use them in the absence of the phenomenal states that they designate. We could think, "Red is like *this*," without imagining or seeing red. That is an unacceptable consequence. Reflecting on what red is like requires having a red experience. Third, Mary could have an innate neutral label that was wired to fire when she encountered red. On Loar's view, it would follow that Mary knows what red is like innately, but this is an unwelcome conclusion, because even if she had such an innate label, she would learn something new on encountering red. These points can be summarized by saying that neutrality implies that we can grasp an experience without having it, and this runs afoul of the have-it-to-know-it principle and hence the possessive knowledge constraint.

Perhaps Loar would concede the point. It might be proposed that phenomenal knowledge consists in the activation of a neutral label *together with* the labeled state. So amended, Loar's proposal begins to look very attractive. But this move cannot fully resuscitate the core of Loar's theory. I have already said that phenomenal knowledge cannot require recognition, so Loar's appeal to *recognitional* concepts can't be right. But one can also take issue with his appeal to *concepts*. First of all, concepts may presuppose recognition. Many authors agree that concepts are tools for reidentification, and someone cannot be credited with having a concept if that person cannot recognize multiple encounters with the same thing (Millikan, 2000). In this usage, a label that cannot be used for recognition cannot be a concept. Thus, the ephemeral knowledge constraint, which says that we can have phenomenal knowledge without recognition abilities, already ruled out the phenomenal concepts strategy. The have-it-to-know-it principle, which motivated possessive knowledge, is also hard to reconcile with the claim that phenomenal knowledge is conceptual. It's commonly believed that concepts are mental representations that can be tokened in the absence of their referents. If phenomenal knowledge depends on phenomenal states, then it also fails on this criterion for concepthood. In short, the two objections that I raised against Loar indicate that a theory of phenomenal knowledge should not posit phenomenal concepts (Prinz, 2007b; see also Tye, 2009).

A critic might respond that this argument against phenomenal concepts depends on a technical definition of what concepts are, and other definitions are available. If concepts require reidentification and object independence, then phenomenal knowledge cannot be conceptual. But suppose we define a concept as any constituent of a thought. Surely, Mary can have thoughts about her experiences. She can have the thought that she expresses by "Red is like that," where the word *that* picks out a visual state. This thought is the canonical expression of what Mary comes to know.

The link between phenomenal knowledge and demonstrative thought is actually central to Loar's account. He argues explicitly that phenomenal concepts are mental demonstratives that point to their referents. The problem is that there is a tension between the appeal to demonstrative reference and the idea of recognitional concepts. It is characteristic of demonstratives that they can point to things, which would not be identified a second time around. Pointing does not entail reidentification. Pointing is also object-dependent in that we cannot point to what isn't there. So demonstratives have precisely the properties we are looking for and precisely the properties that recognitional concepts lack. I would express this by saying that demonstratives (or at least those that don't allow reidentification) are not concepts. But the terminological point isn't what matters. The crucial insight, which is present but overshadowed in Loar, is that phenomenal knowledge involves demonstrative reference.

In summary, I don't think that phenomenal knowledge requires recognitional concepts or any other kind of mental representation that could be called conceptual without inviting confusion. But I do think that Loar's discussion contains an insight that is important enough to express as a constraint:

Demonstrative Knowledge: An adequate account of phenomenal knowledge should say that some kind of mental demonstratives play a role in forming beliefs about what our phenomenal states are like.

I will later offer an account that tries to meet this constraint, but it is also important to see that it faces a daunting hurdle. The most influential approach to demonstratives in the philosophy of language was developed by Kaplan (1989). According to his theory, words such as *this* and *that* do not contain any descriptive content and thus meet Loar's objectives, which I described as Russellian. Russell himself thought that demonstratives refer without the benefit of descriptions, so Loar's appeal to demonstratives further confirms the Russellian spirit of his account. Kaplan agrees that demonstratives are not descriptions, but this very feature leads him to believe that demonstratives cannot refer on their own. They need to be supplemented by what he calls "demonstrations." For example, I might point to a glass of wine and say, "That's just what the doctor ordered." My pointing serves as a reference fixer. It helps my listeners determine what my utterance of *that* refers to. Pointing is a gesture, but it works very much like a description. *That* refers to the object in line with my finger. My listeners must be able to use this property, finger alignment, to figure out what I am talking about. For Kaplan, some such demonstration is needed whenever we use a demonstrative in language, and therefore, linguistic demonstratives refer by means of properties even though they lack descriptive content. If so, linguistic demonstratives are not a promising model for phenomenal knowledge. They fall prey to exactly the same worry that faced the first model of presentation proposal, the worry put forward by Max Black: which properties are used to demonstrate our phenomenal states? Perhaps their phenomenal properties. If so, we'd be back at square one. I think this worry can be addressed, but we can also see why it might be tempting to look for a different approach to phenomenal knowledge.

2.6. ACQUAINTANCE

The predicament can be summarized as follows. We saw two versions of the view that Mary learns a new mode of presentation on her release. According to the first, modes are individuated by properties. The problem here is that those properties would have to be nonphysical, because Mary knows all physical properties before her release, and she can't use those to explain the alleged nonphysical ones. According to the second mode of presentation reply, Mary acquires a mode of presentation with no descriptive content. The problem with this move is that the leading theory of how nondescriptive reference works in language, Kaplan's theory of demonstratives, still indirectly appeals to reference-fixing properties.

Given these worries, we might decide to give the mode of presentation strategy a rest. Rather than saying that knowing WIL is a matter of possessing a mode of presentation, one can say that it is a matter of having *a special kind of epistemic access* to that mode. With this approach, Mary doesn't learn any new properties, but she acquires a new way of knowing. Lewis and Nemirow's ability theory pushed in this direction. They distinguished knowing how from knowing that. This strategy failed, because the abilities they consider are neither necessary nor sufficient for knowing WIL. But there is another distinction to be drawn between two kinds of knowing. We can distinguish knowledge by acquaintance and knowledge by description (Russell, 1912: chap. 5). Many languages mark this difference lexically. There is one epistemic verb that expresses knowledge by acquaintance or familiarity (e.g., *conoscere, conocer, connaitre, kennen*) and another that expresses the mastery of facts (e.g., *sapere, saber, savoir, wissen*). Some authors have suggested that after leaving her room, Mary merely acquires acquaintance with properties she already knew by description (Horgan, 1984; Conee, 1994; Tye, 2009).

This proposal can be used to refute the third premise of the knowledge argument. Jackson assumes that if Mary cannot deduce knowledge of WIL from physical knowledge, then WIL is not physical. But this rests on an equivocation. Knowledge of WIL is not knowledge by description; it is knowledge by acquaintance. One cannot infer acquaintance from descriptive knowledge. Acquaintance occurs only when one has encountered something, and describing something is not the same as encountering it. The fact that we cannot infer acquaintance from description has no important ontological implications. You can describe Timbuktu to me, but I can't become acquainted with Timbuktu without going there; it does not follow that Timbuktu is not physical. Likewise, the fact that Mary's textbooks do not acquaint her with color experiences does not entail that those experiences are not physical.

This move is seductive but problematic. The difficulty is that the gulf between acquaintance and description usually isn't very large. Usually, one can learn so much information by description that acquaintance yields no surprises. Suppose I tell you about my friend Henrietta. I tell you all about her personality, her biography, and her appearance in excruciating detail. Perhaps we have a lot of time on our hands, so I tell you everything there is to know about these facts. Of course, you are not thereby acquainted with Henrietta. You don't know her. Description does not entail acquaintance. Now, suppose I introduce the two of you. You now acquire a new form of knowledge: knowledge by acquaintance. But, I submit, you won't be surprised when you meet her. If my descriptions have been thorough, Henrietta will be just as you would have expected.

The point can be made by saying that acquaintance is an externalist epistemic construct. When you shift from description to acquaintance, the only thing that must be added is some kind of *encounter* with the object of knowledge. The internalist (i.e., mentally represented) information can be entirely descriptive. Encountering something can increase your stock of internal information, but that information is not necessarily qualitatively different from information you could have gotten by description without acquaintance. In other words, a person who is *not* acquainted with something can usually have internal states that are indistinguishable from those of someone who *is* acquainted with that thing. Acquaintance is too epistemically modest to account for Mary's surprise when she leaves the room.

In response, the proponent of the acquaintance strategy might argue that knowing WIL involves a special kind of acquaintance, which is much more than description-plus-encountering. But this move renders the acquaintance proposal empty. What is the special kind of acquaintance that Mary acquires? Well, it's phenomenal acquaintance, of course. Mary's surprise on leaving the room is not merely a consequence of her becoming acquainted with something; the appeal to acquaintance does no explanatory work. Her surprise is rather a consequence of having phenomenal experiences, and the physicalist owes us an explanation of why we can't attain an epistemic state that is internally indistinguishable from those obtained by description alone.

Despite these complaints, something seems right about the acquaintance approach. By focusing on how representations are accessed rather than focusing on the representations themselves, one can overcome some of the objections facing mode of presentation replies to the knowledge argument. What we need is a substantive account of the special epistemic access relation, rather than the unhelpful label "acquaintance." We need to explain what our *direct epistemic access* to experiences consists in.

Coming up with a substantive account of direct access is not going to be easy. There is a challenging puzzle concerning direct access. In cases of indirect epistemic access, we can explain two things: what we know about the entity accessed *and what we don't know*. I have good indirect epistemic access to my shoes, but that is not good enough to tell me about the molecules that make them up. I can't see molecules as such. This failing is explained by a limitation in my representational acuity. But consider direct epistemic access. If we are in direct epistemic contact with the thing itself, then there should be no barrier to accessing any of its essential properties. This is potentially embarrassing for the physicalist. Physicalists claim that experiences are token-identical to brain states. If we have direct access to brain states and direct access makes every essential property available, then we should have direct access to the brainy properties of our experience (such as the morphology and firing pattern of their constituent cells). On the face of it, we have no such access.

This can be brought out by considering the inverse knowledge argument. Inverse Mary is Mary's sister. She is just like us. She knows nothing about the brain, but she knows a lot about experience. She is great at introspecting, and when she experiences red, she likes to focus on the phenomenal qualities of that experience. She knows everything there is to know about the phenomenology of seeing red. Yet she does not know that red experiences are brain states. If she were to read about the underlying cellular activity, she would be extremely surprised. If knowing WIL were a matter of having direct epistemic access to brain states, then one might expect Inverse Mary to be able to discern the brainy properties of her experiences. She should be able to read them off, in much the way that we can describe the brush strokes in a painting by van Gogh. Her inability to do that places some pressure on the direct access thesis and cries out for explanation.

This puzzle about the direct access thesis provides another constraint:

Nonrevelatory Knowledge: An adequate account of phenomenal knowledge should include a substantive theory of direct access that explains why we can't read brainy properties off of our phenomenal states.

Among all of the constraints, this may be the most important. If phenomenal states wore their neural nature on their sleeves, the mind-body problem would have never arisen.

2.7. CONFLICTING CONSTRAINTS

I have identified six constraints that a theory of phenomenal knowledge should meet. Although they are not universally accepted, each enjoys considerable support in the literature. But it is not obvious whether they can be mutually satisfied. As I presented them here, each constraint derives from a problem with a leading response to the knowledge argument. This raises the possibility that no single account can satisfy every constraint. This worry can be brought into focus by considering how the constraints relate to one another and to competing strategies for wrestling with Mary.

Some strategies look unpromising. It's hard to stand behind the radical claim that Mary learns nothing new on leaving the room. But there are three strategies that have considerable appeal. One plausible strategy characterizes Mary's achievement as the acquisition of a new mode of presentation. Another says that Mary gains an ability she didn't have before. A third says that she becomes acquainted with something that she knew only by description. Ostensibly, these strategies are all very different. One posits a new kind of mental representation, another posits a new skill, and the third posits a new epistemic relation. These are entirely different psychological categories, and it might seem that we have to pick among them.

One might try to pick among these strategies by figuring out which one does the best job of meeting all of the constraints. Unfortunately, this isn't so easy. Each strategy seems well suited for some constraints and not others. Consider first the mode of presentation strategy. This fits well with the demonstrative knowledge constraint, since demonstratives are representations. It also fits well with nonrevelatory knowledge, since representations can conceal the essence of what they represent. The mode of presentation strategy is also reasonably well positioned to accommodate ephemeral knowledge, since a representation could come in and out of existence quickly. But it fits less naturally with possessive knowledge, since most representations can occur without possessing the thing they represent. It sheds little light on noticed knowledge, since being represented does not entail awareness (recall the discussion of higher-order theories in chapter 1). The mode of presentation strategy fares even worse when it comes to unmediated knowledge, since modes are, one would think, mediators.

The ability strategy promises to reconcile the tension between nonrevelatory knowledge and unmediated knowledge. An ability to do something need not reveal the nature of that thing; knowing how may come apart from at least some forms of knowing that. At the same time, abilities can be unmediated in some sense; they can be activities carried out directly on some object. The ability strategy also makes sense of possessive knowledge. In this approach, phenomenal knowledge is the exercise of a skill that we have with our phenomenal states, and we cannot exercise a skill with something unless we possess it. But the ability story falls short on other constraints. There is no special link between having abilities (which can be thought of as skills) and noticing something (which is an achievement); thus, the ability strategy sheds little light on noticed knowledge. Furthermore, there is much empirical evidence to suggest that consciousness tends to diminish as skills are acquired. Abilities are also usually enduring, which makes it difficult to see how this approach will deliver on the ephemeral knowledge constraint. Finally, abilities are not representations, so they fail to qualify as demonstrative knowledge.

Acquaintance also has pros and cons. It is explicitly implicated in the formation of the unmediated knowledge constraint. It also does well with possessive knowledge, since we must have a phenomenal state to become acquainted with it. It may also handle the noticed knowledge constraint, since it seems odd to say that we can be acquainted with something that we haven't noticed. It's less clear whether acquaintance call help with ephemeral knowledge, since, in ordinary usage, we ascribe acquaintance as an enduring state; I am acquainted with Miles Davis's Prestige recordings, even though I am not listening to them right now. For reasons indicated earlier, acquaintance also doesn't fit well with standard models of demonstrative knowledge. Russell thought that demonstratives require knowledge by acquaintance, but Kaplan's influential approach suggests that demonstratives are mediated by demonstrations. Worst of all, acquaintance looks flatly incompatible with nonrevelatory knowledge, since unmediated access looks like just the kind of epistemic relation that should reveal essences.

The upshot is that each of the three leading strategies for responding to the knowledge argument can accommodate half of the constraints and cannot accommodate the others. That suggests that these strategies are inadequate as they stand. My survey of responses to Jackson has not been exhaustive, but most extant responses can be classified under one of the strategies that I have been discussing. It would be nice, therefore, to look for a new alternative.

3. Maintaining Mary

3.1. MENTAL MAINTENANCE

Thus far, I have been considering a variety of different theoretical posits that might be used to explain why Mary can't infer WIL from her knowledge of physical facts. We have talked about imagination, mnemonic abilities, modes of presentation, recognitional concepts, and acquaintance. Almost all of these proposals have been generated in a philosopher's armchair with no effort to find empirical support. That is peculiar. After all, the posits in question are substantive. The defenders of these theories are not merely making verbal moves; they are speculating about the architecture of the mind. Armchair speculation is a good way to generate testable theories, but it should be viewed as a starting place, not the final word. We have seen that some of these starting places are nonstarters. None of these posits would be able adequately to answer the knowledge argument, even if they could be empirically confirmed. For example, the ability view cannot explain learning what it's like in the absence of the proposed abilities; the mode of presentation view tends to proliferate properties; and the acquaintance view cannot by itself explain why Mary is incapable of knowing WIL in the absence of actual contact with phenomenal states. Thus, prevailing proposals are doubly flawed: they are empirically unfettered, and they are not able to satisfy all of the constraints on an adequate solution to the knowledge argument. Perhaps if we begin by looking for an empirically motivated theory, we will end up with a better explanation of why Mary doesn't know WIL.

In the previous chapters, I presented an empirically based theory of consciousness. According to that theory, conscious states are AIRs, attended intermediate-level representations. Consciousness arises when an intermediate-level representation is made available for processing in working memory through attentional modulation. Let's assume that this theory is correct and ask how Mary learns what it's like to see red after leaving her room.

Presumably, Mary's first encounter with a red object would, if her parvocellular system had not atrophied, cause vectorwaves in her V4 neurons. If the stimulus were presented long enough for her attention systems to engage, the V4 response would synchronize and propagate forward, sending afferent to brain structures that can temporarily store spectral information. As soon as the V4 cells broadcast to systems higher in the pathway—as soon as their responses become *available*—Mary has a conscious experience of red. That experience is like something.

Strictly speaking, however, Mary might not yet *know* what it's like. Knowing an experience requires having the experience, but merely having the experience does not suffice. There could be creatures for which it is like something but who do not know what it is like. Some readers may want to insist that having an experience constitutes a form of knowing WIL in and of itself. Perhaps. I don't want to quibble too much about the scope of "knowledge" here. I want simply to underscore that there is an epistemic state that goes beyond having an experience. Imagine consciously tasting the tannins in wine before acquiring the ability to identify them as a distinct component of experience. One might say that one has experienced them but doesn't know what they are like. In contrast, if one learned to identify tannins in experience, one would be credited with knowing what they are like. This might imply that knowledge requires possession of a recognitional concept, but I've already rejected this suggestion. Suppose a person notices the tannin in a wine but doesn't store a record of the experience. The person might focus on the experience while it's happening. She might even be told then and there, "That's tannin you are tasting." There and then, she knows what tannin is like. She could even be credited with knowing what tannin is like, there and then, if she didn't know what it was that she was tasting. She might wonder about *that* taste, and that wondering would involve an awareness of the experience that goes beyond the mere having of it.

Likewise, I don't think that Mary merely experiences red on seeing that color for the first time. Perhaps she would merely have the experience if her first color encounter were with a briefly flashed detail from a Seurat painting. She'd have many color experiences in that moment, but she might not have epistemic purchase on any of them. She couldn't have a thought, for example, about any specific color. Or recall Clumsy Mary, who saw a brief flash of red upon hitting her head. But if Mary were able to experience something red for a longer duration, she could learn what it's like. If she were presented with a nice glass of red wine, for example, she could point to the color and say, "*This* is red." Or, bereft of verbal labels, she might wonder what color *this* liquid is that she is looking at.

So now we can ask, what does Mary's new epistemic state consist in? What more is needed beyond experience? Fans of recognitional concepts think that Mary needs an internal state that represents her red experience and can be used to recognize it. Having rejected this view, we will need a successor. Hints are given by the way she expresses her knowledge linguistically. She says that red is like *that*, using a demonstrative. Hints are often given by the folk-psychological terms used to describe Mary's achievement: she *notices* the color or becomes *aware* of it. But these terms cannot substitute for an account. These terms appear in constraints on a theory of phenomenal knowledge; they don't constitute a theory. They are only placeholders that must be filled in. That is to say, we should trade in folk concepts for a specific process that can be measured psychologically and located in brain function.

As a starting place, I want to return to a theme that first arose in chapter 3. There, I distinguished *availability* to working memory from *encoding* in working memory. I argued that consciousness requires mere availability and that awareness involves encoding. Given that phenomenal knowledge entails awareness, it follows that phenomenal knowledge also requires encoding. To have thoughts about experiences, they must be encoded. But what is working memory encoding? A prevailing view in cognitive neuroscience is that working memory is not really a storehouse but a collection of "executive" processes. For example, memory can be used to rotate mental images, draw inferences, make action decisions, or orchestrate strategic deployments of attention. But working memory also has another function that may be a precondition to executive control: working memory can *maintain* a representation of a perceived stimulus (Petrides, 1996; D'Esposito et al., 1999; Glahn et al., 2002). It is by maintaining representations that working memory can keep a stimulus in mind after it has been taken away. Suppose you read a number in a phone book, and then hold it in your head en route to the phone. Working memory is keeping it there. Or suppose you see a crime and keep the assailant's face in mind until the police come. Working memory does that.

Crucially, working memory does not maintain sensory representations by re-representing them. Working-memory encodings are not copies of sensory states. Rather, maintenance works by sustaining activity in sensory systems. A working-memory encoding is an internal state that causes a sensory representation to remain active after the stimulus that caused it has been removed. I would like to suggest that such encodings form the basis of phenomenal knowledge. When Mary thinks, "Red is like *this*," she is holding a red representation in her visual system. The red representation in an intermediate-level visual area that encodes color information becomes available via attention to working memory, and then a working-memory state is generated, which allows Mary to retain that representation for a brief period of time. Mary has access to what red is like as soon as the color representation becomes available, and she can think about what it's like as soon as she is in a position to maintain that representation.

At the psychological level of analysis, the maintenance process might be described as follows. First, attention makes a range of intermediate-level representations available for working memory. Then various factors, including top-down task demands and bottom-up stimulus features, determine which, if any, of the attentionally modulated representations will be encoded. Once an inter-mediate-level representation is selected for encoding, a corresponding high-level representation sends a signal to working memory. The high-level representation is used by working-memory processes to project an image of the intermediate-level representation back into intermediate-level processing systems. Because there is a loss of resolution between intermediate and high levels, the resulting image will not be a perfect copy of the original representation. One possibility is that the image will conform to a prototype. Thus, if the original intermediate-level representation was of a particular shade of red, the image produced by working memory may be a slightly different shade that comes closer to the prototype as determined by either the prior history of red experiences or under-lying default values within the neural mechanisms that implement the process. Executive working-memory structures can alter the image on command. For example, a person can effortfully imagine what a given red would look like if it were brighter or more saturated. As a result of this flexibility, a stored image could reinstantiate the original color, but the person doing this would not know which of the variations was exactly right. The images used in this process are not generated in the same way that ordinary mental images are generated, because they are not drawn from records in long-term memory. Instead, they rely on the fleeting representations generated by the stimulus when it is presented. Thus, it would be misleading to credit the person who stores an item in working memory with the ability to imagine the stored items. It is more accurate to say that the person is able to maintain a recorded item just presented.

The basic outlines of this story are presented in figure 21. Here we see a perceptual hierarchy with attention directed at the intermediate level. Then a high-level representation of the perceived color is sent to working memory, which sends a signal back to the intermediate level, reactivating the input, while also signaling attention systems to retain focus on the input. The result is an intermediate-level representation that has been generated bottom-up but then gets maintained by top-down reactivation and continued attention. Maintenance consists in this reactivation loop.

Within the brain, working memory involves a number of different structures, including sensory areas (e.g., those in the occipital and temporal cortex) and lateral frontal areas that control the maintenance process. A maintained color representation would be a neural activation in color-sensitive portions of

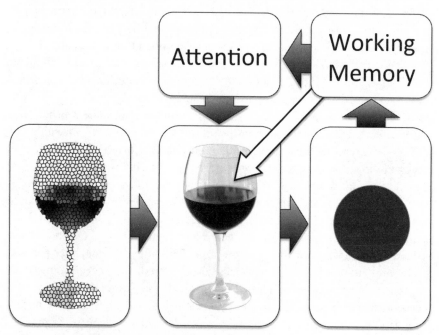

FIGURE 21 Mental maintenance as phenomenal knowledge.

V4 whose activity depended in part on input by frontal feedback. The nature of these activations is a topic of intense investigation. Working memory is associated with oscillations in the theta frequency (4–8 Hz). Fuentemilla et al. (2010) found an increase in frontal and temporal theta activity during the delay period in a working-memory task, and the increase was more pronounced when the memory load was more demanding. This is consistent with studies of monkeys showing theta activity in V4 during working-memory delays (Lee et al., 2005; Hoerzer et al., 2010). Fuentemilla et al. also found that neural patterns associated with the stored stimulus were phase-locked to the theta cycle and that such phase locking correlated with successful performance of the task. These neural patterns may oscillate within the gamma range. Gamma oscillations can be phase-locked to theta (Canolty et al., 2006), and this kind of nesting has been implicated in computational models of working memory (Jensen and Lisman, 1998). (If the brain uses alpha waves to chunk moments in time, then working-memory encodings of temporally extended events may involve alpha-nested gamma activity nested in theta.) However these details work out, the basic picture is clear enough: the brain is able to maintain cellular activity that is similar to the activations caused by a just-seen stimulus with the help of slow oscillations that help convey information at long distances.

Now let's consider this account of working-memory maintenance in the context of the knowledge argument. Prior to leaving the room, Mary knows about the AIR theory. She knows all of the facts about what goes on in the brain when people see red. Nevertheless, these states have never occurred in her brain. V4 representations of red have never been made available to her. On the AIR theory, it follows that she has never had an experience of red. Now, after leaving the room, she has that experience. Mary is also able, after leaving the room, to have the thought expressed by "Red is like *that*." That thought becomes possible only when she is able to notice red, which is a matter of encoding it in working memory. More specifically, she is able to think, "Red is like *that*," when she mentally maintains the red experience. Her word *that* refers to the maintained experience, which she can introspect as long as she is able to maintain it.

Mary learns something new when she is able to maintain her red experience. It would be misleading to say that she learns a new fact, because she already knew about all of the brain events that underlie red experiences. It would also be misleading simply to say that Mary has a new red representation. If Mary had been exposed to red subliminally, she might have already had representations in V4. Instead, Mary *accesses* a representation, by encoding it in working memory. Encoding is maintaining, so Mary's knowledge consists in mental maintenance. By maintaining her neural state, Mary continues to be able to access it, to experience what it's like, and to reflect on that experience. Knowing WIL is maintaining availability.

This account of what Mary learns allows us to see where Jackson's knowledge argument goes wrong. P3 says that if physicalism is true, then Mary should

be able to derive WIL from her knowledge of physical and functional properties of the brain. If the AIR theory is right, then this premise is false. Knowing
WIL is maintaining availability, and knowledge of the brain is not sufficient to
put one in that position. Maintaining availability is an actual neural process,
and Mary cannot undergo that neural process, or any other, by simply reading
about it. P3 presupposes that physicalism is committed to the derivability of
phenomenal knowledge, but the derivability assumption is false. Physicalists
should reject P3, and the AIR theory explains why.

3.2. MEETING THE CONSTRAINTS

The mental maintenance solution to the knowledge argument fares well in
comparison with other proposals. In comparison with the solutions surveyed
above, it alone can satisfy all of the constraints on an adequate theory. Let's
consider each in turn.

> **Possessive Knowledge:** An adequate account of phenomenal knowledge
> should explain why you need to have a phenomenal state in order to know
> what it is like.

Working-memory maintenance requires that there be a state to maintain. It
is not knowledge we have in the absence of the thing known; it is rather a process
carried out on the thing known. Moreover, before a state can be maintained in
working memory, it must be available to working memory, which, according to
the AIR theory, is what makes perceptual states conscious. I also argued in
chapter 4 that consciousness endows sensory states with their qualitative or
phenomenal character. Putting this together, the maintenance account guarantees that the objects of phenomenal knowledge are not only sensory states that
we possess, but they are sensory states that are conscious, and they thereby have
their phenomenal qualities. More succinctly, the account entails that the objects
of phenomenal knowledge are not just sensory states but phenomenal states.

> **Noticed Knowledge:** An adequate account of phenomenal knowledge
> should explain why you need to be aware of a mental state in order to know
> what it is like.

The maintenance account says that phenomenal knowledge arises only
when a sensory state is encoded in working memory. In chapter 3, I suggested
that this is just what awareness consists in. According to AIR, mental states are
conscious when they are available to working memory, and we become aware of
those states when they are encoded.

> **Ephemeral Knowledge:** An adequate account of phenomenal knowledge
> should explain why you can know what a state is like while having it without
> retaining an ability to recall, recognize, or imagine it on another occasion.

In the mental maintenance view, Mary need not acquire the abilities emphasized by Lewis and Nemirow in their response to the knowledge argument. Suppose she sees a strawberry for the first time. She can maintain the percept while staring at the strawberry, but her capacity to recall or recognize that hue on her next encounter might be very low. As noted above, maintenance can be described as a process in which an image of a stimulus is created, but this should be distinguished from ordinary cases of mental imagery, which rely on long-term memory. Mary can learn what the color of strawberries is like without being able to imagine it on a future occasion. By analogy, you might taste a quince for the first time and say, "Quince tastes like this," while maintaining the flavor for a few moments after eating the last bite, but an hour later, you may have no capacity to revisit that taste in imagination.

> **Unmediated Knowledge:** An adequate account of phenomenal knowledge should not suppose that we know what a phenomenal state is like by representing some property of that state.

It is tempting to think of working memory as a representational capacity. In that interpretation, we store items in working memory by forming representations of them in the working-memory areas in the lateral prefrontal cortex. But this is not the right way to think about it. Working memory operates by maintaining states in sensory systems, not by representing such states. The cellular activity in prefrontal cortex would be best regarded as implementing instructions rather than storing information. It would be inaccurate to say that Mary represents her red experience by *representing* how to maintain it; what matters is that she *can* maintain it. When Mary thinks about what red is like, she is not entertaining her working-memory instructions. Rather, she is experiencing the red percept that they maintain. One might be tempted to think of the red percept as a representation of the quality of redness, but this, too, would be a mistake. The maintained red percept does not *represent* the quality of redness; rather, it *exemplifies* that quality. The term *exemplification* was introduced by Goodman (1976) to describe cases in which people communicate by drawing attention to a sample of something. To take a case from Wittgenstein, a dictionary might explain the meaning of a color term by printing a small colored patch. Therefore, I think we should say that Mary does not represent her red experience at all; it simply becomes available for her to think about. If so, there is no worry about her representing red by means of a nonphysical property. Her knowledge is unmediated.

> **Demonstrative Knowledge:** An adequate account of phenomenal knowledge should say that some kind of mental demonstratives play a role in forming beliefs about what our phenomenal states are like.

The claim that Mary has direct knowledge of what her experiences are like might seem to suggest that she lacks demonstrative knowledge of them. After all, demonstratives are usually regarded as mental representations. Moreover, in Kaplan's influential theory, demonstratives are mediated by demonstrations. If Mary's knowledge is direct, then it seems we have to reject the supposition that her knowledge is demonstrative. This presents us in a quagmire. On leaving her room, Mary seems to form demonstrative thoughts about colors. She says, "Red is like that," and these words presumably express a psychological state. What is that state if not a mental demonstrative?

To escape the quagmire, we need a theory of unmediated demonstratives. Kaplan posits demonstrations to explain linguistic demonstratives because the word *that* has no intrinsic content that can fix its referent on any occasion. It needs to be supplemented. If the word *that* were causally linked to a particular object on a given occasion, and listeners could retrace that causal path merely by virtue of hearing the word, then supplementation would be unnecessary. This is impossible to pull off with words, because *that* is unconstrained, but we can achieve something like this with nonverbal behavior. Suppose you ask me what color I plan to use when painting my house, and I respond by lifting up a color chip. This action can be regarded as a kind of demonstrative—a nonverbal way of saying "this color"—but it works by exemplifying the color rather than representing it. Put differently, this response is both a demonstrative and a demonstration. The distinction collapses because I point out the color by means of the color itself. This case can be compared to the working-memory instructions that maintain percepts. Working-memory instructions are caused by percepts, and they also guarantee that a person activating the instructions will have the corresponding percepts. There is no ambiguity about what such instructions are pointing to, since they maintain the percepts to which they point. This pointing works without representing. We might call it a Goodmanian mode of presentation; it works by creating a copy of the demonstrated percept, which then serves as an exemplification of itself. Exemplification collapses the distinction between demonstrative and demonstration. As with the color chip, we point without representing or representational mediation. Maintenance instructions are unmediated demonstratives. Elsewhere I refer to this as mental pointing (Prinz, 2007b).

> **Nonrevelatory Knowledge:** An adequate account of phenomenal knowledge should include a substantive theory of direct access that explains why we can't read brainy properties off of our phenomenal states.

I will spend a bit more time on this constraint because the Inverse Mary case, which motivates it, has received insufficient attention in the literature. Everyone is worried about the fact that we can't infer the phenomenal qualities from neural descriptions, but comparatively few are worried about the fact that we can't infer neural descriptions from phenomenal qualities. Perhaps the neglect stems from the fact that contributors to the consciousness literature assume that this problem has an easy solution. But a quick review of knee-jerk responses suggests that the problem may be harder than it looks:

Proposal 1: Phenomenal states are multiply realizable, and one cannot infer a realizer from a multiply realized state, because there is an open-ended range of realizers.

Reply: It's not obvious that qualia are multiply realized, and in any case, most physicalists accept the token-identity theory. An adequate reply should explain why direct epistemic access to a token phenomenal state does not reveal its braininess.

Proposal 2: We have direct access to brainy properties as such, but we cannot "read them off," because they are nonconceptual and hence inaccessible to cognitive mechanisms.

Reply: Phenomenal states may be nonconceptual, but they are certainly accessible. That is a central tenet of the AIR theory and many others. Also, when we have a vivid conscious experience, we have no difficulty applying concepts to it.

Proposal 3: We have direct access to brainy properties as such, but we don't describe experiences that way, because doing so requires possession of a neuroscientific vocabulary.

Reply: If this were the case, then we should at least be able to describe our experiences using geometrical vocabulary that corresponds to neural structures. That is, we should be able to discern that our experiences decompose into roundish parts that have long branching lines stemming off of them. Later, when we learn the words for cell body and dendrites, we should say, "Oh, that's what those things are!" Of course, we don't do this.

Proposal 4: Phenomenal states are diaphanous. They represent external features of the world, and when we access them, we are aware of those features.

Reply: I argued against representationalism in chapter 1. I think that both representational content and apparent diaphanousness are contingent features of phenomenal states and phenomenal properties are not representational properties. If I am right, this proposal won't fly.

Proposal 5: One might think that the problem of Inverse Mary is based on an unwarranted allegiance to the act-object theory of perception. According to that theory, perception involves an act of awareness directed toward an object that serves as an intermediary between mind and world. In this view, having a phenomenal experience is like staring at a mental painting. If the act-object theory were right, we should be able simply to describe the medium in which our experiences are painted. But the act-object theory is false. Phenomenal states are not objects viewed by a mental eye but vehicles through which we view the external world.

Reply: My answer parallels what I said in response to representationalism. When we have phenomenal experiences, we are, in a sense, aware of *them*, not (merely) of what they represent. Even if we don't view our phenomenal experiences with an inner eye, it doesn't follow that they lack introspectable intrinsic qualities. Suppose we think of experiences as inner paintings with no viewers. Paintings still have qualities, such as their brush-strokes, that go beyond what they represent. So rejecting the act-object theory of perception has no bearing on the question of why we can't dis-cover the neural brushstrokes of our phenomenal states.

I don't presume that these replies are decisive. Some version of one of these proposals might be salvageable. I offer this brief survey to indicate that the so-lution to the inverse knowledge argument is not totally obvious. In any case, I want to propose a different response.

To begin with, I think that the act-object theory of perception contains an important kernel of truth. In the AIR theory, consciousness arises when a per-ceptual representation (an object) is made available to working memory via at-tention (an act of awareness). Structurally, the view conforms to old-fashioned act-object theories, but there are also important differences. Old-fashioned act-object theorists believed in sense-data (e.g., Russell, 1912; Broad, 1925; Price, 1932). Sense-data were presumed to be nonphysical entities that have no inten-tional content and literally have properties such as redness, roundness, and so on. Perceptual representations, in my view, are physically realized states that ordinarily represent features of the world. In these respects, they are quite unlike sense-data. I also depart from the old-fashioned act-object theory in another way. Sense-data enthusiasts claimed that the act of perception involves the assignment of meaning to otherwise meaningless sense-data. Perceptual acts are interpretive acts. In that view, we inspect our sense-data and then figure out what they tell us about the outside world. In the view that I favor, the act of awareness is not an interpretive act; it is the act of maintaining availability. The working-memory states that do this work are not, I have suggested, representa-tions of perceptual states; they are instructions that keep perceptual represen-tations active and accessible. This is an inversion of sense-data theory. In that approach, the objects of perception are contentless, and the acts confer con-tent; in my approach, the objects of perception are (ordinarily) contentful, and the acts are contentless. With this inversion, we can begin to discern a solution to the Inverse Mary problem.

The Inverse Mary problem arises because we seem to be able to inspect our perceptual states. If we are inspecting them, and if inspection is direct, then we should be able to identify their brainy features. But I think that inspection is an illusion. What seems like the inspection of a perceptual state is not a semantic or epistemic act but rather an act of selective entrainment. We maintain one portion of a percept, and then another, and then another, making each avail-able for further processing in turn. What seems like inspecting is just a form of moving about.

When we perceive a red surface, we form a perceptual representation of that surface, and this results in an experience of the phenomenal quality we call "redness." What is it to know what the quality of redness is like? It is to maintain that representation. What is the phenomenal quality of redness? It is the one I attend to in this way. Knowing what redness is like is a matter of knowing how to maintain or focus in on features of a perceptual representation. If I show you a field of colored shapes and say, "Look at the red ones," you will respond by using a stored perceptual template to search for matching features in your perceptual representation, and those matches will lead you to attend selectively to the red shapes. Top-down visual search engages the mechanisms of maintenance. You seek out features by finding your way about. Once you find those features, you can maintain their availability by fixing attention.

Let's suppose this picture is right. We can then explain why Inverse Mary cannot discover brainy features in any of the perceptual states that she experiences. Inverse Mary is directly aware of her perceptual states, which are made conscious through a relation of availability. Her perceptual states *are* brain states, so Inverse Mary is directly aware of her brain states. But her grasp of the "features" in those states is not a matter of representing them; it is a matter of maintaining them. So Mary cannot read off the brainy properties of her experience. She has access to her brain states, because consciousness entails accessibility, and this access can be described as direct, because it is not mediated by representations. But for that very reason, access doesn't reveal essence.

The claim that Mary has direct access to her phenomenal states might appear to imply that she can introspect their essence, but directness actually explains why this is impossible. In other words, unmediated knowledge is the key to explaining nonrevelatory knowledge. Philosophers traditionally try to explain unmediated knowledge by analogy to *directly seeing* our phenomenal states, and this conflicts with the idea that phenomenal knowledge is nonrevelatory. But the mental maintenance explains unmediated knowledge by analogy to the idea of keeping our phenomenal states in place. Phenomenal states are things we have, not things we examine, which is why they don't reveal their essences.

This solution to the Inverse Mary problem resembles the fifth proposal that I canvassed above. In line with that proposal, I am suggesting that conscious states are not inspected objects in a mental gallery. But I am not suggesting that we drop an act-object theory of perception. Conscious perception is characteristically a matter of performing acts of awareness on mental objects. The major fault of the traditional act-object theory is that the acts of awareness were regarded as interpretive. If we drop that assumption, there is no longer any pressure to think that we should be able to inspect the medium of our percepts.

I suggested above that the mental maintenance story can be used to show that the knowledge argument is unsound. In this section, I argued that it also satisfies the constraints on an adequate solution to the knowledge argument. Other replies to Jackson fail to meet one or more constraints. Mental maintenance does better.

3.3. A MIXED STRATEGY

In discussing other replies to Jackson, I said that three explanatory constructs appeared particularly attractive: modes of presentation, abilities, and acquaintance. But I also argued that none of these strategies is adequate, because all do well with some constraints at the expense of others. Since the mental maintenance account can accommodate all of the constraints, it must follow that it differs from these three strategies. Different but not entirely new. By way of conclusion, I want to suggest that mental maintenance can be regarded as a hybrid solution. Each strategy gets something right, but they must be integrated in order to provide a satisfying account of what Mary learns.

Although phenomenal knowledge does not involve new representations in my view, Mary can be said to acquire new demonstrative thoughts when she leaves the room. I said above that these thoughts work by exemplifying phenomenal qualities rather than representing them. On the face of it, the move away from representation may look like a significant departure from the mode of presentational strategy, but that is only because modes of presentation are often equated with inner symbols. The notion of "presentation" need not be equated with representation. It can also subsume cases of exemplification, as when I present a color chip on being asked which color I will use to paint my house. Earlier, I called this a Goodmanian mode of presentation. Mary uses a Goodmanian mode when she mentally points to red.

Even more obviously, Mary gains a new ability. Maintenance is an activity, and knowing how to maintain a percept is a kind of procedural knowledge. When Mary maintains red for the first time, she is exercising an ability she didn't have before. She was able to maintain other experiences but not colors, because you cannot maintain what you have not had.

In addition, Mary can be said to acquire a new epistemic relation to her perceptual states when she leaves the room. When she consciously sees colors, they become available to working memory, and when she encodes them in working memory, she becomes aware of them. This awareness gives her unmediated access to their qualities. This can be regarded as a kind of acquaintance. It is not a kind of acquaintance that can be substituted by descriptive knowledge. It essentially requires a direct causal relation with its object.

Putting this together, Mary acquires a new mode of presentation, a new ability, and a new epistemic relation. The mode of presentation arises on exercising an ability, which acquaints her with a phenomenal quality. This can also be stated using the language of mental pointing. The mode of presentation is the percept that has been pointed to, the ability is the capacity to point, and acquaintance consists in the pointing relation. It's in the nature of pointing that we need all three. Philosophers sometimes ask whether Mary learns a new fact or a new way of representing old facts. Answering this question often involves stipulating a theory of facts, and such stipulations are often used to dictate a response to the knowledge argument. This approach may look like a verbal trick, and I've tried to avoid taking a stance on what facts are. Now I think we can see that the issue of new facts versus new representations is a red herring. In a sense, Mary gains neither. In learning what it's like, Mary simply has an experience and points to it.

The mixed strategy that I am advocating implies that the strategies surveyed above were all on the right track. Each strategy compensates for the shortcomings of the others. For example, the mode of presentation strategy, when taken on its own, fares badly with possessive knowledge, since representation modes can represent objects in their absence. Acquaintance overcomes this limitation. But acquaintance does badly with nonrevelatory knowledge. Abilities solve this problem, because they show that we can know our phenomenal states without inspecting them. Abilities, in turn, stumble when it comes to demonstrative knowledge, but modes of presentation do well with that. And so on. By bringing these together, we can best explain what Mary learns, while blocking the threat to physicalism.

In conclusion, the mental maintenance story has something in common with each of the prevailing strategies for responding to the knowledge argument. Because it borrows from all, it overcomes the problems of each. The mixed strategy is not an unholy jumble but a unified whole. Maintenance is a process (hence ability) of encoding (hence relation) sensory states (presentations). Although it is a cornerstone of memory research, maintenance is not a process that philosophers have thought about. Philosophers have tended to focus on more familiar constructs, such as representation, imagination, and concepts. This limited arsenal has weakened the campaign against dualism. Philosophical argumentation can be used to help show that these tools are too limited and to identify broad constraints on a theory of phenomenal knowledge compatible with physicalism. But empirical investigation of the processes underlying awareness of our phenomenal states adds much to the philosophical discussion. Physicalists can take heart in the discovery that a neurobiologically grounded account of awareness has features that can meet all of the constraints that philosophical theories have had such difficulty satisfying.

Conclusion

AIR COMPARED

Trendiness has its advantages. These last decades have seen a massive interdisciplinary effort to identify the psychological and neural correlates of conscious experience, and those efforts have paid off. Although controversy abounds, there is now an ocean of evidence from which we can distill detailed conclusions about where and when consciousness arises. In these chapters, I offered my take on what the empirical literature shows. The AIR theory is intended as a synthesis. It brings together elements that have been articulated, defended, and tested by many researchers in different fields. The elements have also been challenged, and I've argued that the most obvious objections can be met. There are, of course, other theories of consciousness on the market and other interpretations of the empirical literature. In this concluding chapter, I will review how the AIR theory compares with alternatives and meets the desiderata set out in chapter 1. I will end with a list of unfinished business.

1. The Desiderata

A complete theory of consciousness must take a stance on a number of different issues. In chapter 1, I identified seven issues of particular importance, and for each, I articulated a constraint on what stance should be taken. We can now see how the AIR theory fares.

1.1. QUALIA

A theory of consciousness should deliver an account of what qualia are and how to account for differences between qualitative states. I defended the following desideratum, which a theory of qualia would ideally meet:

Subjective Character. On an adequate theory, qualitative character should be located in states that represent appearances, and those states have their character only when they are conscious.

According to the AIR theory, conscious states are located at an intermediate level of representation within hierarchically organized sensory systems (chapter 2). Here I follow Jackendoff (1987). Let's see now how this story satisfies subjective character.

The first thing to note is that intermediate-level representations represent the world from a particular point of view. This alone does not entail that they represent appearances, because it is conceivable that viewpoints could be represented in a more objective way—think of an overhead map, with an arrow labeled, "You Are Here." Intermediate-level representations are not like that. They are perspectival in at least the weak sense that they capture the world as it appears from a particular position and thus fails to represent the intrinsic structure of a perceived object. When you consciously see a cube, some of its sides are invisible, and its visible sides are rarely square in appearance.

I would submit that intermediate-level representations are also perspectival in a deeper sense. The colors we see do not correspond to natural kinds in the world and are thus response-dependent, and the shapes we encounter in experience have no intrinsic dimensions. The viewpoint-specific representation of a cube may represent its objective size (perhaps each face is one foot square), but it does so by presenting an appearance whose sides cannot be measured in feet or any other objective units. We cannot even specify this geometry by appeal to visual angle, because an object that subtends the same angle may grow or shrink in our visual field as we shift attention. When this happens, the apparent length changes, even though the visual angle remains constant, and none of these apparent lengths can be said to misrepresent the line; they all capture ways in which it appears (see Block, 2010).

The AIR theory also satisfies the second clause of the subjective character desideratum. In chapter 4, I proposed that intermediate-level representations are neurally implemented by populations of neurons, and these populations activate collectively when, and only when, we are conscious. They can still serve perception when they do not activate collectively, but under those conditions, they lack qualitative character. Thus, consciousness is needed for qualia. This is a substantive claim because the theory of qualia that I offered is not defined in terms of consciousness, and the theory of consciousness is not defined with reference to qualia. Other accounts, such as HOT theories, also observe this distinction, noting that it is one thing to specify how a state becomes conscious and another thing to specify its qualitative character (notice that every state becomes conscious in the same way, but conscious states differ in character). But other accounts go too far in cleaving apart character and consciousness, implying that the former can exist without the latter. For example, quality space theories and representationalism imply that unconscious states have a qualitative character. This may be a coherent position, but I see little reason to accept it. Qualitative character is the major source of mystery in consciousness studies: qualia lead us to ask why one mental state feels different from another. But this question never arises for those states that are inaccessible to consciousness. Should we say that those states have qualitative character that we just never learn about? That seems unmotivated. It is more plausible that qualia come into being with consciousness. This rules out representationalism and quality space theory. The AIR theory says that qualitative states represent, but their character is not exhausted by what they represent. Character is a dynamic property of the vehicles that do the representing.

1.2. CONSCIOUSNESS

A theory of qualia specifies which mental states have qualitative character and what that character consists of, but it does not specify when those states become conscious—or, more accurately, the conditions under which mental states that are potentially qualitative become qualitative. For that, we need a theory of what makes mental states conscious. I offered the following constraint:

> **First-Order Consciousness**. An adequate theory should explain how mental states can become conscious without requiring that they are represented by some other mental states.

According to the AIR theory, consciousness arises when and only when intermediate-level representations are modulated by attention (chapter 3). Attention, in turn, is defined as a process that makes these representations available for encoding in working memory. Actual encoding is not necessary, but availability is. This explains why some conscious states are not readily reportable, but all are available to become reportable, which is not true of unconscious states. Reportability entails consciousness because reportable states are those that have gotten into working memory, and getting there requires becoming conscious along the way.

Many consciousness researchers appeal to attention. It plays a central role in some psychological theories (Baars, 1988; Mack and Rock, 1998), neuroscientific theories (Crick and Koch, 1990; Posner, 1994), and philosophical theories (Evans, 1982; Peacocke, 1989; Lycan, 1996; Mole, 2008). These accounts differ in how they define attention and in whether they claim that attention is necessary and sufficient for consciousness, but all agree that attention matters. The account is at odds with those who argue for a strong dissociation between attention and consciousness (e.g., Koch and Tsuchiya, 2007).

Crucially for the desideratum, this is a first-order theory of consciousness. Attention does not involve meta-representation. The AIR theory also rejects the conjecture that consciousness requires concepts, which is a commitment of the HOT theory. It shares with Lycan's HOP theory an emphasis on attention but denies that we have inner monitors that represent perceptual states. AIR also bears a resemblance to dispositional higher-order representational theories, which say that consciousness requires not an actual meta-representation but the mere possibility of one (Carruthers, 2000). But being available to working memory, which AIR requires, is not equivalent to being available for meta-representation. Working memory does not encode perceptual states by representing them. Working-memory representations normally represent the world, not the mind. These representations also have a coarser grain than the intermediate-level states that become conscious.

The AIR theory is closest to other first-order availability theories, such as Tye's (1995) PANIC theory, Kirk's (1994) direct activity theory, or Baars's (1988) global workspace theory. All of these accounts say that consciousness arises when perceptual states become available for use in cognition, but they also imply that actual encoding in cognitive systems is required. Tye (2010) also explicitly denies that attention is what makes availability possible. The AIR theory might be described as a dispositional global workspace theory, although there is one empirical issue that would need to be resolved before that claim could stick. Working memory is sometimes believed to be subdivided into a number of modality-specific storage buffers (Baddeley, 2007). Normally, information in one of these buffers can be used for cognitive tasks and is, in that sense, part of a global workspace. But in principle, we can imagine these buffers operating without globally broadcasting, perhaps as the result of lesions that disconnect them from each other. The global workspace theory can be read as implying that consciousness would break down under such circumstances, but I doubt that this is the case. I think that the global information processing that is permitted by consciousness is both indirect and contingent.

1.3. COGNITION

A theory of consciousness must say something about scope and limits. In particular, it must say whether consciousness is limited to perception or also extends to include thought. In criticizing the global workspace theory, I endorsed:

> **Noncentrality**. An adequate theory should restrict consciousness to processes that lie outside of those systems that underwrite our highest cognitive capacities.

This might be taken to imply that there is no cognitive phenomenology. But that doesn't follow. Rather, noncentrality implies that there is no distinctive cognitive phenomenology; thoughts get felt by producing sensory images.

This is precisely the view that I defend (chapter 5). Cognitive phenomenology is always reducible to sensory features, including the sounds of inner speech. All consciousness is perceptual. Indeed, all consciousness resides at the intermediate level, which means that even our more abstract perceptual states lie outside of consciousness.

The AIR theory differs from those that allow for distinction cognitive phenomenology (e.g., Bayne, 2009; Pitt, 2004; Siewert, 2009). Baars (2002) also suggests that thoughts can be conscious and that consciousness arises with central encoding, although he would admit that most cognitive processes take place outside of consciousness.

AIR echoes those who say that phenomenal states are nonconceptual (e.g., Tye, 1995). However, I think that perceptual states can be used for cognition, so it would be more accurate to say that phenomenal states are always phenomenally type-identical to states that are nonconceptual.

The commitment to noncentrality is also shared with Lamme (2001), who argues that consciousness is brought about by back projections in sensory cortex, and Block (2007), who is sympathetic to Lamme's account and argues that phenomenal states can arise without accessing central systems. Block and Lamme may push too far, however, by implying that availability to central systems is not necessary. Without availability, we would have no way of knowing whether a perceptual state was conscious. All of the evidence for phenomenal consciousness without access consciousness is, of necessity, evidence for states that are available for recognition, just not recognized, such as the unreported letters in the Sperling (1960) studies. Sperling proved that all of these letters were available by asking people to report using poststimulus cues. In sharp contrast, letters that are masked are totally unavailable, and we have no reason to think that they are conscious. In summary, noncentrality should not be taken as the view that central systems are unimportant for phenomenal consciousness.

1.4. FUNCTION

Some researchers believe that consciousness has no function, and others believe that it exists to serve the highest aspects of human cognition. I argued for something in between these extremes:

> **Basic Function**. On an adequate theory, the function of consciousness should be identified with something that is more basic than high-level interpretation.

AIR satisfies this requirement by relating consciousness to action. Conscious states are a menu for practical deliberation. They make perspectival representations available to working memory, because perspectival representations are actionable, and working memory is where deliberative decision making takes place.

This theory of function parallels others in the literature (e.g., James, 1890; Tye, 1995; Glover, 2002). It differs from those that say that consciousness is primarily for object recognition (Milner and Goodale, 1995) or those that say that its functions are primarily, if not exclusively, cognitive (Baars, 2002). I think that there has been too much focus on cognition in consciousness studies. The fact that consciousness is restricted to perspectival representations should be a tipoff that it might have evolved for practical ends. This focus on action also constitutes a point of contact between AIR and enactive theories of consciousness, but I resist going that far (chapter 6). Consciousness contributes to decision making, but once we have decided what to do, the fine-tuned changes in motor actions need not contribute to experience. In fact, given how little control we have over such movements, it might be a bad idea to include them in a stream of information that gains access to decision centers.

The theory of function that I favor differs most dramatically from narrative approaches, which state that consciousness is primarily in the business of self-interpretation (Gazzaniga, 1988). But I actually think that these theories hit on something important. If consciousness is a menu for deliberative action, then the actions we choose have conscious antecedents. Suppose someone asks why you acted in a certain way. A natural response strategy would be to survey, in memory, the conscious states that preceded what you did. Of course, you can't access the actual deliberation process, so the contents of your survey will be incomplete. This leads people to make errors, even confabulations, in explaining action. Thus, Gazzaniga is right to think that consciousness plays a role in action explanation, and he is right to place emphasis on the interpretive nature of that activity. But rather than showing that consciousness is designed to serve self-interpretation, these observations actually point to the conclusion that consciousness plays a more primitive role in action determination.

1.5. THE SELF

There is a Cartesian intuition that consciousness always contains an awareness of the conscious subject. I argued that we should resist this idea and accept:

> **Selfless Experience**. An adequate theory should allow that consciousness can arise without any experience of the self.

In chapter 7, I pushed this even further and argued that all consciousness is selfless in some sense. There is no item in experience that corresponds to the subjective I.

This claim coheres with the AIR theory's ambition to explain all consciousness in terms of intermediate-level perception. The strong form of selfless experience also situates the theory within the Humean tradition of skepticism about the phenomenal self. AIR is incompatible with Cartesian theories, and Kantian theories, in some readings. It also goes against contemporary theories that look for a self in experience, such as same-order representationalism (Kriegel, 2005) and Damasio's (1999) account.

But AIR is not completely selfless. The rejection of a phenomenal I is compatible with the view that experience is implicitly subjective. The strongly

perspectival character of phenomenal states illustrates one way in which consciousness essentially embodies subjectivity. With the AIR theory, every conscious state is a point of view.

1.6. UNITY

In chapter 1, we saw that Crick and Koch (1990) attempt to equate consciousness with binding. I objected that binding is neither necessary nor sufficient for
consciousness but that there is a related form of integration, which any theory
should explain:

> **Conscious Unity**. An adequate theory should explain how states that
> are distributed in space and time get integrated into unified conscious
> experiences.

Unity has often been explained by appeal to a single subject of experience, but
echoing the skepticism about conscious selves in chapter 7, I expressed doubt
about such accounts in chapter 8. I proposed that unity can be explained in
terms of attention. This link has been suggested in the past (see Picard, 1921),
and it deserves a revival. If I am right, unity is not an add-on to the AIR theory
but a consequence of it. If conscious states are AIRs, then conscious states can
be individuated by co-attention. Two experiences are part of a whole if they are
attended together. I argued that co-attention can be identified with resonance;
unified experiences are those that resonate causally under attentional modulation. In neural terms, this means states that are phase-locked in the gamma
band. Thus, Crick and Koch were wrong to equate gamma with binding, but
they weren't far off the mark, given the role of gamma in unity. One might
express this by saying that gamma doesn't explain local binding, but it explains
global binding—the way multiple conscious states can feel as if they are part of
a single conscious state.

The resonance story works for synchronic unity and for unity across time.
But I also argued that unity is not guaranteed. Two conscious states in the same
individual at the same time may fail to resonate. We cannot directly observe
such failures, however, because when we introspectively investigate whether two
states are unified, they begin to resonate. This is a case in which the AIR account leads to a surprising prediction, which may be borne out on reflection by
familiar examples. On reflection, I argued that disunity may be a common
aspect of experience.

1.7. LEVELS

The scientific study of consciousness has been particularly preoccupied with
identifying neural correlates. I suggested that the search be guided by the
following objective:

Multilevel Integration. An adequate theory should identify neural corre-lates of consciousness, and these should help account for some observable aspect(s) of conscious experience.

The AIR theory satisfies this condition in two ways (chapter 4). First, AIR appeals to the empirically supported conjecture that gamma synchrony is a correlate of attention. Once we relate synchrony to attention, we can see that it helps to explain one of the most important psychological characteristics of consciousness: when we attend, information becomes available to working memory. Synchrony provides a mechanism. Synchronized neurons create a strong signal against a noisy neural background; the increase in order allows for communication, making the neurons that fire together candidates for for-ward propagation into brain structures involved in working memory. Many others have conjectured that gamma synchrony is important for conscious-ness (e.g., Crick and Koch, 1990; Engel et al., 1999; Gaillard et al., 2009), and the AIR theory belongs in that tradition. The main contribution is that the AIR theory equates gamma with attention, whereas other researchers, such as Crick and Koch, have mischaracterized gamma as a mechanism for binding.

The second way the AIR theory provides multilevel integration has to do with population coding. Recall that the correlates of perspectival representa-tions are neural populations (chapter 4). As mentioned, when this hypothesis is combined with the claim that consciousness requires synchrony, we can ac-count for the fact that qualia require consciousness, because neural populations operate as such when synchronized. Conversely, consciousness requires qualia, because perspectival neural populations are the cells that become available for working memory when we attend. In many theories, qualia are defined inde-pendently of consciousness—a distinction I wholeheartedly endorse—but no other theory explains why the two go together. We cannot be conscious without qualia, and we cannot have qualia without consciousness. AIR explains this.

The multilevel integration desideratum is stated in a way that implies uni-directional explanation. Neural correlates are said to account for psychological observations. But it must be emphasized that this can also go the other way. The psychological level sheds light on the neuroscience by explaining what all of the microprocesses are up to. Synchrony accounts for attention, but the need for attention, or information flow, also accounts for synchrony. So the desider-atum should really be understood as a plea for multilevel integration. The neu-rofunctional theory of the mind-body relation that I defend in chapter 9 is intended to correct the view that finding neural correlates is somehow more important than finding psychological correlates in the science of consciousness. An adequate theory should be stated at more than one level and should specify how different levels are interrelated. In this respect, the theory differs from those that focus too exclusively on psychological-level descriptions (such as higher-order-representation theories) or on neural realizers (such as Lamme's back-projection account).

1.8. PHENOMENAL KNOWLEDGE

The neurofunctional approach presupposes that consciousness is part of the physical world. Dualists try to refute physicalism using a variety of different arguments, and these tend to hinge on the premise that we can know, conceive, or imagine phenomenal states in a way that does not reveal any physical essences or, conversely, that we can learn about the physical correlates of a conscious state without knowing what it is like. To escape refutation, physicalists must show that this fact is compatible with physicalism:

> **Phenomenal Knowledge**. An adequate theory should provide an account of how we epistemically access phenomenal states that blocks standard arguments for dualism.

There are three common strategies for satisfying this requirement. Some authors have suggested that phenomenal knowledge is a form of know-how and therefore does not involve any descriptive information that would reveal the neural essence of phenomenal states (Lewis, 1988; Nemirow, 1990). Some have suggested that phenomenal knowledge involves a relationship of acquaintance, where acquaintance is defined as nondescriptive (Conee, 1994). Still others have argued that phenomenal knowledge involves a special class of demonstrative concepts that refer by pointing rather than describing (Loar, 1990; Papineau, 2002). I defended a view that integrates all three of these ideas, which I call mental maintenance (chapter 10). It draws on research in cognitive neuroscience, which suggests that we have mechanisms in working memory that sustain perceptual states rather than representing them. These maintenance mechanisms do not reveal anything about the essence of the states to which they point. They allow us to know what our phenomenal states are like without providing any descriptive information that would allow us to infer that those states are physical.

The mental maintenance account builds on leading proposals but compensates for their shortcomings by combining resources. It is also more firmly grounded in empirical research. The account offers a response to dualist arguments, while helping to explain why dualism is so tempting.

These chapters also implicitly argue against dualism by illustrating how richly informative research on the functional and neural correlates can be. Scientific research on consciousness has taught us a tremendous amount about the conditions under which consciousness arises and the neural mechanisms that account for behavioral observations. Given the tremendous success of this research, dualism begins to look quaint. Dualism could be true, but it is not an explanatory theory. It teaches us very little about the nature of consciousness beyond the blanket claim about its metaphysical status. Even if dualism were true, we would learn more about consciousness by studying its physical correlates than by rehearsing metaphysical arguments. This point applies equally to physicalists who spend excessive time battling dualism. I am not suggesting that the discovery of nonphysical properties would lack interest or import, only that, ironically, dualist arguments take us farther away from understanding mentality by raising broad issues about mental essence rather than precise questions about mental activity.

Still, debates about dualism have some benefit. They lead us to theories of phenomenal knowledge, and they help to explain why consciousness seems like such a mystery to begin with. If it weren't for the dualist impulse, this topic would attract less interest. That does not mean that consciousness studies would be uninteresting. I hope to have shown that there are many important debates that have little do with dualism. Can thoughts be conscious? Do we experience the self? Does consciousness depend on attention? Does it have a function? Fortunately, the agenda of consciousness studies has broadened to include such questions. Dualists and physicalists can join forces in tackling these. Those who do quickly discover that they are as contentious, as captivating, and as hard as questions about how minds could be made of matter.

2. What Next?

The theory that I have been defending can be summarized as follows. Conscious states are attended intermediate-level representations, or AIRs. Attention is a neurofunctional kind that allows information to get from perceptual areas to working memory by means of gamma-band neural synchrony. The intermediate level is a neurofunctional kind that can be defined as a perceptual-processing stage that uses viewpoint-specific representations of microfeatures implemented by populations of neurons. All consciousness is perceptual; there is no distinctive cognitive phenomenology or any phenomenal self. The teleological and causal function of consciousness is to serve as a menu for action. We know what our conscious states are like by means of mental maintenance, a form of epistemic access that does not disclose their neural nature.

This is my best assessment of what we've learned from the last quarter-century of consciousness research. The theory builds on many others, developed by linguists, philosophers, psychologists, and neuroscientists. It has been a central aim of this book to establish that we've learned a great deal and that a complete account of the nature of consciousness may be within reach. That said, we must also be mindful of how much work still needs to be done. I conclude with four outstanding questions for consciousness research.

The first question concerns senses other than vision. Almost all of the empirical research reviewed here comes from vision science. In chapter 2, I suggested that an intermediate level can be found in other senses and seems to be privileged with respect to consciousness. But more evidence would be needed to make a strong case. Questions also arise about whether attention has common correlates in all of the modalities and whether intermediate-level representations get synchronized with each other at such long distances. There is evidence for a link between attention and gamma in sound (Debener et al., 2003), touch (Bauer et al., 2006), and perhaps smell (Beshel, Kopell, and Kay, 2007). The account of conscious unity sketched above depends on this, but the evidence lags behind.

The second question, first noted in chapter 3, concerns diffuse attention. The AIR theory assumes that we are conscious of features that are not focally attended. Attention can be allocated to a large region of space, in this view, bringing a richly detailed scene into consciousness even if only one of the items is selected for further processing. To date, there is very little research on diffuse attention (Jonides, 1983; Burnham et al., 2006). It would be nice to establish that diffuse and selective attention involve overlapping mechanisms. One intriguing finding is that meditation seems to induce increased gamma activity, and this has been attributed to the fact that meditation increases attention (Lutz et al., 2004). But unlike most laboratory studies of attention, which require subjects to focus on a specific object or location, the form of attention in meditation is often described as diffuse (e.g., Welwood, 1977).

A third issue, encountered in chapter 4, concerns neural codes. It is humbling to realize how little we know about how neurons communicate. I speculated that population codes underlie conscious experience, but this needs empirical support. There is evidence that population coding is used in taste (Carleton, Accolla, and Simon, 2010), smell (Stopfer, Jayaraman, and Laurent, 2003), touch (Peterson, Panzeri, and Diamon, 2002), and sound (Bartho et al., 2009). The coding strategies across modalities are often similar (e.g., Yau et al., 2009), but it is equally important to investigate whether the codes used across modalities differ in some way that allows us to tell them apart. Further research could also help reveal how the brain distinguishes sensory qualities within a modality, such as blue and red. Are the codes for similar qualities more alike? Do compounds of two qualities preserve the neural population structures associated with each?

Finally, there are ways in which the AIR theory can be applied to answer perennial questions about which creatures are conscious. Are human infants conscious? Are nonhuman animals conscious? It is difficult to answer these questions on the basis of behavior alone. Attention is difficult to distinguish from orienting, and working memory is difficult to distinguish from what ethologists call reference memory, a longer-term storage of objects and their locations (Green and Stanton, 1989). To search for consciousness in infants and animals, it would help to look for the neural signatures of consciousness. In infant brains, connections between areas are underdeveloped (Homae et al., 2010), and this may limit the capacity for allocating attention. The mammalian brain is similar across species, and we do know that gamma activity can be found in rodents (e.g., Vianney-Rodrigues, Iancu, and Welsh, 2011). But there are also differences across mammalian brains. At a cellular level, human visual streams are even subtly different from those of great apes and monkeys (Preuss and Coleman, 2002). We don't yet know whether these differences have functional implications or implications for consciousness, but given the large numbers of similarities, it is likely that primates and perhaps all mammals are conscious. Many of the experiments cited in developing the AIR theory were performed on mammals, and the extraordinary lessons we have learned from that research may ultimately bear on the ethics of its continuation. What about birds? Their brains are built out of structures that are related to the mammalian subcortex, but these structures have evolved to function like the mammalian neocortex, resulting in working-memory and attention capacities that look surprisingly similar to our own (Güntürkün, 2005; Kirsch et al., 2008; Milmine, Rose, and Colombo, 2008). Cephalopods engage in strategic hunting behavior, and that may require attending to and briefly storing information about the spatial locations of their prey. The brain mechanisms of octopus working memory have been explored (Shomrat et al., 2008). There has also been work on the neural mechanisms of short-term memory in crabs (Tomsic, Berón de Astrada, and Sztarker, 2003). Pushing things even farther, there are studies of attention in fruit flies, and their capacity to attend is linked to genes that allow for short-term memory (van Swinderen, 2007). Obviously, there is also great variation between us and these other creatures. Given the doubts raised about multiple realizability in chapter 9, it wouldn't be surprising to discover that only mammals have what it takes to be conscious on the AIR theory. But there is also astonishing continuity across animal phyla, so it is important to investigate the extent of similarity with respect to the mechanisms of consciousness. Then we can decide whether we can eat octopuses with impunity.

These are just a few of the important puzzles that remain. The AIR theory raises more questions than it answers. More work lies ahead of us than behind. But I hope that the theory also shows how far consciousness research has come. We can envision theories emerging that gain widespread acceptance and enjoy powerful empirical support. We can imagine textbooks on consciousness that report a received view rather than counting controversies and multiplying mysteries. I'd like to think that AIR, in part or in whole, will be woven into the textbook story, but even if it isn't, the science on which it builds can be seen as a stairway that is taking us to that destination.

REFERENCES

Adolphs, R. (2002). Recognizing emotion from facial expressions: Psychological and neurological mechanisms. *Behavioral and Cognitive Neuroscience Reviews* 1: 21–62.

Aglioti, S., DeSouza, J.F.X., & Goodale, M.A. (1995). Size-contrast illusions deceive the eye but not the hand. *Current Biology* 5: 679–685.

Aha, D.W., & Goldstone, R.L. (1992). Concept learning and flexible weighting. *Proceedings of the 14th Annual Conference of the Cognitive Science Society*, 534–539. Hillsdale, NJ: Lawrence Erlbaum.

Akins, K. (2001). More than mere coloring: A dialog between philosophy and neuroscience on the nature of spectral vision. In S. Fitzpatrick & J.T. Breur, eds., *Carving Our Destiny*, 77–114. Washington, DC: Joseph Henry.

Andrews, T.J., & Schluppeck, D. (2004). Neural responses to Mooney images reveal a modular representation of faces in human visual cortex. *Neuroimage* 21: 91–98.

Angell, J.A. (1911). Imageless thought. *Psychological Review* 18: 295–322.

Anton-Erxleben, K., Henrich, C., & Treue, S. (2007). Attention changes perceived size of moving visual patterns. *Journal of Vision* 7: 1–9.

Armstrong, D. (1968). *A Materialist Theory of Mind*. London: Routledge and Kegan Paul.

Arnell, K.M., Killman, K.V., & Fijavz, D. (2007). Blinded by emotion: Target misses follow attention capture by arousing distractors in RSVP. *Emotion* 7: 465–477.

Ashby, F.G., & Casale, M. (2003). The cognitive neuroscience of implicit category learning. In L. Jimenez, ed., *Attention and Implicit Learning*, 108–141. Amsterdam: John Benjamins.

Awh, E., Vogel, E.K., & Oh, S.H. (2006). Interactions between attention and working memory. *Neuroscience* 139: 201–208.

Ayotte, J., Peretz, I., Rousseau, I., Bard, C., & Bojanowski, M. (2000). Patterns of music agnosia associated with middle cerebral artery infarcts. *Brain* 123: 1926–1938.

Baars, B.J. (1988). *A Cognitive Theory of Consciousness*. Cambridge, UK: Cambridge University Press.

———. (2002). The conscious access hypothesis: Origins and recent evidence. *Trends in Cognitive Science* 6: 47–52.

Baars, B.J., & Franklin, S. (2009). Consciousness is computational: The LIDA model of Global Workspace Theory. *International Journal of Machine Consciousness* 1: 23–32.

Bach-y-Rita, P. (1972). *Brain Mechanisms in Sensory Substitution*. New York: Academic.

Backus, B.T., Fleet, D.J., Parker, A.J., & Heeger, D.J. (2001). Human cortical activity correlates with stereoscopic depth perception. *Journal of Neurophysiology* 86: 2054–2068.

Baddeley, A.D. (2007). *Working Memory, Thought and Action*. Oxford: Oxford University Press.

Bahrami, B., Carmel, D., Walsh, V., Rees, G., & Lavie, N. (2008). Spatial attention can modulate unconscious orientation processing. *Perception* 37: 1520–1528.

Bahrami, B., Vetter, P., Spolaore, E., Pagano, S., Butterworth, B., & Rees, G. (2010). Unconscious numerical priming despite interocular suppression. *Psychological Science* 21: 224–233.

Ballard, D.H. (1991). Animate vision. *Artificial Intelligence* 48: 57–86.

Ballard, D.H., Hayhoe, M.M., & Pelz, J.B. (1994). Memory representations in natural tasks. *Journal of Cognitive Neuroscience* 7: 66–80.

Bao, Y., Zhou, J., & Fu, L. (2004). Aging and the time course of inhibition of return in a static environment. *Acta Neurobiologiea Experimentalis* 64: 403–414.

Barbas, H., & Mesulam, M.M. (1981). Organization of afferent input to subdivisions of area 8 in the rhesus monkey. *Journal of Comparative Neurology* 200: 407–431.

Barsalou, L.W. (1999). Perceptual symbol systems. *Behavioral and Brain Sciences* 22: 577–660.

Bartho, P., Curto, C., Luczak, A., Marguet, S.L., & Harris, K.D. (2009). Population coding of tone stimuli in auditory cortex: Dynamic rate vector analysis. *European Journal of Neuroscience* 30: 1767–1778.

Bauer, M., Oostenveld, R., Peeters, M., & Fries, P. (2006). Tactile spatial attention enhances gamma-band activity in somatosensory cortex and reduces low-frequency activity in parieto-occipital areas. *Journal of Neuroscience* 26: 490–501.

Baylis, G.C., & Driver, J. (2001). Shape-coding in IT cells generalizes over contrast and mirror reversal, but not figure-ground reversal. *Nature Neuroscience* 4: 937–942.

Bayne, T. (2004). Self-consciousness and the unity of consciousness. *Monist* 87: 219–236.

———. (2006). Phenomenology and the feeling of doing: Wegner on the conscious will. In S. Pockett, W.P. Banks, & S. Gallagher, eds., *Does Consciousness Cause Behavior?* 169–186. Cambridge, MA: MIT Press.

———. (2009). Perception and the reach of phenomenal consciousness. *Philosophical Quarterly* 59: 385–404.

Bayne, T., & Chalmers, D.J. (2003). What is the unity of consciousness? In A. Cleeremans, ed., *The Unity of Consciousness*, 23–58. Oxford: Oxford University Press.

Beanland, V., & Pammer, K. (2010). Looking without seeing or seeing without looking? Eye movements in sustained inattentional blindness. *Vision Research* 50: 977–998.

Bechtel, W. (2001). Cognitive neuroscience: Relating neural mechanisms and cognition. In P. Machamer, P. McLaughlin, & R. Grush, eds., *Philosophic Reflections on the Methods of Neuroscience*, 55–79. Pittsburgh: University of Pittsburgh Press.

Bechtel, W., & McCauley, R.N. (1999). Heuristic identity theory (or back to the future): The mind-body problem against the background of research strategies in cognitive neuroscience. In M. Hahn & S.C. Stones, eds., *Proceedings of the 21st Meeting of the Cognitive Science Society*, 67–72. Mahwah, NJ: Lawrence Erlbaum.

Bechtel, W., & Mundale, J. (1999). Multiple realizability revisited: Linking cognitive and neural states. *Philosophy of Science* 66: 175–207.

Beck, D.M., Rees, G., Frith, C.D., & Lavie, N. (2001). Neural correlates of change awareness and change blindness. *Nature Neuroscience* 4: 645–650.

Behrmann, M., & Tipper, S.P. (1994). Object-based attentional mechanisms: Evidence from patients with unilateral neglect. In C. Umilta & M. Moscovitch, eds., *Attention and Performance, Vol. 15: Conscious and Nonconscious Processing and Cognitive Functioning*, 351–375. Cambridge, MA: MIT Press.

Bermúdez, J.L. (1995). Nonconceptual content: From perceptual experience to subpersonal computational states. *Mind and Language* 10: 333–369.

Bertelson, P., Vroomen, J., De Gelder, B., & Driver, J. (2000). The ventriloquist effect does not depend on the direction of deliberate visual attention. *Perception and Psychophysics* 62: 321–332.

Berti, A., & Rizzolatti, G. (1992). Visual processing without awareness: Evidence from unilateral neglect. *Journal of Cognitive Neuroscience* 4: 345–351.

Berti, A., Oxbury, S., Oxbury, J., Affanni, P., Umilta, C., & Orlandi, L. (1999). Somatosensory extinction for meaningful objects in a patient with right hemispheric stroke. *Neuropsychologia* 37: 333–343.

Bertini, C., Leo, F., Avenanti, A., & Ladavas, E. (2010). Independent mechanisms for ventriloquism and multisensory integration as revealed by theta-burst stimulation. *European Journal of Neuroscience* 31: 1791–1799.

Beshel, J., Kopell, N., & Kay, L.M. (2007). Olfactory bulb gamma oscillations are enhanced with task demands. *Journal of Neuroscience* 27: 8358–8365.

Bhattacharya, J., Shams, L., & Shimojo, S. (2002). Sound-induced illusory flash perception: Role of gamma band responses. *NeuroReport* 13: 1727–1730.

Bickle, J. (1998). *Psychoneural Reduction: The New Wave*. Cambridge, MA: MIT Press.

Biederlack, J., Castelo-Branco, M., Neuenschwander, S., Wheeler, D.W., Singer, W., & Nikolic, D. (2006). Brightness induction: Rate enhancement and neuronal synchronization as complementary codes. *Neuron* 52: 1073–1083.

Biederman, I. (1987) Recognition-by-components: A theory of human image understanding. *Psychological Review* 94: 15–47.

Binda, P., Cicchini, G.M., Burr, D.C., & Morrone, M.C. (2009). Spatiotemporal distortions of visual perception at the time of saccades. *Journal of Neuroscience* 29: 13147–13157.

Binder, J.R., Frost, J.A., Hammeke, T.A., Bellgowan, P.S., Springer, J.A., Kaufman, J.N., & Possing, E.T. (2000). Human temporal lobe activation by speech and nonspeech sounds. *Cerebral Cortex* 10: 512–528.

Biran, I., & Chatterjee, A. (2004). Alien hand syndrome. *Archives of Neurology* 61: 292–294.

Bisiach, E. (1992). Understanding consciousness: Clues from unilateral neglect and related disorders. In A.D. Milner & M.D. Rugg, eds., *The Neuropsychology of Consciousness*, 113–139. London: Academic.

Bisiach, E., & Rusconi, M.L. (1990). Break-down of perceptual awareness in unilateral neglect. *Cortex* 26: 643–649.

Blakemore, S.-J., Wolpert, D.M., & Frith, C.D. (2000). Why can't you tickle yourself? *NeuroReport* 11: R11–16.

———. (2002). Abnormalities in the awareness of action. *Trends in Cognitive Science* 6: 237–242.

Blanke, O., & Metzinger, T. (2009). Full-body illusions and minimal phenomenal selfhood. *Trends in Cognitive Science* 13: 7–13.

Blatt, G.J., Andersen, R.A., & Stoner, G.R. (1990). Visual receptive field organization and cortico-cortical connections of the lateral intraparietal area (area LIP) in the macaque. *Journal of Comparative Neurology* 299: 421–445.

Block, N.J. (1978). Troubles with functionalism. In C.W. Savage, ed., *Minnesota Studies in the Philosophy of Science*, Vol. 9, 261–325. Minneapolis: University of Minnesota Press.

———. 1995. On a Confusion about the Function of Consciousness. *Behavioral and Brain Sciences* 18: 227–287.

————. (1996). Mental paint and mental latex. *Philosophical Issues* 7: 19–50.

————. (1998). Is experiencing just representing? *Philosophy and Phenomenological Research* 58: 663–670.

————. (2002). The harder problem of consciousness. *Journal of Philosophy* 99: 391–425.

————. (2005). Review of Alva Noë, *Action in Perception. Journal of Philosophy* CII: 259–272.

————. (2007). Consciousness, accessibility, and the mesh between psychology and neuroscience. *Behavioral and Brain Sciences* 30: 481–548.

————. (2010). Attention and mental paint. *Philosophical Issues* 20: 23–63.

————. (2011). Perceptual consciousness overflows cognitive access. *Trends in Cognitive Sciences* 15: 567–575.

Block, N.J., & Fodor, J. (1972). What psychological states are not. *Philosophical Review* 81: 159–181.

Block, N.J., & Stalnaker, R. (1999). Conceptual analysis, dualism, and the explanatory gap. *Philosophical Review* 108: 1–46.

Boatman, D., Freeman, J., Vining, E., Pulsifer, M., Miglioretti, D., Minahan, R., Carson, B., Brandt, J., & McKhann, G. (1999). Language recovery after left hemispherectomy in children with late-onset seizures. *Annals of Neurology* 46: 579–586.

Bodegard, A., Geyer, S., Grefkes, C., Zilles, K., Roland, P.E. (2001). Hierarchical processing of tactile shape in the human brain. *Neuron* 31: 317–328.

Bohlhalter, S., Fretz, C., & Weder, B. (2002). Hierarchical versus parallel processing in tactile object recognition: A behavioural-neuroanatomical study of apperceptive tactile agnosia. *Brain* 125: 2537–2548.

Bonneh, Y.S., Cooperman, A., & Sagi, D. (2001). Motion-induced blindness in normal observers. *Nature* 411: 798–801.

Bonnel, A.M., & Hafter, E.R. (1998). Divided attention between simultaneous auditory and visual signals. *Perception and Psychophysics* 60: 179–190.

Botvinick, M., & Cohen, J. (1998). Rubber hands "feel" touch that eyes see. *Nature* 391: 756.

Bouvier, S.E., & Engel, S.A. (2006). Behavioral deficits and cortical damage loci in cerebral achromatopsia. *Cerebral Cortex* 16: 183–191.

————. (2011). Delayed effects of attention in visual cortex as measured with fMRI. *Neuroimage* 57: 1177–1183.

Boyer, J.L., Harrison, S., & Ro, T. (2005). Unconscious processing of orientation and color without primary visual cortex. *Proceedings of the National Academy of the Sciences USA* 102: 16875–16879.

Braddick, O.J. (1973). The masking of apparent motion in random-dot patterns. *Vision Research* 13: 355–369.

Braun, A.R., Balkin, T.J., & Wesensten, N.J. (1997). Regional cerebral blood flow throughout the sleep-wake cycle: An H250 PET study. *Brain* 120: 1173–1193.

Breitmeyer, B.G., Ogmen, H., & Chen, J. (2004). Unconscious priming by color and form: Different processes and levels. *Consciousness and Cognition* 13: 138–157.

Bridge, H., Harrold, S., Holmes, E.A., Stokes, M., & Kennard, C. (2011). Vivid visual mental imagery in the absence of the primary visual cortex. *Journal of Neurology*. In press.

Brincker, M. (2010). *Moving beyond mirroring: A social affordance model of sensorimotor integration during action perception.* Doctoral dissertation, City University of New York, Department of Philosophy.

Bristow, D., John-Dylan Haynes, J-D., Sylvester, R., Frith, C.D., & Rees, G. (2005). Blinking suppresses the neural response to unchanging retinal stimulation. *Current Biology* 15: R554–R556.

Broad, C.D. (1925). *The Mind and Its Place in Nature*. London: Routledge and Kegan Paul.

Brook, A. (1994). *Kant and the Mind*. Cambridge, UK: Cambridge University Press.

Brooks, R.A. (1991). Intelligence without representation. *Artificial Intelligence* 47: 139–159.

Brouwer, G.J., & Heeger, D.J. (2009). Decoding and reconstructing color from responses in human visual cortex. *Journal of Neuroscience* 29, 13992–14003.

Bruner, J.S., & Goodman, C.C. (1947). Value and need as organizing factors in perception. *Journal of Abnormal and Social Psychology* 42: 33–44.

Bubl, E., Kern, E., Ebert, D., Bach, M., & Tebartz van Elst, L. (2010). Seeing gray when feeling blue? Depression can be measured in the eye of the diseased. *Biological Psychiatry* 68: 205–208.

Budd, J.M.L. (1998). Extrastriate feedback to primary visual cortex in primates: A quantitative analysis of connectivity. *Proceedings of the Royal Society of London B* 265: 1037–1044.

Buffalo, E.A., Fries, P., Landman, R., Buschman, T.J., & Desimone, R. (2011). Laminar differences in gamma and alpha coherence in the ventral stream. *Proceedings of the National Academy of Sciences USA* 108: 11262–11267.

Buffalo, E.A., Fries, P., Landman, R., Liang, H., & Desimone, R. (2010) A backward progression of attentional effects in the ventral stream. *Proceedings of the National Academy of Sciences USA* 107: 361–365.

Buia, C.I., & Tiesinga, P.H. (2008). Role of interneuron diversity in the cortical microcircuit for attention. *Journal of Neurophysiology* 99: 2158–2182.

Burnett, L.R., Stein, B.E., Perrault, T.J., & Wallace, M.T. (2007). Excitotoxic lesions of the superior colliculus preferentially impact multisensory neurons and multisensory integration. *Experimental Brain Research* 179: 325–338.

Burnham, B.R., Neely, J.H., Walker, P.B., & Neill, W.T. (2006). Interference from irrelevant colour-singletons during serial search depends on visual attention being spatially diffuse. *Visual Cognition* 14: 75–78.

Burr, D.C., & Santoro, L. (2001). Temporal integration of optic flow, measured by contrast and coherence thresholds. *Vision Research* 41: 1891–1899.

Busse, L., Roberts, K.C., Crist, R.E., Weissman, D.H., & Woldorff, M.G. (2005). The spread of attention across modalities and space in a multisensory object. *Proceedings of the National Academy of Sciences USA* 102: 18751–18756.

Byrne, A. (2001). Intentionalism defended. *Philosophical Review* 110: 199–239.

Campbell, J. (1999). Schizophrenia, the space of reasons and thinking as a motor process. *Monist* 82: 609–625.

Canolty, R.T., Edwards, E., Dalal, S.S., Soltani, M., Nagarajan, S.S., Kirsch, H.E., Berger, M.S., Barbaro, N.M., & Knight, R.T. (2006). High gamma power is phase-locked to theta oscillations in human neocortex. *Science* 313: 1626–1628.

Caplovitz, G.P., Barroso, D.J., Hsieh, P.J., & Tse, P.U. (2008). fMRI reveals that non-local processing in ventral retinotopic cortex underlies perceptual grouping by temporal synchrony. *Human Brain Mapping* 29: 651–661.

Cariani, P. (1999). Temporal coding of periodicity pitch in the auditory system: An overview. *Neural Plasticity* 6: 147–172.

Carleton, A., Accolla, R., & Simon, S.A. (2010). Coding in the mammalian gustatory system. *Trends in Neurosciences* 33: 326–334.

Carmichael, L.P., Hogan, H.P., & Walter, A.A. (1932). An experimental study of the effect of language on the reproduction of visually perceived form. *Journal of Experimental Psychology* 15: 73–86.

Carrasco, M., Ling, S., & Read, S. (2004). Attention alters appearance. *Nature Neuroscience* 7: 308–313.

Carruthers, P. (2000). *Phenomenal Consciousness: A Naturalistic Theory*. Cambridge, UK: Cambridge University Press.

———. (2002a). The cognitive functions of language. *Behavioral and Brain Sciences* 25: 657–719.

———. (2002b). Conscious thinking: Language or elimination? *Mind & Language* 13: 457–476.

Catmur, C., Walsh, V., & Heyes, C.M. (2007). Sensorimotor learning configures the human mirror system. *Current Biology* 17: 1527–1531.

Chalmers, D.J. (1996). *The Conscious Mind: In Search of a Fundamental Theory*. New York: Oxford University Press.

———. (1997). Availability: The cognitive basis of experience? *Behavioral and Brain Sciences* 20: 148–149.

———. (1999). Materialism and the metaphysics of modality. *Philosophy and Phenomenological Research* 59: 473–493.

———. (2004a). Phenomenal concepts and the knowledge argument. In P. Ludlow, Y. Nagasawa, & D. Stoljar, eds., *There's Something about Mary*, 269–298. Cambridge, MA: MIT Press.

———. (2004b). The representational character of experience. In B. Leiter, ed., *The Future for Philosophy*, 153–181. Oxford: Oxford University Press.

Chalmers, D.J., & Jackson, F. (2001). Conceptual analysis and reductive explanation. *Philosophical Review* 110: 315–361.

Chambers, D., & Reisberg, D. (1985). Can mental images be ambiguous? *Journal of Experimental Psychology: Human Perception and Performance* 11: 317–328.

———. (1992). What an image depicts depends on what an image means. *Cognitive Psychology* 24: 145–174.

Chao, L.L., Haxby, J.V., & Martin, A. (1999). Attribute-based neural substrates in posterior temporal cortex for perceiving and knowing about objects. *Nature Neuroscience* 2: 913–919.

Chatterjee, A., & Southwood, M.H. (1995). Cortical blindness and visual imagery. *Neurology* 12: 2189–2195.

Chen, L.M., Friedman, R.M., & Roe, A.W. (2005). Optical imaging of S1 topography in anesthetized and awake squirrel monkeys. *Journal of Neuroscience* 25: 7648–7659.

Cheselden, W. (1728). An account of some observations made by a young gentleman, who was born blind, or lost his sight so early, that he had no Remembrance of ever having seen, and was couch'd between 13 and 14 years of age. *Philosophical Transactions of the Royal Society of London B* 35: 447–450.

Chorlian, D.B., Porjesz, B., & Begleiter, H. (2006). Amplitude modulation of gamma band oscillations at alpha frequency produced by photic driving. *International Journal of Psychophysiology* 61: 262–278.

Churchland, P.M. (1985). Reduction, qualia, and the direct introspection of brain states. *Journal of Philosophy* 82: 8–28.

————. (2007). On the reality (and diversity) of objective colors: How color-qualia space is a map of reflectance-profile space. *Philosophy of Science* 74: 119–149.

Churchland, P.S. (1986). *Neurophilosophy*. Cambridge, MA: MIT Press.

Churchland, P.S., Ramachandran, V.S., & Sejnowski, T.J. (1994). A critique of pure vision. In C. Koch & J.L. Davis, eds., *Large Scale Neuronal Theories of the Brain*, 23–60. Cambridge, MA: MIT Press.

Cicchini, G.M., & Morrone, M.C. (2009). Shifts in spatial attention affect the perceived duration of events. *Journal of Vision* 9: 1–13.

Clark, A. (1993). *Sensory Qualities*. Oxford: Oxford University Press.

————. (2001). Visual experience and motor action: Are the bonds too tight? *Philosophical Review* 110: 495–519.

Cole, J. (1995). *Pride and a Daily Marathon*. Cambridge, MA: MIT Press.

Colgin, L.L., Denninger, T., Fyhn, M., Hafting, T., Bonnevie, T., Jensen, O., Moser, M., & Moser, E.I. (2009). Frequency of gamma oscillations routes flow of information in the hippocampus. *Nature* 462: 353–357.

Conee, E. (1994). Phenomenal knowledge. *Australasian Journal of Philosophy* 72: 136–150.

Connor, C.E., Egeth, H.E., & Yantis, S. (2004). Visual attention: Bottom-up versus top-down. *Current Biology* 14: R850–R852.

Conway, B.R., & Tsao, D.Y. (2006). Color architecture in alert macaque cortex revealed by FMRI. *Cerebral Cortex* 16: 1604–1613.

————. (2009). Color-tuned neurons are spatially clustered according to color preference within alert macaque posterior inferior temporal cortex. *Proceedings of the National Academy of Sciences USA* 106: 18034–18039.

Coolidge, F.L., & Wynn, T. (2009). *The Rise of Homo Sapiens: The Evolution of Modern Thinking*. New York: Wiley.

Corbetta, M., & Shulman, G.L. (2002). Control of goal-directed and stimulus-driven attention in the brain. *Nature Neuroscience* 3: 215–229.

Corbetta, M., Miezin, F.M., Dobmeyer, S., Shulman, G.L., & Petersen, S.E. (1990). Attentional modulation of neural processing of shape, color, and velocity in humans. *Science* 248: 1556–1559.

Cotterill, R. (1998). *Enchanted Looms: Conscious Networks in Brains and Computers*. Cambridge, UK: Cambridge University Press.

Cowan, N. (1995). *Attention and Memory: An Integrated Framework*. New York: Oxford University Press.

Cowey, A., & Heywood, C.A. (1997). Cerebral achromatopsia: Color blindness despite wavelength processing. *Trends in Cognitive Science* 1: 133–139.

Crane, T. (1992). The nonconceptual content of experience. In T. Crane, ed., *The Contents of experience*. Cambridge, UK: Cambridge University Press.

Craver, C. (2007). *Explaining the Brain: Mechanisms and the Mosaic Unity of Neuroscience*. New York: Oxford University Press.

Crick, F. (1995). *Astonishing Hypothesis: The Scientific Search for the Soul*. New York: Scribner.

Crick, F., & Koch, C. (1990). Towards a neurobiological theory of consciousness. *Seminars in Neuroscience* 2: 263–275.

————. (1995). Consciousness and neuroscience. *Cerebral Cortex* 8: 97–107.

————. (2000). The unconscious homunculus. In T. Metzinger, ed., *The Neural Correlates of Consciousness*, 103–110. Cambridge, MA: MIT Press.

Critchley, H.D., Wiens, S., Rotshtein, P., Ohman, A., & Dolan, R.J. (2004). Neural systems supporting interoceptive awareness. *Nature Neuroscience* 7: 189–195.

Crottaz-Herbette, S., Anagnoson, R.T., & Menon, V. (2004). Modality effects in verbal working memory: Differential prefrontal and parietal responses to auditory and visual stimuli. *Neuroimage* 21: 340–351.

Cummins, R.E. (1985). *The Nature of Psychological Explanation.* Cambridge, MA: MIT Press.

Damasio, A.R. (1994). *Descartes's Error: Emotion, Reason, and the Human Brain.* New York: Putnam's.

———. (1999). *The Feeling of What Happens: Body and Emotion in the Making of Consciousness.* New York: Harcourt Brace.

Damasio, A.R., & Van Hoesen, G.W. (1983). Emotional disturbances associated with focal lesions of the limbic frontal lobe. In K.M. Heilman & P. Satz, eds., *Neuropsychology of Human Emotion,* 85–110. New York: Guilford.

Darden, L. (2001). Discovering mechanisms: A computational philosophy of science perspective. In K.P. Jantke & A. Shinohara, eds., *Discovery Science,* 3–15. New York: Springer-Verlag.

Debener, S., Herrmann, C.S., Kranczioch, C., Gembris, D., & Engel, A.K. (2003). Top-down attentional processing enhances auditory evoked gamma band activity. *NeuroReport* 14: 683–686.

De Brigard, F. (2011). Reconstructing memory. Doctoral dissertation, University of North Carolina, Chapel Hill, Department of Philosophy.

De Brigard, F., & Prinz, J.J. (2010). Attention and consciousness. *Wiley Interdisciplinary Reviews: Cognitive Science* 1: 51–59.

De Bruyn, B., & Orban, G.A. (1988). Human velocity and direction discrimination measured with random dot patterns. *Vision Research* 28: 1323–1335.

De Gelder, B. (2010). Uncanny sight in the blind. *Scientific American* 302: 60–65.

De Gelder, B., Morris, J.S., & Dolan, R.J. (2005). Unconscious fear influences emotional awareness of faces and voices. *Proceedings of the National Academy of Sciences* 102: 18682–18687.

Dehaene, S., & Changeux, J.P. (2005). Ongoing spontaneous activity controls access to consciousness: A neuronal model for inattentional blindness. *PLoS Biology* 3: 910–927.

Dehaene, S., & Naccache, L. (2001). Towards a cognitive neuroscience of consciousness: Basic evidence and a workspace framework. *Cognition* 79: 1–37.

Dehaene, S., Changeux, J.P., Naccache, L., Sackur, J., & Sergent, C. (2006). Conscious, preconscious, and subliminal processing: A testable taxonomy. *Trends in Cognitive Science* 10: 204–211.

Demiralp, T., Bayraktaroglu, Z., Lenz, D., Junge, S., Busch, N.A., Maess, B., Ergen, M., & Herrmann, C.S. (2007). Gamma amplitudes are coupled to theta phase in human EEG during visual perception. *International Journal of Psychophysiology* 64: 24–30.

Dennett, D.C. (1969). *Content and Consciousness.* London: Routledge and Kegan.

———. (1978). *Brainstorms: Philosophical Essays on Mind and Psychology.* Cambridge, MA: MIT Press.

———. (1991). *Consciousness Explained.* New York: Penguin.

———. (2003). *Freedom Evolves.* New York: Viking.

Dennett, D.C., & Kinsbourne, M. (1995). Time and the observer: The where and when of consciousness in the brain. *Behavioral and Brain Sciences* 15: 183–247.

De Ridder, D., Van Laere, K., Dupont, P., Menovsky, T., & Van de Heyning, P. (2007). Visualizing out-of-body experience in the brain. *New England Journal of Medicine* 357: 1829–1833.

Descartes, R. (1633/1984). The treatise on man. In J. Cottingham, R. Stoothoff, & D. Murdoch, eds., *The Philosophical Writings of Descartes*, Vol. 1, 99–108. Cambridge, UK: Cambridge University Press.

———. (1649/1988). The passions of the soul. In J. Cottingham, R. Stoothoff, & D. Murdoch, trans. and eds., *Selected Philosophical Writings of René Descartes*, Vol. 1, 325–403. Cambridge: Cambridge University Press.

DeSchepper, B., & Treisman, A. (1996). Visual memory for novel shapes: Implicit coding without attention. *Journal of Experimental Psychology: Learning, Memory, and Cognition* 22: 27–47.

Desmurget, M., & Sirigu, A. (2009). A parietal-premotor network for movement intention and motor awareness. *Trends in Cognitive Science* 13: 411–419.

Desmurget, M., Reilly, K.T., Richard, N., Szathmari, A., Mottolese, C., & Sirigu, A. (2009). Movement intention after parietal cortex stimulation in humans. *Science* 324: 811–813.

D'Esposito, M., & Postle, B.R. (1999). The dependence of the mnemonic components of working memory on prefrontal cortex. *Neuropsychologia* 37: 89–101.

D'Esposito, M., Postle, B.R., Ballard, D., & Lease, J. (1999). Maintenance versus manipulation of information held in working memory: An event-related fMRI study. *Brain and Cognition* 41: 66–86.

Di Lollo, V. (1980). Temporal integration in visual memory. *Journal of Experimental Psychology: General* 109: 75–97.

Di Lorenzo, P.M., Chen, J., & Victor, J.D. (2009). Quality time: Representation of a multi-dimensional sensory domain through temporal decoding. *Journal of Neuroscience* 29: 9227–9238.

Di Lorenzo, P.M., Hallock, R.M., & Kennedy, D.P. (2003). Temporal coding of sensation: Mimicking taste quality with electrical stimulation of the brain. *Behavior and Neuroscience* 117: 1423–1433.

Dijksterhuis, A., Bos, M.W., Nordgren, L.F., & van Baaren, R.B. (2006). On making the right choice: The deliberation-without-attention effect. *Science* 311: 1005–1007.

Dixon, N.F., & Spitz, L. (1980). The detection of auditory visual desynchrony. *Perception* 9: 719–721.

Dodell-Feder, D., Koster-Hale, J., Bedny, M., & Saxe, R. (2011). fMRI item analysis in a theory of mind task. *Neuroimage* 55: 705–712.

Doesburg, S.M., Roggeveen, A.B., Kitajo, K., & Ward, L.M. (2008). Large-scale gamma-band phase synchronization and selective attention. *Cerebral Cortex* 18: 386–396.

Doricchi, F., & Galati, G. (2000). Implicit semantic evaluation of object symmetry and contralesional visual denial in a case of left unilateral neglect with damage of the dorsal paraventricular white matter. *Cortex* 36: 337–350.

Dretske, F. (1995). *Naturalizing the Mind*. Cambridge, MA: MIT Press.

Driver, J., & Mattingly, J.B. (1998). Parietal neglect and visual awareness. *Nature Neuroscience* 1: 17–22.

Driver, J., & Vuilleumier, P. (2001). Perceptual awareness and its loss in unilateral neglect and extinction. *Cognition* 79: 39–88.

Du Boisgueheneuc, F., Levy, R., Volle, E., Seassau, M., Duffau, H., Kinkingnehun, S., Samson, Y., Zhang, S., & Dubois, B. (2006). Functions of the left superior frontal gyrus in humans: A lesion study. *Brain* 129: 3315–3328.

Eagleman, D.M., & Sejnowski, T.J. (2000). Motion integration and postdiction in visual awareness. *Science* 287: 2036–2038.

Edelman, G.M. (1992). *Bright Air, Brilliant Fire*. New York: Basic.

Edelman, G.M., & Tononi, G. (2000). *A Universe of Consciousness: How Matter Becomes Imagination*. New York: Basic.

Edwards, E., Soltani, M., Deouell, L.Y., Berger, M.S., & Knight, R.T. (2005). High gamma activity in response to deviant auditory stimuli recorded directly from human cortex. *Journal of Neurophysiology* 94: 4269–4280.

Ehrenstein, W.H. (1977). Geometry in visual space: Some method dependent (arti)facts. *Perception* 6: 657–660.

Eichenbaum, H., Morton, T.H., Potter, H., & Corkin, S. (1983). Selective olfactory deficits in case H.M. *Brain* 106: 459–472.

Enç, B. (1983). In defense of the identity theory. *Journal of Philosophy* 80: 279–298.

Engel, A.K., Fries, P., Brecht, M., & Singer, W. (1999). Temporal binding, binocular rivalry and consciousness. *Consciousness and Cognition* 8: 128–151.

Enns, J.T., & Di Lollo, V. (2000). What's new in visual masking? *Trends in Cognitive Sciences* 4: 345–352.

Evans, G. (1982). *The Varieties of Reference*. Oxford: Oxford University Press.

Fang, F., & He, S. (2005). Cortical responses to invisible objects in the human dorsal and ventral pathways. *Nature Neuroscience* 8: 1380–1385.

Farah, M.J. (1990). *Visual Agnosia: Disorders of Object Recognition and What They Tell Us about Normal Vision*. Cambridge, MA: MIT Press.

Farrell, B.A. (1950). Experience. *Mind* 234: 170–198.

Farrer, C., Franck, N., Georgieff, N., Frith, C.D., Decety, J., & Jeannerod, M. (2003). Modulating the experience of agency. *Neuroimage* 18: 324–333.

Feigl, H. (1958). The "mental" and the "physical." In H. Feigl, M. Scriven, & G. Maxwell, eds., *Concepts, Theories and the Mind-Body Problem*, 3–36. Minneapolis: University of Minnesota Press.

Felleman, D.J., & Van Essen, D.C. (1991). Distributed hierarchical processing in primate visual cortex. *Cerebral Cortex* 1: 1–47.

Festinger, L., Allyn, M.R., & White, C.W. (1971). The perception of color with achromatic stimulation. *Vision Research* 11: 591–612.

Ffytche, D.H., Howard, R.J., Brammer, M., David, A., Woodruff, P.W., & Williams, S. (1998). The anatomy of conscious vision: An fMRI study of visual hallucinations. *Nature Neuroscience* 1: 738–742.

Fine, I., Smallman, H.S., Doyle, P., & MacLeod, D. (2002). Visual function before and after the removal of bilateral congenital cataracts in adulthood. *Vision Research* 42: 191–210.

Finke, K., Bublak, P., & Zihl, J. (2006). Visual spatial and visual pattern working memory: Neuropsychological evidence for a differential role of left and right dorsal visual brain. *Neuropsychologia* 33: 649–661.

Fischer, B. (1986). The role of attention in the preparation of visually guided eye movements in monkey and man. *Psychological Research* 48: 251–257.

Fletcher, P.C., & Henson, R.N.A. (2001). Frontal lobes and human memory: Insights from functional neuroimaging. *Brain* 124: 84 –881.

Fodor, J. (1974). Special sciences, or the disunity of science as a working hypothesis. *Synthese* 28: 97–115.

———. (1985). Fodor's guide to mental representations: The intelligent auntie's vademecum. *Mind* 373: 76–100.

Fougnie, D., & Marois, R. (2007). Executive load in working memory induces inattentional blindness. *Psychonomic Bulletin & Review* 14: 142–147.

Foxe, J.J., Simpson, G.V., & Ahlfors, S.P. (1998). Parieto-occipital approximately 10 Hz activity reflects anticipatory state of visual attention mechanisms. *NeuroReport* 9: 3929–3933.

Franz, V.H., Fahle, M., Bülthoff, H.H., & Gegenfurtner, K.R. (2001). Effects of visual illusions on grasping. *Journal of Experimental Psychology: Human Perception and Performance* 27: 1124–1144.

Friedman, D.P., Murray, E.A., O'Neill, J.B., & Mishkin, M. (1986). Cortical connections of the somatosensory fields of the lateral sulcus of macaques: Evidence for a corticolimbic pathway for touch. *Journal of Comparative Neurology* 252: 323–347.

Fries, P. (2005). A mechanism for cognitive dynamics: Neuronal communication through neuronal coherence. *Trends in Cognitive Sciences* 9: 474–480.

Fries, P., Reynolds, J.H., Rorie, A.E., & Desimone, R. (2001). Modulation of oscillatory neuronal synchronization by selective visual attention. *Science* 291: 1560–1563.

Fries, P., Roelfsema, P.R., Engel, A.K., König, P., & Singer, W. (1997). Synchronization of oscillatory responses in visual cortex correlates with perception in interocular rivalry. *Proceedings of the National Academy of Sciences USA* 94: 12699–12704.

Frith, C.D., Blakemore, S.-J., & Wolpert, D.M. (2000). Abnormalities in the awareness and control of action. *Philosophical Transactions of the Royal Society of London B* 355: 1771–1788.

Fuentemilla, L., Penny, W.D., Cashdollar, N., Bunzeck, N., & Düzel, E. (2010). Theta-coupled periodic replay in working memory. *Current Biology* 20: 606–612.

Funahashi, S., Bruce, C.J., & Goldman-Rakic, P.S. (1989). Mnemonic coding of visual space in the monkey's dorsolateral prefrontal cortex. *Journal of Neurophysiology* 61: 331–349.

Fuster, J.M. (2004). Upper processing stages of the perception-action cycle. *Trends in Cognitive Sciences* 8: 143–145.

Gaillard, R., Dehaene, S., Adam, C., Clemenceau, S., Hasboun, D., Baulac, M., Cohen, L., & Naccache, L. (2009). Converging intracranial markers of conscious access. *PLoS Biology* 7: e61.

Gallistel, C.R. (1980). *The Organization of Action: A New Synthesis*. Hillsdale, NJ: Erlbaum.

Gazzaniga, M.S. (1988). *Mind Matters*. Boston: Houghton Mifflin.

———. (1992). *Nature's Mind*. New York: Basic.

———. (2002). The split brain revisited. *Scientific American* 12: 27–31.

Gazzaniga, M.S., & LeDoux, J.E. (1978). *The Integrated Mind*. New York: Plenum.

Georgopoulos, A.P., Schwartz, A.B., & Kettner, R.E. (1986). Neuronal population coding of movement direction. *Science* 233: 1416–1419.

Gerstner, G.E., & Fazio, V.A. (1995). Evidence for a universal perceptual unit in mammals. *Ethology* 101: 89–100.

Ghazanfar, A.A., Maier, J.X., Hoffman, K.L., & Logothetis, N.K. (2005). Multisensory integration of dynamic faces and voices in rhesus monkey auditory cortex. *Journal of Neuroscience* 25: 5004–5012.

Gibson, J.J. (1979). *The Ecological Approach to Visual Perception*. Boston: Houghton Mifflin.

Glahn, D.C., Kim, J., Cohen, M.S., Poutanen, V.P., Therman, S., Bava, S., Van Erp, T.G., Manninen, M., Huttunen, M., Lönnqvist, J., Standertskjöld-Nordenstam, C.G., & Cannon T.D. (2002). Maintenance and manipulation in spatial working memory: Dissociations in the prefrontal cortex. *Neuroimage* 17: 201–213.

Glennan, S.S. (1996). Mechanisms and the nature of causation. *Erkenntnis* 44: 49–71.

Glover, S.R. (2002). Visual illusions affect planning but not control. *Trends in Cognitive Sciences* 6: 288–292.

Glover, S.R., & Dixon, P. (2001). Dynamic illusion effects in a reaching task: Evidence for separate visual representations in the planning and control of reaching. *Journal of Experimental Psychology: Human Perception and Performance* 27: 560–572.

Gogel, W.C. (1990). A theory of phenomenal geometry and its applications. *Perception & Psychophysics* 48: 105–123.

Goldberg, I.I., Harel, M., & Malach, R. (2006). When the brain loses itself: Prefrontal inactivation during sensorimotor processing. *Neuron* 50: 329–339.

Goldenberg G., Müllbacher W., & Nowak A. (1995). Imagery without perception: A case study of anosognosia for cortical blindness. *Neuropsychologia* 33: 1373–1382.

Goldsmith, M. (1998). What's in a location? Comparing object-based and space-based models of feature integration in visual search. *Journal of Experimental Psychology: General* 12: 189–219.

Goldstone, R.L. (2004). Believing is seeing. *American Psychological Society Observer* 17: 23–26.

Gonzalez Andino, S., Michel, C., Thut, G., Landis, T., & de Peralto, R.G. (2005). Prediction of response speed by anticipatory high-frequency (gamma band) oscillations in the human brain. *Human Brain Mapping* 24: 50–58.

Goodale, M.A., & Milner, A.D. (1992). Separate visual pathways for perception and action. *Trends in Neurosciences* 15: 20–25.

———. (2005). *Sight Unseen: An Exploration of Conscious and Unconscious Vision*. Oxford: Oxford University Press.

Goodman, N. (1976). *Languages of Art*. Indianapolis: Hacket.

Graham, C.H., & Hsia Y. (1958). The discriminations of a normal and a color blind eye in the same person. *Proceedings of the American Philosophical Society* 102: 168–173.

Gray, C.M. (1999). The temporal correlation hypothesis of visual feature integration: Still alive and well. *Neuron* 24: 31–47.

Gray, C.M., König, P., Engel, A.K., & Singer, W. (1989). Oscillatory responses in cat visual cortex exhibit inter-columnar synchronization which reflects global stimulus parameters. *Nature* 338: 334–337.

Gray, J. (2004). *Consciousness: Creeping Up on the Hard Problem*. Oxford: Oxford University Press.

Gray, K., Knobe, J., Sheskin, M., Bloom, P., & Barrett, L. (2012). More than a Body: Mind Perception and the Nature of Objectification. *Journal of Personality and Social Psychology* 101: 1207–1220.

Green, R.J., & Stanton, M.E. (1989). Differential ontogeny of working memory and reference memory in the rat. *Behavioral Neuroscience* 103: 98–105.

Greenberg, S., Carvey, H., Hitchcock, L., & Chang, S. (2003). Temporal properties of spontaneous speech: A syllable-centric perspective. *Journal of Phonetics* 31: 465–485.

Grèzes, J., Armony, J.L., Rowe, J., & Passingham, R.E. (2003). Activations related to "mirror" and "canonical" neurones in the human brain: An fMRI study. *Neuroimage* 18: 928–937.

Grimsley, G. (1943). A study of individual differences in binocular color fusion. *Journal of Experimental Psychology* 32: 82–87.

Gross, D.W., & Gotman, J. (1999). Correlation of high-frequency oscillations with the sleep-wake cycle and cognitive activity in humans. *Neuroscience* 94: 1005–1018.

Grossberg, S. (2007). Consciousness CLEARS the mind. *Neural Networks* 20: 1040–1053.

Güntürkün, O. (2005). The avian "prefrontal cortex" and cognition. *Current Opinion in Neurobiology* 15: 686–693.

Gur, M., & Snodderly, D.M. (1997). A dissociation between brain activity and perception: Chromatically opponent cortical neurons signal chromatic flicker that is not perceived. *Vision Research* 37: 377–382.

Güzeldere, G. (1997). The many faces of consciousness: A field guide. In N. Block, O. Flanagan, & G. Güzeldere, eds., *The Nature of Consciousness: Philosophical Debates*, 1–67. Cambridge, MA: MIT Press.

Haggard, P., & Eimer, M. (1999). On the relation between brain potentials and the awareness of voluntary movements. *Experimental Brain Research* 126: 128–133.

Halberstadt, J., Winkielman, P., Niedenthal, P., & Dalle, N. (2009). Emotional conception: How embodied emotion concepts guide perception and facial action. *Psychological Science* 20: 1254–1261.

Halsey, R., & Chapanis, A. (1951). On the number of absolutely identifiable spectral hues. *Journal of the Optical Society of America* 41: 1057–1058.

Hameroff, S.R. (2006). Consciousness, neurobiology and quantum mechanics: The case for a connection. In J. Tuszynski, ed., *The Emerging Physics of Consciousness*, 193–253. Berlin: Springer.

———. (2007). The brain is both neurocomputer and quantum computer. *Cognitive Science* 31: 1035–1045.

Hansen, T., Olkkonen, M., Walter, S., & Gegenfurtner, S. (2006). Memory modulates color appearance. *Nature Neuroscience* 9: 1367–1368.

Hardin, C.L. (1988). *Colors for Philosophers: Unweaving the Rainbow*. Indianapolis: Hackett.

———. (1997). Reinverting the spectrum. In D. Hilbert & A. Byrne, eds., *Readings on Color: The Philosophy of Color*, Vol. 1, 289–312. Cambridge, MA: MIT Press.

Harman, G. (1990). The intrinsic quality of experience. In J. Tomberlin, ed. *Philosophical Perspectives 4: Action Theory and Philosophy of Mind*, 31–52. Atascadero, CA: Ridgeview.

Harris, C.S. (1965). Perceptual adaptation to inverted, reversed, and displaced vision. *Psychological Review* 72: 419–444.

Harrison, S.A., & Tong, F. (2009). Decoding reveals the contents of visual working memory in early visual areas. *Nature* 458: 632–635.

Hart, J.T. (1965). Memory and the feeling-of-knowing experience. *Journal of Educational Psychology* 56: 208–216.

Hartmann, J., Wolz, W., Roeltgen, D., & Loverso, F. (1991). Denial of visual perception. *Brain and Cognition* 16: 29–40.

Hassin, R.R., Bargh, J.A., Engell, A., & McCulloch, K.C. (2009). Implicit working memory. *Consciousness and Cognition* 18: 665–678.

Hatfield, E., Cacioppo, J.T., & Rapson, R.L. (1993). Emotional contagion. *Current Directions in Psychological Science* 2: 96–99.

Heath, R.G., Carpenter, M.B., Mettler, F.A., & Kline, N.S. (1949). Visual apparatus: Visual fields and acuity, color vision, autokinesis. In F.A. Mettler, ed., *Selective Partial Ablation of the Frontal Cortex: A Correlative Study of Its Effects on Human Psychotic Subjects*, 480–491. New York: P.B. Hoeber.

Held, R., & Hein, A. (1963). Movement-produced stimulation in the development of visually guided behavior. *Journal of Comparative and Physiological Psychology* 56: 872–876.

Held, R., Ostrovsky, Y., de Gelder, B., Gandhi, T., Ganesh, S., & Sinha, P. 2011. The newly sighted fail to match seen with felt. *Nature Neuroscience* 14: 551–553.

Heywood, C.A., Cowey, A., & Newcombe, F. (1994). On the role of parvocellular (P) and magnocellular (M) pathways in cerebral achromatopsia. *Brain* 117: 245–254.

Hill, C.S. (1997). Imaginability, conceivability, possibility, and the mind-body problem. *Philosophical Studies* 87: 61–85.

Hillyard, S.A., Squires, K.C., Bauer, J.W, & Lindsav, P.H. (1971). Evoked potential correlates of auditory signal detection. *Science* 172: 1357–1360.

Hoerzer, G.M., Liebe, S., Schloegl, A., Logothetis, N.K., & Rainer, G. (2010). Directed coupling in local field potentials of macaque V4 during visual short-term memory revealed by multivariate autoregressive models. *Frontiers in Computational Neuroscience* 4: 14.

Hohwy, J. (2007). The sense of self in the phenomenology of agency and perception. *Psyche* 13: 1–20.

Holz, E.M., Glennon, M., Prendergast, K., & Sauseng, P. (2010). Theta-gamma phase synchronization during memory matching in visual working memory. *Neuroimage* 52: 326–335.

Homae, F., Watanabe, H., Otobe, T., Nakano, T., Go, T., Konishi, Y., & Taga, G. (2010). Development of global cortical networks in early infancy. *Journal of Neuroscience* 30: 4877–4882.

Hooker, C. (1981). Towards a general theory of reduction. Part III: Cross-categorial reductions. *Dialogue* 20: 496–529.

Horgan, T. (1984). Functionalism, qualia, and the inverted spectrum. *Philosophy and Phenomenological Research* 44: 453–469.

———. (2000). Narrow content and the phenomenology of intentionality. Presidential address delivered at the annual meeting of the Society for Philosophy and Psychology, New York.

Horowitz, T., & Treisman, A. (1994). Attention and apparent motion. *Spatial Vision* 8: 193–219.

Hötting, K., & Röder, B. (2004). Hearing cheats touch but less in the congenitally blind than in sighted individuals. *Psychological Science* 15: 60–64.

Howard, M.W., Rizzuto, D.S., Caplan, J.B., Madsen, J.R., Lisman, J., Aschenbrenner-Scheibe, R., Schulze-Bonhage, A., & Kahana, M.J. (2003). Gamma oscillations correlate with working memory load in humans. *Cerebral Cortex* 13: 1369–1374.

Hsieh, P.-J., Colas, J.T., & Kanwisher, N. (2011). Pop-out without awareness: Unseen feature singletons capture attention only when top-down attention is available. *Psychological Science* 22: 1220–1226.

Hubel, D.H., & Wiesel, T.N. (1962). Receptive fields, binocular interaction and functional architecture in the cat's visual cortex. *Journal of Physiology* 160: 106–115.

Huebner, B. (2010). Commonsense concepts of phenomenal consciousness: Does anyone care about functional zombies? *Phenomenology and the Cognitive Sciences* 9: 133–155.

Hume, D. (1739/1978). *A Treatise of Human Nature.* P.H. Nidditch, ed. Oxford: Oxford University Press.

Humphrey, G.K., James, T.W., Gati, J.S., Menon, R.S., & Goodale, M.A. (1999). Perception of the McCollough effect correlates with activity in extrastriate cortex: A resonance imaging study. *Psychological Science* 10: 444–448.

Humphrey, N. (1992). *A History of the Mind.* New York: Simon & Schuster.

Hurlburt, R. (1990). *Sampling Normal and Schizophrenic Inner Experience.* New York: Plenum.

Hurley, S.L. (1998). *Consciousness in Action.* Cambridge, MA: Harvard University Press.

Hurley, S., & Noë, A. (2003). Neural plasticity and consciousness. *Biology and Philosophy* 18: 131–168.

Husain, M., & Kennard, C. (1996). Visual neglect associated with frontal lobe infarction. *Journal of Neurology* 243: 652–657.

Husain, M., & Nachev, P. (2007). Space and the parietal cortex. *Trends in Cognitive Sciences* 11: 30–36.

Hyun, J-S., Woodman, G.F., & Luck, S.J. (2009). The role of attention in the binding of surface features to locations. *Visual Cognition* 17: 10–24.

Ito, M., Tamura, H., Fujita, I., & Tanaka, K. (1995). Size and position invariance of neuronal responses in monkey inferotemporal cortex. *Journal of Neurophysiology* 73: 218–226.

Jackendoff, R. (1987). *Consciousness and the Computational Mind.* Cambridge, MA: MIT Press.

Jackson, F. (1982). Epiphenomenal qualia. *Philosophical Quarterly* 32: 127–136.

———. (1986). What Mary didn't know. *Journal of Philosophy* 83: 291–295.

———. (1998). *From Metaphysics to Ethics: A Defense of Conceptual Analysis.* Oxford: Oxford University Press.

———. (2003). Mind and illusion. In A. O'Hear, ed., *Minds and Persons: Royal Institute of Philosophy Supplement,* 251–271. Cambridge, UK: Cambridge University Press.

James, W. (1884). What is an emotion? *Mind* 9: 188–205.

———. (1890). *The Principles of Psychology,* Vol. 1. New York: Holt.

Jensen, O., & Lisman, J.E. (1998). An oscillatory short-term memory buffer model can account for data on the Sternberg Task. *Journal of Neuroscience* 18: 10688–10699.

Jiang, Y., Costello, P., Fang, F., Huang, M. & He, S. (2006). A gender- and sexual orientation-dependent spatial attentional effect of invisible images. *Proceedings of The National Academy of Sciences USA,* 103: 17048–17052.

Jiang, Y., Zhou, K., & He, S. (2007) Human visual cortex responds to invisible chromatic flicker. *Nature Neuroscience* 10: 657–662.

John, E.R., & Prichep, L.S. (2005). The anesthetic cascade: A theory of how anesthesia suppresses consciousness. *Anesthesiology* 102: 447–471.

Johnson, H., & Haggard, P. (2005). Motor awareness without perceptual awareness. *Neuropsychologia* 43: 227–237.

Jokisch, D., & Jensen, O. (2007). Modulation of gamma and alpha activity during a working memory task engaging the dorsal or ventral stream. *Journal of Neuroscience* 27: 3244–3251.

Jonides, J. (1983). Further toward a model of the mind's eye's movement. *Bulletin of the Psychonomic Society* 21: 247–250.

Kaas, J.H. (1993). The functional organization of the somatosensory cortex in primates. *Annals of Anatomy* 175: 509–518.

Kaas, J.H. (1997). Topographic maps are fundamental to sensory processing. *Brain Research Bulletin* 44: 107–112.

Kaas, J.H., & Hackett, T.A. (2000). Subdivisions of auditory cortex and processing streams in primates. *Proceedings of the National Academy of Sciences USA* 97: 11793–11799.

Kammer, T., Puls, K., Erb, M., & Grodd, W. (2005). Transcranial magnetic stimulation in the visual system. II: Characterization of induced phosphenes and scotomas. *Experimental Brain Research* 160: 129–140.

Kanai, R., Muggleton, N.G., & Walsh, V. (2008). TMS over the intraparietal sulcus induces perceptual fading. *Journal of Neurophysiology* 100: 3343–3350.

Kanayama, N., Sato, A., & Ohira, H. (2007). Crossmodal effect with rubber hand illusion and gamma-band activity. *Psychophysiology* 44: 392–402.

———. (2009). The role of gamma band oscillations and synchrony on rubber hand illusion and crossmodal integration. *Brain and Cognition* 69: 19–29.

Kandell, E.R., Schwartz, J.H., & Jessel, T.M. (2000). *Principles of Neural Science*, 4th ed. New York: McGraw-Hill.

Kant, I. (1781/1998). *Critique of Pure Reason*. P. Guyer & A.W. Wood, trans. Cambridge, UK: Cambridge University Press.

Kanwisher, N. (2001). Neural events and perceptual awareness. *Cognition* 79: 89–113.

Kaplan, D. (1989). Demonstratives. In J. Almog, J,. Perry, & H. Wettstein, eds., *Themes from Kaplan*, 481–564. New York: Oxford University Press.

Karnath, H.O., Baier, B., & Nagele, T. (2005). Awareness of the functioning of one's own limbs mediated by the insular cortex? *Journal of Neuroscience* 25: 7134–7138.

Kawamura, S. (1998). Multiple streams of time consciousness: A new model of retrospective timing. *Perceptual and Motor Skills* 86: 1119–1122.

Kayaert, G., Biederman, I., & Vogels, R. (2003). Shape tuning in macaque inferior temporal cortex. *Journal of Neuroscience* 23: 3016–3027.

Kazanovich, Y., & Borisyuk, R. (2006). An oscillatory neural model of multiple object tracking. *Neural Computing* 18: 1413–1440.

Keller A. (2011). Attention and olfactory consciousness. *Frontiers in Consciousness Research* 2: 380.

Kelly, S.P., Lalor, E.C., Reilly, R.B., & Foxe, J.J. (2006). Increases in alpha oscillatory power reflect an active retinotopic mechanism for distracter suppression during sustained visuospatial attention. *Journal of Neurophysiology* 95: 3844–3851.

Kentridge, R.W., Nijboer, T.C.W., & Heywood, C.A. (2008). Attended but unseen: Visual attention is not sufficient for visual awareness. *Neuropsychologia* 46: 864–869.

Keysers, C., Wicker, B., Gazzola, V., Anton, J.L., Fogassi, L., & Gallese, V. (2004). A touching sight: SII/PV activation during the observation and experience of touch. *Neuron* 42: 335–346.

Kim, J. (1972). Phenomenal properties, psychophysical laws, and the identity theory. *Monist* 56: 177–192.

———. (1998). *Mind in a Physical World*. Cambridge, UK: Cambridge University Press.

Kind, A. (2003). What's so transparent about transparency? *Philosophical Studies* 115: 225–244.

Kinomura, S., Larsson, J., Gulyas, B., & Roland, P.E. (1996). Activation by attention of the human reticular formation and thalamic intralaminar nuclei. *Science* 271: 512–515.

Kirk, R. (1994). *Raw Feeling: A Philosophical Account of the Essence of Consciousness*. New York: Oxford University Press.

Kirk, R. (2005). *Zombies and Consciousness*. New York: Oxford University Press.

Kirsch, J.A., Güntürkün, O., & Rose, J. (2008). Insight without cortex: Lessons from the avian brain. *Consciousness and Cognition* 17: 475–483.

Kitcher, Patricia (1982). Kant on self-identity. *Philosophical Review* 91: 41–72.

Kitcher, Philip (1982). Genes. *British Journal for the Philosophy of Science* 33: 337–359.

Klein, K., & Acevedo, C. (2002). Working memory and inattentional blindness. Poster presented at the annual meeting of the North Carolina Cognition Group, Chapel Hill, NC.

Kline, K.A., & Eagleman, D.M. (2008). Evidence against the snapshot hypothesis of illusory motion reversal. *Journal of Vision* 8: 1–5.

Knobe, J., & Prinz, J. (2008). Intuitions about consciousness: Experimental studies. *Phenomenology and the Cognitive Sciences* 7: 67–85.

Knudsen, E.I. (2007). Fundamental components of attention. *Annual Review of Neuroscience* 30: 57–78.

Kobayakawa, T., Ogawa, H., Kaneda, H., Ayabe-Kanamura, S., Endo, H., & Saito, S. (1999). Spatio-temporal analysis of cortical activity evoked by gustatory stimulation in humans. *Chemical Senses* 24: 201–209.

Koch, C. (2004). *The Quest for Consciousness: A Neurobiological Approach*. Englewood, NJ: Roberts.

Koch, C., & Braun, J. (1996). Towards the neuronal correlate of visual awareness. *Current Opinion in Neurobiology* 6: 158–164.

Koch, C., & Tsuchiya, N. (2007). Attention and consciousness: Two distinct brain processes. *Trends in Cognitive Science* 11: 16–22.

Koechlin, E., & Summerfield, C. (2007). An information theoretical approach to prefrontal executive function. *Trends in Cognitive Sciences* 11: 229–235.

Köhler, W. (1923). Zur Theorie des Sukzessivvergleichs und der Zeitfehler. *Psychologische Forschung* 4: 115–175.

Koivisto, M., Hyona, J., & Revonsuo, S. (2004). The effects of eye movements, spatial attention, and stimulus features on inattentional blindness. *Vision Research* 44: 3211–3221.

Komatsu, H., Kinoshita, M., & Murakami, I. (2000). Neural responses in the retinotopic representation of the blind spot in the macaque V1 to stimuli for perceptual filling-in. *Journal of Neuroscience* 20: 9310–9319.

Konen, C., & Kastner, S. (2008) Two hierarchically organized neural systems for object information in human visual cortex. *Nature Neuroscience* 11: 224–231.

Konkle, T., Wang, Q., Hayward, V., & Moore, C.I. (2009). Motion aftereffects transfer between touch and vision. *Current Biology* 19: 745–750.

Kopala, L.C., Campbell, C., & Hurwitz, T. (1992). Olfactory deficits in neuroleptic naive patients with schizophrenia. *Schizophrenia Research* 8: 245–250.

Kopell, N., Ermentrout, G.B., Whittington, M.A., & Traub, R.D. (2000). Gamma rhythms and beta rhythms have different synchronization properties. *Proceedings of the National Academy of Sciences USA* 97: 1867–1872.

Koreimann, S., Strauß, S., & Vitouch, O. (2009). Inattentional deafness under dynamic musical conditions. In J. Louhivuori, T. Eerola, S. Saarikallio, T. Himberg, & P.S. Eerola, eds., *Proceedings of the 7th Triennial Conference of European Society for the Cognitive Sciences of Music.* Jyväskylä, Finland: University of Jyväskylä.

Kosslyn, S. (1994). *Image and Brain: The Resolution of the Imagery Debate.* Cambridge, MA: MIT Press.

Kosslyn, S.M., Thompson, W.L., Costantini-Ferrando, M.F., Alpert, N.M., & Spiegel, D. (2000). Hypnotic visual illusion alters color processing in the brain. *American Journal of Psychiatry* 157: 1279–1284.

Kotake, Y., Morimoto, H., Okazaki, Y., Fujita, I., & Tamura, H. (2009). Organization of color-selective neurons in macaque visual area v4. *Journal of Neurophysiology* 102: 15–27.

Kouider, S., de Gardelle, V., Sackur, J., & Dupoux, E. (2010). How rich is consciousness? The partial awareness hypothesis. *Trends in Cognitive Sciences* 14: 301–307.

Kouider, S., Dehaene, S., Jobert, A., & Le Bihan, D. (2007). Cerebral bases of subliminal and supraliminal priming during reading. *Cerebral Cortex* 17: 2019–2029.

Kreiman, G., Fried, I., & Koch, C. (2002). Single neuron correlates of subjective vision in the human medial temporal lobe. *Proceedings of the National Academy of Sciences USA* 99: 8378–8383.

Kriegel, U. (2005). Naturalizing subjective character. *Philosophy and Phenomenological Research* 71: 23–57.

Kriegel, U., & Williford, K., eds. (2006). *Consciousness and Self-Reference.* Cambridge, MA: MIT Press.

Kripke, S. (1979). A puzzle about belief. In A. Margalit, ed., *Meaning and Use,* 239–283. Dordrect: Reidel.

Kripke, S. (1980). *Naming and Necessity.* Oxford: Blackwell.

Kuehni, R.G., & Hardin, C.L. (2010). Churchland's metamers. *British Journal for the Philosophy of Science* 61: 81–92.

Kühn, S., & Brass, M. (2009). Retrospective construction of the judgment of free choice. *Consciousness and Cognition* 18: 12–21.

Kunimoto, C., Miller, J., & Pashler, H. (2001). Confidence and accuracy of near-threshold discrimination responses. *Consciousness and Cognition* 10: 294–340.

Kusunoki, M., Moutoussis, K., & Zeki, S. (2006). Effect of background colors on the tuning of color-selective cells in monkey area V4. *Journal of Neurophysiology,* 95, 3047–3059.

Kuznetsova, A.Y., & Deth, R.C. (2008). A model for modulation of neuronal synchronization by D4 dopamine receptor-mediated phospholipid methylation. *Journal of Computational Neuroscience* 24: 314–329.

Lamme, V.A. (1995). The neurophysiology of figure-ground segregation in primary visual cortex. *Journal of Neuroscience* 15: 1605–1615.

———. (2001). Blindsight: The role of feedforward and feedback corticocortical connections. *Acta Psychologica* 107: 209–228.

———. (2003). Why visual attention and awareness are different. *Trends in Cognitive Sciences* 7: 12–18.

————. (2006). Zap! Magnetic tricks on conscious and unconscious vision. *Trends in Cognitive Sciences* 10: 193–195.

————. (2010). How neuroscience will change our view on consciousness. *Cognitive Neuroscience* 1: 204–220.

Lamme, V.A., & Spekreijse, H. (1998). Neuronal synchrony does not represent texture segregation. *Nature* 396: 362–366.

Lane, R.D. (2000). Neural correlates of conscious emotional experience. In R.D. Lane & L. Nadel, eds., *Cognitive Neuroscience of Emotion*, 345–370. New York: Oxford University Press.

LaRock, E. (2007). Disambiguation, binding, and the unity of visual consciousness. *Theory and Psychology* 17: 747–777.

Lau, H.C. (2008). A higher-order Bayesian decision theory of perceptual consciousness. *Progress in Brain Research* 168: 35–48.

Lau, H., & Rosenthal, D. (2011). Empirical support for higher-order theories of conscious awareness. *Trends in Cognitive Sciences* 15: 365–373.

Lau, H.C., Rogers, R.D., & Passingham, R.E. (2007). Manipulating the experienced onset of intention after action execution. *Journal of Cognitive Neuroscience* 19: 81–90.

Lê, S., Cardebat, D., Boulanouar, K., Hénaff, M.A., Michel, F., Milner, D., Dijkerman, C., Puel, M., & Démonet, J.-F. (2002). Seeing, since childhood, without ventral stream: A behavioural study. *Brain* 125: 58–74.

Lecours, A.R., & Joanette Y. (1980). Linguistic and other psychological aspects of paroxysmal aphasia. *Brain and Language* 10: 1–23.

Lee, C.L., & Federmeier, K.D. (2006). To mind the mind: An event-related potential study of word class and semantic ambiguity. *Brain Research* 1081: 191–202.

Lee, H., Simpson, G., Logothetis, N.K., & Rainer, G. (2005). Phase locking of single neuron activity to theta oscillations during working memory in monkey extrastriate visual cortex. *Neuron* 45: 147–156.

Leopold, D.A., & Logothetis, N.K. (1999). Multistable phenomena: Changing views in perception. *Trends in Cognitive Sciences* 3: 254–264.

Levine, J. (1983). Materialism and qualia: The explanatory gap. *Pacific Philosophical Quarterly* 64: 354–361.

Lewis, C.I. (1929). *Mind and the World-Order: An Outline of a Theory of Knowledge*. New York: Scribner's.

Lewis, D. (1972). Psychophysical and theoretical identifications. *Australasian Journal of Philosophy* 50: 249–258.

————. (1980). Mad pain and Martian pain. In N. Block, ed., *Readings in Philosophy of Psychology*, 216–222. Cambridge, MA: Harvard University Press.

————. (1988). What experience teaches. *Proceedings of the Russellian Society* 13: 29–57.

Libet, B. (1999). Do we have free will? *Journal of Consciousness Studies* 6: 47–57.

Libet, B., Gleason, C.A., Wright, E.W., & Pearl, D.K. (1983). Time of conscious intention to act in relation to onset of cerebral activity (readiness-potential): The unconscious initiation of a freely voluntary act. *Brain* 106: 623–642.

Lichtenberg, G.C. (1765–1799/1990). *The Waste Books*. R.J. Hollingdale, trans. New York: New York Review of Books.

Lima, B., Singer, W., Chen, N.H., & Neuenschwander, S. (2010). Synchronization dynamics in response to plaid stimuli in monkey V1. *Cerebral Cortex* 20: 1556–1573.

Linden, D.E., Kallenbach, U., Heinecke, A., Singer, W., & Goebel, R. (1999). The myth of upright vision: A psychophysical and functional imaging study of adaptation to inverting spectacles. *Perception* 28: 469–481.

Lipps, M. (2002). How people take pictures: Understanding consumer behavior through eye tracking before, during, and after image capture. Research report, Visual Perception Laboratory Center for Imaging Science, Rochester Institute of Technology.

Liu, T., Slotnick, S.D., Serences, J.T., & Yantis, S. (2003). Cortical mechanisms of feature-based attentional control. *Cerebral Cortex* 13: 1334–1343.

Liu, Y., Yttri, E.A., & Snyder, L.H. (2010). Intention and attention: Different functional roles for LIPd and LIPv. *Nature Neuroscience* 13: 495–500.

Livermore, A., & Laing, D. (1998). The influence of odor type on the discrimination and identification of odorants in multicomponent odor mixtures. *Physiology & Behavior* 65: 311–320.

Llinás, R. (2002). *I of the Vortex: From Neurons to Self*. Cambridge, MA: MIT Press.

Llinás, R., & Ribary, U. (1993). Coherent 40-Hz oscillation characterizes dream state in humans. *Proceedings of the National Academy of Sciences USA* 90: 2078–2081.

Loar, B. (1990). Phenomenal states. *Philosophical Perspectives* 4: 81–108.

Locke, J. (1690/1979). *An Essay concerning Human Understanding*. P.H. Nidditch, ed. Oxford: Oxford University Press.

Logothetis, N.K., Pauls, J., & Poggio, T. (1995). Shape representation in the inferior temporal cortex of monkeys. *Current Biology* 5: 552–563.

Lopes, D.M. (2000). What is it like to see with your ears? The representational theory of mind. *Philosophy and Phenomenological Research* 60: 439–453.

Lormand, E. (1996). Nonphenomenal consciousness. *Noûs* 30: 242–261.

Lotto, R., & Purves, D. (2002). The empirical basis of color perception. *Consciousness and Cognition*, 11, 609–629.

Luauté, J., Schwartz, S., Rossetti, Y., Spiridon, M., Rode, G., Boisson, D., & Vuilleumier, P. (2009). Dynamic changes in brain activity during prism adaptation. *Journal of Neuroscience* 29: 169–178.

Luck, S.J., Hillyard, S.A., Mangun, G.R., & Gazzaniga, M.S. (1989). Independent hemispheric attentional systems mediate visual search in split-brain patients. *Nature* 342: 543–545.

Luck, S.J., Woodman, G.F., & Vogel, E.K. (2000). Event-related potential studies of attention. *Trends in Cognitive Sciences* 4: 432–440.

Lumer, E.D., & Rees, G. (1999). Covariation of activity in visual and prefrontal cortex associated with subjective visual perception. *Proceedings of the National Academy of Sciences USA* 96: 1669–1673.

Lutz, A., Greischar, L.L., Rawlings, N.B., Ricard, M., & Davidson, R.J. (2004). Long-term meditators self-induce high-amplitude gamma synchrony during mental practice. *Proceedings of the National Academy of Sciences USA* 101: 16369–16373.

Lycan, W.G. (1987). *Consciousness*. Cambridge, MA: MIT Press.

———. (1991). Homuncular functionalism meets PDP. In W. Ramsey, S.P. Stich, & D. Rumelhart, eds., *Philosophy and Connectionist Theory*, 259–286. Hillsdale, NJ: Lawrence Erlbaum.

———. (1996). *Consciousness and Experience*. Cambridge, MA: MIT Press.

———. (2001). A simple argument for a higher-order representation theory of consciousness. *Analysis* 61: 3–4.

————. (2004). The superiority of HOP to HOT. In R. Gennaro, ed., *Higher-Order Theories of Consciousness*, 115–136. Amsterdam: John Benjamins.

Macaluso, E., & Driver, J. (2001). Spatial attention and crossmodal interactions between vision and touch. *Neuropsychologia* 39: 1304–1316.

Machamer, P., Darden, L., & Carver, C. (2000). Thinking about mechanisms. *Philosophy of Science* 67: 1–25.

Mack, A., & Rock, I. (1998). *Inattentional Blindness*. Cambridge, MA: MIT Press.

Macdonald, J.S.P., & Lavie, N. (2011). Visual perceptual load induces inattentional deafness. *Attention, Perception & Psychophysics* 73: 1780–1789.

MacKay, D.M. (1962). Theoretical models of space perception. In C.A. Muses, ed., *Aspects of the Theory of Artificial Intelligence*, 83–104. New York: Plenum.

Mack, A., Pappas, Z., Silverman, M., & Gay, R. (2002). What we see: Inattention and the capture of attention by meaning. *Consciousness & Cognition* 11: 488–506.

Maier, J.X., Chandrasekaran, C., & Ghazanfar, A.A. (2008). Integration of bimodal looming signals through neuronal coherence in the temporal lobe. *Current Biology* 18: 963–968.

Maldonado, P., Babul, C., Singer, W., Rodriguez, E., Berger, D., & Grün, S. (2008). Synchronization of neuronal responses in primary visual cortex of monkeys viewing natural images. *Journal of Neurophysiology* 100: 1523–1532.

Malt, B.C. (1994). Water is not H2O. *Cognitive Psychology* 27: 41–70.

Mandik, P. (1999). Qualia, space, and control. *Philosophical Psycholology* 12: 47–60.

Mann, E.O., Suckling, J.M., Hajos, N., Greenfield, S.A., & Paulsen, O. (2005). Perisomatic feedback inhibition underlies cholinergically induced fast network oscillations in the rat hippocampus in vitro. *Neuron* 45: 105–117.

Marks, C. (1980). *Commissurotomy, Consciousness, and Unity of Mind*. Cambridge, MA: MIT Press.

Marois, R., & Ivanoff, J. (2005). Capacity limits of information processing in the brain. *Trends in Cognitive Sciences* 9: 296–305.

Marr, D. (1982). *Vision*. San Francisco: Freeman.

Marshall, J.C., & Halligan, P.W. (1988). Blindsight and insight in visiospatial neglect. *Nature* 336: 766–767.

Martin, A. (2007). The representation of object concepts in the brain. *Annual Review of Psychology* 58: 25–45.

Martínez, A., Anllo-Vento, L., Sereno, M.I., Frank, L.R., Buxton, R.B., Dubowitz, D.J., Wong, E.C., Hinrichs, H., Heinze, H.J., & Hillyard, S.A. (1999). Involvement of striate and extrastriate visual cortical areas in spatial attention. *Nature Neuroscience* 2: 364–369.

Mathewson, K.E., Gratton, G., Fabiani, M., Beck, D.M., & Ro, T. (2009). To see or not to see: Prestimulus alpha phase predicts visual awareness. *Journal of Neuroscience* 29: 2725–2732.

Maturana, H.R., & Varela, F.J. (1973). Autopoiesis: The organisation of the living. In H.R. Maturana & F.J. Varela, eds., *Autopoiesis and Cognition: The Realization of the Living*, 63–123. Boston: Reidel.

Maunsell, J.H.R., & Gibson, J.R. (1992). Visual response latencies in striate cortex of the macaque monkey. *Journal of Neurophysiology* 68: 1332–1344.

McClurkin, J.W., Zarbock, J.A., & Optican, L.M. (1996). Primate striate and prestriate cortical neurons during discrimination. II: Separable temporal codes for color and pattern. *Journal of Neurophysiology* 75: 496–507.

McGinn, C. (1991). *The Problem of Consciousness*. Oxford: Blackwell.

McGurk, H., & MacDonald, J. (1976). Hearing lips and seeing voices. *Nature* 264: 746–748.

McKeefry, D.J., Burton, M.P., Vakrou, C., Barrett, B.T., & Morland, A.B. (2008). Induced deficits in speed perception by transcranial magnetic stimulation of human cortical areas V5/MT+ and V3A. *Journal of Neuroscience* 28: 6848–6857.

McKyton, A., & Zohary, E. (2007). Beyond retinotopic mapping: The spatial representation of objects in the human lateral occipital complex. *Cerebral Cortex* 17: 1164–1172.

Mehta, A.D., & Schroeder, C.E. (2000). Intermodal selective attention in monkeys I: Distribution and timing of effects across visual areas. *Cerebral Cortex* 10: 343–358.

Meister, I.G., Wienemann, M., Buelte, D., Grünewald, C., Sparing, R., & Dambeck, N. (2006). Hemiextinction induced by transcranial magnetic stimulation over the right temporo-parietal junction. *Neuroscience* 142: 119–123.

Mele, A.R. (2009). *Effective Intentions: The Power of Conscious Will*. Oxford: Oxford University Press.

Melloni, L., Molina, C., Pena, M., Torres, D., Singer, W., & Rodriguez, E. (2007). Synchronization of neural activity across cortical areas correlates with conscious perception. *Journal of Neuroscience* 27: 2858–2865.

Mendez, M.F. (2001). Generalized auditory agnosia with spared music recognition in a left-hander: Analysis of a case with a right temporal stroke. *Cortex* 37: 139–150.

Mendola, J.D., Dale, A.M., Fischl, B., Liu, A.K., & Tootell, R.B.H. (1999). The representation of illusory and real contours in human cortical visual areas revealed by functional magnetic resonance imaging. *Journal of Neuroscience* 19: 8560–8572.

Merleau-Ponty, M. (1962). *Phenomenology of Perception*. New York: Humanities.

Metzger, W. (1930). Optische Untersuchungen am Ganzfeld. *Psychologische Forschung* 13: 6–29.

Metzinger, T., ed. (2000). *Neural Correlates of Consciousness: Empirical and Conceptual Questions*. Cambridge, MA: MIT Press.

Michotte, A. (1963). *The Perception of Causality*. New York: Basic.

Miller, S.M., Liu, G.B., Ngo, T.T., Hooper, G., Riek, S., Carson, R.G., & Pettigrew, J.D. (2000). Interhemispheric switching mediates perceptual rivalry. *Current Biology* 10: 383–392.

Millikan, R. (1984). *Language, Thought, and Other Biological Categories*. Cambridge, MA: MIT Press.

———. (2000). *On Clear and Confused Ideas*. Cambridge, UK: Cambridge University Press.

Milmine, M., Rose, J., & Colombo, M. (2008). Sustained activation and executive control in the avian prefrontal cortex. *Brain Research Bulletin* 76: 317–323.

Milner, A.D., & Goodale, M.A. (1995). *The Visual Brain in Action*. Oxford: Oxford University Press.

Mitchell, J.F., Stoner, G.R., & Reynolds, J.H. (2004). Object-based attention determines dominance in binocular rivalry. *Nature* 429: 410–413.

Mitchell, J.F., Sundberg, K.A., & Reynolds, J.H. (2007). Differential attention-dependent response modulation across cell classes in macaque visual area V4. *Neuron* 55: 131–141.

Mitroff, S.R., Simons, D.J., & Levin, D.T. (2004). Nothing compares two views: Change blindness can occur despite preserved access to the changed information. *Perception & Psychophysics* 66: 1268–1281.

Mizrahi, V. (2009). Is colour composition phenomenal? In D. Skusevich & P. Matikas, eds., *Color Perception: Physiology, Processes and Analysis*, 185–202. New York: Nova Science.

Mole, C. (2008). Attention and consciousness. *Journal of Consciousness Studies* 15: 86–104.

Monrad-Krohn, G.H. (1947). Dysprosody or altered "melody of language." *Brain* 70: 405–415.

Montero, B. (1999). The body problem. *Noûs* 33: 183–200.

Moore, J.W., Lagnado, D., Deal, D.C., & Haggard, P. (2009). Feelings of control: Contingency determines experience of action. *Cognition* 110: 279–283.

Moran, J., & Desimone, R. (1985). Selective attention gates visual processing in the extrastriate cortex. *Science* 229: 782–784.

Mordkoff, J.T., & Halterman, R. (2008). Feature integration without visual attention: Evidence from the correlated flankers task. *Psychonomic Bulletin & Review* 15: 385–389.

Morin, A. (2005). Possible links between self-awareness and inner speech: Theoretical background, underlying mechanisms, and empirical evidence. *Journal of Consciousness Studies* 12: 115–134.

Morita, T., Kochiyama, T., Okada, T., Yonekura, Y., Matsumura, M., & Sadato, N. (2004). The neural substrates of conscious color perception demonstrated using fMRI. *NeuroImage* 21: 1665–1673.

Moro, V., Zampini, M., & Aglioti, S.M. (2004). Changes in spatial position of hands modify tactile extinction but not disownership of contralesional hand in two right brain-damaged patients. *Neurocase* 10: 437–443.

Morrot, G., Brochet, F., & Dubourdieu, D. (2001). The color of odors. *Brain and Language* 79: 309–320.

Morsella, E. (2005). The function of phenomenal states: Supramodular interaction theory. *Psychological Review* 112: 1000–1021.

Mosimann, U.P., Müri, R.M., Burn, D.J., Felblinger, J., O'Brien, J.T., & McKeith, I.G. (2005). Saccadic eye movement changes in Parkinson's disease dementia and dementia with Lewy bodies. *Brain* 128: 1267–1276.

Most, S.B., Scholl, B.J., Clifford, E., & Simons, D.J. (2005). What you see is what you set: Sustained inattentional blindness and the capture of awareness. *Psychological Review* 112: 217–242.

Mueller, S.T., & Krawitz, A. (2009). Reconsidering the two-second decay hypothesis in verbal working memory. *Journal of Mathematical Psychology* 53: 14–25.

Murray, M.M., Wylie, G.R., Higgins, B.A., Javitt, D.C., Schroeder, C.E., & Foxe, J.J. (2002). The spatiotemporal dynamics of illusory contour processing: Combined high-density electrical mapping, sources analysis, and functional magnetic resonance imaging. *Journal of Neuroscience* 22: 5055–5073.

Naccache, L., & Dehaene, S. (2001). Unconscious semantic priming extends to novel unseen stimuli. *Cognition* 80: 215–229.

Naccache, L., Blandin, E., & Dehaene, S. (2002). Unconscious masked priming depends on temporal attention. *Psychological Science* 13: 416–424.

Naccache, L., Gaillard, R., Adam, C., Hasboun, D., Clémenceau, S., Baulac, M., Dehaene, S., & Cohen, L. (2005). A direct intracranial record of emotions evoked by subliminal words. *Proceedings of the National Academy of Sciences USA* 102: 7713–7717.

Nagel, T. (1974). What is it like to be a bat? *Philosophical Review* 83: 435–450.

Nair, K.U., & Ramnarayan, S. (2000). Individual differences in need for cognition and complex problem solving. *Journal of Research in Personality* 34: 305–328.

Nakatani, C., Ito, J., Nikolaev, R.A., Gong, P., & van Leeuwen, C. (2005). Phase synchronization analysis of EEG during attentional blink. *Journal of Cognitive Neuroscience* 17: 1969–1979.

Nemirow, L. (1990). Physicalism and the cognitive role of acquaintance. In W. Lycan, ed., *Mind and Cognition*, 490–499. Oxford: Blackwell.

Newman, J., & Baars, B.J. (1993). A neural attentional model for access to consciousness: A global workspace perspective. *Concepts in Neuroscience* 4: 255–290.

Nikolić, D., Hausler, S., Singer, W., & Maass, W. (2009). Distributed fading memory for stimulus properties in the primary visual cortex. *PLoS Biology* 7: e1000260.

Nisbett, R., & Wilson, T. (1977). Telling more than we can know: Verbal reports on mental processes. *Psychological Review* 84: 231–259.

Noë, A. (2005). *Action in Perception*. Cambridge, MA: MIT Press.

———. (2010). Vision without representation. In N. Gangopadhyay, M. Madary, & F. Spicer, eds., *Perception, Action, and Consciousness: Sensorimotor Dynamics and Two Visual Systems*, 245–256. Oxford: Oxford University Press.

O'Doherty, J.P., Deichmann, R., Critchley, H.D., & Dolan, R.J. (2002). Neural responses during anticipation of a primary taste reward. *Neuron* 33: 815–826.

O'Regan, J.K., & Noë, A. (2001). A sensorimotor account of vision and visual consciousness. *Behavioral and Brain Sciences* 24: 939–1031.

O'Reilly, R., Busby, R., and Soto, R. (2003). Three forms of binding and their neural substrates: Alternatives to temporal synchrony. In A. Cleeremans, ed., *The Unity of Consciousness: Binding, Integration, and Dissociation*, 168–192. Oxford: Oxford University Press.

Orgs, G., Lange, K., Dombrowski, J.-H., & Heil, M. (2006). Conceptual priming for environmental sounds and words: An ERP study. *Brain and Cognition* 65: 162–166.

Osipova, D., Hermes, D., Jensen, O., & Rustichini, A. (2008). Gamma power is phase-locked to posterior alpha activity. *PLoS ONE* 3: 1–7.

Ostrowsky, K., Magnin, M., Ryvlin, P., Isnard, J., Guenot, M., & Maugiére, F. (2002). Representation of pain and somatic sensation in the human insula: A study of responses to direct electrical cortical stimulation. *Cerebral Cortex* 12: 376–385.

Pacherie, E. (2001). Agency lost and found. *Philosophy Psychiatry Psychology* 8: 173–176.

Palmer, S.E. (1999). Color, consciousness, and the isomorphism constraint. *Behavioral and Brain Sciences* 22: 923–989.

Palva, S., & Palva, J.M. (2007). New vistas for α-frequency band oscillations. *Trends in Neurosciences* 30: 150–158.

Panzeri, S., Brunel, N., Logothetis, N.K., & Kayser, C. (2010). Sensory neural codes using multiplexed temporal scales. *Trends in Neuroscience* 33: 111–120.

Papineau, D. (2002). *Thinking about Consciousness*. Oxford: Oxford University Press.

Parr, W.V., White, K.G., & Heatherball, D.A. (2004). Exploring the nature of wine expertise: What underlies wine experts' olfactory recognition memory advantage? *Food Quality and Preference* 15: 411–420.

Pasupathy, A., & Connor, C.E. (2002). Population coding of shape in area V4. *Nature Neuroscience* 5: 1332–1338.

Patterson, K., Nestor, P.J., Rogers, T.T. (2007). Where do you know what you know? The representation of semantic knowledge in the human brain. *Nature Neuroscience* 8: 976–987.

Paus, T., Zatorre, R., Hofle, T., Caramanos, Z., Gotman, J., Petrides, M., & Evans, A. (1997). Time-related changes in neural systems underlying attention and arousal during the performance of an auditory vigilance task. *Journal of Cognitive Neuroscience* 9: 392–408.

Peacocke, C. (1983). *Sense and Content*. Oxford: Oxford University Press.

———. (1998). Conscious attitudes, attention, and self-knowledge. In C. Wright, B. Smith, and C. Macdonald, eds., *Knowing Our Own Minds*, 63–98. Oxford: Oxford University Press.

———. (2007). Mental action and self-awareness. In B.P. McLaughlin & J.D. Cohen, eds., *Contemporary Debates in Philosophy of Mind*, 358–376. Oxford: Blackwell.

Pellisson, D., Prablanc, C., Goodale, M.A., & Jeannerod, M. (1986). Visual control of reaching movements without vision of the limb. II: Evidence of fast unconscious processes correcting the trajectory of the hand to the final position of a double-step stimulus. *Experimental Brain Research* 62: 303–311.

Penfield, W., & Evans, J. (1935). The frontal lobe in man: A clinical study of maximal removals. *Brain* 58: 115–133.

Peretz, I. (1993). Auditory agnosia: A functional analysis. In S. McAdams & E. Bigand, eds., *Thinking in Sound*, 199–230. Oxford: Oxford University Press.

Peretz, I., Blood, A.J., Penhune, V., & Zatorre, R.J. (2001). Cortical deafness to dissonance. *Brain* 124: 928–940.

Perkel, D.J., Bullier, J., & Kennedy, H. (1986). Topography of the afferent connectivity of area 17 of the macaque monkey: A double labeling study. *Journal of Comparative Neurology* 253: 374–402.

Perrett, D.I., Oram, M.W., Harries, M.H., Bevan, R., Hietanen, J.K., Benson, P.J., & Thomas, S. (1991). Viewer-centered and object-centered coding of heads in the macaque temporal cortex. *Experimental Brain Research* 86: 159–173.

Peru, A., Moro, V., Avesani, R., & Aglioti, S. (1996). Overt and covert processing of left-side information in unilateral neglect investigated with chimeric drawings. *Journal of Clinical and Experimental Neuropsychology* 18: 621–630.

Pessiglione, M., Schmidt, L., Draganski, B., Kalisch, R., Lau, H., Dolan, R.J. & Frith, C.D. (2007). How the brain translates money into force: A neuroimaging study of subliminal motivation. *Science* 316: 904–906.

Petersen, R.S., Panzeri, S., & Diamon, M.E. (2002). Population coding in somatosensory cortex. *Current Opinion in Neurobiology* 12: 441–447.

Petrides, M. (1996). Specialized systems for the processing of mnemonic information within the primate frontal cortex. *Philosophical Transactions of the Royal Society of London B* 351: 1455–1462.

Phan, K.L., Wager, T., Taylor, S.F., & Liberzon, I. (2002). Functional neuroanatomy of emotion: A meta-analysis of emotion activation studies in PET and fMRI. *Neuroimage* 16: 331–348.

Picard, M. (1921). The unity of consciousness. *Journal of Philosophy* 18: 347–357.

Pitt, D. (2004). The phenomenology of cognition, or, what is it like to think that P? *Philosophy and Phenomenological Research* 69: 1–36.

Pizzighello, S., & Bressan, P. (2008). Auditory attention causes visual inattentional blindness. *Perception* 37: 859–866.

Place, U.T. (1956). Is consciousness a brain process? *British Journal of Psychology* 47: 44–50.

Platz, T. (1996). Tactile agnosia: Casuistic evidence and theoretical remarks on modality-specific meaning representations and sensorimotor integration. *Brain* 119: 1565–1574.

Plendl, H., Paulus, W., Roberts, I.G., Gotzel, K., Towell, A., Pitman, J.R., Scherg, M., & Halliday, A.M. (1993). The time course and location of cerebral evoked activity associated with the processing of color stimuli in man. *Neuroscience Letters* 150: 9–12.

Polger, T. (2004). *Natural Minds*. Cambridge, MA: MIT Press.

Pons, T.P., Garraghty, P.E., Friedman, D.P., & Mishkin, M. (1987). Physiological evidence for serial processing in somatosensory cortex. *Science* 237: 417–420.

Pöppel, E. (1971). Oscillations as possible basis for time perception. *Studium Generale* 24: 85–107.

———. (1988a). The measurement of music and the cerebral clock: A new theory. *Leonardo* 22: 83–89.

———. (1988b). *Mindworks: Time and Conscious Experience*. New York: Harcourt Brace Jovanovich.

———. (1994). Temporal mechanisms in perception. *International Review of Neurobiolology* 37: 185–202.

———. (2009). Pre-semantically defined temporal windows for cognitive processing. *Philosophical Transactions of the Royal Society of London B* 364: 1887–1896.

Posner, M.I. (1980). Orienting of attention. *Quarterly Journal of Experimental Psychology* 32: 3–25.

———. (1994). Attention: The mechanisms of consciousness. *Procedures of the National Academy of Sciences USA* 91: 7398–7403.

Posner, M.I., & Gilbert, C.D. (1999). Attention and primary visual cortex. *Proceedings of the National Academy of Sciences USA* 96: 2585–2587.

Posner, M.I., & Raichle, M.E. (1994). *Images of Mind*. New York: Scientific American.

Price, H.H. (1932). *Perception*. London: Methuen.

Priebe, N.J., & Lisberger, S.G. (2004). Estimating target speed from the population response in visual area MT. *Journal of Neuroscience* 24: 1907–1916.

Prinz, J.J. (2000a). The duality of content. *Philosophical Studies* 100: 1–34.

Prinz, J.J. (2000b). A neurofunctional theory of visual consciousness. *Consciousness and Cognition*, 9: 243–259.

———. (2002). *Furnishing the Mind: Concepts and Their Perceptual Basis*. Cambridge, MA: MIT Press.

———. (2003). Level-headed mysterianism and artificial experience. *Journal of Consciousness Studies* 10: 111–132.

———. (2004a). The fractionation of introspection. *Journal of Consciousness Studies* 11: 40–57.

———. (2004b). *Gut Reactions: A Perceptual Theory of Emotion*. New York: Oxford University Press.

———. (2005). A neurofunctional theory of consciousness. In A. Brook & K. Akins, eds., *Cognition and the Brain: Philosophy and Neuroscience Movement*, 381–396. Cambridge, UK: Cambridge University Press.

———. (2006a). Beyond appearances: The content of sensation and perception. In T.S. Gendler & J. Hawthorne, eds., *Perceptual Experiences*, 434–460. Oxford: Oxford University Press.

———. (2006b). Putting the brakes on enactive perception. *Psyche* 12: 1–19.

———. (2007a). All consciousness is perceptual. In B. McLaughlin & J. Cohen, eds., *Contemporary Debates in Philosophy of Mind*, 335–357. Oxford: Blackwell.

———. (2007b). Mental pointing: Phenomenal knowledge without concepts. *Journal of Consciousness Studies* 14: 184–211.

———. (2008). Is consciousness embodied? In P. Robbins & M. Aydede, eds., *Cambridge Handbook of Situated Cognition*. Cambridge, UK: Cambridge University Press.

———. (2010). When is perception conscious? In B. Nanay, ed., *Perceiving the World: New Essays on Perception*, 310–332. New York: Oxford University Press.

Preuss, T.M., & Coleman, G.Q. (2002). Human-specific organization of primary visual cortex: Alternating compartments of dense Cat-301 and calbindin immunoreacitivity in layer 4A. *Cerebral Cortex* 12: 671–691.

Pruett, J.R., Sinclair, R.J., & Burton, H. (2000). Response patterns in second somatosensory cortex (SII) of awake monkeys to passively applied tactile gratings. *Journal of Neurophysiology* 84: 780–797.

Ptito, M., Moesgard, S.M., Gjedde, A., & Kupers, R. (2005). Cross-modal plasticity revealed by electrotactile stimulation of the tongue in the congenitally blind. *Brain* 128: 606–614.

Purves, D., & Lotto, R.B. (2003). *Why We See What We Do: An Empirical Theory of Vision*. Sunderland, MA: Sinauer.

Putnam, H. (1967). Psychological predicates. In W.H. Capitan & D.D. Merrill, eds., *Art, Mind, and Religion*, 37–48. Pittsburgh: University of Pittsburgh Press.

Quine, W.V.O. (1951). Two dogmas of empiricism. *Philosophical Review* 60: 20–43.

Raffman, D. (1995). On the persistence of phenomenology. In T. Metzinger, ed., *Conscious Experience*, 293–308. Paderborn, Germany: Imprint Academic.

Ramachandran, V.S. (1995). Anosognosia in parietal lobe syndrome. *Consciousness and Cognition* 4: 22–51.

Ramachandran, V.S., & Hirstein, W. (1997). Three laws of qualia: Clues from neurology about the biological functions of consciousness and qualia. *Journal of Consciousness Studies* 6: 15–41.

———. (1998). The perception of phantom limbs. *Brain* 121: 1603–1630.

Ramsden, B.M., Chou, P.H., and Roe, A.W. (2001). Real and illusory contour processing in area V1 of the primate: A cortical balancing act. *Cerebral Cortex* 11: 648–665.

Rao, R., Eagleman, D., & Sejnowski, T. (2001). Optimal smoothing in visual motion perception. *Neural Computing* 13: 1243–1253.

Ratcliff, G., & Davies-Jones, G.A.B. (1972). Defective visual localization in focal brain wounds. *Brain* 95: 49–60.

Rauschecker, J.P. (1998). Cortical processing of complex sounds. *Current Opinion in Neurobiology* 8: 516–521.

Ray, S., Niebur, E., Hsiao, S.S., Sinai, A., & Crone, N.E. (2008). High-frequency gamma activity (80–150 Hz) is increased in human cortex during selective attention. *Clinical Neurophysiology* 119: 116–133.

Recanzone, G.H., Merzenich, M.M., & Schreiner, C.E. (1992). Changes in the distributed temporal response properties of SI cortical neurons reflect improvements in performance on a temporally based tactile discrimination task. *Journal of Neurophysiology* 67: 1071–1091.

Reddy, L., Reddy, L., & Koch, C. (2006). Face identification in the near-absence of focal attention. *Vision Research* 46: 2336–2343.

Reed, C.L., Caselli, R.J., & Farah, M.J. (1996). Tactile agnosia: Underlying impairment and implications for normal tactile object recognition. *Brain* 119: 875–888.

Reed, C.L., Shoham, S., & Halgren, E. (2004). Neural substrates of tactile object recognition: An fMRI study. *Human Brain Mapping* 21: 236–246.

Rees, G., Wojciulik, E., Clarke, K., Husain, M., Frith, C., & Driver, J. (2000). Unconscious activation of visual cortex in the damaged right hemisphere of a parietal patient with extinction. *Brain* 123: 1624–1633.

Reeves, A.J., Amano, K., & Foster, D.H. (2008). Color constancy: Phenomenal or projective? *Perception & Psychophysics* 70: 219–228.

Reeves, A., Fuller, H., & Fine, E. (2005). The role of attention in binding shape to color. *Vision Research* 45: 3343–3355.

Reid, T. (1764/1970). *An Inquiry into the Human Mind.* Chicago: University of Chicago Press.

Rensink, R.A., O'Regan, J.K., & Clark, J.J. (1997). To see or not to see: The need for attention to perceive changes in scenes. *Psychological Science* 8: 368–373.

Rey, G. (1988). A question about consciousness. In H. Otto & J. Tuedio, eds., *Perspectives in Mind: From Objective Function to Subjective Reference*, 5–24. Dordrecht: Reidel.

Reynolds, J.H., Chelazzi, L., & Desimone, R. (1999). Competitive mechanisms subserve attention in macaque areas V2 and V4. *Journal of Neuroscience* 19: 1736–1753.

Rivière, J., & Lécuyer, R. (2002). Spatial cognition in young children with spinal muscular atrophy. *Developmental Neuropsychology* 21: 273–283.

Rizzolatti, G., & Craighero, L. (2004). The mirror-neuron system. *Annual Reviews Neuroscience* 27: 169–192.

Robertson, L.C. (2003). Binding, spatial attention and perceptual awareness. *Nature Neuroscience* 4: 93–102.

Rock, I., & Gutman, D. (1981). The effect of inattention on form perception. *Journal of Experimental Psychology: Human Perception & Performance* 7: 275–285.

Rock, I., Linnett, C.M., Grant, P., & Mack, A. (1992). Perception without attention: Results of a new method. *Cognitive Psychology* 24: 502–534.

Rohenkohl, G., & Nobre, A.C. (2010). Alpha band oscillations track temporal orienting of attention. Poster presentation, 16th Annual Meeting of the Organization for Human Brain Mapping, Barcelona.

Roland, P.E., & Mortensen, E. (1987). Somatosensory detection of microgeometry, macrogeometry and kinesthesia in man. *Brain Research* 434: 1–42.

Rolls, E.T. (2004). *A higher order syntactic thought (HOST) theory of consciousness.* In R.J. Gennaro, ed., *Higher Order Theories of Consciousness*, 137–172. Philadelphia: John Benjamins.

Rolls, E.T., & Tovée, M.J. (1994). Processing speed in the cerebral cortex, and the neurophysiology of backward masking. *Proceedings of the Royal Society of London B* 257: 9–15.

Rolls, E.T., Yaxley, S., & Sienkiewicz, Z.J. (1990). Gustatory responses of single neurons in the caudolateral orbitofrontal cortex of the macaque monkey. *Journal of Neurophysiology* 64: 1055–1066.

Rols, G., Tallon-Baudry, C., Girard, P., Bertrand, O., & Bullier, J. (2001). Cortical mapping of gamma oscillations in areas V1 and V4 of the macaque monkey. *Visual Neuroscience* 18: 527–540.

Romei, V., Gross, J., & Thut, G. (2010). On the role of prestimulus alpha rhythms over occipito-parietal areas in visual input regulation: Correlation or causation? *Journal of Neuroscience* 30: 8692–8697.

Rosenthal, D.M. (1986). Two concepts of consciousness. *Philosophical Studies* 49: 329–359.

———. (1997). A theory of consciousness. In N. Block, O. Flanagan, & G. Güzeldere, eds., *The Nature of Consciousness: Philosophical Debates*, 729–753. Cambridge, MA: MIT Press.

———. (2005). *Consciousness and Mind*. Oxford: Oxford University Press.

———. (2008). Consciousness and its function. *Neuropsychologia* 46: 829–840.

Rounis, E., Maniscalco, B., Rothwell, J.C., Passingham, R.E., & Lau, H. (2010). Theta-burst transcranial magnetic stimulation to the prefrontal cortex impairs metacognitive visual awareness. *Cognitive Neuroscience* 1: 165–175.

Ruben, J., Schwiemann, J., Deuchert, M., Meyer, R., Krause, T., Curio, G., Villringer, K., Kurth, R., & Villringer, A. (2001) Somatotopic organization of human secondary somatosensory cortex. *Cerebral Cortex* 11: 463–473.

Rubens, A.B., & Benson, D.F. (1971). Associative visual agnosia. *Archives of Neurology* 24: 305–316.

Ruby, P., & Decety, J. (2001). Effect of the subjective perspective taking during simulation of action: A PET investigation of agency. *Nature Neuroscience* 4: 546–550.

Russell, B. (1912). *Problems of Philosophy*. Oxford: Oxford University Press.

Rüttiger, L., Braun, D.I., Gegenfurtner, K.R., Petersen, D., Schoenle, P., & Sharpe, L.T. (1999). Selective color constancy deficits after circumscribed unilateral brain lesions. *Journal of Neuroscience* 19: 3094–3106.

Ryle, G. (1949). *The Concept of Mind*. London: Penguin.

Sacks, O. (1995). To see and not to see. In *An Anthropologist on Mars: Seven Paradoxical Tales*, 108–152. New York: Knopf.

———. (1996). *The Island of the Colorblind*. New York: Vintage.

Sadato, N., Pascual-Leone, A., Grafman, J., Ibanez, V., Deiber, M.P., Dold, G., & Hallett, M. (1996). Activation of the primary visual cortex by Braille reading in blind subjects. *Nature* 380: 526–528.

Sahraie, A., Weiskrantz, L., Barbur, J.L., Simmons, A., Williams, S.C.R., & Brammer, M.J. (1997). Pattern of neuronal activity associated with conscious and unconscious processing of visual signals. *Proceedings of the National Academy of Sciences USA* 94: 9406–9411.

Salinas, E., & Sejnowski, T.J. (2001). Correlated neuronal activity and the flow of neural information. *National Review of Neuroscience* 2: 539–550.

Samonds, J.M., Zhou, Z., Bernard, M.R., & Bonds, A.B. (2006). Synchronous activity in cat visual cortex encodes collinear and cocircular contours. *Journal of Neurophysiology* 95: 2602–2616.

Sauseng, P., Hoppe, J., Klimesch, W., Gerloff, C., & Hummel, F. (2007). Dissociation of sustained attention from central executive functions: Local activity and interregional connectivity in the theta range. *European Journal of Neuroscience* 25: 587–593.

Sauseng, P., Klimesch, W., Stadler, W., Schabus, M., Doppelmayr, M., Hanslmayr, S., Gruber, W.R., & Birbaumer, N. (2005). A shift of visual spatial attention is selectively associated with human EEG alpha activity. *European Journal of Neuroscience* 22: 2917–2926.

Sauvan, X.M., & Peterhans, E. (1999). Orientation constancy in neurons of monkey visual cortex. *Visual Cognition* 6: 43–54.

Savic, I., & Berglund, H. (2004). Passive perception of odors and semantic circuits. *Human Brain Mapping* 21: 271–278.

Savic, I., Gulyas, B., Larsson, M., & Roland, P. (2000). Olfactory functions are mediated by parallel and hierarchical processing. *Neuron* 26: 735–745.

Saxe, R., & Powell, L.J. (2006). It's the thought that counts: Specific brain regions for one component of theory of mind. *Psychological Science* 17: 692–699.

Schellenberg, S. (2007). Action and self-location in perception. *Mind* 116: 603–631.

Schiff, N.D. (2008). Central thalamic contributions to arousal regulation and neurological disorders of consciousness. *Annals of the New York Academy of Science* 1129: 105–118.

Schiller, P.H., & Carvey, C.E. (2005). The Hermann grid illusion revisited. *Perception* 34: 1375–1397.

Schira, M., Fahle, M., Donner, T., Kraft, A., & Brandt, S. (2004). Differential contribution of early visual areas to the perceptual process of contour processing. *Journal of Neurophysiology* 91: 1716–1721.

Schleidt, M., & Kien, J. (1997). Segmentation in behavior and what it can tell us about brain function. *Human Nature* 8: 77–111.

Schmolesky, M.T., Wang, Y., Hanes, D.P., Thompson, K.G., Leutgeb, S., Schall, J.D., & Leventhal, A.G. (1998). Signal timing across the macaque visual system. *Journal of Neurophysiology* 79: 3272–3278.

Schneider, R.J., Friedman, D.P., & Mishkin, M. (1993). A modality-specific somatosensory area within the insula of the rhesus monkey. *Brain Research* 621: 116–120.

Schnyer, D., Nicholls, L., & Verfaellie, M. (2005). The role of VMPC in metamemorial judgments of content retrievability. *Journal of Cognitive Neuroscience* 17: 832–846.

Schnyer, D.M., Ryan, L., Trouard, T., & Forster, K. (2002). Masked word repetition results in increased fMRI signal: A framework for understanding signal changes in priming. *NeuroReport* 13: 281–284.

Schoenfeld, M.A., Hopf, J.M., Martínez, A., Mai, H.M., Sattler, C., Gasde, A., Heinze, H. -J., & Hillyard, S.A. (2007). Spatio-temporal analysis of feature-based attention. *Cerebral Cortex* 17: 2468–2477.

Schroeder, T. (2004). *Three Faces of Desire*. New York: Oxford University Press.

Schubert, R., Blankenburg, F., Lemm, S., Villringer, A., & Curio, G. (2006). Now you feel it—now you don't: ERP correlates of somatosensory awareness. *Psychophysiology* 43: 31–40.

Schurger, A., Cowey, A., & Tallon-Baudry, C. (2006). Induced gamma-band oscillations correlate with awareness in hemianopic patient GY. *Neuropsychologia* 44: 1796–1803.

Scott, M. (2007). Distinguishing the senses. *Philosophical Explorations* 10: 257–262.

Scott, T.R., Yaxley, S., Sienkiewicz, Z.J., & Rolls, E.T. (1986). Gustatory responses in the frontal opercular cortex of the alert cynomolgus monkey. *Journal of Neurophysiology* 56: 876–890.

Searle, J. (1992). *The Rediscovery of Mind*. Cambridge, MA: MIT Press.

Sederberg, P.B., Schulze-Bonhage, A., Madsen, J.R., Bromfield, E.B., Litt, B., Brandt, A., & Kahana, M.J. (2007). Gamma oscillations distinguish true from false memories. *Psychological Science* 18: 927–932.

Seghier, M., Dojat, M., Delon-Martin, C., Rubin, C., Warnking, J., Segebarth C., and Bullier, J. (2000). Moving illusory contours activate primary visual cortex: An fMRI Study. *Cerebral Cortex* 10: 663–670.

Seguin, E.G. (1886). A contribution to the pathology of hemianopsis of central origin (cortex-hemianopsia). *Journal of Nervous and Mental Diseases* 13: 1–38.

Senkowski, D., Schneider, T.R., Foxe, J.J., & Engel, A.K. (2008). Crossmodal binding by neural coherence: Implications for multisensory processing. *Trends in Neurosciences* 31: 401–409.

Senkowski, D., Talsma, D., Grigutsch, M., Herrmann, C.S., & Woldorff, M.G. (2007). Good times for multisensory integration: Effects of the precision of temporal synchrony as revealed by gamma-band oscillations. *Neuropsychologia* 45: 561–571.

Serences, J.T., Ester, E.F., Vogel, E.K., & Awh, E. (2009). Stimulus-specific delay activity in human primary visual cortex. *Psychological Science* 20: 207–214.

Sereno, M.I., Pitzalis, S., & Martinez, A. (2001). Mapping of contralateral space in retinotopic coordinates by a parietal cortical area in humans. *Science* 294: 1350–1354.

Sevush, S. (2006). Single-neuron theory of consciousness. *Journal of Theoretical Biology* 238: 704–725.

Sewards, T.V., & Sewards, M.A. (1999). Alpha-band oscillations in visual cortex: Part of the neural correlate of visual awareness? *International Journal of Psychophysiology* 32: 35–45.

Shadlen, M.N. (2002). Rate versus temporal coding of information in the cerebral cortex. In *Encyclopedia of Cognitive Science*. New York: Macmillan.

Shadlen, M.N., & Movshon, J.A. (1999). Synchrony unbound: A critical evaluation of the temporal binding hypothesis. *Neuron* 24: 67–77.

Shams, L., Kamitani, Y., & Shimojo, S. (2000). What you see is what you hear. *Nature* 408: 788.

Shapiro, L. (2000). Multiple realizations. *Journal of Philosophy* 97: 635–654.

Sheinberg, D.L., & Logothetis, N.K. (1997). The role of temporal cortical areas in perceptual organization. *Proceedings of the National Academy of Sciences USA* 94: 3408–3413.

Shergill, S.S., Bullmore, E.T., Brammer, M.J., Williams, S.C.R., Murray, R.M., and McGuire P.K. (2001). A functional study of auditory verbal imagery. *Psychological Medicine* 31: 241–253.

Sheth, B., Nguyen, H., & Whittaker, G. (2010). Effect of sleep on color perception. Poster presented at the 24th annual meeting of the Associated Professional Sleep Societies, San Antonio, TX.

Shimojo, S., & Shams, L. (2001). Sensory modalities are not separate modalities: Plasticity and interactions. *Current Opinion in Neurobiology* 11: 505–509.

Shimojo, S., Kamitani, Y., & Nishida, S. (2001). Afterimage of perceptually filled-in surface. *Science* 293: 1677–1680.

Shipko, S. (1982). Alexithymia and somatization. *Psychotherapy and Psychosomatics* 37: 193–201.

Shoemaker, S. (1981). Some varieties of functionalism. *Philosophical Topics* 12, 93–119.

Shomrat, T., Zarrella, I., Fiorito, G., & Hochner, B. (2008). The octopus vertical lobe modulates short-term learning rate and uses LTP to acquire long-term memory. *Current Biology* 18: 337–342.

Sidtis, J.J. (1988). Dichotic listening after commissurotomy. In K. Hugdahl, ed., *Handbook of Dichotic Listening*, 161–184. New York: Wiley.

Siegel, S. (2006). Which properties are represented in perception? In T.S. Gendler & J. Hawthorne, eds., *Perceptual Experiences* 481–503. Oxford: Oxford University Press.

Siewert, C.P. (1998). *The Significance of Consciousness*. Princeton, NJ: Princeton University Press.

———. (2009). Consciousness and conceptual thought. In T. Bayne, ed., *The Oxford Companion to Consciousness*, 167–168. Oxford: Oxford University Press.

Silverman, M., & Mack, A. (2001). Priming from change blindness [abstract]. *Journal of Vision* 1: 13a.

Simons, D., & Chabris, C. (1999). Gorillas in our midst: Sustained inattentional blindness for dynamic events. *Perception* 28: 1059–1074.

Simons, D.J., & Levin, D.T. (1997). Change blindness. *Trends in Cognitive Science* 1: 261–267.

Singer, W. (1999). Neuronal synchrony: A versatile code for the definition of relations? *Neuron* 24: 49–65.

Singer, W., & Gray, C.M. (1995). Visual feature integration and the temporal correlation hypothesis. *Annual Review of Neuroscience* 18: 555–586.

Sirigu, A., Daprati, E., Ciancia, S., Giraux, P., Nighoghossian, N., Posada, A., & Haggard, P. (2003). Altered awareness of voluntary action after damage to the parietal cortex. *Nature Neuroscience* 7: 80–84.

Sligte, I.G., Vandenbroucke, A.R.E., Scholte, H.S., & Lamme, V.A.F. (2010). Detailed sensory memory, sloppy working memory. *Frontiers in Psychology* 1: 12.

Sligte, I.G., Wokke, M.E., Tesselaar, J.P., Scholte, H.S., & Lamme, V.A.F. (2011) Magnetic stimulation of the dorsolateral prefrontal cortex dissociates fragile visual short tem memory from visual working memory. *Neuropsychologia* 49: 1578–1588.

Sloman, S.A., & Malt, B.C. (2003). Artifacts are not ascribed essences, nor are they treated as belonging to kinds. *Language and Cognitive Processes* 18: 563–582.

Slotnick, S.D., Thompson, W.L., & Kosslyn, S.M. (2005). Visual mental imagery induces retinotopically organized activation of early visual areas. *Cerebral Cortex* 15: 1570–1583.

Small, D.M., Zald, D.H., Jones-Gotman, M., Zatorre, R.J., Pardo, J.V., Frey, S., and Petrides, M. (1999). Human cortical gustatory areas: A review of functional neuroimaging data. *NeuroReport* 10: 7–14.

Smart, J.J.C. (1959). Sensations and brain processes. *Philosophical Review* 68: 141–156.

Smith, E.E., Jonides, J., Koeppe, R.A., Awh, E., Schumacher, E., & Minoshima, S. (1995). Spatial versus object working memory: PET investigation. *Journal of Cognitive Neuroscience* 7: 337–356.

Sohal, V.S., & Huguenard, J.R. (2005). Inhibitory coupling specifically generates emergent gamma oscillations in diverse cell types. *Proceedings of the National Academy of Sciences USA* 102: 18638–18643.

Solomon, R.C., ed. (2004). *Thinking about Feeling: Contemporary Philosophers on Emotions*. Oxford: Oxford University Press.

Soon, C.S., Brass, M., Heinze, H.J., & Haynes, J.D. (2008). Unconscious determinants of free decisions in the human brain. *Nature Neuroscience* 11: 543–545.

Soto, D., Mäntylä, T., & Silvanto, J. (2011). Working memory without consciousness. *Current Biology* 21: R912–R913.

Sperling, G. (1960). The information available in brief visual presentations. *Psychological Monographs* 74: 1–29.

Spillmann, L., Laskowski, W., & Lange, K.W. (2000). Stroke-blind for colors, faces, and locations: Partial recovery after three years. *Restorative Neurology and Neuroscience* 17: 89–103.

Steinmetz, P.N., Roy, A., Fitzgerald, P.J., Hsiao, S.S., Johnston, K.O., & Niebur, E. (2000). Attention modulates synchronized neuronal firing in primate somatosensory cortex. *Nature* 404: 187–190.

Stetson, C., Fiesta, M., & Eagleman, D.M. (2007). Does time really slow down during a frightening event? *PLoS ONE* 2: 1295.

Stevenson, R.J., & Wilson, D.A. (2007). Odour perception: An object-recognition approach. *Perception* 36: 1821–1833.

Stewart, L., von Kriegstein, K., Warren, J.D., & Griffiths, T.D. (2006). Music and the brain: Disorders of musical listening. *Brain* 129: 2533–2553.

Stoerig, P., & Cowey, A. (1997). Blindsight in man and monkey. *Brain* 120: 535–559.

Stopfer, M., Jayaraman, V., & Laurent, G. (2003). Intensity versus identity coding in an olfactory system. *Neuron* 39: 991–1004.

Stratton, G.M. (1897). Vision without inversion of the retinal image. *Psychological Review* 4: 341–360, 463–481.

Strawson, G. (1999). Self and body: Self, body, and experience. *Proceedings of the Aristotelian Society* 73: 307–332.

———. (2009). *Selves: An Essay in Revisionary Metaphysics*. Oxford: Oxford University Press.

Strawson, P.F. (1966). *The Bounds of Sense*. London: Methuen.

Sugita, Y. (1996). Global plasticity in adult visual cortex following reversal of visual input. *Nature* 380: 523–526.

Summerfield, C., Jack, A.I., & Burgess, A.P. (2002). Induced gamma activity is associated with conscious awareness of pattern masked nouns. *International Journal of Psychophysiology* 44: 93–100.

Suzuki, S., & Grabowecky, M. (2003). Attention during adaptation weakens negative afterimages. *Journal of Experimental Psychology: Human Perception and Performance* 29: 793–807.

Szczepanowski, R., & Pessoa, L. (2007). Fear perception: Can objective and subjective awareness measures be dissociated? *Journal of Vision* 7: 1–17.

Szelag, E. (1997). Temporal integration of the brain as studied with the metronome paradigm. In H. Atmanspacher & E. Ruhnau, eds., *Time, Temporality, Now*, 107–120. Berlin: Springer.

Tallon-Baudry, C., & Bertrand, O. (1999). Oscillatory gamma activity in humans and its role in object representation. *Trends in Cognitive Science* 3: 151–162.

Tallon-Baudry, C., Bertrand, O., Delpuech, C., & Pernier, J. (1997). Oscillatory g-band activity (30–70 Hz) induced by a visual search task in human. *Journal of Neuroscience* 17: 722–734.

Tanaka, K. (1997). Mechanisms of visual object recognition: Monkey and human studies. *Current Opinion in Neurobiology* 7: 523–529.

Taraborelli, D., & Mossio, M. (2008). On the relation between the enactive and the sensorimotor approach to perception *Consciousness and Cognition* 17: 1343–1344.

Tarr, M.J., & Gauthier, I. (2000). FFA: A flexible fusiform area for subordinate-level visual processing automatized by expertise. *Nature Neuroscience* 3: 764–769.

Thiele, A., & Stoner, G. (2003). Neuronal synchrony does not correlate with motion coherence in cortical area MT. *Nature* 421: 366–370.

Thompson, B. (2006). Colour constancy and Russellian representationalism. *Australasian Journal of Philosophy* 84: 75–94.

Thompson, K.G., Biscoe, K.L., & Sato, T.R. (2005). Neuronal basis of covert spatial attention in the frontal eye field. *Journal of Neuroscience* 26: 9479–9487.

Thut, G., Nietzel, A., Brandt, S.A., & Pascual-Leone, A. (2006). Alpha-band electroencephalographic activity over occipital cortex indexes visuospatial attention bias and predicts visual target detection. *Journal of Neuroscience* 26: 9494–9502.

Tiippana, K., Andersen, T.S., & Sams, M. (2004). Visual attention modulates audiovisual speech perception. *European Journal of Cognitive Psychology* 16: 457–472.

Tolias, A.S., Moore, T., Smirnakis, S.M., Tehovnik, E.J., Siapas, A.G., & Schiller, P.H. (2001). Eye movements modulate visual receptive fields of V4 neurons. *Neuron* 29: 757–767.

Tomsic, D., Berón de Astrada, M., & Sztarker, J. (2003). Identification of individual neurons reflecting short- and long-term visual memory in an arthropod. *Journal of Neuroscience* 23: 8539–8546.

Tootell, R.B.H., Reppas, J.B., Dale, A.M., Look, R.B., Sereno, M.I., Malach, R., Brady, T.J., and Rosen, B.R. (1995). Visual motion after effect in human cortical area MT revealed by functional magnetic resonance imaging. *Nature* 11: 139–141.

Treisman, A. (1998). Feature binding, attention and object perception. *Philosophical Transactions of the Royal Society of London B* 353: 1295–1306.

Treisman, A., & Gelade, G. (1980). A feature integration theory of attention. *Cognitive Psychology* 12: 97–136.

Treisman, A., & Schmidt, H. (1982). Illusory conjunctions in the perception of objects. *Cognitive Psychology* 14: 107–141.

Trevarthen, C. (1984). Biodynamic structures, cognitive correlates of motive sets and the development of motives in infants. In W. Prinz & A.F. Sanders, eds., *Cognition and Motor Processes*, 327–350. Berlin: Springer-Verlag.

Tsakiris, M. (2010). My body in the brain: A neurocognitive model of body-ownership. *Neuropsychologia* 48: 703–712.

Tsao, D.Y., Vanduffel, W., Sasaki, Y., Fize, D., Knutsen, T.A., Mandeville, J.B., Wald, L.L., Dale, A.M., Rosen, B.R., Van Essen, D.C., Livingstone, M.S., Orban, G.A., & Tootell, R.B. (2003). Stereopsis activates V3a and caudal intraparietal areas in macaques and humans. *Neuron* 39: 555–568.

Tse, P.U., Intriligator, J., Rivest, J., & Cavanagh, P. (2004). Attention and the subjective expansion of time. *Perception & Psychophysics* 66: 1171–1189.

Tse, P.U., Martinez-Conde, S., Schlegel, A., & Macknik, S. (2005). Visibility and visual masking of simple targets are confined to areas in the occipital cortex beyond human V1/V2. *Proceedings of the National Academy of Sciences USA* 102: 17178–17183.

Tucker, M., & Ellis, R. (1998). On the relations between seen objects and components of potential actions. *Journal of Experimental Psychology: Human Perception and Performance* 24: 830–846.

Tukker, J.J., Fuentealba, P., Hartwich, K., Somogyi, P., & Klausberger, T. (2007). Cell type-specific tuning of hippocampal interneuron firing during gamma oscillations in vivo. *Journal of Neuroscience* 27: 8184–8189.

Tunik, E., Lo, O.-Y., & Adamovich, S.V. (2008). Transcranial magnetic stimulation to the frontal operculum and supramarginal gyrus disrupts planning of outcome-based hand-object interactions. *Journal of Neuroscience* 28: 14422–14427.

Turner, F., & Pöppel, E. (1988). Metered poetry, the brain, and time. In I. Rentschler, B. Herzberger, & D. Epstein, eds., *Beauty and the Brain: Biological Aspects of Aesthetics*, 71–90. Basel: Birkhäuser.

Tye, M. (1983). Functionalism and type physicalism. *Philosophical Studies* 44: 161–174.

———. (1992). Visual qualia and visual content. In T. Crane, ed., *The Contents of Experience*, 105–135. Cambridge, UK: Cambridge University Press.

———. (1995). *Ten Problems of Consciousness*. Cambridge, MA: MIT Press.

———. (2000). *Consciousness, Color, and Content*. Cambridge, MA: MIT Press.

———. (2003). *Consciousness and Persons: Unity and Identity*. Cambridge, MA: MIT Press.

———. (2009). *Consciousness Revisited: Materialism without Phenomenal Concepts*. Cambridge, MA: MIT Press.

———. (2010). Attention, seeing and change blindness. *Philosophical Issues* 20: 410–437.

Umino, O., & Ushio, T. (1998). Spatio-temporal receptive fields in carp retinal horizontal cells. *Journal of Physiology* 508: 223–236.

Ungerleider, L.G., & Mishkin, M. (1982). Two cortical visual systems. In D.J. Ingle, M.A. Goodale, & R.J.W. Mansfield, eds., *Analysis of Visual Behavior*, 549–586. Cambridge, MA: MIT Press.

Van Boxtel, J.J.A., Tsuchiya, N., & Koch, C. (2010). Opposing effects of attention and consciousness on afterimages. *Proceedings of the National Academy of Sciences USA* 107: 8883–8888.

———. (2011). Consciousness and attention: On sufficiency and necessity. *Frontiers in Psychology* 1: 1–13.

Vandenbroucke, A.R.E., Sligte, I.G., & Lamme, V.A.F. (2011). Manipulations of attention dissociate fragile visual short-term memory from visual working memory. *Neuropsychologia* 49: 1559–1568.

Van den Bussche, E. Hughes, G., van Humbeeck, N., and Reynvoet, B. (2010). The relation between consciousness and attention: An empirical study using the priming paradigm. *Consciousness and Cognition* 19: 86–89.

Van den Bussche, E., Van den Noortgate, W., Reynvoet, B. (2009). Mechanisms of masked priming: A meta-analysis. *Psychological Bulletin* 135: 452–477.

Van Dijk, H., Schoffelen, J.M., Oostenveld, R., & Jensen, O. (2008). Prestimulus oscillatory activity in the alpha band predicts visual discrimination ability. *Journal of Neuroscience* 28: 1816–1823.

Van Gulick, R. (1993). Understanding the phenomenal mind: Are we all just armadillos? In M. Davies & G. Humphreys, eds., *Consciousness: Psychological and Philosophical Essays*, 137–154. Oxford: Blackwell.

———. (2004). Higher-order global states (HOGS): An alternative higher- order model of consciousness. In R. Gennaro, ed., *Higher-Order Theories of Consciousness*. Amsterdam: Benjamins.

———. (2006). Mirror mirror—Is that all? In U. Kriegel & K. Williford, eds., *Self-Representational Approaches to Consciousness*. Cambridge, MA: MIT Press.

Vanni, S. (1999). Neural synchrony and dynamic connectivity. *Consciousness and Cognition* 8: 159–163.

VanRullen, R., & Koch, C. (2003). Competition and selection during visual processing of natural scenes and objects. *Journal of Vision* 3: 75–85.

VanRullen, R., Reddy, L., & Koch, C. (2005). Attention-driven discrete sampling of motion perception. *Proceedings of the National Academy of Sciences USA*, 102, 5291–5296.

Van Swinderen, B. (2007). Attention-like processes in Drosophila require short-term memory genes. *Science* 315: 1590–1593.

Varela, F.J. (1991). Perception and the origin of cognition: A cartography of current ideas. In F. Varela & J.P. Dupuy, eds., *Understanding Origins*, 235–265. Boston: Kluwer.

Varela, F.J., Thompson, E., & Rosch, E. (1991). *The Embodied Mind: Cognitive Science and Human Experience*. Cambridge, MA: MIT Press.

Verstraten, F.A.J., Cavanagh, P., & Labianca, A.T. (2000). Limits of attentive tracking reveal temporal properties of attention. *Vision Research* 40: 3651–3664.

Vianney-Rodrigues, P., Iancu, O.D., & Welsh, J.P. (2011). Gamma oscillations in the auditory cortex of awake rats. *European Journal of Neuroscience* 33: 119–129.

Victor, J.D., & Purpura, K.P. (1996). Nature and precision of temporal coding in visual cortex: A metric-space analysis. *Journal of Neurophysiology* 76: 1310–1326.

Vignolo, L.A. (1982). Auditory agnosia. *Philosophical Transactions of the Royal Society of London B* 298: 49–57.

Von der Heydt, R., Peterhans, E., and Baumgartner, G. (1984). Illusory contours and cortical neuron responses. *Science* 224: 1260–1262.

Von der Malsburg, C. (1997). The coherence definition of consciousness. In M. Ito, Y. Miyashita, & E.T. Rolls, eds., *Cognition, Computation and Consciousness*, 193–204. Oxford: Oxford University Press.

Von der Malsburg, C., & Schneider, W. (1986). A neural cocktail-party processor. *Biological Cybernetics* 54: 29–40.

Von Stein, A., & Sarnthein, J. (2000). Different frequencies for different scales of cortical integration: From local gamma to long range alpha/theta synchronization. *International Journal of Psychophysiology* 38: 301–313.

Von Stein, A., Rappelsberger, P., Sarnthein, J., & Petsche, H. (1999). Synchronization between temporal and parietal cortex during multimodal object processing in man. *Cerebral Cortex* 9: 137–150.

Vosgerau, G., & Newen, A. (2007). Thoughts, motor actions, and the self. *Mind & Language* 22: 22–43.

Vroomen, J., & de Gelder, B. (2004). Temporal ventriloquism: Sound modulates the flash-lag effect. *Journal of Experimental Psychology: Human Perception and Performance* 30: 513–518.

Vroomen, J., Driver, J., & de Gelder, B. (2001). Is cross-modal integration of emotional expressions independent of attentional resources? *Cognitive, Affective, and Behavioral Neuroscience* 1: 382–387.

Vuilleumier, P., Henson, R.N., Driver, J., & Dolan, R.J. (2002). Multiple levels of visual object constancy revealed by event-related fMRI of repetition priming. *Nature Neuroscience* 5: 491–499.

Vuilleumier, P., Sagiv, N., Hazeltine, E., Poldrack, R.A., Swick, D., Rafal, R.D., & Gabrieli, J. (2001). Neural fate of seen and unseen faces in visuospatial neglect: A combined event-related functional MRI and event-related potential study. *Proceedings of the National Academy of Sciences USA* 98: 3495–3500.

Wachtler T., Sejnowski, T.J., & Albright, T.D. (2003). Representation of color stimuli in awake macaque primary visual cortex. *Neuron* 37: 681–691.

Walsh, V. (1999). How does the cortex construct color? *Proceedings of the National Academy of Sciences USA* 96: 13594–13596.

Walsh, V., & Cowey, A. (2000). Transcranial magnetic stimulation and cognitive neuroscience. *Nature Neuroscience* 1: 73–79.

Wardak, C., Olivier, E., & Duhamel, J.R. (2011). The relationship between spatial attention and saccades in the frontoparietal network of the monkey. *European Journal of Neuroscience* 33: 1973–1981.

Watanabe, M., Cheng, K., Murayama, Y., Ueno, K., Asamizuya, T., Tanaka, K., & Logothetis, N. (2011). Attention but not awareness modulates the BOLD signal in the human V1 during binocular suppression. *Science* 334: 829–831.

Wede, J., & Francis, G. (2007). Attentional effects on afterimages: Theory and data. *Vision Research* 47: 2249–2258.

Wegner, D.M. (2002). *The Illusion of Conscious Will.* Cambridge, MA: MIT Press.

Wegner, D.M., & Wheatley, T.P. (1999). Apparent mental causation: Sources of the experience of will. *American Psychologist* 54: 480–492.

Weigelt, S., Singer, W., & Muckli, L. (2007). Separate cortical stages in amodal completion revealed by functional magnetic resonance adaptation. *BMC Neuroscience* 8: 70.

Weiskrantz, L. (1986). *Blindsight: A Case Study and Implications.* Oxford: Oxford University Press.

———. (1997). *Consciousness Lost and Found.* Oxford: Oxford University Press.

Welch, R.B., & Warren, D.H. (1986). Intersensory interactions. In K.R. Boff, L. Kaufman, & J.P. Thomas, eds., *Handbook of Perception and Human Performance, Vol. 1: Sensory Processes and Perception,* 1–36. New York: Wiley.

Welwood, J. (1977). Meditation and the unconscious: A new perspective. *Journal of Transpersonal Psychology* 9: 1–26.

Wen, L., Moallem, I., Paller, K., & Gottfried, J. (2007). Subliminal smells can guide social preferences. *Psychological Science* 18: 1044–1049.

Wertheimer, M. (1912). Experimentelle Studien über das Sehen von Bewegung. *Zeitschrift für Psychologie* 61: 161–265.

Wessinger, C.M., VanMeter, J., Tian, B., Van Lare, J., Pekar, J., & Rauschecker, J.P. (2001). Hierarchical organization of the human auditory cortex revealed by functional magnetic resonance imaging. *Journal of Cognitive Neuroscience* 13: 1–7.

Williams, L.M., Liddell, B., Rathjen, J., Shevrin, H., Gray, J.A., Phillips, M.L., Young, A.W., Brown, K., & Gordon, E. (2004). Mapping the time course of nonconscious and conscious perception of fear: An integration of central and peripheral measures. *Human Brain Mapping* 21: 64–74.

Wilson, T.D. (2002). *Strangers to Ourselves: Discovering the Adaptive Unconscious.* Cambridge, MA: Harvard University Press.

Wimsatt, W. (1976). Reductive explanation: A functional account. In A.C. Michalos, C.A. Hooker, G. Pearce, & R.S. Cohen, eds., *Philosophy of Science Association 1974,* 671–710. Dordrecht: Reidel.

Winkielman, P., Berridge, K.C., & Wilbarger, J.L. (2005). Unconscious affective reactions to masked happy versus angry faces influence consumption behavior and judgments of value. *Personality and Social Psychology Bulletin* 1: 121–135.

Wolfe, J.M. (1999). Inattentional amnesia. In V. Coltheart, ed., *Fleeting Memories*, 71–94. Cambridge, MA: MIT Press.

Wolpert, D.M., Ghahramani, Z., & Jordan, M.I. (1995). An internal model for sensorimotor integration. *Science* 269: 1880–1882.

Womelsdorf, T., Schoffelen, J.M., Oostenveld, R., Singer, W., Desimone, R., Engel, A.K., & Fries, P. (2007). Modulation of neuronal interactions through neuronal synchronization. *Science* 316: 1609–1612.

Woodworth, R.S. (1906). Imageless thought. *Journal of Philosophy* 3: 701–708.

———. (1915). A revision of imageless thought. *Psychological Review* 22: 1–27.

Woody, E., & Szechtman, H. (2002). The sensation of making sense: Motivational properties of the "fringe." *Psyche* 8: 20.

Wörgötter, F., Suder, K., Zhao, Y., Kerscher, N., Eysel, U.T., & Funke, K. (1998). State-dependent receptive-field restructuring in the visual cortex. *Nature* 396: 165–168.

Wyart, V., & Tallon-Baudry, C. (2008). A neural dissociation between visual awareness and spatial attention. *Journal of Neuroscience* 28: 2667–2679.

Xu, F., & Carey, S. (1996). Infants' metaphysics: The case of numerical identity. *Cognitive Psychology* 30: 111–153.

Yantis, S., & Nakama, T. (1998). Visual interactions in the path of apparent motion. *Nature Neuroscience* 1: 508–512.

Yantis, S., Schwarzbach, J., Serences, J.T., Carlson, R.L., Steinmetz, M.A., Pekar, J.J., & Courtney, S.M. (2002). Transient neural activity in human parietal cortex during spatial attention shifts. *Nature Neuroscience* 5: 995–1002.

Yardly, L. (1990). Contribution of somatosensory information to perception of the visual vertical with body tilt and rotating visual field. *Perception and Psychophysics* 48: 131–134.

Yau, J.M., Pasupathy, A., Fitzgerald, P.J., Hsiao, S.S., & Connor, C.E. (2009). Analogous intermediate shape coding in vision and touch. *Proceedings of the National Academy of Sciences USA* 106: 16457–16462.

Yaxley, S., Rolls, E.T., & Sienkiewicz, Z.J. (1990). Gustatory responses of single neurons in the insula of the macaque monkey. *Journal of Neurophysiology* 63: 689–700.

Young, B.D. (2011). Olfaction: Smelling the content of consciousness. Doctoral dissertation, City University of New York, Department of Philosophy.

Yun, R., Krystal, J., & Mathalon, D. (2010). Working memory overload: Fronto-limbic interactions and effects on subsequent working memory function. *Brain Imaging and Behavior* 4: 96–108.

Zangwill, N. (1992). Variable reduction not proven. *Philosophical Quarterly* 42: 214–218.

Zatorre, R.J., Bouffard, M., & Belin, P. (2004). Sensitivity to auditory object features in human temporal neocortex. *Journal of Neuroscience* 24: 3637–3642.

Zhang, W., & Luck, S.J. (2009). Sudden death and gradual decay in visual working memory. *Psychological Science* 20: 423–428.

Zeki, S. (1990). A century of cerebral achromatopsia. *Brain* 113: 1721–1777.

———. (1991). Cerebral akinetopsia (visual motion blindness): A review. *Brain* 111: 811–824.

———. (1993). *A Vision of the Brain*. Oxford: Blackwell.

Zeki, S., & Bartels, A. (1998). The asynchrony of consciousness. *Proceedings of the Royal Society of London B* 265: 1583–1585.

Zeki, S., and Moutoussis, K. (1997). Temporal hierarchy of the visual perceptive systems in the Mondrian world. *Proceedings of the Royal Society of London B* 264: 1415–1419.

Zeki, S., Aglioti, S., McKeefry, D., & Berlucchi, G. (1999). The neurological basis of conscious color perception in a blind patient. *Proceedings of the National Academy of Sciences USA* 96: 14124–14129.

Zellner, D.A., Bartoli, A.M., & Eckard, R. (1991). Influence of color on odor identification and liking ratings. *American Journal of Psychology* 104: 547–561.

INDEX